STUDIES ON BEHAVIOR
IN ORGANIZATIONS

A Research Symposium

In their original form the chapters in this book were presented as part of a Research Conference on Behavior in Organizations at the University of Georgia.

This symposium provides a utilitarian approach to the subject of basic research in the area of organizational effectiveness and its results emphasize the necessity of understanding behavioral patterns in organizations. Included are reports on the results of completed work and discussions on the problems of conceptualization or method.

The editor has arranged the chapters into three categories: conceptual essays, empirical studies (substantive or methodological), and computer-simulation experiments. This arrangement should facilitate analysis of the ideas a sented in the studies.

STUDIES ON BEHAVIOR

IN ORGANIZATIONS

A Research Symposium

The chapters of this volume resulted from papers presented at a conference on "Behavior in Organizations," as part of an AFOSR Research Contract with the Social Science Research Institute of the University of Georgia.

Studies on Behavior
in Organizations

A Research Symposium

Edited by
RAYMOND V. BOWERS

WITH A FOREWORD BY

CHARLES E. HUTCHINSON

UNIVERSITY OF GEORGIA PRESS

ATHENS

To My

MOTHER AND FATHER

Acknowledgements

The editor is most grateful to Dr. Elizabeth Brownell for her skilled and patient assistance in preparing this volume for publication, and to Mrs. Janis Hughes for the work she accomplished so well in connection with it. Also his appreciation goes to Drs. Robert Brown and Clifton Bryant and to Mrs. Joanna Parsons for their assistance in managing the conference at which these papers were read.

Contents

COMPUTER SIMULATION EXPERIMENTS

POSTLUDE

Foreword

ONE of the major justifications for research conferences is the guidance they provide to the sponsoring organization. The Research Conference on Behavior in Organizations coincided in time and purpose with a staff review of the Air Force Office of Scientific Research program of research in the area of organizational effectiveness. Our holdings at that time were largely concentrated in the small group field, although our share in the support of this area was quite small and only a fraction of the total research effort on small groups.

We had directed our efforts into the small group field for a number of reasons. Small group research was "safe" because it was generally carried on in laboratories and did not inconvenience functioning organizations. It was scientifically defensible because it made greater efforts to attain methodological elegance than other areas of the social sciences. And, additionally, there was a ten-year backlog of solid effort which promised that the field was ripe for the development of principles that might serve as the base for broadly applicable generalizations. From the inception of our program in 1956 to 1960, our support of this field was dictated by expectations for major advances in the field. While four years is a short span in the development of a discipline, it is not too short to permit the reevaluation of the potential contribution of a research area as a part of a broad program of sponsored research.

After reviewing the potential contributions of research to the development of knowledge of greatest promise for the improvement of Air Force organizational effectiveness, and after weighing the results of the Conference on Behavior in Organizations, we reduced our support for new research to be performed in laboratory settings and began to emphasize studies of functioning organizations. In the development of the program we wished to encourage investigators proposing new approaches to the study of large-scale bureaucratic organizations. We concentrated effort on the management of research because this is a large and significant area of military management, and one in which there is limited experience in regard to management.

At the same time, we became sensitized to the problem of transmitting the results to potential users in management. This, we felt, was one of the difficulties of the small group area. It did not supply information in a form readily useful to managers, nor did it supply feedback to group members that was helpful to them in estimating their role as group participants. To insure that there would be channels for transmission of results from the investigator to the Air Force manager, we began to insist that the research sponsored by us must at some stage involve the study of Air Force units and subjects. We are persuaded that investigations which deal directly with military activities are more apt to provide understandings useful to Air Force executives than studies based on other populations and organizations.

Our approach to basic research in the area of organizational effectiveness is frankly utilitarian for a number of reasons, but above all because it will be impossible to perform studies of functioning organizations without providing some immediate and useful information to managers and group members.

In the short run, our objective is to collect the kinds of data that are essential for the analysis and understanding of functioning organizations and of the behavior of people in organizational settings. In the long run, we hope that it will be possible to develop some generalizations useful in the management of organizations of a military or research type, and to produce techniques and instruments that can be used by management engineers whose professional specialization is in the area of management rather than in behavioral research.

We are indebted to Dr. Raymond V. Bowers for his persistent efforts to organize, manage, and bring to fruition the working conference on behavior in organizations. We believe that he and the panel of research specialists have produced a report which speaks to the issues involved in the guidance of research programs in the area of organizational effectiveness. We are pleased that it is possible to share the results of this conference with others whose interests converge on the problems here addressed.

Charles E. Hutchinson

Air Force Office of Scientific Research
Washington, D. C.

Introduction

RAYMOND V. BOWERS

THE sponsorship of basic research in the behavioral sciences by the Department of Defense is now well into its second decade. The original stimulus was a combination of Congressional mandate, expressed in the National Security Act of 1947, requiring the Secretary of Defense to establish a Research and Development Board in his office to stimulate the use of science for military purposes, and of the farsightedness of Dr. Vannevar Bush, the Board's first chairman, in supporting the inclusion of the sciences of human behavior in that mandate. Thus a Committee on Human Resources was established in 1947 to review military requirements and research projects in the behavioral science fields, and to recommend the additional types and levels of military research effort considered necessary to ensure that the requirements would be adequately met.*

Among the behavioral science areas needing much basic research support, according to the Committee's report, the highest priority was given those concerned with problems of organizing and managing human groups. Problems of leadership, human relations and morale, unit effectiveness, the administration of growth and change, military-civilian relations, psychological warfare, and many others pointed to the need to know more about the nature of human organizations from small aircraft crews on the one hand to large, potentially hostile nation-states on the other.

The Air Force, as did the other services, reviewed the Committee's recommendations in the light of its own particular needs and

---

*The Committee's original members were: Donald Marquis, Chairman, Walter Hunter, William Menninger, Carroll Shartle, and Samuel Stouffer. The Panel on Human Relations and Morale, whose responsibility covered the area of this volume, had as members: Charles Dollard, Chairman, Leland DeVinney, Carl Hovland, Alexander Leighton, and Hans Speier. The Committee's original full-time civilian staff consisted of Lyle Lanier, Raymond Bowers, Dwight Chapman, and Henry Odbert.

initiated research on some of these problems as early as 1949. The original programs, a mixture of in-service and contract research, were developed primarily at the Air University Human Resources Research Institute, Maxwell Air Force Base, Alabama, under this writer's direction. However, since 1956 the basic research contract part of the work has been the responsibility of the Air Force Office of Scientific Research, the co-sponsor of this Conference, and, specifically of AFOSR's Behavioral Sciences Division, whose Chief, Dr. Charles E. Hutchinson, is the author of the Foreword to this volume.

The participants in the Conference included most of those who have had contracts with AFOSR on problems of human organization. They were joined by Mr. Cecil Goode of the U. S. Bureau of the Budget, Dr. Robert Hall of the National Science Foundation, Dr. E. Kenneth Karcher, Jr., of the Army Research Office, Dr. Paul Van Riper of Cornell University, and Dr. Jerry S. Kidd, consultant, all interested in the theory and practice of human organizations as applied to governmental systems; by Drs. Beatrice and Sydney Rome, interested in computer simulation research on organizational problems; and by Drs. Hutchinson and Herman J. Sander of AFOSR. The purpose was to discuss research problems and share research experiences in order to maximize the effectiveness of the AFOSR program.

The papers presented at the Conference, and included in this volume, represent projects at various stages of completion. Some are descriptions of completed work, others are limited to problems of conceptualization or method. Since the projects were chosen for support by AFOSR on grounds of their technical promise and relevance to future Air Force problems rather than how they would fit together in the table of contents of a volume such as this, the editor has had to face the alternative of imposing probably more order on the papers than actually existed or submitting to the "no order" of an alphabetical listing by author. His choice of the former may not please everyone, but it does provide some reasonable guidance to the busy reader who is usually harrassed enough without facing a table of random contents. Moreover, the laudable fact that the AFOSR program, even though small in funds, is making contributions to general theory and methodology beyond what is coming out of its empirical studies should be made a matter of note. Thus, the papers have been classified under the following rubrics: Conceptual Essays; Empirical Studies (Substantive and Methodological); and Computer Simulation Experiments; followed by a Postlude comprising Mr. Goode's paper on "Putting Organizational Research to Use."

Conceptual Essays

The four papers in this section are contributions to varied aspects of organization theory.

Van Riper directs attention to the taxonomy problem and proposes a typology of organizations based on where each stands with reference to eleven "great (organizational) issues" or basic organizational variables such as "centralization — decentralization," or "authoritarianism — permissiveness." He sees each of these "issues" as a continuum of values and suggests that any organization's degree of internal cohesiveness is related to the consistency of its ratings along the eleven continua. Ratings consistently at one end yield organizations devoted almost wholly to the establishment of control from the top, while those at the other end yield organizations so resistant to such controls as to be near anarchy. Thus his typology is based on the consistency with which the "degree of power or control is exercised from the top—by an elite—over the mass of personnel in the organization," and he proceeds to isolate and describe six types along this complex continuum.

Guetzkow is concerned with another general problem—a typology of interactional relations between (rather than within) organizations, and he suggests a somewhat comprehensive conceptual framework within which the study of these inter-organizational relations may proceed. He classifies them, first of all, as taking place at three locations: *within* each other's boundary (what he terms "interpenetrations"); *at* the boundary, and *beyond* the boundary (through supra-organizational processes), and gives a range of examples for each. He then discusses the conflicting tendencies of all organizations to pursue both autonomy and interdependency, and he points out that the latter often involves interference as well as facilitation.

Altman's essay is addressed to a quite different consideration— the proposition that large scale organizational study might profit from the substantive findings of small group research. As one example, he points out that large organizations contain many small work groups, and hence the research findings, errors, and blind alleys uncovered in the small group field might prove useful in the study of the larger settings. The paper describes the Altman-McGrath schema for classifying small group research findings and gives actual examples of how the information might be used by the student of large organizations.

Finally, *Vollmer's* paper tackles an important problem in the field of theory building—the need for researchers to state their conclusions in some formal manner to permit more reliable comparisons of results from one study to another, thus facilitating the accumulation of knowledge about social systems. His proposal is to use structural-functional analysis as a method (rather than as a substantive theory) and to put all hypotheses and conclusions in the form of structural-functional propositions, stating, in each case, the property, requirement, mechanisms, and situational conditions involved. Vollmer then compares this method with the historical-causal method, pointing out the strengths and weaknesses of each, and faces up to the need for a more rigorous method for testing structural-functional propositions, offering as one answer an application of the method of elaboration.

EMPIRICAL STUDIES: SUBSTANTIVE AND METHODOLOGICAL

The six papers in this section have been grouped together because they are primarily concerned with the empirical scene, either as pieces of research themselves or as comments on research methodology.

Seashore's paper, for example, concerns a major methodological problem in empirical research—how to conduct field experiments in on-going complex organizations. His discussion begins with demarcating field experiments from simulations, case studies, correlation studies, and ex post facto comparisons, proceeds to a statement of the research dilemmas to be faced in doing field experiments, and ends with some suggestions regarding their research design and execution.

McGrath's paper is also concerned with research strategy but with reference to a special segment of the empirical world—the process of negotiation. After defining this process, the author discusses the three major strategies available for studying it, indicating his preference for what he terms "experimental simulation." He then presents a "conceptual framework of the negotiation situation to serve as a tentative model for [his] studies" and an experimental paradigm for carrying out the studies, both illustrated by his first three experiments.

The *Pepinsky-Riner-Weick-Moll* paper is a progress report regarding the functioning of work teams in a large organization, specifically of two small research teams in a large research organization. The description of events transpiring in this empirical situation was obtained by analyzing some 3,400 statements (obtained through lengthy recorded interviews with all team members) in terms of an explicitly defined conceptual framework involving the tasks that were preferred, the pairings of persons with the tasks, and the pairings of persons affected by the tasks.

The *McClintock* report is of a completed classical type experiment in the militarily important field of leadership. The purpose was "to ascertain, in the course of an experimentally manipulated social situation, whether individuals with previous experience in filling leadership roles behaved differently from those without such experience, under conditions of group support and non-support."

The *Haas-Hall-Johnson* study addresses itself to the taxonomy problem that was also of concern to Van Riper. However, the Haas group attempted to go beyond the integration of existing knowledge and insights to what they term an "empirically derived taxonomy." Data were collected from 75 organizations on 99 relatively distinct organizational dimensions, and a computer program was developed to compare the attribute profiles of the organizations to determine what clusters existed, if any. The results exhibit interesting parallels to zoological taxonomy.

The *Bowers-Brown-Bryant* project regarding the impact of technological change on careers in large scale organizations was at the data collecting stage when the Conference was held and the paper included here is limited to the conceptualization of the study and the design of the research schedule. One hundred intensive interviews were conducted with executives and professional personnel to supplement the rather meager existing literature as background for selecting the independent (change) variables and the dependent (career) variables. In addition, a number of presumed intervening variables were included for control purposes. Samples of middle management personnel from a number of industrial, governmental, and military organizations, totaling some 4,000 individuals, constituted the subjects of the study.

COMPUTER SIMULATION EXPERIMENTS

Although *Beatrice and Sydney Rome's* unique research on large scale organizations was not a part of the AFOSR program, it seemed most desirable to have it represented at the conference.

Their experiments have involved a conceptual framework, a laboratory facility, and a set of computer programs. The conceptual schema represents organizational actions, their assessment in terms of established criteria, and the feed back of these assessments to the actions themselves. It is used to translate the every day complexity of an organization's activity into "a multi-dimensional typology amenable to investigation in a computerized laboratory." The result is an artificial society operating in a laboratory, the society combining live subjects in managerial roles with artificial agents in implementing roles. Three simulations using this methodology are discussed in the *Leviathan* paper, which is devoted to describing the theoretical and experimental aspects of the program.

However, the Romes also see their work as having practical or developmental applications, and in their second paper, "Automated Learning Process," they provide an example of this potential. In it they "describe a plan or design for modelling a real college or school system on a digital computer," and show how the model assists in such specific areas as curriculum planning, teacher training, administrative policies, and student learning.

POSTLUDE

The final paper in the volume, *Cecil Goode's* suggestions for putting organizational research to use, is another useful addition to the AFOSR contributions. Mr. Goode's position in the Executive Office of the President provides him an unusual opportunity to see both the organizational problems of the federal government and such governmental efforts as the AFOSR program. In his paper he speaks of the importance of bringing the fruits of the latter to bear on the former through such steps as integrating the findings of the research, learning how to communicate such integrations to the management practitioners, and assisting the practitioners to become more knowledgeable about such findings.

In agreeing to have their papers published together in such a volume as this, the participants at the Conference hope to increase interest in many facets of the study of complex organizations. The general picture painted by them is that of a scientific frontier where the questions are still more numerous than the answers and where many of the most significant ones have probably not yet been adequately formulated. Through such penetrations as are represented here, it is hoped that the explorations will proceed at an accelerated pace.

At the time of the conference this writer was Director of the Social Science Research Institute and Chairman of the Division of Social Sciences at the University of Georgia. As director of the local co-sponsoring organization he served as chairman of the Conference.

Tucson, Arizona
January 26, 1966

Organizations: Basic Issues and a Proposed Typology

PAUL P. VAN RIPER*

THIS report, like Gaul, is divided into three parts. It has about as much unity. In a general way most of my remarks pertain to aspects of research concerning large scale organization. Beyond this, the connectives are tenuous indeed. The three parts are these: a brief presentation of what I will here call "The Great Issues within Organizations;" "A Typology of Organizations," and finally some remarks which can only be termed "miscellaneous."

GREAT ISSUES WITHIN ORGANIZATIONS

A few years ago I was perusing Leslie Lipson's book on *The Great Issues of Politics* (1)[1] when it occurred to me that his "great issues" were indeed often *the* issues so far as the internal "politics" of almost any organization was concerned. But Lipson's issues—they are only five in number—did not seem quite adequate, nor did I feel that all of them were stated properly for the more universal purpose I had in mind. Actually, at that time (about 1957) I was looking for a general guide to policy formulation within organizations —any organizations. The basic texts in either business or public administration were (and are) inadequate on this subject.

What is to follow then is "Van Riper out of Lipson." I present this list of "issues" as a tentative typology of those problems which tend to divide or perplex almost all organizations. As I view it, however, the list is reasonably complete only with respect to *basic*

---

*Professor Van Riper was invited to the Conference as participant observer and commentator. His prepared comments are presented in this chapter. Dr. Van Riper is Professor of Administration, Graduate School of Business and Public Administration, Cornell University, Ithaca, New York.

[1]Numbers in parentheses refer to items in the bibliography at the end of the chapter.

matters, and only with respect to those policy problems which are *internal* rather than external as far as the given organization is concerned.

Finally, my "issues" are not presented as components with a single orientation, but rather as continua between extremes. This has another advantage to which I will allude after presenting the issues themselves. Without attempting to put them in any hierarchical order, they are:

1. PRIVILEGE _____ ("to" or "versus") _____ EQUALITY
   This concerns everything from pay to office space and water carafes.
2. AUTHORITARIANISM _____ PERMISSIVENESS
   This refers to the relative emphasis on force as a method of influence within the organization.
3. CENTRALIZATION _____ DECENTRALIZATION
   Lipson refers to this as "concentration" or "dispersion" of power. I have chosen "centralization," etc., as it conveys a sense of both power and organization structure.
4. EXPANSIONISM _____ STATIC CONDITION
   This refers to the tendency toward territorial expansion, including the absorption (by implication) of other people(s) as well.
5. GROUP _____ INDIVIDUAL
   Again a matter of relative emphasis, with the word "group" encompassing groups of various size up to and including the "state" or "society."
6. MONISM _____ PLURALISM
   This refers to the range of toleration of ideas. Some might prefer an "absolutistic-pragmatic" continuum, but "monistic-pluralistic" seems a bit less ambiguous.
7. SYMBOLIC REPRESENTATION _____
   _____ REAL REPRESENTATION
   Concerns the relationship of leaders to "the led."
8. STATUS _____ CONTRACT
   This refers to the freedom of movement of individuals within the organization or social structure.
9. JUSTICE _____ MERCY
   This relates to the enforcement of law — whether by rules of general application or by exception based on personal situation.
10. ORDERLY TRANSFER OF POWER _____
    _____ NO RECOGNIZED MEANS FOR SUCH
    This concerns the problem of succession among leaders, par-

ticularly at death, incapacity, retirement, or change of preferences.

11. REPRESENTATIVE ART _____ ABSTRACT ART
This concerns the range of aesthetic preferences.

Perhaps there are "great issues" other than these which deserve to be included, but the above is my list after some years of thinking about the problem and of trying out such a list on various types of students, some of them at the executive level. I would be interested to consider any suggestions for additions or deletions, or suggestions relating to better phraseology, semantics, etc., in my choice of key words to symbolize the various issues.

Once the issues are established, it should be noted that it is possible to chart the situation within any given organization in terms of its place on each of the various continua. This facilitates certain other conceptions. For example, the movement of an organization (with respect to place on each continuum) back and forth between extremes of left or right is a measure of social change within the organization. Speed of movement is a measure of equilibrium as well as of the rapidity of social change. The proportion of the eleven variables which, for any given organization, may be plotted at or about the same point on the continua is a measure of integration or cohesiveness. Finally, all variables represent major policy problems which must be solved in some manner. Considered from this manipulative point of view, the "great issues" offer a basis for relatively immediate administrative (or social, etc.) action.

Again, I would welcome comments aimed at refinement of this conceptual scheme.

A TYPOLOGY OF ORGANIZATIONS

The above leads naturally into the matter of organization types. It seems to me that one of the most pressing needs in administrative theory is for an adequate (useful) organizational typology. Here again, I have found my training in political science to be suggestive.

But to come back to the great issues for a moment, note that adding up the variables in terms of the words and phrases on the left side of the various continua produces a set of conditions highly related to our general concepts of *totalitarian* society. Those on the right side suggest *anarchy,* which, by definition, implies almost no formal organization at all. Considered from another point of view, the variables at the left symbolize an organization devoted almost wholly to "control" while those at the right symbolize an almost chaotic individualism or absence of control.

All this has suggested to me a typology, one of whose main

characteristics involves the scaling of organizational types according to the relative strength of the control over individuals in the name of the group. Stated still another way, this involves scaling according to the relative strength of power relations of the few over the many.

A useful typology of organizations must, however, meet other criteria. It should, if possible, be all-inclusive, or nearly so; that is, it should be capable, with little distortion, of being used to classify all types of known organizational entities no matter how tight or loose, formal or informal, they may be. It should be helpful in organizing present knowledge for both theoretical and practical purposes. And, hopefully, it should be useful—or its components useful—in their suggestivity with respect to the formulation of new organizational concepts. In short, to be of maximum utility any such typology should be capable of being used for various types of predictive and creative purposes.

Some specific comments on the typology I shall describe here are perhaps in order. I have used Types 2, 3, and 5 in connection with various classroom and lecture discussions since the winter of 1956-57 and found that the students (at both college and executive levels) felt they were quite useful in categorizing and to some extent explaining certain organizational phenomena within their experience but which most existing literature on administration had failed to mention. Type 4 became impressed on my mind as the result of directing a doctoral dissertation on the subject of manufacturer-dealer relations in certain industries, but it also derives to some extent from our political concepts of federalism. Type 1 occurred to me just recently. As a useful typology should, it suggested to me that there must be a form of organization concerned with control almost solely for its own sake; and, indeed, as I think back over history, there are actual historical counterparts of this type. Type 6 represents an effort to round out the typology, this time from the right (or anarchic) side of the continuum. I am least satisfied with Type 6, for I am inclined to think that it may consist of two or more types.

But enough for the past. What is the typology? My present conception is of six distinctly different types of organization, presented here in order of degree of power or control exercised from the top— by an elite—over the mass of personnel in any given organization:

1. *CONTROL* organizations. Here the prime purpose of the organization can perhaps best be expressed as "maintenance of orthodoxy," with examples from ancient empires, certain present-day totalitarian efforts, and from the religious spheres (the Spanish Inquisition, for example.) The prime organizational characteristic of such an entity

lies in the division of authority among several hierarchies, each checking to some extent on the other, with the top of all hierarchies coinciding in the same person or very small group of persons (Pope or Presidium). Diagrammatically, this type of organization can be expressed as follows:

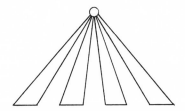

In a CONTROL organization the minimum number of such hierarchies is two. There is no theoretical maximum, but the practical maximum is probably in the range of four to a dozen depending upon the complexity of the social system comprehended by the organization. Certainly, today, the Soviet government involves at least four clear and distinct hierarchies, the main purpose of two being simply that of checking on the activities of the other two: these are the relatively permanent civil establishment, the traditional uniformed military, the secret police, and the Communist Party. All four of these are separate, but there is some interlocking of the last two with the first two, and of the last with the others; but there is almost no interlocking of the first two with each other. If one wishes to break down the Soviet apparatus into its relatively separate Army, Navy, and Air Force components, and the civil establishment into several functionally separate ministries, the Soviet pyramid can be broken down into the dozen or so hierarchies suggested above as a possible maximum.

The hazard in such a system lies, of course, first, in the wastes involved in such interlocking controls, many of which may be overdone; and second, in the tendency, pointed out by Dr. Sydney Rome,* toward so many, often contradictory, controls that no one at the top really has any idea of what is going on below, with a resulting sort of libertarianism at the bottom which was not intended. It should also be noted that a secret police (a sort of countervailing power, if viewed from the standpoint of a dictator) is a necessity for control purposes when there is no free press or free public discussion to bring to light waste, inefficiency, and "unorthodoxy" at all levels.

---

*Reference is to Dr. Rome's presentation on Leviathan at the Conference, see Chapter 11.

It must be stressed that the central problem in any CONTROL organization derives from its very emphasis on orthodoxy, its primary goal. Such an organization may be productive in the sense of the following Type 2, but productivity is not and cannot be its primary goal. This can be seen most clearly in Soviet agriculture, where productivity has been sacrificed for control in the name of orthodoxy (Marxist-Leninist theory.) This suggests, in turn, that for an organization to be most productive (especially in an economic sense) one must to some extent sacrifice both control and orthodoxy. Here lie the roots of the administrative argument against any totalitarian or absolutistic effort, as well as the roots of the major Soviet dilemma of today. Control—and orthodoxy—may, however, be the prelude to productivity, for the latter requires an effort which must in many respects be unified. In other words, only in the short run can productivity and control in the name of orthodoxy walk arm in arm. In the long run, one must follow or precede the other.

2. *PRODUCTION* organizations. For this type, some might prefer the designation of "bureaucratic," for the basic component is the Weberian pyramid with a small center of power at the top. But I have chosen the term "production," for in this type of organization the simple functionalism, hierarchy, and span of control of bureaucratic thought are often combined in the world of today with the military's line and staff mechanism, to form a much more complex organizational type than is implied by any stretch of the imagination in Weber's famous essay (5). There are two ways of graphically portraying this type:

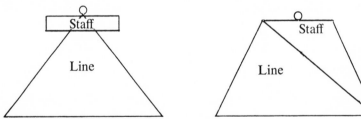

Basically, this is a single, often monolithic organizational structure, although in some very large organizations which use what is often termed the "profit center" system, the major pyramid may be tied by various means (usually financial) to subordinate pyramids, all of which are essentially like the top control pyramid.

Here, as in the first type, the goal is both known and relatively specific, with the principal means toward its accomplishment also relatively well known and understood. The problem is to organize others to produce what some central person or group desires to have produced and for which he or they can provide the capital, organizing talent and, in turn, the power to motivate and move the entire mechanism. It is in describing and dissecting this type of organization —typical of business, civil government, the military, and parts of the Catholic Church—that present textbooks are most precise and helpful. This is, in our society at least, by far the predominant form of organized endeavor.

More specifically, this type has all of Weber's characteristics, plus many of those of the military. It emphasizes communication downward; it normally utilizes "production line" methods and techniques involving repetitive processes and interchangeable parts, both material and personal; it knows reasonably clearly what it wants to do and sets out to bring people into the organization for *its* purposes and only secondarily, at best, for theirs.

The problem inherent in this type of organization lies in its tendency to metamorphose into Type 1 from which it differs little except in number of hierarchies. Indeed, numbers of 19th century and pre-Depression 20th century American business firms, with their complements of spies and industrial police, closely resembled Type 1. Human relations research and theory have produced a variety of gadgetry to aid an administrator who is more concerned about productivity than with maintaining control, orthodoxy or set procedures. He may use such devices as decentralization, employee participation, delegation of control from the top, or encouragement of communication from the bottom. But such a program is by no means easy to accomplish and a great deal depends upon the personal idiosyncrasies and preferences of top management. That is, a PRODUCTION organization may vary in pattern between the limits of McGregor's Theory X and Theory Y, which, however, are in fact not very far apart (2). Nor can they be very far apart when the principal goals are all set by the top, and the principal requirements for their accomplishment are determined and implemented from the top.

3. *BARGAINING* organizations. Perhaps this type is best approached through the two major examples of (a) manufacturer-dealer systems, and of (b) various types of federal systems where the lesser units have clear and determinable "rights." BARGAINING organizations represent marriages of convenience between or among various units, all of which are likely (individually) to resemble Type 2. Some sort of "constitution" (contract) governs the association; each party recognizes certain rights and obligations vis-à-vis other parties; and while there is usually recognition of the predominant position of one pyramid among all the pyramids involved, there is some limit beyond which the major pyramid may not coerce subordinate units. Graphically, this type may be thought of as clusters of pyramids,

the majority of them small, with all pyramids somewhat overlapping one or more other pyramids in patterns which change considerably —often kaleidoscopically—through time. Basically, any capitalistic system represents only a variation—albeit extremely complex—of this type.

The problem here is maintenance of the "constitution" or "contract" so that the relationship of pyramids remains fairly stable, without larger pyramids swallowing smaller ones and without the distribution of the rewards of cooperative effort varying too much from the expectations shared at the time cooperation was implemented. That is, in such a system cooperation may fairly easily turn into coercion as larger units utilize to their own advantage the power which is in fact theirs and which no "contract" can completely or effectively control. Actually, private enterprises of this type often depend upon government as an umpire, in the manner that federal governments of this type often depend upon Supreme Courts. This problem is best seen in government where, as a wag once noted, the United States "Supreme Court has been as impartial an umpire in national-state disputes as one of the members of two contending teams could be expected to be."

4. *REPRESENTATIVE* organizations. Here again it is perhaps best to begin by arguing from analogy. Typical REPRESENTATIVE organizations are found in political parties, some trade unions and some religious organizations (mainly certain types of Protestant groups), trade associations, most fraternal organizations, and some civic agencies. While these are membership organizations, the members are not employees; the relationship of the bottom (the members) to the top (paid secretariat) is the reverse of the previous types. That is, the members band together to employ one or more persons to represent them and to do their bidding. I will not go into details of this type of organization, for there is a vast amount of literature on the problems of representation and of developing representative democracies; there is much less literature, however, on trade association organizations and the like. Nevertheless the techniques are essentially similar in many ways.

The problem of REPRESENTATIVE organization is to keep the top responsible to the bottom and prevent the bottom from becoming nothing more than an echo or sounding board for the top. The principal error often made in membership organizations is to develop them in the model of Type 2 (PRODUCTION organization.) This almost ensures that the organization will become a tool of the central secretariat. I have sometimes felt that Michels' "iron law of oligarchy" (3) was developed from observations about membership organizations (in Michels' case, political parties) which were simply organized incorrectly from the standpoint of the members—that is, organized as Type 2 rather than Type 4. Of course, the organizations may have gravitated into the control of the central secretariats, but this was the result not of necessity but simply of either poor or calculated organizational techniques. Membership organizations, as any good political scientist knows, need not turn into oligarchies of the kind posited by Michels.

5. *RESEARCH* organizations. The basic purpose of what, for lack of a better word, I call RESEARCH organizations is innovation, creativity, discovery of the unknown. Examples are found in universities, advertising agencies, the movie industry, other creative arts, and the standard sorts of research efforts we are all familiar with—in short, any organization especially dedicated to novelty. The most effective design of such organizations is still a matter of considerable dispute, even though there is a growing literature on the subject.

About all one can say is that a RESEARCH organization works best if it is relatively flat, cellular in work group formation, flexible (to the point of chaos) in communication system, and, for any given project, relatively small. That is, excessive supervisory hierarchies and control by non-experts are nonsense in any technical area (typical universities have only three basic levels of personnel—students, faculty, and deans.) Work groups must be capable of extensive face-to-face relationships. The cellular organization and communication systems should be so flexible as almost to defy being called an organization. All this suggests a relatively small organization or a larger mechanism which, however, is essentially a loose-knit amalgam of small units.

The problem of RESEARCH organizations stems from the tendency of such an organization to gravitate either toward Type 2 or toward Type 6. That is, it may easily become over-controlled, or it may go so far in the other direction as to become a group of warring, uncooperative, and often secretive factions. Organizing for creativity is almost, but not quite, a contradiction in terms. Therein lies the dilemma of what is now termed "research administration."

6. *COMMUNAL* organizations. Here I have in mind a catch-all for a number of forms of relatively informal organization, varying from some kinds of families to neighborhoods or even larger "societies" —all, however, without presidents, chairmen of the board, official representatives, and most of the other paraphernalia of formal organizations. Man is simply a gregarious animal. This form of organization tends to operate (where it "operates" at all) more by a sort of Quaker "sense of the meeting" than by any more formal type of endeavor. Anything more formal should be classified under the other types outlined above.

Let us now consider this typology again as a whole. The types vary from those which are fully administered from the top down to those where there is almost no organization at all of any formal character. Among the first five (formal) types, number 2 (PRODUCTION organization) is most common, but Types 1, 2, 4, and 5 are by no means uncommon in the modern or earlier worlds. Our tendency, however, has been to teach organization and administration as if everything should be administered like Type 2. This has made for vast confusions not only from the standpoint of the active administrator but also of the researcher.

Now it should also be understood that many very complex organizations may contain within their total framework more than one type of organization. General Motors, for example, is clearly a combination of Types 2, 3, and 5. The Grange League Federation Cooperative in upstate New York (annual sales over $300,000,000), represents a mixture of Types of 2, 4, and 5. An immense mechanism such as the United States national government involves all types. Unfortunately, organization theory thus far is almost silent on methods of combining various types of organization or on analysis of the results of such combinations.

Finally, it seems to me there has been much confusion resulting from our traditional tendency to classify organizations according to clientele, membership, secondary functions (manufacturing, sales, military), size and so forth. That is, we have tended to think of all religious organizations as somehow really different from business organizations. All this has greatly obscured our thinking, which, for the further fruitful study of organization, needs in my opinion to be directed toward organization as a mechanism of control and power, capable of being subdivided into types which vary widely in degree and form of control and power and in relationships of leaders to led. The typology presented here permits us to see that some religious organizations are Type 1, while others may be of Types 2, 4 or even 5 and 6. Families may operate as any one of the various types: the family as a social organism is not one but many. Our political and economic institutions, too, run the gamut of possibilities. I am arguing, thus, that the key to organization analysis lies not in classification as political, economic, family, service, or manufacturing, but in a classification which permits clear delineation and understanding of organizational and social *power* as it affects the individual, either as a member of an elite or simply as one of the mass. Moreover, it should be noted that the proposed typology makes no distinctions according to size of organization, however size may be defined. All types may be of varying sizes. It is presumed, however, that very large organizations, up to and including an entire society, are likely to represent combinations of types rather than a single type.

MISCELLANEOUS COMMENTS

Is Organization Amoral?

This question has bothered me for some time. I noted that during the entire conference no one considered the problem of the relationship of various forms of organization (or administration) as having anything to do with broad decisions of an "ought to be" character. This is one of the matters on which I would hope consideration of the typology of organizations given in this paper might shed some light. You will note that some types of organization leave little room for individual freedom. Others presuppose a great deal of this freedom. In the light of this I pose a general hypothesis: that large social systems (organizations) have reciprocal effects with respect to the smaller social systems composing them. More precisely, I think one cannot long have an over-all democratic social system unless most of the component social systems (organizations) are gradually predisposed (changed) to function like the larger system. That this is in fact happening in the United States is, I think, the real meaning of human relations research—that is, participation is an overriding characteristic of our over-all political (social) system, and this characteristic stimulates the development of so-called "democracy in administration" in nearly all of our component social systems. This may work in reverse, of course—for example, one of our main hopes with respect to the Soviet Union is that some limited freedom is likely to result in an irreversible (under present conditions) movement toward more and more freedom (as in the Protestant Revolution after Martin Luther).

In other words, it seems quite clear to me that organizational form makes a great deal of difference to anyone interested in moral and ethical problems to which any question concerning "desirable" forms of general (national) social systems relates. Organization is not and cannot be considered as neutral with respect to considerations of what "ought to be."

The Problem of Large-Scale Organization.

Here I would like to quote from a talk I made some years ago before a meeting of the Society for Personnel Administration:

"Peter Drucker is right when he wrote recently in the January 1959 issue of *Harper's Magazine* of 'the crisis in government.' One of his theses, to put it very simply, is that we have in fact no really workable, teachable theory of organization for large scale purposes. We have done a lot of theorizing about organization recently, especially in small groups—group dynamics and the like—but the world's problems lie today in large scale organization, concerning which we have at best three kinds of conceptions, no one of them very satis-factory.

"We have first of all the concept of pluralism which is essentially *decentralization*—a basic aspect of capitalism—but we are not quite sure how or when to do it, although everyone is for decentralization. Second, we have the opposite number of this, the concept of *bureaucracy* outlined by Max Weber, or, as one of his opponents, von Hayek, has termed it, a concept of the world as organized like one gigantic pre-Summerfield post office, in a neat hierarchic pattern with Heaven knows how many layers from bottom to top. Third, we have the *line* and *staff* formula, which works beautifully in organizations up to a half million or so but which even in the military has not been followed in its classic form above the Field Army level. We have nothing teachable or usable for organizations of over one million persons" (4).

This expresses what I feel to be one of our most crucial problems today. The Communists are no better off than we are, perhaps even worse off—for Karl Marx was terrible when it came to such matters as administrative theory. His was the post office system plus something he called the "classless society"—the Communist version of Heaven; and he was no more able to prescribe how to get to that Heaven than we are to ours. Indeed, his very theory of organization, which essentially is that of Max Weber (5) modified into Type 1 outlined earlier in this paper, stands solidly in the way of innovation by the Communists in this matter.

So, as one of the topics for a future conference, I propose "the problem of large scale organization" in which all papers should be concerned with organizational and administrative problems found in organizations involving no less than a half million persons!

BIBLIOGRAPHY

1. Lipson, Leslie. *The Great Issues of Politics; An Introduction to Political Science.* Englewood Cliffs, N.J.: Prentice-Hall, Inc., 1954
2. McGregor, Douglas. *The Human Side of Enterprise.* New York: McGraw-Hill Book Co., 1960
3. Michels, Robert. *Political Parties.* Glencoe, Ill.: The Free Press, 1949
4. Van Riper, Paul P. "Some Approaches to Education for the Public Service," *Personnel Administration,* XXIII (January-February, 1960) 29-36
5. Weber, Max. "Bureaucracy," in *From Max Weber,* by Hans Gerth and C. Wright Mills. New York: Oxford University Press, Inc., 1946

Relations Among Organizations*

HAROLD GUETZKOW**

ONE does not know *a priori* whether a theory of relations among organizations will consist of little more than the social theory of processes occurring within organizations until both have been developed. Blau and Scott's recent essay on this matter treats "Interorganizational Processes" in the context of the broader social system, rather than focusing on the interactions between organizations per se (11, pp. 214-221). Let us attempt to develop aspects of a somewhat comprehensive framework within which the study of the relations among organizations might proceed.

Although the article on "One Hundred Definitions of Organization" has not yet been written, such would be useful. After despairing with the state of definitional affairs, Kaufman asserts: "The term organization will refer to all sets of human beings who exhibit the following five processes: boundary demarcation, replenishment, elicitation of effort, coordination of effort, and channels of distribution." But then he leaves his definitional posture by tagging on a quasi-empirical proposition, "If one of these functions ceases entirely, so, in short order, do the others. And if they cease, the set of people affected no longer constitutes an organization" (42, p. 39). With caution dictated by our abysmal ignorance of the functioning of organizations, as

---

*This research was supported by the Behavioral Sciences Division, Air Force Office of Scientific Research, under Contract No. AF 49(638)-742. This paper was developed as a part of the author's activity as a Master Fellow of the Economics Development and Administration group within the Ford Foundation, 1958-1963. Grateful acknowledgement is made of the exemplary aid given by Mr. Larry A. Eberhardt in its preparation.

**Dr. Guetzkow is Professor of Sociology and Political Science, and Co-Director of the International Relations Program, Northwestern University, Evanston, Illinois.

documented in our inventory of the literature (54), it seems unwise as yet to follow Kaufman's lead in delineating requisite functions.

It would seem well rather to define organizations by denotation, allowing our empirical analyses then to determine how the phenomenological entities that we use in common speech have operational existence, too, as has been suggested by Campbell (12). Thus, by *organizations*, let us designate those groups of individuals in which interaction is mediated and indirect (but not excluding the direct), of somewhat enduring continuity, falling in size between face-to-face clusters and the larger collectivities, such as cities, states, and societies. One may point to schools and universities, to government units and political parties, to business and industrial enterprises, to hospitals and prisons, and to professional associations, religious bureaucracies, and other voluntary membership groupings. This formulation avoids inclusion by definition *per se* of such characteristics as "cooperative relationship," "collective goal(s) or output(s)," and maintenance of "hierarchical structure," as is assumed by Strother (73, p. 23).

Description of Interaction Among Organizations

The frequency of the interactions would seem to be of importance, because organizations with many interactions may be more likely to develop patterns in their interrelationships than those whose relationship consists of but single or occasional events. Given a volume of interactions, the distribution of acts in time—be they continuous or lumped in intermittent spurts—also would seem to be a determinant of the way an organization relates to other groups in its environment.

There seem to be at least three classes of such interactions: (1) those developing by virtue of the interpenetration of groups; (2) those deriving from the specialized roles and teams delineated to handle interaction across organizational boundaries; and (3) those growing from indirect mediations of supraorganizational processes.

The Interpenetration of Organizations

The boundaries of organizations are of wide variety, most of them being at least somewhat permeable. Often one thinks of the boundary of an organization in terms of its membership, with exclusiveness of the barriers to membership as a sign of impermeability, as Hemphill and Westie found in their factor analysis of group descriptions (35, p. 327). They found that groups described as less permeable were also groups of decided status hierarchy (*"stratification"*), which possessed "primary significance" for their members (*"potency"*) and in which the members applied considerable "time and effort to group activities" (*"participation"*) (35, p. 327 and Table 5, p. 334).

But organizations may be penetrated in other ways. The domain of one organization intermittently may be invaded physically by the men and machines of another, as in the widespread practice of industrial catering of food, and by the presence of governmental examiners in private banks. The penetration also may occur through the diffusion of technology, as is illustrated in the internal organizational changes induced by the use of United States nuclear technicians with allied military groups. The activities themselves may be actually conducted by another unit. For instance, some personnel functions of a company are sometimes handled by a consulting firm; or, the shoe department of a large retail establishment may be leased as a concession to another firm.

Simmel's discussion of the boundary in conflicts within the Catholic and Protestant church contrasts its importance in groups which are elastic and those which are rigid. Simmel argues that throughout the centuries the organizational boundary confined the "monastic orders by means of which mystical or fanatical impulses of the Catholic Church (as of all religions) could live themselves out in a way completely harmless and unconditionally subordinate to it. In Protestantism, on the contrary, with its sometimes much greater dogmatic intolerance, these same impulses often led to separatist splinter groups which detracted from its unity" (70, pp. 93-94).

Sometimes there is simultaneous membership in two organizations, which at times may be identical for a whole group of persons, as in the union-company nexus. Other times, there is but partial overlap in membership, as occurs in ideological movements in which a core group of individuals seems to operate through "fronts." The phenomenon of interlocking directorates has long been a noted feature of the American corporate scene. Then there is interpenetration of organizations into the very fountainhead of each other, as occurs within the British "Establishment."

In American communities, "key leaders" characteristically serve in the offices and committees of many voluntary organizations, thus providing opportunity for the interrelation of private and quasi-public social institutions (60, p. 281). In U. S. foreign affairs Alger has noted how such relations between organizations through simultaneous memberships have developed role patterns, which he designates as the organization's "external bureaucracy" (1, p. 52 and p. 77). Perhaps one of the crucial differences between an emerging society and a politically developed one is the relatively low degree of membership interpenetration among the organizations of the former. As Coleman summarizes the process, "The strength and tenacity of communal and similar groupings militates against the emergence of functionally specific [interest] groups . . ." in which there is overlapping membership (3, p. 548).

National governments even attempt secret penetration of one another through their intelligence and infiltration operations. The agents of the initiating organization bribe individuals or sub-groups belonging to the target organization to frustrate or blunt the effectiveness of the latter's activities. Surprise in innovative product and pricing is an important weapon in marketing. Thus, stores maintain "shoppers" who inform their employers about new merchandising policies within rival firms. The incentives which "traitors" receive are not necessarily material. They may be psychological, as when the lower levels of both union and management organizations evade the formal contract worked out by the top levels of their respective organizations (17, pp. 611-619, passim). The making of personal side-payments was an honored tool in the repertoire of diplomats up until the end of the 19th century. The phenomenal ability of agents to penetrate the boundaries of nations even when they are at war with each other is reflected in the 1945 budget of the Office of Strategic Services of some fifty-seven million dollars, part of which was devoted to its "special operations, a term covering espionage, counter-intelligence in foreign nations, sabotage, commando raids, guerrilla and partisan-group activity—in conjunction with such as the French *maquis,* Italian anti-fascists, anti-Nazis within Germany, Kachins in Burma . . ." (66, pp. 64-65).

Such interpenetrations also may take place over time, as in the case when there is a gradual exchange of important legal personnel between a government regulatory agency and the top law firms serving clients who are regulated by that agency. With the accelerated development of a more professionalized manager who specializes in administration and organization, the inter-transfer of such executives among competing organizations may result at times in unusual relations among managements because of personal friendships across company boundaries.

There may be ideological penetration (43). Propaganda may be defined as persuasion through the instruments of communication, with the goal of modifying the expectations and/or identifications of members of *target* organizations. As interaction through mass media—the press, radio, etc.,—propaganda may be directed also toward publics with the hope of eliciting reactions as desired by the initiating organization (64, p. 27). Such ideological penetration attempts to affect a large segment of the target organization's membership, as Holt and van de Velde so vividly describe in telling about American psychological operations in Italy in both war (1943-45) and peace (1948)

(37, Chapters V and VI). Yet usually relatively few members of the initiating organization are involved in the interaction, since the propaganda development is often promulgated by a specialized sub-unit within that organization. In this mode of interaction there is an asymmetry between the initiating organization and the target organization with regard to the number of members involved. This asymmetry tends to endow the initiating organization with an advantage that the target organization can overcome only by directing propaganda of its *own* toward the initiating organization or toward its *own* membership to counteract the effect.

Nevertheless, propaganda may have costs for the initiating organization, too. The broadcast manipulation of symbols may result in unintended and undesired feedback on the membership of the initiating organization or on strategic third parties. This has occurred within Russia and among its satellite states when the Soviet foreign aid apparatus has attempted to present itself to neutral nations in a humanitarian role. The broadcast manipulation of symbols may also strengthen adverse predispositions among target memberships. For example, Russian propaganda initiatives designed to bully the West sometimes have strengthened the cohesion of Western allies in the North Atlantic Treaty Organization.

Ideological penetration may be overt, as when professional associations develop norms for personnel in operating organizations. For instance, the American Medical Association provides standards for the conduct of the medical staff in a local community hospital. Or the penetration may be more covert, as is the case when bureaucrats without formal membership in "client organizations" use such organizations as reference groups, modeling their own behaviors in terms of their suppositions about behaviors prescribed by such reference groups. In the post-World War II period, European nationalism surreptitiously permeates the underdeveloped countries, despite their antagonism to colonialism, which itself was mothered by such nationalistic tendencies. Reference groups used by memberships as bases for social status comparisons may be a source for an even more subtle kind of ideological invasion. For example, Blanksten, Plank, and Guetzkow found dissatisfaction with personnel practices on the part of members of the Organization of American States Secretariat because the OAS personnel believed the salaries and benefits of the UN Secretariat were far superior to theirs (9).

Perhaps the most effective type of boundary penetration in terms of changing the goals of the organization being invaded is when the penetration involves both membership and ideology. Witness the way in which the Communists have operated within trade unions, as is illustrated in the study of Max Kampelman on the informal and formal actions of the C.I.O. in expelling its communist-dominated unions in the 1940's (41). On the other hand, much dual penetration may actually benefit the organization being intruded upon; the co-optation of members of the larger community by an organization encourages their ideological transformation, so that they subsequently tend to carry the ideology of the co-opting organization into their many other membership groups, thereby inducing community support (69, pp. 13-16). In the extreme, one finds the closed shop, in which all workers are members both of the company and the union. But as Purcell found in his empirical study of workers' attitudes in packing plants, although members simultaneously hold feelings of loyalty to both organizations, periodically during times of contract negotiation, positive attitudes toward union dominate attitudes toward the company (63).

Interactions at Boundaries of Organizations

There is a wide variety of ways in which organizations interact with their environments, both social and material. They have special service units for interacting with their clients and customers; they have special receiving and shipping departments for expediting material exchanges with the environment. Their personnel offices serve to make contact with individual members of the surrounding community for recruitment purposes. Organizations have differentiated public relations and information groups which handle the relations of the organization to their various publics. It is interesting to note that within the last decade or two, many corporations have special units devoting effort to communication with their stockholders, because of the increasing segregation which has occurred between management and ownership. Yet, even in as important a boundary role as that of the Representative in the United States Congress, despite the energies devoted to relations with constituency, Miller and Stokes' empirical investigation suggests there is little "effective communication between Congressman and district . . . . The Representative has very imperfect information about the issue preferences of his constituency, and the constituency's awareness of the policy stands of the Representative ordinarily is slight" (55, p. 56).

When there is resistance to interaction at the boundary, the public display of force or resources may be used, (1) to demonstrate feelings and attitudes by one organization to another, and possibly (2) to increase or decrease the boundary permeability of one or more of the organizations. For example, the maneuvering of naval units in foreign waters at times constitutes an important vehicle for the interaction of nation-states. Commodore Perry's naval demonstration in

Japanese waters in 1853 induced the Tokugawa elite to broaden the range of Japan's interactions with the outside world, ultimately resulting in boundary penetrations as well as in expanded interorganizational linkages. Congregations of peoples before presidential palaces may be thought of as mob actions directed toward the communication of sentiments. Clearly, demonstrations in many cases need only be aimed at decision-makers in the target organization in order to be effective. It is interesting to note that in labor-management interaction, when conflict between the two units becomes intense, particularly during a strike, picket lines both have propaganda value and serve as an important tool for reducing the permeability of the physical boundary between the two groups.

Often there is little difference in the way organizations deal with individuals or with other organizations in the environment. But sometimes specialized boundary roles are developed to handle the interrelations among organizations, analogous to that noted for the husband-father as he simultaneously occupies interpenetrating roles in both occupational and family systems (61, p. 13). A particular person will be designated as liaison to a particular organization. Since 1949 there has been a permanent Congressional Relations Office providing the Department of State with liaison with the Congress; Robinson has described the nature of this liaison net in exciting detail (67, Chapters V and VI). Special liaison groups, such as coordination committees between governmental agencies, may be established (31). Sometimes *ad hoc* teams are instituted for the negotiation of contracts between organizations. This may occur in labor-management relations, as Goldner has noted (30). Organizations on occasion maintain such close connections with each other that "opposite numbers" are differentiated. The roles of these boundary specialists become extremely routinized, thereby reducing the likelihood of interorganizational conflicts accruing from threats to the status of organizational representatives. This development has reached a climax in the relations between states. Elaborate codes have routinized much of this day-to-day diplomatic activity in national capitals (8), whereby each desk officer soon learns to work with his opposite numbers in the embassies of those countries assigned to him (25, pp. 19-44).

These roles are not new. The designation of individuals with powers-of-attorney to act in behalf of business entities is a legal device that has existed in varying forms in western societies for centuries. Similarly, the profession of the diplomat is at least as old as ancient Greece, although permanent diplomatic missions did not originate until about the end of the fifteenth century. The relations among diplomats were not formally institutionalized until the Congress of Vienna in

1815 (58, p. 32). Only recently, however, has the rôle of representative been studied in a systematic fashion (7). Most impressive is the comparative empirical work which has been done on the state legislator's roles for California, New Jersey, Ohio, and Tennessee by Wahlke, Eulau, Buchanan and Ferguson (77). Eulau has indicated how the legislator may serve as "trustee," "politico," or "delegate," as he represents his constituency within the state legislature (77, Chapter 12). Wahlke describes how the legislator relates at the boundary to his pressure-groups, as "facilitator," as "resister," or as a "neutral" (77, Chapter 14). Then in the chapter on "The Network of Legislative Role Orientations," Eulau demonstrates how these roles "interpenetrate" each other, as for example when he notes that in all chambers, "the trustee orientation predominates among the three pressure-group-role types, but somewhat more so among the neutrals. Neutrals, being less involved in the politics of interest groups, are apparently more likely to fall back on their own convictions or judgments in groping their way among divergent and conflicting groups" (77, p. 399).

Individuals who operate at the boundaries of their organizations are subject to important strains, as has been elaborated by Stouffer (72) and others. The literature on marginal man contains insights as to how individuals handle the problem of competing and contradictory role requirements. The consequences of these various devices, viewed from the perspective of the organization, are many. Since there is no clear presentation of organizational image, response to conflicting role demands by alternation of response tends to make for confusion of interorganizational expectations. The device of resolving role conflict by withdrawal will tend to reduce contact at the boundary. When there is inner conflict-grounded aggression against counterparts across the organizational boundary, there may be induction of counter-aggression by the representatives of other organizations. In his examination of the labor-relations representatives of a firm, men who are employed as staff experts for dealing with unions, Goldner notes "soon were seen by line management as representing the union viewpoint. The unions also regarded them with suspicion and thus they became marginal men, working for the firm and with the union but not accepted by either" (30).

Some of these reactions to counterpressures at the boundary are seen in the diplomatic outpost. At times the diplomat is torn between professional norms on the one hand and expediential considerations relevant for his future career mobility on the other hand. We have in mind the choice between reporting what his superiors in the foreign office want to hear and what in fact they should learn if they are to form veridical images of other organizations. This particular type of role conflict is especially pronounced when the organizations involved are highly motivated by ideological considerations. For example, when the American foreign policy organization was subject to abnormally high domestic ideological pressures in the early 1950's, the adequacy of United States diplomacy along its informational dimension was impaired as some American diplomats resolved their role conflicts by either "playing it safe" or by leaving the Foreign Service. Because of ideological indoctrination, considerable perceptual and cognitive distortion is said to occur in the Soviet foreign policy organization (34, pp. 31-32). That conflicting role demands confront the man at the boundary is noted in another context in Etzioni's commentary on institutionalized attitudes in production-oriented organizations which are adverse to client interests: "To be client-oriented and to transmit clients' demands upward seems to be relatively unrewarding in many organizations" (27, p. 259). Or, given the position of the group within the organization as a whole, the reaction may be the inverse, as when a sales division manages to induce changes in the style or quality of the article for the customer, despite the problems created internally for production.

These "men-in-the-middle" would seem to be aided in handling their boundary relations by a number of devices. The use of uniforms for purposes of organizational identification of individuals at the boundary is one device widely adopted by companies and governments. Because of the conflicts which continuously are aroused in those having interactions at the margins of their organizations, it would seem important that they be given more indoctrination with respect to organizational goals. Thorough knowledge of organizational procedures and operations would be useful in resolving the blur which ambiguous role prescriptions enhance.

Occupants of boundary-roles may be prevented from developing unwanted identifications with groups in the organizational environment by the deliberate, periodic shifting of personnel from one segment of the organizational boundary to another. In the monolithic Communist Party apparatus a potentially unstable boundary role is found in the person of the Party deputy in parliamentary bodies. In order to prevent the Communist deputy from turning his constituency into a personal stronghold, the French Party organization usually chooses candidates from outside the district that they will be called upon to represent. Sometimes deputies are uprooted from one constituency and placed in another (20, p. 199). A reason for the periodic shifting of diplomatic personnel from one country to another is to prevent over-identification with any particular host country.

The problem of intra-individual role strains at the boundary may be avoided by the employment of non-affiliated "fixers" for the handling of interorganizational relations. These individuals, lacking clear organizational identifications, have a freedom of movement that is denied those who are embedded in particular organizations. Furthermore, organizations which want to avoid what they regard as premature boundary commitments may prefer the use of neutral individuals for "sounding out" the environment. Neutral "fixers" or "go-betweens" are present in diverse institutional and cultural milieus, from the inter-familial marriage broker in Japan to a third state's assumption of the role of "good offices" in international relations, as when President Theodore Roosevelt proffered good offices to the belligerents in the Russo-Japanese War in 1905. To the extent that a "go-between" exercises independent initiative, he becomes what Long has termed an "entrepreneur of ideas" and may, as such, play an extremely important role in structuring the network of interorganizational relationships (50, p. 258).

Interactions through Supraorganizational Processes

As the interactions between organizations become dense and stabilized, these very processes may become institutionalized, sometimes assuming supraorganizational forms. The studies of ten cases, reported in summary by Karl Deutsch and his colleagues on the development of political integration among separate political entities, as the unification of Germany and Italy, indicate how such intimate relations among component units occur. Although the process is complex, the most frequent method employed was promotion of the "emergence of strong core areas of amalgamation—either in the form of some one particularly large or strong political unit, or of an increasingly closely-knit composite of smaller units" (18, p. 72). The relations of nation-states over the past two and one-half centuries dramatically illustrate the way in which binary-type relations through special diplomatic representatives have so increased in intensity and regularity as now to take form in international organizations, such as in the United Nations complex (13, Chapters 2, 3 and 4).

The degree of interdependence among organizations may vary from very loose arrangements to tightly bound associations, in which units have membership as organizations rather than as individuals. Examples may be found in trade associations and in councils of governmental agencies. These associations aid organizations in presenting more standardized behaviors toward client or employee groups. Or they may be useful in obtaining goal achievements which each organization alone could not accomplish, as in the contracting consortium, where the magnitude of physical construction tasks on occasion may exceed the capital and labor resources of any existing enterprise. These coalitions for limited purposes and for limited periods of time in turn may create new organizations, often replete with management and operating staffs. The use of "task forces" by the (Hoover) Commission on Organization of the Executive Branch of the Government constituted *ad hoc* supraorganizational devices, having tremendous impact on the interorganizational arrangements among units of the federal government of the United States, as provided in the Reorganization Act of 1949 (15).

As was intimated above, at times a new organization is created to serve as a vehicle through which organizations may interact. For example, stock exchanges enable brokerage firms to conduct their interactions with other houses in an expeditious manner. Commercial clearing houses enable banks to exchange funds among themselves. Social service agencies have established client clearing procedures, to avoid cross-purpose and duplicative services to their "hard core" cases. The United Nations often serves as a vehicle for bilateral diplomatic contacts (2).

Perhaps one of the most important ways in which organizations relate to each other and to their social and material environments is through regulatory supraorganizations, such as commissions and boards. These regulatory relations may be mandatory, as when organizations resolve conflicts through a court system or through quasi-private arbitration association. Good offices, conciliation and inquiry, mediation, and finally, various degrees and types of compulsory adjudication are familiar forms along an institutionalization continuum.

Modes and Media of Interaction Among Organizations

The relations among organizations are affected by the media through which they are conducted, be they things or symbols. When organizations are interacting through material objects and by rendering personal services, transportation processes are involved. When organizations are interacting by means of symbols, communication facilities determine the speed and volume of messages which may be interchanged. In this case, the physical characteristics of the symbol vehicles are not as important as the cultural context through which they are interpreted by the members of the organizations.

In instances of interaction through materials and services, as well as through the interchange of symbols, organizations may relate to each other through special organizations whose very function it is to provide such interconnections. The transportation and communication industries represent aggregations of such specialized organizations. For example, the newspaper is an important connecting link among organizations in the local community. Cohen indicates the role of the "prestige press" in bringing coordination "in a de-

centralized policy-making process" within our United States government
(14, p. 227). Organizations sometimes serve as vehicles of interorganizational communication processes as a byproduct of nominally unrelated service functions. For instance, the local country club provides a geographic setting for the face-to-face interaction of organizational leaders.

Our treatment above of specializations at the boundary indicates
the directness that interrelations can assume. In such instances, interface
characteristics play a large part in determining the way in which the
organizations will interact. In primitive situations, one organization
may attempt to confront the other directly, as when political groups
conduct mass demonstrations in front of government offices. In more
differentiated situations, interest groups will operate on behalf of their
organizations indirectly through the mass media as well as through
"influence" channels within the governments' bureaucracies and
legislatures. Costs of communication and transportation — costs defined broadly to include non-material items such as potential loss
of prestige or of strategic position—will determine the volume of
interaction which develops among organizations. McClelland has indicated how such interactions among nations may be analyzed in the
course of the development and demobilization of crises (52, 53).

INSTITUTIONALIZATION OF INTERACTION

Over time, the interactions among organizations become institutionalized. Ways of behaving across boundaries and within alien organizations become routinized and formalized. The folkways, mores, and
legal standards prescribing relations among organizations derive not
only from the organizations themselves, but they come as extrapola-
tions from the infra-units, such as the family and work group, as
well as from the society as a whole. Most groups have norms about
the proper conduct of themselves vis-a-vis out-groups; witness the
ubiquity of customs about appropriate relations to strangers (79).

Other things being equal, it would seem that the greater the
frequency of interaction, the greater will be the degree of institutionalization of the relations among organizations. A factor in the gradual
institutionalization of labor-management relations in the United States
has been the frequency of contact between union and management
representation both at formal negotiations and during the interim
periods between such sessions.

These norms about the proper relations of organizations have
wide variation in content, however. Some of them are directed toward
the acceptance by each group of the existence of others, a fact which
is not always taken for granted as the controversies over "union
recognition" indicate. In the law of nations, such distinctions as that

between *de facto* and *de jure* recognition of the governments of other states play an important role in international politics. Other norms are directed toward the regulation of the interaction among the nations, prescribing how the groups shall compete or cooperate with each other. These "rules of the game" may over-regulate the functioning of the internal structure of each of the organizations. One illustration of this occurs when unions are permitted to use the communication system of the company for purposes which often are at odds with management goals.

Regularizing of the interaction among organizations permits one to delineate a variety of forms which the interaction may take. Attention now will be turned to these forms.

FORMS OF INTERACTION

Organizations tend to have some degree of autonomy; otherwise, observers hardly could label them as distinct social units. Such partial freedom from dependence on other groups occurs by definition within the areas of group maintenance activities to a greater extent than with respect to those activities of the organization in which there are input and output relations vis-à-vis the external environment.

When an organization is autonomous, it has few relations with other organizations in its environment. Yet even in such social isolation, the organization itself may enlarge or contract, depending upon its internal processes and its relation to material and people resources. The complete isolation of an organization occurs but rarely in a given society, as has been implied above in discussing the interactions which occur between organizations. Even in a primitive society, tribes or lineages have fairly regular relationships with other tribes or lineages.

It may be useful first to consider the interdependencies among organizations against their inclination toward autonomy. Then later the confluence of interrelationships which develop among them may be discussed.

Autonomy

Our purpose now is not to describe the roots of the tendencies of organizations toward autonomy. Instead our focus is to be on the ways organizations isolate themselves from each other. In their factor analysis of characteristics, as described for some 35 groups, Hemphill and Westie found that "autonomy" emerged as a reliable dimension, being defined as "the degree to which a group functions independently of other groups and occupies an independent position in society" (35, p. 326). The tendencies of organizations toward self-sufficiency have been sketched out in some detail already by others. Kaufman indicates how organizations, originally conceived as instruments for the development of outputs, acquire non-instrumental value for their sub-units as well as their aggregate membership (42, pp. 53-66). The sub-units acquire a vested interest in the stability of intraorganizational relationships. The phenomena of striving toward autonomy are high-lighted as independence in nation-states where the concept of sovereign-ty long has had descriptive referents in state behaviors (57, p. 315). Yet despite the surface cogency of this speculation, Hemphill and Westie found that groups which were described as autonomous tended also to be perceived ($r = .46$) as permeable (35, Table 5, p. 334).

There would seem to be need for insulating devices to secure the isolation of organizations from one another. The mechanical isolation of the organizations, both in terms of physical distance and in terms of a lack of communication channels, aids in the maintenance of autonomy. The use of violence at the organization's boundaries, as in the Mafia, often effectively prevents interpenetration. But perhaps even more interesting are the social devices which have been developed to insure the isolation of organizations. These social processes seem to be of two kinds, those seated within the organizations themselves and those located within supraorganizational processes.

Organizational norms may proscribe multiple memberships, there-by obviating serious interpenetration of one organization by another. Nation-states have used this device, as have many religious groups. Even when overlapping membership is permitted, formal or informal rules preserve the integrity of the roles that are associated with each of the separate memberships. A concrete example is the legal restriction of the political activities of federal civil servants that is embodied in the Hatch Act. Positions held by persons with overlapping member-ships may be stripped of decision-making power, so as to avoid an invasion of the organization's autonomy. The post of trustee, for instance, may be made honorific, thereby securing the insulation of the institution from external influence at its top. In Nazi Germany, there was a separation between the foreign affairs experts of Wilhelm-strasse and the party leaders, thereby developing the so-called "ring of silence" which supposedly isolated Hitler from external sources of information (68, pp. 90-110).

Devices to preserve cultural autonomy have been proliferated in the course of time in many organizational systems. Caste prohibitions regarding social contact in traditional India have prevented the merger of social groups. Customs with respect to the division of labor may prescribe "appropriate" activities which may be undertaken by one group but not by another, as is exemplified in jurisdictional disputes between unions. The persons and customs of out-groups are often thought of as "strange" and "dirty," aversions which aid in insulating organizations from each other.

The very process of applying autonomy-reducing pressure upon organizations may serve instead to enhance their autonomies. Blau and Scott relate that "business firms often go to great lengths to inform some segment of their set about the pressures and demands made by other segments" (11, p. 196). This device is employed in government, too, as Ehrmann points out in his study of demands of interest groups on the French civil service. He notes, "In some cases conflicting pressures entail the possibility of disregarding them altogether" (22, p. 547). In inter-nation diplomacy, the autonomous role of many small states is safeguarded at times by the fact that they manifestly are unable to satisfy the expectations of one Great Power without arousing the enmity of another (28).

Should the outside pressure be quite disruptive, Kaufman indicates that the organization may encapsulate disturbances in its environment, thus assuring absorption of external uncertainties (42, pp. 55-57). Through the device of "vertical integration," in which the firm secures control over its inputs by acquiring other units which process its raw materials and control over its outputs by owning its distribution outlets, the organization may considerably dampen the impact of the environment by such expansion at its boundaries.

When the supraorganizational processes have been institutionalized, they may be directed exactly toward the preservation of the autonomous character of the organizations for which they provide background. This is the purpose of anti-trust legislation. Because many of the decisions of supra-units regulating organizations are based on precedents, there is a tendency toward the preservation of earlier, more autonomous structures.

Interdependency

These currents toward autonomy are counterbalanced by interdependencies. It is important to note the forms which such interactions take as organizations wax and wane.

Interdependency often takes the form of *cooperation*. The organizations involved perform one or more of their internal and/or external activities through interactions with each other. Young's definition is typical: cooperation is defined as "joint striving with another or others for a good, goal, or value" (81, p. 64). A facilitative relationship may hold among organizations, even though each might well have incorporated within itself without disadvantage a range of activities which are being performed jointly. It seems useful to determine by empirical study rather than by *a priori* definition whether the cooperation is actually increasing individual unit rewards.

When there is interference in the activities of the other organization(s), interdependency may be described as *conflict*. Such interference may take the specialized form of *competition,* in which the interference is of a constant-sum type—whatever objective one organization achieves necessarily reduces the accomplishment of the other.

These interdependencies often are thought of as symmetric. This is not necessarily the case, however. Depending upon the relative resources of the interacting organizations, conflict itself may be quite asymmetric, impinging upon the very autonomy of the one organization and having but marginal effects upon the other. Likewise, the mutual benefits seemingly derived from cooperation may be minute for one unit and of survival impact for the other. These asymmetries are apparent in the relationship of large and small states. For instance, whereas the economic boycott of Cuba, begun after the emplacement of Russian nuclear weapons on the island in 1962, has had a marginal impact on the American economy, it is apparently having a deleterious effect on Cuba's. Similarly, the alliance between Greece and the theocratic Republic of Athos yielded considerably fewer benefits to the former than to the latter.

Before discussing "interfering" and "facilitating" types of interdependency separately, it may be useful to remind ourselves briefly that interdependency may result from the constraints imposed by underlying realities of the situation in which the organizations find themselves, or they may be induced by actions of the organization's decision-makers based upon their expectations as to how organizations can and/or should be interrelated. Although both sets of forces are realities, the former are seated in the objective requirements of the situations while the latter derive from the cultural milieu provided by the society in which the organizations operate.

Reality roots of the interdependency also may be found internal to each organizational unit. One phase of this problem is discussed by Jacob and Teune when they consider the extent to which the internal integration of a political unit determines its ability to participate in a larger community of such units—as in metropolitan grouping of local governments (40, pp. 38-42). In historical work on ten nations Deutsch and his associates observe that "amalgamation did not come to pass because the government of the participating units had become weaker or more inefficient . . . Rather, amalgamation occurred after a substantial increase in the capabilities of at least some of the participating units, or sometimes of all of them," as was the case before the union of the American colonies in 1789 (18, p. 39).

Another background consideration which may aid in understanding relations among organizations is the kind of division of labor which exists among them. Some division of activity may seem trivial. Note, for instance, the case of a division of work with respect to location, as when the same product is multiplicated in different plants throughout the world in seemingly unrelated units. As Phillips points out in his theory of interfirm organization, besides the consciously recognized oligopolistic relations among firms, there often is diffuse but complex interdependence in the market among large numbers of coexisting firms of which the individual entrepreneurs may be largely unaware (62, pp. 24-25). The specialization that occurs with respect to product and clientele often contains seeds for autonomy and interdependence. When there is functional specialization of activity, organizations necessarily interrelate with others, in order successfully to accomplish their over-all tasks. Quite different degrees of interdependence seem to be implied by these varying kinds of division of labor.

For the nonce, conflict and cooperation among organizations will be treated as contrasts in their traditional juxtaposition. However, it seems unwise to think of organizations as being entirely conflicting or entirely cooperative in their relations to each other. Perhaps it is the mix itself which gives rise to interesting properties in the patterns which hold among organizations.

1. Interferences among Organizations

Because organizations exist in physical and social space and draw their inputs from and discharge their outputs into a common environment, non-facilitative types of interdependencies are bound to occur fairly frequently. But should there be no scarcity of the materials or people in the environment from which all may draw, conflict is unlikely to be aroused. Indeed, coexistence without tensions would seem entirely possible were there no lack of clientele or space for outputs.

Organizations may be in competition with respect to their inputs and/or their outputs. When there are insufficient resources, the activity of each organization may suffer because of lack of adequate raw materials, capital goods, and/or labor. On the other hand, there may be inadequate facilities for distribution and—one step removed—too few consumers of the organization's goods or services. In the words of Luce and Raiffa, "Many conflict situations . . . can be considered formally to be games against nature" (51, p. 309). In both of these situations the "game" is against nature itself and/or against other organizations.

But even when competition over environmental resources is unnecessary, the structure of social relations which has been built up in the organization's contacts with its resources—its prerogatives with respect to access to suppliers, workers, and clientele—may tone its relations with conflict. As Harrison White has illustrated, within a firm, even when a quasi-autonomous department expands without any intention of destroying another departmental organization, such growth is often perceived by parallel units in the firm as a source of chronic conflict (78, p. 187). In laboratory work on the simulation of the relations among nations, Noel has noted that ideological presuppositions may transform objectively non-competitive situations into situations of conflict and threat (59, p. 91). Particularistic parties, "concerned in a separatist fashion with selected ethnic groups or regions and including some form of secession among their statements of political objectives, have from time to time filled major roles in the Americas. Indeed, this is one of the reasons why what were once only eight Spanish colonies are now eighteen independent states" (10, p. 486).

When the competition between organizations involves divergent belief systems, incompatibility is due to ideological contradictions as much as to objective scarcities. A political party and a religious organization may compete for votes and vows, of which there are but a limited number in a society. Furthermore, the creeds themselves often contain norms that prescribe the inferiority of contradictory beliefs. Hence, by basic postulation, coexisting ideologies often are defined as rivalrous by their proponents. And once these creeds have clashed violently, future interactions among organizations may be powerfully influenced by the earlier struggles. In studying the causes of industrial conflict in two Pacific Coast industries, Eliel submits, "Industrial conflicts which are climaxed by violence produce a reaction which is carried forward through the years and which makes more difficult the establishment of normal relations" (26, p. 488).

2. Facilitation among Organizations

Organizations may relate to one another in a mutually facilitative manner. Such cooperation may be marginal; then it is useful but not necessary for the survival of the organizations. In other cases, the division of labor among organizations may be so highly differentiated and the interaction so tightly articulated that failure in cooperation may be disastrous for both, as occurs between part suppliers and automobile assemblers. Such cooperation among organizations usually takes place through what Levine and White have conceptualized as exchange relations, in which each component derives locomotion toward its goals during the course of the interchange of outputs (48, p. 588). When there is interpenetration of one organization by another, due to the intimacy necessary for close cooperation, one may consider the organizations symbiotic.

*Concomitant Variation in _Interdependency_ and _Differentiation_*

Eberhardt has summarized the combinations of kinds of interdependency, i.e., cooperation and competition, with the extremes of differentiation among organizations, i.e., duplication vs. specialization (21). This is done in a six-fold classification presented in Figure 1. The table includes speculations about frequency with which the various combinations occur in the relations among organizations.

Figure 1

CONJECTURES ON FREQUENCY OF OCCURRENCES OF RELATIONS AMONG ORGANIZATIONS

	largely cooperative	mixture of cooperation and competition	largely competitive
largely identical activities	seldom	seldom	often (commensal)
highly specialized and differentiated activities	often (symbiotic)	most often	seldom

Social scientists have done little in developing a vocabulary for the description of the states of affairs exhibited in Figure 1. The human ecologists have borrowed terms from the biologists, in tagging the "highly specialized"-and-"largely cooperative" cell *symbiosis* and the "largely identical"-and-"largely competitive" cell *commensalism*. Although sociologists continue to work on urbanism, little research has been done in the last decade and a half in developing the early concepts used in human ecology for understanding the mutual relations of organizations and their environments, since they were sketched briefly in 1950 by Hawley (33) and Quinn (65).

The Admixture of Interference and Facilitation

Often the interdependency of organizations simultaneously involves facilitation and interference. And for both relations among organizations some kind of over-riding coordinative or regulatory mechanism often evolves. Even in groups at war, supraorganizational units and processes such as the Geneva Convention and the Red Cross have developed to control violent interactions. In fact, opposing armies contain elaborate boundary processes to insure coordination when one nation physically attacks another. In less rivalrous situations, there are often agreements with respect to the domains of each organization's activities. On the other hand, in cooperative situations there often are elements of competition. And even when organizations have symbiotic relationships, there is sometimes competition between the organizations for a larger share of the "profits" of the total enterprise and a lesser share of the "costs."

The degree of coordination which exists among organizations may vary from minimal, tacit arrangements of coexistence to maximal, highly explicit contractual arrangements of almost complete integration. The interlocking of competition and cooperative tendencies is accomplished through a variety of means, some of which are relatively loose and informal and others of which are quite formalized, involving at times separate coordinating organizations.

1. Minimal, Tacit Coordinations

It seems useful to note that the consensus reached by organizations with reference to the domains of their operations often is quite minimal and tacit in nature. In a condition of relative abundance of resources, prior organizational claims on the environment often are recognized with little dispute. In situations of mild conflict, the more clearly the claims have been established, the more easily do the organizations reach accommodation. Sometimes tacit coordination is achieved almost inadvertently because of the nature of the social context within which the organizations exist. One empirical study by Minnis has shown that voluntary associations may be differentiated in terms of membership in line with the social stratification of the community (56). Could it be that the community's structure limits organizational competition along the membership dimension, so that persons of one social class tend not to seek membership in a voluntary group composed of persons of another class? Further, it seems probable that status differences between memberships promote a division of task activity based on the relative prestige of the tasks. The traditions of an occupation, its "professional ethics," often serve also as a normative structure through which some coordination is achieved among its organizations. Thus, it is not considered "good medical practice" for hospitals to advertise for patients, even when wards are operating below capacity, while other hospitals are queuing the inflow of patients. Note that these coordinations with respect to domain operate through the mechanism of reducing potential interferences.

It is fascinating to observe how unions and contractors in the construction industries have developed tacit agreements with respect to outsiders, insuring both labor and management a local monopoly. As Bell indicates, "Thus, on many local projects, outside contractors are kept out because the unions refuse to supply them with labor." When an outsider invades and wins a contract, such contractors "find themselves afflicted by strikes or slowdowns" (5, p. 211).

2. Coordination through Domination

Ecological features of an organization's material and social environment may provide for relations among organizations which allow one unit to dominate the other to varying extents. Often the dominance exercised will be based upon controls applied at the boundaries of the other organization. Sometimes the dominance is established by outright invasion of one organization by another. At times the penetration is so extreme as to constitute merger or acquisition.

Hawley argues, "Dominance attaches to the unit that controls the conditions necessary to the functioning of other units" (33, p. 221). The dominant organization may provide boundary conditions for the functioning of other units by regulating inputs into the subordinate units and then serving as gatekeeper for the subordinate organization's outputs. An example of moderate dominance may be found in newspapers, which may screen the inputs into local communities and simultaneously monitor the informational outputs of its organizations in terms of such criteria as newsworthiness. Large retailing corporations have relationships with suppliers in which there are long term contracts with specified profit margins based on reasonable returns. Tentative billings are made during the year, with the actual determination of profits decided at the end of the year in a meeting of executives of both firms. As Houser explains, "There are many tens of thousands of manufacturers, and their employees, who could not exist were it not for their affiliation with a large corporate retailer" (39, p. 44). At the national public level, Young explains how agenda formulation within the United States Congress is determined in most important ways by messages and actions of the American Executive (82, pp. 112-113). In international relations it has been customary for great powers to provide boundary controls over subjugated states (legally known as protectorates) by handling their foreign affairs *in toto*.

The asymmetry of interdependence mentioned earlier provides leverage for the development of dominance hierarchy. An example is found in the large branch of a national corporation operating in a small town without other industries. The resource needs of such a branch are to a large extent supplied by non-local units. On the other hand, small businesses in the community depend for their survival on the company payroll; private or semi-public welfare agencies depend on the company's cooperation in the solicitation of funds from employees as well as on direct corporate giving; and local governments rely on corporate taxes.

Open and explicit forms of control, such as adjudication, occur in the regulation of some competitive relationships. A relationship between the existence of a competitive nexus and the endowment of the coordinating unit with adjudicatory power has been observed in the case of both labor unions and welfare agencies. In the instance of labor unions, a number of locals is likely to exist in a formal alliance against employers. Yet at the same time each local unit may be a potential competitor of every other local for jobs. In the event of such latent competition a dominant, intermediate unit with adjudicatory functions composes inter-union differences in the face of the larger bargaining relationship with management. On the other hand, "Where the locals of the same union in the same area are not potential direct competitors, the intermediate body is more likely to be a service agent of the locals" (44, p. 178). Litwak and Hylton suggest that if there is local competition for resources—as is the case with respect to financial support among welfare agencies—then "there is good reason to predict the growth and continued existence of co-ordinating agencies such as the community chest" (49, p. 410). In addition to the institutional structure of our courts, there are also within both state and federal governments the ever-active independent regulatory commissions which serve as sites for informal adjudicatory functions when the competition for resources is national (80).

At times, the domination of one organization over another makes possible the extension of controls into the internal activities of the subordinate organization. Smiley indicates how in Canada the exercise of federal spending power on objects usually regarded as local responsibilities has considerably reduced provincial autonomy merely through the interaction developed among federal and local units, "rather than through formal constitutional amendment or through an evolving pattern of judicial interpretation of the British North American Act" (71, p. 59). The development of the United States federal government demonstrates a similar phenomenon. Sometimes the tendencies toward autonomy within a unit are so great that there is usurpation of the functions of another organization, as Harrison White found in his study of conflicts among departments of a manufacturing concern with respect to research and development activities (78, pp. 187-196).

Modern technologies make possible greater amounts of centralization, providing means for control by the more dominant unit within a system of interrelated units. The provision of cheap and rapid means of communication and transportation for executive decision-makers in organizations makes possible a volume of interactions which facilitates the exercise of control in vast networks of interdependency. In the political arena modern military technologies reinforce existing hierarchies of dominance by providing overwhelming instruments of coercion, together with great mobility in their deployment. In Latin American countries, for instance, the hegemony of groups in the capital city is enforced by the mobility of troops into the provinces. The huge outlays involved in modern technology, exemplified by the large amounts of capital needed in the collection, editing, printing, and distribution of information, makes it difficult for new organizations to challenge the dominance—and at times, near monopoly—of established, on-going enterprises.

Dominance relationships may exist within cooperative as well as within competitive interdependencies. Decades ago Durkheim stressed that functional differentiation is an important way of resolving competition among units with similar demands upon their environment. In the process of the development of cooperation, as Blau and Scott point out, former competitors may develop ancillary roles by which weaker units become dependent upon those who have gained command over the resource supply or the clientele (11, pp. 217-218).

On occasion the preponderance of one unit over another is so complete that the relationship becomes indistinguishable from the ordinary bonds which tie sub-units into larger wholes. "Mergers" may develop for any variety of reasons, with payoffs to all units constituting the combine. Such amalgamation processes in the development of nation-states have been described by Karl Deutsch and his colleagues for a number of historical situations, as, for example, the union of Scotland and England in the 17th century, and the unification of Italy in the 19th century (18, pp. 46-59).

3. Coordination through the Proliferation of New Organizations

But at times, the costs involved in the domination of one organization by another are too great, given the benefits to be obtained from the exercise of such intimate controls by the superior unit. Rigidities from cumbersome executive devices may induce slowness in response to the environment. Decentralization of the decision-making then may be instituted, with controls being exercised by the central, coordinating unit only after the monitoring of feedback procedures has signaled important deviances from general, over-all organizational policy. If the environment demands very specialized adaptations to local conditions, as in the case of the overseas units of corporate enterprises, there may be a proliferation of quasi-detached sub-organizations. In fact, the decentralization may proceed with respect to so many activities of the organization, including its ownership in the case of some industrial enterprises, that the unit has in fact "budded" off the corporate-mother unit. The joint venture in international business—whether it involve investment equity or consist merely in management or construction contracts—is an attempt to coordinate entrepreneurial efforts across national and cultural barriers. As described in their wide variety by Friedmann and Kalmanoff, such enterprises seem to encompass the range from firms dominated by either their local or their foreign partner to firms in which there is a partnership of collaboration (29).

The process may work in a reverse direction, too. A number of units existing in quasi-isolation may find themselves confronting a common threat, as when a number of small, independent retailers in a community are faced by the "invasion" of a multi-line discount house. General Foods developed in some measure as a defensive alliance of a number of smaller firms who found that chain-store organizations were formidable in their bargaining with food processors. If there has been competition among the organizations, joint action, as Hawley writes, "requires a reduction of competition and ultimately . . . competition must be brought under control . . . . This takes the form of rules of procedure, parceling out of territory, definition of the common interest, and other similar devices" (33, p. 211). Even in an industry in which the gamut of legal processes involved in trust-busting has sought to prevent collaboration, some twenty-two companies in the steel industry recently united to establish Blast Furnace Research, Inc., a cooperative, non-profit research venture (4, p. 8).

Sometimes supraorganizational devices become far more elaborate than the trade association common in the American business community, and they may in fact receive deliberate governmental sanction. This is exemplified by the development of formal agreements between businessmen faced by the common threat of the Great Depression, under the auspices of the National Recovery Administration. Our United States Constitution provides that states may not enter into "agreement or compact with any other state" without the consent of Congress, in its so-called Compact Clause (Article I, Section 10). Yet, even the difficulties of securing Congressional approval have not deterred an accelerated use of the compact agency within the last half-century, as was dramatized in the early success of the Port of New York Authority in the 1920's. Leach and Sugg describe the operation of some thirty interstate agencies created by compact, ranging from the Atlantic States Marine Fisheries Commission to the Western Interstate Commission on Higher Education (46). As Thursby points out, herein is "one method of tackling supra-state, sub-national problems . . . to avoidance of an overladen general government" (75, p. 149). In the European cartel one has an example of a supraorganizational device which seems to have been quite effective in the inter-war years in disciplining its membership in quasi-governmental fashion.

Sometimes the coordination of units with important interdependencies may be accomplished by quasi-self-enforcing mechanisms such as markets and exchanges. But even in these instances, as the history of banking institutions and currency reforms in the United States indicates, the problems involved in developing supraorganizations to facilitate the relations among component organizations are not small. In his description of the bases of political development, Eisenstadt notes that "only in modern political systems do these different interest groups and movements tend to become integrated into the framework of a common continuous political activity and organization . . . namely in political parties" (23, p. 102). When the rivalry between organizations is severe, it is necessary to embed the interaction among them in frameworks of force; thus the development of judicial systems under the aegis of governments is a vital instrument of social development and control.

The growth in size and complexity of supraorganizations and client organizations tends to be mutually reinforcing. Lane has pointed out that in government, "the establishment of a public agency serving a more or less unorganized clientele has served as a catalyst for the more effective grouping of the interests concerned, as well as those of interests which might be disadvantaged by the new agency's activities" (45, p. 106). Frequently, the establishment of a government regulatory agency provokes commensurate groupings of the organizations being regulated. By playing the role of arbitrator in interorganizational conflict, government helps to consolidate "business" and "labor" into supraorganizations of their own. The consolidation and growth of interest groups, in turn, prompts the extension of governmental organization in order to (1) balance "the public interest" over against "organized private interests" and (2) fulfill the functions that interest groups assign to it (6, pp. 202-203). Thus, there are mutually reinforcing relationships between client organizations and supraorganizations.

This reinforcement process seems to differ from the one widely noted and so well codified by Coser in his Proposition 16, "Conflict leads to the formation of associations and coalitions between previously unrelated parties" (16, p. 140). David Truman notes that heretofore unorganized interest groups in American society are likely to solidify into special interest associations in waves; the organization of one interest prompts the organization of competing interests (76, pp. 59f). This mechanism also seems operative in established, ongoing organizations, as is demonstrated in labor-management relations. One student observes that "centralization in the industrial relations policies of management generates a corresponding tendency within the unions dealing with that management, and, similarly, management tends to react in the same direction to union centralizing developments" (47, p. 116). Alliance seems to lead to counter-alliance. As Coser summarizes the matter, "Alliance, even when not formed for the purpose of conflict, may seem to other groups a threatening and unfriendly act. This very perception, however, leads to the creation of new associations and coalitions . . ." (16, p. 149).

Changes in Mixed Relations

Thus, there is a wide range of coordinative and control devices developed as organizations evolve in their relations with each other, from weak, tacit linkages to enforced, explicit bonds. The extent to which the cooperation and competition exist in the relations among organizations fluctuates. Subordinate units may attempt to improve their positions by forming coalitions with other subordinate units of differing functions against a dominant, central organization. Thus, they may become more cooperative with their erstwhile competitors and more antagonistic to a supraorganization which can no longer so easily control its cooperative relations.

The problem of tension induced by the simultaneous existence of cooperative and competitive relations was noted early by Sumner and designated as "antagonistic cooperation" (74, pp. 16-18). At times there are seemingly ineradicable conflicts which together create interaction leading to cooperation. Such antagonistic cooperation may characterize the state of affairs between the USA and USSR in the mid-20th century. Achievement of effectiveness in nuclear deterrence implies that cooperation coexists with antagonism. Friedmann and Kalmanoff describe how "basic problems of joint ventures arise from a mixture of harmonies and conflicts of interest" (29, p. 5) in a series of fascinating case studies of such companies operating in Latin America and the Far and Middle East (29, pp. 281-548).

As Dubin points out, "Antagonistic co-operation in union-management relations involves the collaboration of two organized groups . . ." (19, p. 197). The zero-sum aspects of the economic goals of union and management provide the backdrop of fundamental antagonism, even when the two organizations cooperatively attempt to increase the "size of the pie" by transforming the relationship into a non-zero-sum game. This antagonism sometimes is heightened by the immersion of union leadership in an ideology of class conflict which portrays labor as the "underdog" (5, p. 213). Yet the fact that the two sets of decision-makers possess an overlapping membership induces cooperation in relations among the organizations. Bell indicates that "in the evolution of the labor contract, the union becomes part of the 'control system of management' . . . and often takes over the task of disciplining the men, when management cannot" (5, p. 211-212). And vice versa, management provides a framework within which minorities of workers may be coerced to insure the stability of the union, as through the check-off and closed shop. Superimposed upon these exchange-of-services is the friendship and cooperation which arises out of the constant interaction of supervisors and workers, following Homans's hypothesis, "If the interactions between the members of a group are frequent in the external system, sentiments of liking will grow up between them, and these sentiments will lead in turn to further interactions, over and above the interactions of the external system" (38, p. 112). Coser notes, however, that such transformations are more likely "in associations where the members of the alliance are individuals rather than groups. In coalitions, each of the coalesced groups is anxious to maintain its boundaries and the exclusive loyalty of its members" (16, p. 146).

  Little wonder that in contemporary American life—and perhaps in other cultures at other times, also, as Eisenstadt (24) so vividly documents in his study of the historical bureaucratic empires—with its bevies of interdependencies, one should find antagonistic cooperation so pervasive.

BIBLIOGRAPHY

1. Alger, Chadwick F. "The External Bureaucracy in United States Foreign Affairs," *Administrative Science Quarterly,* VII (June, 1962) 50-78
2. _____"Personal Contact in Intergovernmental Organizations," in *International Behavior,* ed. by Herbert C. Kelman. (New York: Holt, Rinehart and Winston, 1965)
3. Almond, Gabriel A., and Coleman, James S. et al. *The Politics of the Developing Areas.* Princeton: Princeton University Press, 1960
4. Anonymous. "The Fourth R: Production Research," *Steelways,* XVIII (November, 1962) 8-11
5. Bell, Daniel. *The End of Ideology.* Glencoe, Ill.: The Free Press, 1960
6. Bendix, Reinhard. "Bureaucracy and the Problem of Power," *Public Administration Reveiw,* V (Summer, 1945) 194-209
7. Blake, Robert R., and Mouton, Jane S. "Loyalty of Representatives to Ingroup Positions during Intergroup Competition," *Sociometry,* XXIV (June, 1961) 177-183
8. Bland, Sir Nevile (ed.). *Satow's Guide to Diplomatic Practice.* 4th ed. London: Longmans, Green and Co., 1957
9. Blanksten, George I., Guetzkow, Harold, and Plank, John N.

The Organization of American States. A Study prepared for the Sub-Committee on American Republic Affairs of the Committee on Foreign Relations, U. S. Senate. Washington: Government Printing Office, 1959

10. Blanksten, George I. "The Politics of Latin America," in *The Politics of the Developing Areas,* ed. by Gabriel A. Almond and James S. Coleman. (Princeton, N. J.: Princeton University Press, 1960) 455-531

11. Blau, Peter M., and Scott, W. Richard. *Formal Organizations: A Comparative Approach.* San Francisco: Chandler Publishing Co., 1962

12. Campbell, Donald T. "Common Fate, Similarity, and Other Indices of the Status of Aggregates of Persons as Social Entities," *Behavioral Science,* III (January, 1958) 14-25

13. Claude, Inis L. Jr. *Swords into Plowshares: The Problems and Progress of International Organization.* New York: Random House, 1956

14. Cohen, Bernard C. "Foreign Policy Makers and the Press," in *International Politics and Foreign Policy,* ed. by James N. Rosenau. (New York: The Free Press of Glencoe, 1961) 220-228

15. Commission on Organization of the Executive Branch of the Government. *Reports.* Washington, D. C.: Government Printing Office, 1949

16. Coser, Lewis A. *The Function of Social Conflict.* London: Routledge and K. Paul, 1956

17. Dalton, Melville. "Unofficial Union-Management Relations," *American Sociological Review,* XV (October, 1950) 611-619

18. Deutsch, Karl W. et al. *Political Community and the North Atlantic Area: International Organization in the Light of Historical Experience.* Princeton: Princeton University Press, 1957

19. Dubin, Robert. "Union-Management Co-operation and Productivity," *Industrial and Labor Relations Review,* II (January, 1949) 195-209

20. Duverger, Maurice. *Political Parties.* New York: John Wiley and Sons, Inc., 1954

21. Eberhardt, Larry A. Personal communication, April, 1962

22. Ehrmann, Henry W. "French Bureaucracy and Organized Interests," *Administrative Science Quarterly,* V (March, 1961) 534-555

23. Eisenstadt, S. N. "Bureaucracy and Political Development," in *Bureaucracy and Political Development,* ed. by Joseph La Palombara. (Princeton: Princeton University Press, 1963) 96-119

24. _____ *The Political Systems of Empires: The Rise and Fall of Bureaucratic Societies.* New York: The Free Press, 1963

25. Elder, Robert E. *The Policy Machine: The Department of State and American Foreign Policy.* New York: Syracuse University Press, 1960

26. Eliel, Paul. "Industrial Peace and Conflict: A Study of Two Pacific Coast Industries," *Industrial and Labor Relations Review,* II (July, 1949) 477-501

27. Etzioni, Amitai. "Administration and the Consumer," *Administrative Science Quarterly,* III (September, 1958) 251-264

28. Fox, Annette Baker. *The Power of Small States; Diplomacy in World War II.* Chicago: University of Chicago Press, 1959

29. Friedmann, Wolfgang G., and Kalmanoff, George (eds.) *Joint International Business Ventures.* New York: Columbia University Press, 1961

30. Goldner, Fred H. "Organizations and Their Environment: Roles at Their Boundary," paper read at the meetings of the American Sociological Association, New York, 1960, quoted in Blau and Scott (11, p. 197)

31. Guetzkow, Harold. "Interagency Committee Usage," *Public Administration Review,* X (Summer, 1950) 190-196

32. _____, Brody, Richard A., Driver, Michael J., and Beach, Phillip F. *An Experiment on the N-Country Problem through Simulation.* St. Louis, Mo.: The Social Institute, Washington University, 1960

33. Hawley, Amos H. *Human Ecology; A Theory of Community Structure.* New York: The Ronald Press Co., 1950

34. Hayter, Sir William. *The Diplomacy of the Great Powers.* London: Hamish Hamilton, 1960

35. Hemphill, J. K., and Westie, C. M. "The Measurement of Group Dimensions," *Journal of Psychology,* XXIX (April, 1950) 325-342

36. _____ *Group Dimensions: A Manual for their Measurement.* Columbus, Ohio: Bureau of Business Research, College of Commerce and Administration, Ohio State University, 1956. Research Monograph # 87

37. Holt, Robert T., and van de Velde, Robert W. *Strategic Psychological Operations and American Foreign Policy.* Chicago: University of Chicago Press, 1960

38. Homans, George C. *The Human Group.* New York: Harcourt, Brace and Co., 1950

39. Houser, Theodore V. *Big Business and Human Values.* New York: McGraw-Hill Publ. Co., 1957

40. Jacob, Philip E., and Teune, Henry. "The Integrative Process: Guidelines for Analysis of the Bases of Political Community,"

in *The Integration of Political Communities,* ed. by Philip E. Jacob and James V. Toscano (Philadelphia: J. B. Lippincott, 1964), pp. 1-45

41. Kampelman, Max M. *The Communist Party vs. the C.I.O.; A Study in Power Politics.* New York: Frederick A. Praeger, 1957

42. Kaufman, Herbert. *Why Organizations Behave as They Do: An Outline of a Theory.* Interdisciplinary Seminar on Administrative Theory, March 20-21, 1961, University of Texas, Austin, Texas, 37-71

43. Klapper, Joseph T. *The Effects of Mass Communication.* Glencoe, Ill.: The Free Press, 1960

44. Lahne, Herbert J. "The Intermediate Union Body in Collective Bargaining," *Industrial and Labor Relations Review,* VI (January, 1953) 163-179

45. Lane, Edgar. "Interest Groups and Bureaucracy," *Annals of the American Academy of Political and Social Science,* CCXCII (March, 1954) 104-111

46. Leach, Richard H., and Sugg, Redding S., Jr. *The Administration of Interstate Compacts.* Baton Rouge: Louisiana State University Press, 1959

47. Lester, Richard A. *As Unions Mature: An Analysis of the Evolution of American Unionism.* Princeton: Princeton University Press, 1958

48. Levine, Sol, and White, Paul E. "Exchange as a Conceptual Framework for the Study of Interorganizational Relationships," *Administrative Science Quarterly,* V (March, 1961) 583-601

49. Litwak, Eugene and Hylton, Lydia F. "Interorganizational Analysis: A Hypothesis on Co-ordinating Agencies," *Administrative Science Quarterly,* VI (March, 1962) 395-420

50. Long, Norton E. "The Local Community as an Ecology of Games," *American Journal of Sociology,* LXIV (November, 1958) 251-261

51. Luce, R. Duncan, and Raiffa, Howard. *Games and Decisions: Introduction and Critical Survey.* A Study of the Behavioral Models Project, Bureau of Applied Social Research, Columbia University. New York: John Wiley and Sons, Inc., 1957

52. McClelland, Charles A. "The Acute International Crisis," *World Politics,* XIV (October, 1961) 182-204

53. _____ "Action Structures and Communication in Two International Crises: Quemoy and Berlin," *Background,* VII (February, 1964) 201-215

54. March, James G., and Simon, Herbert A., with the collaboration of Harold Guetzkow. *Organizations.* New York: John Wiley and Sons, Inc., 1958

55. Miller, Warren E., and Stokes, Donald E. "Constituency Influence in Congress," *American Political Science Review,* LVII (March, 1963) 45-61

56. Minnis, Mhyra S. "Cleavage in Women's Organizations: A Reflection of the Social Structure of a City," *American Sociological Review,* XVIII (February, 1953) 47-53

57. Morgenthau, Hans J. *Politics among Nations; The Struggle for Power and Peace.* New York: Alfred A. Knopf, 3rd ed., 1960

58. Nicolson, Hon. Harold George. *Diplomacy: A Basic Guide to the Conduct of Contemporary Foreign Affairs.* London: Thornton Butterworth, Ltd., 1939; 2nd ed. Oxford Univ. Press, London 1950

59. Noel, Robert C. "Evolution of the Inter-Nation Simulation," in *Simulation in International Relations: Developments for Research and Teaching,* by Harold Guetzkow, C. F. Alger, R. A. Brody, R. C. Noel and R. C. Snyder (Englewood Cliffs, N. J.: Prentice-Hall, 1963), pp. 69-102

60. Olmsted, Donald W. "Organizational Leadership and Social Structure in a Small City," *American Sociological Review,* XIX (June, 1954) 273-281

61. Parsons, Talcott, and Bales, Robert F. *Family, Socialization and Interaction Process.* Glencoe, Ill.: The Free Press, 1955

62. Phillips, Almarin. *Market Structure, Organization and Performance: An Essay on Price Fixing and Combinations in Restraint of Trade.* Cambridge, Mass.: Harvard University Press, 1962

63. Purcell, T. V. *The Worker Speaks His Mind on Company and Union.* Cambridge, Mass.: Harvard University Press, 1953

64. Qualter, Terence H. *Propaganda and Psychological Warfare.* New York: Random House, 1962. (Studies in Political Science PS # 41)

65. Quinn, James A. *Human Ecology.* New York: Prentice-Hall, 1950

66. Ransom, Harry Howe. *Central Intelligence and National Security.* Cambridge, Mass.: Harvard University Press, 1958

67. Robinson, James A. *Congress and Foreign Policy-Making: A Study in Legislative Influence and Initiative.* Homewood, Ill.: Dorsey Press, Inc., 1962

68. Seabury, Paul. *The Wilhelmstrasse.* Berkeley: University of California Press, 1954

69. Selznick, Philip. *TVA and the Grass Roots: A Study in the Sociology of Formal Organization.* Berkeley: University of California Press, 1949. (Univ. of California Publications in Culture and Society, vol. iii)

70. Simmel, Georg. *Conflict* and *The Web of Group Affiliations.* Glencoe, Ill.: The Free Press, 1955

71. Smiley, D. V. "The Rowell-Sirois Report, Provincial Autonomy, and Post-War Canadian Federalism," *The Canadian Journal of Economics and Political Science,* XXVIII (February, 1962) 54-69

72. Stouffer, Samuel A., et al. *Studies in Social Psychology during World War II,* vols. i and ii: *The American Soldier.* Princeton: Princeton University Press, 1949

73. Strother, George B. "Problems in the Development of a Social Science of Organization," in *The Social Science of Organizations: Four Perspectives,* ed. by Harold J. Leavitt. (Englewood Cliffs, N. J.: Prentice-Hall, Inc., 1963) 1-37

74. Sumner, William Graham. *Folkways: A Study of the Sociological Importance of Usages, Manners, Customs, Mores, and Morals.* Boston: Ginn and Co., 1906

75. Thursby, Vincent V. *Interstate Cooperation; A Study of the Interstate Compact.* Washington: Public Affairs Press, 1953

76. Truman, David B. *The Governmental Process; Political Interests and Public Opinion.* New York: Alfred A. Knopf, 1951

77. Wahlke, John C., Eulau, Heinz, Buchanan, William, and Ferguson, Leroy C. *The Legislative System: Exploration in Legislative Behavior.* New York: John Wiley and Sons, 1962

78. White, Harrison. "Management Conflict and Sociometric Structure," *American Journal of Sociology,* LXVII (September, 1961) 185-199

79. Wolff, Kurt H. (ed.) *The Sociology of Georg Simmel.* Glencoe, Ill.: The Free Press, 1950

80. Woll, Peter. *Administrative Law; The Informal Process.* Berkeley and Los Angeles: University of California Press, 1963

81. Young, Kimball. *Sociology: A Study of Sociology and Culture.* 2nd ed. New York: American Book Co., 1949

82. Young, Roland. *The American Congress.* New York: Harper and Bros., 1958

Structural-Functional Analysis as a Method*

HOWARD M. VOLLMER**

IN present day studies of complex organizations we have gained many insights about specific types of organized behavior, but little sense of progressive accomplishment. Findings from one study are often difficult to compare with findings from another study. This difficulty derives not so much from the fact that research inquiries may focus attention upon widely different types of organizations, but rather from the fact that research findings are frequently expressed in an essay style that is not comparable from study to study without considerable interpolation on the part of the reader.

It appears to the author that the only way to get around this difficulty is for researchers to summarize their conclusions in some formal manner which allows an easy comparison of findings from one study to another, thus facilitating cumulative knowledge about social systems. For this purpose this paper discusses certain aspects of the use of formal propositions in structural-functional analysis.

"Structural-functional analysis," as generally used in sociological studies, refers to the analysis of factors that support or undermine characteristics of social systems. However, much confusion is prevalent in discussions about structural-functional analysis in sociological research. Persons expressing various points of view on this matter are sometimes unclear on just what structural-functional analysis is, what its peculiar advantages and disadvantages are, and how one may go about maximizing its usefulness for research purposes.

*This paper was produced as part of an ongoing study of Adaptations of Scientists in Different Organizational Contexts, sponsored by the Behavioral Sciences Division of the Air Force Office of Scientific Research under Contract AF No. 49 (638) - 1028.

**Dr. Vollmer is Research Sociologist, Stanford Research Institute, Menlo Park, California.

In this paper I suggest that the structural-functional viewpoint can be used either as a method of study or as a substantive theory about the nature of social phenomena. However, it seems to me that the usefulness of the structural-functional viewpoint is maximized when it is used primarily as a *method* of analysis of social phenomena, rather than as a *substantive theory* about the nature of phenomena. It also appears that structural-functional analysis has certain distinct advantages over historical-causal analysis, a principal methodological alternative, although these advantages certainly do not diminish the necessity of using causal-historical analysis for certain types of problems.

The general form of structural-functional propositions and a procedure for testing such propositions against empirical data are described herein from this point of view.

ADVANTAGES AND LIMITATIONS OF STRUCTURAL-FUNCTIONAL ANALYSIS

First, we might devote some attention to the peculiar advantages and limitations this method has and contrast it with historical-causal analysis. I hope to show that both methods are equally necessary for the development of sociological theory.

Historical-causal analysis attempts to specify the long-run historical as well as the immediate environmental conditions which preceded in time the occurrence of some phenomenon. Historical-causal analysis, insofar as it involves more than a simple historical description, presents propositions to the effect that wherever these specified preconditions occur, all other relevant factors being considered constant, the phenomenon under study as the dependent variable may be expected to occur.

Structural-functional analysis, in contradistinction to historical-causal analysis, is basically a-historical—its propositions do not have a sequential time reference. A structural-functional proposition simply asserts that a given phenomenon under study fulfills or undermines a requirement of a social system referent (i.e., a special and recurrent characteristic of a goal-oriented pattern of human activities). We shall examine the form of these propositions in more detail later.

Structural-functional analysis seems to have advantages over historical-causal analysis both in *breadth* of analysis and in *depth* of analysis. Structural-functional analysis has a tendency to direct the researcher to a broader scope of attention by emphasis upon *system referents* and upon *alternative mechanisms*. The system referent concept induces a social scientist to study the dependent variable within the context of a larger social system and its complex pattern of social variables, rather than simply studying the relationship between two or more variables in temporal sequence abstracted out of a larger social context. What is sought is cumulative knowledge about the system referent, rather than knowledge about isolated interrelationships between variables. As Robert K. Merton has pointed out in his well-known essay on "Manifest and Latent Functions," structural-functional analysis tends to prevent a researcher from merely exploring the relationship between one empirically prominent mechanism and its system referent—instead he is impelled to look for *alternative mechanisms,* which may substitute for, or supplement, each other (7, p. 52-53).

This is not to imply that a sophisticated historical-causal analysis does not also frequently take into account the broader environmental context as well as situations where substitutions of independent variables occur. However, wherever such breadth and depth occur in historical-causal analysis, it is the result of the particular sensitivity and perceptiveness of the researcher and thus is dependent upon his background of research experience—it is not a result of inherent methodological requirements.

The structural-functional method also predisposes a researcher to analyses which tend to exceed those of a historical-causal nature in depth as well as breadth. As Philip Selznick has pointed out, when using a structural-functional approach we are not satisfied merely with asking *what* do men do (the problem of description), or *why* did they do it (the problem of historical-causal analysis); but rather, we are concerned with the deeper problem of why *must* men do what they do (the problem of structural-functional analysis) (12, p. 31). In other words we are interested in getting at underlying generic factors which impose structural limitations and constraints upon human action—the kinds of factors Emile Durkheim referred to as "social facts."

I propose that we can best understand the operation of such normative and structural "social facts" in a framework of structural-functional analysis, whereby we examine the functions of empirical phenomena as mechanisms related to the requirements of larger social systems. Historical-causal analysis predisposes a researcher to concentrate upon finding larger correlations between observable, manifest phenomena; structural-functional analysis induces a researcher to look beyond the appearances of overt phenomena to an assessment of the significance of these phenomena within the contextual framework of systematic interrelationships between structural and functional factors. This, in turn, enables him to generalize his findings from a study of a particular social system so that they apply to other contexts which appear on the surface to be widely different.

As was pointed out earlier, structural-functional analysis as a method of study is not without certain important limitations and difficulties. A major source of difficulty is that the *method* of structural-functional analysis is often confused with *substantive theory* about a given social system. This problem will be discussed in more detail later.

If we consider structural-functional analysis simply as a method of approach to structuring and understanding social phenomena, it can be criticized for its inability to handle, in its own terms, problems of unique historical development. This structural-functional framework of analysis cannot account for *why* one specific mechanism developed in a given historical context to fulfill a certain system requirement; a researcher may actually find other mechanisms developing in other historical contexts to fulfill the same system requirement. Analysis of the conditions which give rise to such differences is properly a historical-causal problem, and is the way in which structural-functional analysis and historical-causal analysis must be related for a comprehensive study. An important example of the interweaving of these two approaches is found in Lipset, Trow, and Coleman's study of the International Typographical Union. The authors wrote in this regard:

> It is clear . . . that any analysis of such a unique set of social forces and relationships as is represented by the two-party system in the ITU requires interpretation on two levels—the historical and the functional. We must consider both the historical conditions which gave rise to this social structure and the factors which support and maintain it as a going system (6, pp. 17-18).

METHOD VERSUS SUBSTANTIVE THEORY

Lack of a clear distinction between structural-functional analysis as a *method of study* and as a *substantive theory* about the nature of social phenomena has led to two types of claims about a structural-functional approach. It is suggested that those who use it are predisposed to make premature judgments about the nature or character of the phenomena studied, and, second, that they are predisposed to take ideological positions which impair objective analysis of these phenomena.

Merton has discussed these claims. He criticized both Radcliffe-Brown and Malinowski for emphasizing the following in their works: *the functional unity of society*—the assumption that standardized social or cultural items are necessarily functional for society as a whole; *universal functionalism*—the assumption that *all* social and cultural items are equally functional; and *functional indispensability*—the assumption that items of functional importance are consequently indispensable (7, pp. 27-38). In each case these assumptions refer to judgements about the nature of human society and thus are a part of a substantive theory—they are not an inherent part of the structural-functional method of analysis. Where structural-functional analysis is used as a method rather than a substantive theory, the researcher directs himself to such questions as the following: *To what extent* is the given social item under study of functional importance to the society as a whole? *To what extent* is it merely important for a subsystem within the larger society? *To what extent* are a variety of items under study of similar functional importance? *To what extent* may given items be substituted for other items within the same functional context? Asking these questions is within the scope of structural-functional analysis as a method. The answers the researcher obtains to such questions are not predetermined by his method, but rather are dependent upon the way the data appear in the empirical investigation itself.

Similarly, Merton has pointed out that charges of ideological bias are not inherent in the method of structural-functional analysis (7, p. 38-39). The problem of ideological bias is an old bone of contention in debates about the merits and limitations of structural-functional analysis. Myrdal and Nisbet are among those who have claimed that functionalism is inherently *conservative* in its approach, being principally concerned with how given structures resist change (8, p. 1056; 9). On the other hand, LaPiere proposed a somewhat more novel view that structural-functional analysis is inherently *radical,* since it questions the utility and value of existing social arrangements:

> The functional approach to collective behavior will, undoubtedly, affront all those who believe that specific socio-psychological structures have inherent values. Thus, to those who believe that a church service is good because it is a church service, the statement that some church services are formal motions which are devoid of religious significance, that others are functionally comparable to theater performances, and that still others are a form of revelry and are therefore comparable to a drunken spree will be an affront to common sense, an attack upon the integrity of decent people, or at least, the ravings of a poor fool (5, pp. 55-56).

Merton has claimed that neither the radical nor the conservative position is inherent in structural-functional analysis, so long as it is used as a method, and by a researcher who attempts to be as sensitive to functional alternatives and contradictory disfunctions as he is to mechanisms supporting the stability of social phenomena (7, pp. 40-43).

Nevertheless, we are confronted by the fact that most researchers who have used the structural-functional approach *have* been more concerned with problems of stability than with problems of social change. I submit that this is not because of a predisposition inherent in their method, but rather because of a predisposition inherent in their preconceptions about the nature of the phenomena they studied. For example, if one views social systems as Talcott Parsons has, i.e., primarily in terms of *equilibrium,* then any change in the system which departs from some constant or cyclical pattern must have its origins outside the system itself—it results from an "input" into the system rather than from any inherent conflict or contradiction within the system (10, pp. 164-165).* If we accept the principles of inertia, action and reaction, acceleration, and system-integration suggested by Parsons, then we are making certain assumptions about phenomena in the empirical world which are not methodological assumptions. Indeed, we may make other types of judgments or prejudgments about the nature of empirical phenomena which are equally compatible with the same methodological perspective. Merton, for example, pointed out how a Marxian-dialectical view of the world is compatible with structural-functional analysis (7, pp. 41-43). Similarly, Selznick has shown how inherent stresses and strains within social organizations have dynamic consequences within the organizations themselves (15). In this manner new needs, new goals, and structural changes are generated by what happens within the social system itself and not only by inputs from outside the system. It appears that insofar as a researcher can be sensitive both to the conditions of stability and the conditions of dynamic change in social systems, he can analyze such systems using the structural-functional method of analysis, without falling prey to ideological biases.

Therefore, I would disagree with the implications of Bernard Barber's statement that "structural-functional analysis is in part a body of substantive sociological concepts and theories, in part a method of analyzing the relations among the several structural constituent of a social system" (1, p. 130). Of course, there is a minimal number of substantive assumptions about the nature of the phenomenon studied which are implicit in any method. For example, historical-causal analysis, insofar as it represents an attempt to develop generalizations, assumes that there are certain sequential regularities in the real world. Similarly, structural-functional analysis assumes that there are determinate relationships between properties of systems, system requirements, and mechanisms. I am maintaining here that it is unnecessary—in fact it is undesirable—for a researcher to make any prejudgments about the nature of such determinate relationships

---

*In this work Parsons seems to deal with certain types of constant or recurrent change in social systems. However, in my opinion, the scheme presented here does not deal with *emergent* factors associated with change in social systems.

before he investigates them to see whether they tend to maintain stability or to promote change.

THE FORM OF STRUCTURAL-FUNCTIONAL PROPOSITIONS

The essence of the structural-functional method is the construction of structural-functional propositions about interrelationships among empirical phenomena. The key elements involved in structural-functional propositions are the following: (1) a *property* of a given system; (2) a system *requirement* which must be fulfilled in order to maintain the system property under consideration; (3) *mechanisms* which fulfill the specified system requirement; and (4) *situational conditions* which specify the set of circumstances under which given mechanisms fulfill particular system requirements.

System Property

A system property is the basic structural item in structural-functional analysis. We distinguish between different types of social systems, indeed between any kind of systems, in terms of their distinctive properties. The distinctive properties of any given social system, taken together, may be said to define the unique character of that system. In speaking of "character" in this manner, we are following Selznick's usage; in this regard he wrote:

> In studying character we are interested in the *distinctive competence or inadequacy* that an organization has acquired. In doing so, we look beyond the formal aspects to examine the commitments that have been accepted in the course of adaptation to internal and external pressures (15, p. 42).

Selznick has given examples of the defining properties in two types of social organization. He characterized the Extension Service of the Tennessee Valley Authority very specifically in terms of: the involvement of the county agricultural agent in local "courthouse" politics; the intimate relation between the Extension Service and the American Farm Bureau Federation; the tendency of extension agents to deal with the relatively more prosperous elements of the local farm population and to reflect the attitudes of the latter toward farm tenancy; and a shift in the role of the Extension Service from a primarily educational emphasis to an acceptance of responsibility for "action" programs. Selznick described the basic character of the Bolshevik type of party organization in the following more general terms:

> The distinctive competence of the Bolshevik "combat" party lies in its ability to transform members of a voluntary association into disciplined and deployable agents (14, pp. 42-45).

In a paper on religious orders in the Roman Catholic Church I compared the Jesuit Order with the Benedictine Order and characterized the Jesuit organization as having a greater degree of centralization, adaptability, and expendability (16, pp. 21-22). In one part of a preliminary report on the study of the role of scientists in research organizations, I have suggested that organizations may be characterized in terms of their adaptability to social and technological change in either a short-run or long-run time period (17, Sect. III).

These, then, are some examples of the ways in which different types of social systems may be characterized in terms of one or more important properties. Once we have identified such properties, we may then go on to indicate the requirements necessary for their support.

System Requirements

This concept refers to the requirements or needs of a given system which support its development with respect to the system property under consideration. In the study of religious orders, previously mentioned, it was found that the peculiar character of such organizations requires the following elements: first, a particularly intensive form of socialization involving both personal alienation from previous interpersonal attachments, ways of action, and ideological patterns, and also intensive personal identification with the way of life of the religious order; and, second, a system of social control focused either upon predominant commitment to a particular ideology or predominant commitment to a particular pattern of authority (16, pp. 14-21).

Another example of the peculiar requirements of one type of social system is found in Selznick's study of the Communist Party. In this work he pointed out that whether the Bolshevik type of party is able to operate effectively as an "organizational weapon" is dependent in part upon the recruitment of mass members and fellow travelers whose association with the party can be described as follows: participation motivated by alienation from existing values rather than positive belief; the lack of a deep personal commitment to ideals and institutions; participation on the basis of stereotyped political codes and symbols; *Realpolitik,* including a radical bifurcation of means and ends; and a search for security substitutes in political action (14, Chap. 7).

In the study of scientists, an example of a functional requirement related to a given property of a larger organizational system is provided by the statement that "the longer range adaptability of a complex organization to social and technological change requires more emphasis upon basic research in research and development activities than upon applied research and development" and by the statement that "the immediate adaptability of a complex organization to short run social and technological change requires more emphasis upon development and applied research in research and development activities than upon basic research" (17, Sect. III).

However, a structural-functional analysis is not completed by merely indicating the requirements for supporting certain properties in given systems. One must go still further and examine the mechanisms which in given situations serve to fulfill such requirements.

Mechanisms

Merton has pointed out in regard to mechanisms:

Functional analysis in sociology, as in other disciplines like physiology and psychology, calls for a "concrete and detailed" account of the mechanisms which operate to perform a given function. This refers, not to psychological, but to social mechanisms (e.g., role-segmentation, insulation of institutional demands, hierarchic orderings of values, social division of labor, ritual and ceremonial enactments, etc.) (7, p. 52).

It is necessary that a clear distinction be made between "mechanisms" and "requirements" in structural-functional analysis. Mechanisms initially may be said to refer to specific structural items or processes which fulfill a general system requirement (or requirements). For example, in the case of the Jesuit Order, the general requirement that members be socialized in a manner which leads them to become intensively identified with the life of the religious order is achieved in part through the repetitive practice of the "Exercises of Loyola." In the same organization, the general requirement that members be socialized in a manner which leads them to become alienated from all attachment to past "wordly" ways of thinking and acting is achieved in part through the practice of "stoning," whereby errors of thought and action are publicly confessed and criticized by fellow novices (16, pp. 15-17).

A well-known example of an organizational defense mechanism is the process of "co-optation," which Philip Selznick has defined as: ". . . the process of absorbing new elements into the leadership or policy-determining structure of an organization as a means of averting threats to its stability or existence" (12, p. 34). Selznick made extensive use of the concept of co-optation to explain how the Tennessee Valley Authority in its early stages of development channelized its agricultural program through local agencies in areas affected by this program (13).

In connection with our study of scientists, employing more scientists relative to engineers might be considered as an example of a mechanism for fulfilling the requirement for more emphasis upon basic research in organizations characterized by long-run adaptability (17, Sect. III). Or the process of "bootlegging" basic research ideas on applied research contracts might be considered as an example of a mechanism for adjusting organizational requirements to certain professional needs of individual research scientists (17, Sect. IV).

We may now systematically indicate the nature of the relationship between these three essential items in structural-functional propositions. We define "mechanisms" (M) as the specific factors which serve to support a "property" (P) of a system insofar as these factors fulfill a general function "requirement" (R). Therefore we may schematically represent a structural-functional proposition initially as follows:

(M) fulfills (R) which supports (P).

However, as was pointed out previously, structural-functional analysts are inclined by the nature of their analysis to be dissatisfied with such simple generalizations. They are also disposed to look for alternative mechanisms in other situations involving the same type of social system (with similar properties and requirements). To take this into account, we may elaborate the basic propositional form as follows:

(M) fulfills (R) which supports (P)

(M') fulfills (R) which supports (P)

(M'') fulfills (R) which supports (P)

Etc.

In such a form M, M', M'', etc. represent specific or unique instances (let us say, among the Jesuits, Benedictines, Franciscans, etc.) of more generalized categories of mechanisms (such as mysticism, asceticism, etc.). Or M and M' might represent such alternative mechanisms as employing proportionately more scientists compared to engineers or allocating proportionately more funds to basic compared to applied research, to fulfill an organizational requirement for relatively more emphasis upon basic research compared to applied research or development.

Up to this point we have not included the historical dimension of the analysis. We need to know something about the conditions under which mechanism (M) may develop in one system context, (M') in another context, (M'') in a third, etc.

Situational Conditions

Merton has pointed out that the range in variation in alternative mechanisms fulfilling a given system requirement is not unlimited, but is in turn dependent upon the context constituting the relevant external and internal environment of the system (7, p. 53). To assume otherwise ignores the fact that behavioral systems at any level of analysis do not exist in vacuums, but are simultaneously shaped by the character of the larger systems of which they are a part, and by the smaller systems contained within their boundaries. Thus, as Warner and Low pointed out, an understanding of the social system of the modern factory is affected by the organization and culture of the surrounding community (18). Reinhard Bendix went a step further and showed the relevance of the social structure of entire national societies to the development of industrial organization and ideology (2). Regarding smaller systems contexts, Roethlisberger and Dickson's well-known report on the Hawthorne studies is an example of a description of the relationship between industrial organization and the systems of informal relations which may exist within the factory itself (11). In each of these studies the authors were dealing with a historical-causal problem—the conditions in the external and internal environment which preceded the development of the items or mechanisms under investigation.

To take into account various complexes of situational conditions (S, S', S'', etc.),* the basic form of structural-functional propositions may be modified as follows:

(M) under conditions of (S) fulfills (R) which supports (P)
(M') under conditions of (S') fulfills (R) which supports (P)
(M'') under conditions of (S'') fulfills (R) which supports (P)
Etc.

Up to this point we have described the nature of structural-functional propositions and discussed their utility in a methodological orientation toward empirical research. However, we have not yet discussed what is perhaps the most neglected problem in structural-functional analysis—how does one go about testing structural-functional propositions against what happens in the real world? If we are to have a firm empirical grounding for structural-functional analysis, we must be prepared to submit our formulations to the traditional scientific ordeal—what are the facts?

Critics of the structural-functional method have claimed that the propositions developed through this method too often have been imputations in the mind of some researcher and not propositions which have been derived from and tested against empirical data. They claim that other analysts might have come to different conclusions using the same data.** To meet this problem, structural-functional analysts must have a rigorous method for testing their propositions which will establish conclusively their validity or lack of validity.

---

*It should be noted that (S) in most instances does not represent a single factor, but rather a complex of environmental factors.
**This is the type of criticism leveled by Harry C. Bredemeeir against Kingsley Davis' analysis of the incest taboo (3, pp. 173-174).

TESTING STRUCTURAL-FUNCTIONAL PROPOSITIONS

Kendall and Lazarsfeld in a notable paper on survey analysis have outlined a basic procedure for the "elaboration" of empirical relationships derived from survey data (4). Harry C. Bredemeier has suggested that this procedure could be as useful for testing structural-functional propositions as it is for testing historical-causal propositions (3). It is the objective of the following discussion to describe a systematic form of application of the method of elaboration to the verification of structural-functional propositions.

For illustrative material, we draw from the work of Lipset, Trow, and Coleman on *Union Democracy* (6). Among other things, they noticed certain interesting phenomena in their study of the International Typographical Union: for example, that the members frequently associated with each other informally off the job in leisure clubs and organizations, that they also associated informally with each other frequently on the job, that the range of occupational roles which were involved in informal interaction was very broad, that the union itself provided a great number and variety of functions for its membership, and that the membership had a high degree of personal identification with their occupation (6, esp. pp. 415-416). Moreover, the researchers found that the International Typographical Union was more "democratic" than most other American unions. They were interested in formulating the relationship between the phenomena they observed occurring within the ITU and its characteristic property of being a particularly "democratic" voluntary organization. Thus in formal terms it might be hypothesized that informal association *off* the job (what the authors described as an "occupational community") acted as a mechanism (M) to support "democracy" (P) in the union; similarly that informal association *on* the job provided another mechanism (M') to support "democracy" (P); and similarly that a broad range of occupational roles involved in such informal associations acted as still another mechanism (M'') to support "democracy" (P); etc.

If such hypotheses are sustained by the data, then the empirical relationships between each one of these alternative mechanisms and the property of the system under study should look something like the cross tabulation indicated schematically in Figure 1. Here the variables involved have been represented for simplicity as dichotomous attributes of, let us say, union locals classified according to whether or not they are "democratic" on one hand and whether or not their members participate in informal relations off the job (occupational communities), on the other hand.

The hypothesis that there is a positive relationship between occupational communities and democracy in union locals would be sustained

Figure 1

(P)
Is the union local "democratic"?

		Yes	No
(M) Are there occupational communities?	Yes	1 X	2
	No	4	3 X

if the preponderance of cases appeared in cells 1 and 3; the hypothesis would not be supported if any other pattern developed in the data.* The same would be true for other hypotheses involving (M'), (M''), etc.

However, the structural-functional analyst would not stop here. He would also want to know more about *how* occupational communities are related to union democracy. In order to advance his understanding, he would attempt to identify the functional requirement(s) of union democracy which is met by the mechanism of occupational communities.

In this regard, the authors of *Union Democracy* found that a high degree of membership interest and voluntary participation in union activities was one of the important requirements for the support of democracy in trade unions. They stated this in the form of the following empirical generalization:

The greater the members' interest in their union, and the greater their voluntary participation in union affairs, the greater the chances for democracy in the union (6, pp. 415-416).

However, in this form, this empirical generalization only expresses an association between two variables, although it hints at two functional requirements which might be expressed in the following terms:
Democracy in unions (P) requires membership interest (R) and membership participation (R).

*Insofar as there are several other mechanisms beside occupational communities associated with union democracy, there might be considerable dispersion of cases throughout the four cells of Figure 1, thus showing only a low degree of association between any one mechanism, such as occupational communities, and union democracy.

Whether such a statement of functional requirements is subject to verification or not, depends of course first upon whether "democracy" as a property or characteristic of trade union is defined operationally in terms independent of membership interest and participation. As an example, this problem might be solved if we conceived of "democracy" in terms of frequency of leadership turnover as a result of membership action through an electoral process.

Assuming that we have established independent operational definitions of the property and the requirement under study, we might test the hypothesized structural-functional relationship of membership interest and democracy in terms of the simplified pattern indicated in Figure 2.

Figure 2

(P)
Is the union local "democratic"?

		Yes	No
(R) Is the membership interested in union activities?	Yes	1 X	2
	No	4 (no cases)	3 X

Again, if the preponderance of cases falls into cells 1 and 3, the hypothesis is sustained that membership interest and participation in union activities is a functional requirement of union democracy.

Since membership interest is considered to be a requirement of union democracy, rather than just a correlate, we would further expect no cases to fall into cell 4 of Figure 2. Any cases that did fall into cell 4 either would have to be considered as resulting from errors of measurement of union democracy or of membership interest, or would have to be taken as cause to reject membership interest as a requirement (R) of union democracy.

At the same time, if membership participation in occupational communities acts as a mechanism to support membership interest in union activities, we would expect the results of an investigation of this relationship to look like Figure 3.

Figure 3

(R)

Is the membership interested in
union activities?

		Yes	No
(M) Are there occupational communities?	Yes	1 X	2
	No	4	3 X

This, in fact, is what the researchers in *Union Democracy* found. They summarized this finding in terms of the following empirical generalization:

The more that workers in the same union associate with each other off the job, informally and in various leisure time clubs and organizations, the greater is likely to be their interest and participation in the affairs of their union (6, p. 415).

They made similar generalizations about the support for membership interest in union activities obtained from alternative mechanisms, such as informal association on the job, the broad range of occupational roles involved in such informal associations, and others and the like.

So far, what has been said has been relatively simple and has not really been an application of the subtle aspects of the Kendall-Lazarsfeld elaboration technique (4). We have shown how one might determine whether there is a positive relationship between membership participation in informal relationships off the job, on the one hand, and membership interest in union activities and union democracy, on the other. We have not yet shown a method for determining whether the relationship between occupational communities and union democracy can be explained in terms of a structural-functional proposition of the following type:

(M) fulfills (R) which supports (P); or union democracy (P) requires that the membership of the union be highly interested in union affairs (R), which in turn is supported by the mechanism of occupational communities (M).

We would be able to determine if (R) in fact "explains" the relationship between (M) and (P), noted originally in Figure 1, if the original relationship between (M) and (P) was substantially reduced when the sample of union locals was stratified according to (R), as illustrated schematically in Figure 4.

Figure 4

(R) Is the membership interested in union activities?

Yes	No

(P)
Is the local union democratic?

(P)
Is the local union democratic?

		Yes	No				Yes	No
(M) Are there occupational communities?	Yes	1 X	2 X	(M) Are there occupational communities?	Yes	1 X	2 X
	No	4 X	3 X		No	4 X	3 X

Thus if the elaboration of the original observed relationship between (M) and (P) in terms of (R) yielded a result of more dispersion of cases in all cells in the "stratified" comparison, rather than a concentration of cases in cells 1 and 3, then the functional proposition that union democracy requires the membership of the union to be highly interested in union affairs and that this in turn is supported by the mechanism of occupational communities, is verified by the data.

If this finding were substantiated, the structural-functional analyst would then be able to go a step further; he would wish to take into account the situational conditions which might affect the operation of occupational communities and which would enable him to specify the historical circumstances permitting alternative mechanisms to perform similar functions. We have already mentioned what some of the alternative mechanisms were in the case of the ITU: informal relations on the job, a broad range of occupational roles involved in informal relations, union provision of a wide variety of functions for its membership, a high degree of membership identification with their occupation, etc. We earlier represented schematically the effect of such situational conditions as follows:

(M) under conditions of (S) fulfills (R) which supports (P)
(M') under conditions of (S) fufills (R) which supports (P)
(M'') under conditions of (S) fulfills (R) which supports (P)
Etc.

We may then conceive of (S) as a test factor which, in Kendall-Lazarsfeld terminology, may be introduced to further "specify" the basic relationship between (M) and (R), as illustrated in Figure 3.* In this regard Lipset, Trow, and Coleman found that members of the ITU who worked in large shops were more likely to be involved and interested in union politics than small shop men—regardless of whether they participated in the printers' occupational community and thus associated with other members' outside work (6, p. 150f). Thus for the ITU, shop size (S) influenced the effectiveness of informal relations off the job (M) in support of union democracy (P), or more specifically in support of interest in union affairs (R). Figure 5 illustrates the pattern of data which would support this hypothesis.

Figure 5

(S) Shop Size

Large shops	Small shops
(R) Is the membership interested in union activities?	**(R)** Is the membership interested in union activities?

		Yes	No				Yes	No
(M) Are there occupational communities?	Yes	1 XX	2		**(M)** Are there occupational communities?	Yes	1 X	2 X
	No	4	3 XX			No	4 X	3 X

Then if the trend in the data shown in terms of Figure 5 indicates that the original relationship between (M) and (R) reported in Figure 3 is increased in large shops and decreased in small shops, the hypothesis is substantiated that shop size is an important conditional factor affecting the original structural-functional relationship. As we specify more and more of these types of situational conditions in research studies, the structural-functional analysis may be put into historical perspective and at the same time our sensitivity to alternate mechanisms is increased.

---

*Actually, in the ITU case, most of the alternative mechanisms cited above operate simultaneously under similar conditions, but this does not vitiate the form of analysis we might use to study situational variations in the effectiveness of these mechanisms.

We may summarize this discussion of the application of the Kendall-Lazarsfeld scheme of "elaboration" to the empirical verification of functional propositions in two statements as follows:

1. The empirical verification of propositions relating mechanisms to properties of systems through the fulfillment of system requirements may be achieved through the process of "interpretation."*

2. The empirical verification of propositions which indicate the situational conditions under which the fulfillment of system requirements by given mechanisms is strengthened or weakened may be achieved through the process of "specification."**

In conclusion, it may be pointed out that the suggested application of the structural-functional method to a description of the findings of studies such as that reported in *Union Democracy* makes a minimum of assumptions about the substantive nature of the phenomenon studied, e.g., about the stability of the ITU, about the "boundaries" of the union as a social system, about the degree of integration of parts within the system, etc. This method does, however, attempt to produce meaningful propositions about structural-functional attributes of a given type of social system which can, in turn, be tested, verified, and/or modified in further research.

BIBLIOGRAPHY

1. Barber, Bernard. "Structural-Functional Analysis: Some Problems and Misunderstandings," *American Sociological Review,* XXI (April, 1956) 129-135

2. Bendix, Reinhard. *Work and Authority in Industry; Ideologies of Management in the Course of Industrialization.* New York: John Wiley & Sons, Inc. 1956

3. Bredemeier, Harry C. "The Methodology of Functionalism," *American Sociological Review,* XX (April, 1955) 173-180

4. Kendall, P. L., and Lazarsfeld, P. F. "Problems of Survey Analysis," in *Continuities in Social Research: Studies in the Scope and Method of 'The American Soldier',* ed. by Robert K. Merton and Paul F. Lazarsfeld (Glencoe, Ill.: The Free Press, 1950) 133-196

---

*This process of analysis Kendall and Lazarsfeld refer to as "M type interpretation," whereby an original relationship between two variables is the result of the marginal terms (4, pp. 154-158).

**This process of analysis is referred to as "P type specification," whereby an original relationship between two variables is a weighted average of the two partial relationships (4). This type of elaboration is especially useful for introducing the historical dimension into otherwise structural-functional propositions wherever a sequential relationship may be established to indicate that (S) precedes (M) in temporal occurrence.

5. LaPiere, Richard T. *Collective Behavior.* New York: McGraw-Hill Book Co., 1938

6. Lipset, Seymour M., Trow, Martin A., and Coleman, James S. *Union Democracy: The Internal Politics of the International Typographical Union.* Glencoe, Ill.: The Free Press, 1956. (A Report of the Bureau of Applied Social Research, Columbia University)

7. Merton, Robert K. *Social Theory and Social Structure; Toward the Codification of Theory and Research.* Glencoe, Ill.: The Free Press, 1949 (Enl. ed., Glencoe Free Press, 1957)

8. Myrdal, Gunnar. *An American Dilemma: The Negro Problem and Modern Democracy.* 2 vols. New York: Harper and Brothers, 1944

9. Nisbet, Robert A. "Conversation and Sociology," *American Journal of Sociology,* LVIII (September, 1952) 167-175

10. Parsons, Talcott, Bales, Robert F., and Shils, Edward A. *Working Papers in the Theory of Action.* Glencoe, Ill.: The Free Press, 1953

11. Roethlisberger, F. J., and Dickson, W. J. *Management and the Worker.* Cambridge, Mass.: Harvard University Press, new ed. 1950. (An account of a research program conducted by The Western Electric Co., Hawthorne Works, Chicago, with the assistance and collaboration of Harold A. Wright. 1st ed. 1943)

12. Selznick, Philip. "Foundations of the Theory of Organization," *American Sociological Review,* XIII (February, 1948) 25-35

13. _____ *TVA and the Grass Roots; A Study in the Sociology of Formal Organization.* Berkeley: University of California Press, 1949. (University of California, Publications in Culture and Society, vol. iii)

14. _____ *The Organizational Weapon: A Study of Bolshevik Strategy and Tactics.* New York: McGraw-Hill Book Co., 1952

15. _____ *Leadership in Administration; A Sociological Interpretation.* Evanston, Ill.: Row, Peterson & Co., 1957

16. Vollmer, Howard M. "Member Commitment and Organizational Competence in Religious Orders," *Berkeley Publications in Society and Institutions,* III (1957) 13-25

17. _____ *A Preliminary Investigation and Analysis of the Role of Scientists in Research Organizations.* Phase I, Technical Research Report to the Air Force Office of Scientific Research, 1962

18. Warner, W. Lloyd, and Low, J. O. *The Social System of the Modern Factory.* New Haven: Yale University Press, 1947

The Small Group Field: Implications for Research on Behavior in Organizations*

IRWIN ALTMAN**

GENERALIZATION of results from small group research to behavior in complex organizations is neither completely appropriate nor directly possible. Historically, small group research has been concerned with groups of individuals behaving in concert with respect to some goal, where the size of the group has ranged from two-man teams to groups of 15-20 members. Many organizations involve much larger numbers of people working with respect to a goal, and who are often members of subgroups whose aims and organizations are often very diverse. In addition, small group research has not been very deeply concerned with relationships *between* groups, whereas in larger organizations intergroup dynamics are often critical. Nevertheless, the small group field can potentially be of importance to students of behavior in organizations for several reasons. First, many interpersonal processes occurring in small groups such as power and status

*This paper is based on results of a research program supported by the Behavioral Sciences Division, Air Force Office of Scientific Research under Contract No. AF (638) -269 and conducted by the author and Dr. Joseph E. McGrath, principal investigator. The paper draws heavily from technical reports produced in the program. A book describing the program and findings, with title *Small Group Research; Synthesis and Critique,* is forthcoming in 1965 (Holt, Rinehart and Winston).

While Dr. McGrath has had a key role in influencing many of the ideas to be discussed, the author assumes sole responsibility for the contents of this paper. In addition, the opinions and statements contained herein are not to be construed as official or reflecting the views of the Navy Department or the Naval Service at large.

**Dr. Altman is currently Research Psychologist at the Naval Medical Research Institute, Bethesda, Maryland.

relationships, negotiation and bargaining processes, work-team effectiveness factors, leader-follower relations, face-to-face communication and breakdowns in communication, to name just a few, occur in subgroups of large organizations. Research findings, errors, and blind alleys uncovered in the small group field, therefore, may be of use to the researcher concerned with behavior in organizations. Second, the small group field has been a meeting ground for many disciplines such as social psychology, sociology, and more recently mathematics and political science. These disciplines are bringing new concepts and methodologies to bear on small group phenomena, which in turn could have application to research on behavior in organizations. Third, a moderate amount of pre- and post-World War II research on small groups has been devoted to military and industrial work teams and therefore has direct relevance to organizational phenomena. These are just a few of the possible reasons why the substantive findings of small group research may be useful to the student of behavior in complex organizations. The present chapter provides a broad treatment of the history of the small group field and some research findings having to do with group and member performance.

In addition, we shall summarize the rationale, procedure, and results of a five-year program to develop a system for classifying the voluminous outpouring of small group research information. Since similar productivity is being shown in research on behavior in organizations, it might be useful to consider our attempt at synthesis and organization of information as a case history in the classification of scientific knowledge. We therefore offer a description of our program in the hope of stimulating consideration of research on the classification of knowledge being accrued about behavior in organizations.

HISTORICAL BACKGROUND OF SMALL GROUP RESEARCH

It is through an understanding of the history of a field that one gains some appreciation of how certain areas came to be studied and others neglected, how various methods of study were adopted at the expense of others, and how researchers came to travel down certain philosophical, theoretical, and empirical paths. In addition, a sense of history makes the gaps and limitations of a field as well as its capabilities more manifest. For the researcher himself, an understanding of his intellectual ancestry may help him better assess his own position and aspirations and may provide some slight opportunity for leverage on his own future. To understand present-day small group research one should be sensitive to its past.

The history of small group research parallels that of social psychology and certain areas of sociology and, in many respects, is the child of both these disciplines. Although roots can be traced to Greek philosophy and to European scholars of the sixteenth, seventeenth, and eighteenth centuries, modern social psychological and sociological thinking about behavior in small groups may be said to have had its beginnings in the early years of this century and in the waning years of the nineteenth century. This was a period when men like Tarde and Le Bon in France were concerned with the pathological group—the mob, crowd, and herd. Ross in America, along with the other sociologists Cooley and Mead were investigating the nature of social interaction processes—the two-person dyad as the basic social unit, the family as a primary group, etc. These formative years of social psychology and indirectly of sociology were turbulent. Students were interested in the fundamental "why" and "how" of social behavior at the simplest level possible. The tendency of the times was to search for basics, assumptions, and primitive terms and concepts much as the book of Genesis in its early pages was a search for answers to questions about man's origins and basic nature. Scholars stood at conceptual poles regarding the essence of social behavior, with the environmentalist-behaviorist adherents at one end and the nativist proponents at the other.

The earlier dominant approach offered by instinct theorists was gradually undermined by the empiricist school of thought in psychology and sociology. Empiricists offered a philosophy of objectivity—to deal only with observables and to reject concepts like the soul, mind, and unconscious. The turmoil of this early period ended with the behavioristically oriented researchers holding sway.

In the 1920's the social psychologist and small group researcher withdrew to the laboratory, no longer swept up in grand philosophical issues, but concerned with developing rigorous methodology and with the study of narrow delimited aspects of man's social behavior. It was in this period, typified by the work of Allport on social facilitation, that the methodological seeds of the years to come were sown. A new norm was established in the decade of the 1920's, not with regard to substance, but with regard to methodology.

The 1930's saw the small group researcher swept along by the field as a whole, emerging out of the laboratory and beginning to deal with real problems, perhaps partly stimulated by the great depression. As the agents of history, researchers began to study mass movements, lynchings, prejudice, rumor flow, and a host of problems relevant to the extra-laboratory secular world. The well-known Hawthorne Western Electric studies dramatically demonstrated the social-psychological dynamics of small groups in a real work setting. Perhaps most important, the beginnings of the group dynamics approach, under the leadership of Kurt Lewin, signified the tenor of the years to come. For it was not only the germination of theory in small group research that made Lewin's contribution significant, but the tackling of real-world problems of frustration, goal achievement, leadership styles, etc. in an experimental fashion. The marriage of theoretically based ideas, real-world problems, and experimental methodology had not occurred before in small group research.

The 1940's were years of important development for social psychology and the small group field. Work expanded on two fronts— methodology development and accumulation of empirical knowledge in several areas, the most noteworthy being leadership—although the contribution to theory was less pronounced. By the end of the decade, small group research had become a popular area of study.

In the 1950's the research boom continued to grow and although attention to theory was generally low there were rumblings to the contrary. Festinger's work on uniformity pressures (7) and social comparison processes (8), Thibaut and Kelley's cost/reward theory of group phenomena (22), and the theoretical analyses of leadership compiled by Petrullo and Bass (18) were some of the major attempts to reverse the trend.

With the stock-piling of empirical knowledge and the relative neglect of integrating theory, a need soon arose to answer the question "What do we know about small group phenomena?" In the middle 1950's several people addressed themselves to this question, as reflected in reviews of the literature by Roseborough (20), Riecken and Homans (19) and others. At about the same time Hare, Borgatta and Bales (13) and Cartwright and Zander (5) edited volumes which were collections of research publications, organized to reflect dominant thinking, methodology and findings of the field. These latter works were primarily reference sources; they were not intended to be critical, to induce theory, or to evaluate existing theory. As research continued, the tone of the integrators and literature reviewers changed somewhat. Thibaut and Kelley (22) offered a theoretical analysis of small group phenomena which included integration of a large amount of prior work and suggested some fruitful areas of work derived from their theory; Golembiewski (10) produced a philosophical-methodological critique of the field along with an integration of many research findings; and Hare (12) published a handbook which reviewed a large amount of research organized around major variables.

It was this cultural milieu that led to our work. As agents of the times, we too felt the need for a "summing up." We hoped not only for description and cataloging, but also for something that would allow identification of gaps in knowledge, which would have predictive value, which could lead to new theory, and which could absorb new findings when they appeared. Thus, we found ourselves as much concerned with the problem of developing a method and rationale for classifying scientific knowledge as with the problem of integrating the substantive findings of the small group field. With this setting of the stage, let us now consider in detail the goals, strategy and procedures used to develop a system to integrate the rapidly accruing fund of knowledge about small groups.

THE CLASSIFICATION APPROACH

To say that the 1950's and 1960's were productive years for the small group field is a gross understatement. A bibliography accumulated during our program contained some 2,000 items, the great majority dated during the period 1950-1962 (21), and it is estimated that the field is accruing new reports of research at the rate of several hundred per year. This fact, coupled with the absence of any broad general theory, led to a situation where a great deal of scattered and unintegrated information was being generated about small group phenomena.

One major goal of our research program was to develop a system for classifying research information in a systematic fashion which would allow for the absorption of new research information and would provide guidelines for future research in high-payoff, provocative, unclear, and untapped areas. These general goals implied some desirable characteristics which we attempted to build into the system. First, we sought a means for comparing any research finding with any other finding, regardless of the terminology or esoteric nature of the research information. This led to an approach which initially ignored "substance" or "content" descriptions of variables and focused on developing classification categories and dimensions based on operational properties of data. In addition, the desired property of being able to compare research results led to a multidimensional classification system in which each finding or variable was assigned to a single point in a common multidimensional classification "space" rather than to a set of unrelated classes. The system sought would "never" have to add new major classification categories, although further distinctions were to be possible within the general system. In short, the aim was to develop a general language of data into which the vast array of semantically unrelated research findings and variables could be translated.

A second general goal of the program was to produce a classification system which would have predictive as well as descriptive value. That is, we aimed toward a scheme which would allow for the prediction, in advance of empirical knowledge, of the probability of association between any two variables. The achievement of such a capability implies, of course, that the ordering principles of the classification system are also fundamental ordering principles for the empirical phenomena to which the classification system refers. The advantages of a system that is both predictive and descriptive over one that is only descriptive are many. For one, the extent to which the system is capable of prediction in the direction specified is one test of the "validity" of the system and its usefulness as a classificatory device. Secondly, a predictive classification system would enable hypothesizing about as yet untested relationships between variables. To do this would be extremely useful to the small group field, for it would permit projection into areas of study which may not have been tapped, with some prediction as to the likelihood of finding strong, weak or ambiguous relationships. Such a capability could obviously assist tremendously in theory construction and the design of individual research studies. Hence let us consider next the terms of the classification system, its application, evaluation, modification, and implications for behavior in complex organizations.

The Classification System

The classification system is described in detail in Altman and McGrath (1). The basic unit of research information was assumed to be a statement of results of an empirical or statistical test of relationship between two variables. Each such statement has three parts: *a resultant variable* whose variation is to be accounted for; *an agent variable* which is presumed or predicted to account for all or some of the variation in the resultant variable; and *a relational term* in the form of the results of a statistical test of significance, ordinarily a statement of the probability of the variables being associated. The classification system is designed to describe the operational data properties of the variables of a relationship and to describe the nature and form of the relationship itself.

Variables of a relationship are operationally defined in terms of combinations of *items of data.* Items of data are individual responses or judgments. Data items are combined to represent a given variable. The theory underlying the distinction between variables and data items, and the ways in which individual items of data are combined is discussed in detail elsewhere (1). The basic terms of the classification system have to do with the operational characteristics of the data items which underlie a given variable.

The classification system postulates six fundamental *operational properties or parameters of data,* each with a number of levels or categories. These six parameters are used to describe any item of data and, therefore, any agent or resultant variable. The parameters of data, their definitions and categories are as follows:

1. *Object.* The object of a data item is the level of reference of the entity to which that response or judgment refers. For example, if a data item deals with a characteristic of a number of the group, then it is at the individual or member level of reference. If the data item referent is the group as a whole, then its object is at the group level of reference. Major categories for the object parameter are: *member* (self, other); *group; environment* (individuals outside the group, other groups, objects).

2. *Mode.* The mode of a data item refers to the type of characteristic which is being judged or recorded in the data item. The mode parameter is a modifier of the object parameter. If the data item refers to a static or persevering property of the object, e.g., a trait, its mode is designated as *state.* If it refers to an action or change in behavior, the mode is designated as *action.* The state-action distinction is analogous to the biologist's distinction between organ structure and organ function, between the nerve and the nerve impulse, etc. While there is not always a conceptually clear difference between the state-action categories, states typically include biographical, attitudinal, personality, etc. properties of members and groups, and describe the object as an entity at a point in time. Actions, on the other hand, refer to dynamic properties of objects and depict events that occur during a specified interval of time, e.g., group or member performances, communications, interactions, etc.

3. *Source.* The person or instrument making the response or providing the judgment is the source of the data item. If the data item is based on a report by a member of the group, then the source is designated as member. If the data item is based on a report or judgment by two or more members of the group, then the source of the data item is group. Categories on the source parameter are: *member; group; environment* (investigator, investigator surrogate such as expert judge or an objective recording instrument).

4. *Viewpoint.* This parameter is a modifier of the source parameter and refers to the frame of reference the source takes in making a judgment about the data object. If a group member makes a judgment from a subjective or personal point of view, the data item is characterized as *subjective.* If he attempts to estimate the judgment of another member of the group or the group as a whole, the viewpoint is categorized as *projective.* If a group member or the investigator, as source, responds or makes a judgment from an impersonal or objective frame of reference, the data item viewpoint is classified as *objective.*

5. *Task.** The task parameter refers to the type of judgment or

---

*The task parameter is identical to Coombs' distinction between Task A and Task B; the distinction between relative and irrelative judgments is also adopted from Coombs' theory of data (6).

response made about an object. If the judgment or response involves specification of the amount or degree of a property possessed by the object, then it falls in the *description* category of the task parameter. If the item of data involves a judgment of the extent to which the object departs or deviates from some ideal or standard, it is classified as an *evaluation*. Thus, evaluation involves a statement of the difference between the amount of an attribute possessed by an object and the amount of that attribute which is judged to be ideal, desirable or correct. On the other hand, description only involves specification of the amount of the attribute possessed by the object.

6. *Relativeness.** For either description or evaluation, a judgment may be a comparative or *relative* one in which the object of concern is compared with one or more other objects. *Irrelative* items of data involve absolute judgments about an object.

The Classification of Variables

Each data item is classified into one of the categories on each of the six parameters. Thus, the number of theoretically possible classes of data is the product of the number of categories on the six parameters. Every item of data is described in terms of the same set of properties and therefore the exact similarity or difference of any item of data from any other one can be specified using the language of the classification system.

Items of data are the building blocks from which variables are formed.** A variable may be composed of a single data item or a combination of different types of data items. For example, the variable "amount of talking in the group" involves summation of a series of judgments or items of data referring to discrete occurrences of conversation between group members. All data items so described would have the same properties in the classification system and would form a variable class containing homogeneous data items. On the other hand, the variable "self-esteem" often consists of two different data items combined to operationally define the variable. For example, self-esteem is frequently defined as the difference between a person's judgment of his own characteristic on some trait and his statement of the "ideal" level on the trait. Since these two judgments would probably be classified differently in the system, self-esteem would be a complex variable containing more than one type of data item.

---

*Ibid.
**A more detailed discussion of the arithmetic and statistical operations employed in combining data items to form variable classes and the use of such operations as another dimension of the classification system are discussed in Altman and McGrath (1).

There are as many simple or homogeneous variable classes as there are combinations of values on the parameters of data. There is, of course, a much larger number of complex classes of variables. Since in our work most variable classes are composed of homogeneous data items, the discussion to follow applies largely to these.

Because the classification approach postulates that variables defined similarly in terms of their values on the six parameters of data are similar regardless of the content label applied to them, it becomes possible to compare and pool data from different studies using the same language and level of abstraction. By pooling information from different studies, with variables now defined in terms of the language of the classification system, it is possible to identify areas in which a great deal of research has been done as well as areas of sparse activity. It is also possible to specify the probability of association between variables in terms of the proportion of relationships between any given pair which is statistically reliable at some level of significance, e.g., the .05 level. The proportion of significant relationships at the .05 level of confidence is termed the "batting average" of a relationship class and is considered to be an estimate of the probability that any given pair of variables will be related to one another. It is through analysis of the batting averages of relationships that the usefulness of the classification system is examined.

The Principle of Operational Concordance

The classification system, designed to be a descriptive and predictive device, has an intrinsic means for partially testing its usefulness as reflected in the hypothesis of operational concordance. This principle states that the more alike two variables are in their operational or data properties the greater the probability of their being associated with one another.

As noted above, it was presumed that variables categorized in terms of the six parameters of the classification system are directly comparable with one another. One index of similarity between variables so classified is the number of category parameters on which they have similar values, which can range from six when they are identical on all parameters, to zero when they assume different values on all parameters of the classification system. A simple count of their similarity on parameters, then, is one indicator of the operational concordance level.*

---

*The index of concordance is more complicated for complex relationships. It is also possible to develop several other measures of concordance by weighting the various parameters and categories. However, results using a variety of weighting methods are so similar that the simple counting procedure suffices for the present discussion. See McGrath (16).

Using this index it is possible to order all relationships into one of seven levels of operational concordance.

It is a basic hypothesis of the classification system that the greater the level of operational concordance between two variables, the greater the probability of their being associated, as indicated by tests of significance. The greater the extent to which this hypothesis is confirmed by recourse to empirical data from the small group field, the more confidence can be placed in the classification system as a predictive device and the more the parameters of data can be trusted as useful means for describing research information in the small group field. If the general hypothesis is confirmed, then, it offers the possibility that the probability of occurrence of significant associations between untested variables can be predicted in advance of empirical study. And if confirmed, the usefulness of the classification system for theory development and study design, as well as for description and integration of existing knowledge, would be partly demonstrated.

Application and Evaluation of the Classification System

After the classification system was tried out on a small number of studies and coder reliability was established (1), it was applied to the research information of a random sample of 200 small group studies and a special sample of 50 studies containing measures of individual and/or group performance effectiveness. The total sample was chosen from a bibliography of some 2,000 small group studies previously compiled (21). Trained coders extracted the empirical information from these studies and coded all variables in terms of the six parameters of the classification system. Substantive or content descriptions of the variables were also recorded, along with detailed information about study procedure and methodology, statistical test information, etc. These 250 studies generated a pool of approximately 12,000 empirical relationships, which constituted the raw data of the research program from which (a) the hypothesis of operational concordance was evaluated (16), (b) the systematic study annotations were prepared (3), (c) the research information was organized by variables (4), and (d) the system was broadened and modified to allow more ready entree and integration of the field (17).

In order to evaluate the fundamental hypothesis underlying the classification system, all relationships in the sample were assigned operational concordance values according to the degree of similarity between the variables of the relationship. The range of concordance values was from six in cases where the variables had identical values on the six parameters to zero where variables assumed different values on all parameters. Following this, the 'batting average' associated with each concordance level was computed, i.e., the proportion of relationships within a concordance level which were statistically significant at or below the .05 level of confidence. The results of this analysis are summarized in Figure 1 as reported in McGrath (16).

Figure 1

ASSOCIATION BETWEEN CONCORDANCE LEVEL AND "BATTING AVERAGE" FOR 7500 SMALL GROUP RELATIONSHIPS

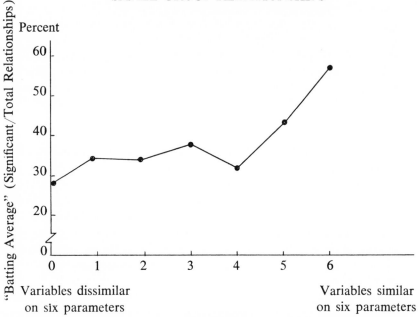

Concordance Level (Parameters that Variables had in Common)

The data of Figure 1 were based on over 7,500 simple relationships, i.e., those that contained homogeneous items of data. Since the data were very similar for 1,500 complex relationships, the discussion is limited to the simple type relationships.* As the data of Figure 1 show, the basic hypothesis of operational concordance is confirmed, in that the more similarity there is between variables of a relationship in terms of operational or data properties (i.e. parameters of the classification system), the greater the incidence of their being as-

---

*While the total pool of relationships in the sample was 12,000, the statistical significance of some 3,000 relationships was not available, thus making it impossible to include them in the analysis.

sociated. In addition to suggesting that we had identified some of the important dimensions of small group data, these results lent support to the predictive potential of the classification approach.

The next step in the analysis was to assess the differential contribution of the various parameters to the over-all relationship between concordance level and batting average. The results showed first the Object parameter and second the Mode parameter to be most important. That is, concordance or similarity on these parameters taken alone led to a much higher incidence of significant associations than did nonconcordance on these parameters. Concordance or lack of concordance on the Task parameter did not affect the batting average, suggesting the lack of importance of this parameter as a classificatory dimension. The Source and Viewpoint parameters, although highly distinct conceptually, were empirically correlated in the data they generated and thereby are best conceived of as a single parameter. The Source-Viewpoint distinction was intermediate in discriminating between concordant and non-concordant cases. The Relativeness parameter was omitted from the analysis because the great preponderance of data was in only one of the two categories of the parameter-relative judgment. From these analyses, it was concluded that similarity or difference on the Object, Mode and Source-Viewpoint parameters are the major contributors to the probability of variables being significantly associated with one another. Interestingly, plotting batting average against degree of concordance using *only* these three parameters yielded a straight linear function with a batting average of approximately 25% in the case of non-concordance on all three parameters and approximately 60% when the variables of a relationship were wholly concordant on the Object, Mode and Source-Viewpoint parameters.

The possibility of non-additive combinations of the three parameters as contributors to the over-all concordance-batting average function was also explored. These analyses showed that the Object parameter is clearly the major one, with the Mode and Source-Viewpoint parameters playing different roles as a function of concordance and non-concordance on the Object parameter. When, for example, the objects of a relationship are concordant, similarity or dissimilarity on the Source-Viewpoint parameter does not affect the batting average at all. Similarity on the Mode parameter, however, does; it yields a higher batting average for Object and Mode concordant cases than it does for Object Concordant, Mode non-concordant cases. Thus, if the objects of a relationship are concordant, then Source-Viewpoint parameter similarity or dissimilarity does not make a difference, whereas Mode parameter concordance has a marked effect on batting average. Turning to relationships in which data objects are non-concordant, the picture is reversed. Here similarity of difference on the Source-Viewpoint parameter is important and does affect the magnitude of the batting average. Object therefore is the dominant parameter, with the Mode and Source-Viewpoint parameters playing roles which depend on the concordance of the objects of the relationships.

It should be noted that the general results obtained here are somewhat similar to those obtained earlier by Guttman (11) and Foa (9). They have developed an approach, facet analysis, which is conceptually very similar to ours, their facets being analogous to parameters and Guttman's contiguity hypothesis analogous to the principle of operational concordance. This system is far more sophisticated, mathematically, than our approach, but it is encouraging that our results are somewhat similar to those obtained by other workers.

Modification of the Classification System for Descriptive Purposes.

In general then, the results of these analyses led to some confidence that aspects of the system developed were potentially useful for description and integration of small group research information and for prediction, study design and theory development. Based on these analyses, the classification system was modified to reflect the dominant role of Object, Mode and Source-Viewpoint parameters. This classification, also modified to bring in certain substantive or content distinctions, is shown in Table 1, as adopted from McGrath (17).

Table 1

LIST OF VARIABLE CLASSES OF
A REVISED CLASSIFICATION SYSTEM

Variable Classes	*Major* *Data Parameters Underlying* *the Revised System*
100 Properties of Group Members	
110 Biographical characteristics of members	Member state
120 Personality characteristics of members	Member state
130 Abilities of members	
131 General abilities of members	Member state
132 Task abilities of members	Member state
140 Attitudes of members	
141 Attitudes toward the task	Surround state
142 Attitudes toward the situation	Surround state

Variable Classes	*Major* *Data Parameters Underlying* *the Revised System*
143 Attitudes toward non-group persons and other groups	Surround state
144 Attitudes toward issues, concepts, ideologies	Surround state
150 Positions of members in the group	
151 Social position in the group	Member state
152 Task or physical position in the group	Member state
200 Properties of the Group	
220 Group capabilities	
221 Group abilities	Group state
222 Group training and experience	Member/Group state
230 Interpersonal relations in the group	Member/Group state
240 General structural properties of the group	Group state
300 Conditions Imposed on the Group	
310 Social conditions	
311 Influence and conformity pressures	Group state
312 Induced social conditions	Group state
320 Task and operating conditions	
321 Stimulus properties of the task	Surround state
322 Feedback and reinforcement conditions	Member/Group state
323 Induced task conditions	Group state
400 Interaction Process	
410 Content of interaction	Member/Group state
420 Patterns of interactions	Member/Group state
430 Outcomes of interaction	Member/Group action
500 Subjective Measures of Member and Group Performance	
510 Perceptions of task performance of self and others	Member action
520 Perceptions of social behavior of self and others	Member action

	Major
Variable Classes	*Data Parameters Underlying*
	the Revised System

600 Objective Measures of Member and
    Group Performance
    610 Leadership performance   Member action
    620 Task performance of members
        621 Member task performance
            in experimental settings   Member action
        622 Member task performance
            in operational settings:
            global measures   Member action
        623 Member task performance
            in operational settings: spe-
            cific measures   Member action
    630 Task performance of groups
        631 Group task performance in
            experimental settings   Group action
        632 Group task performance in
            operational settings: global
            measures   Group action
        633 Group task performance in
            operational settings: spe-
            cific measures   Group action

It can be seen that the six major classes of variables listed in the table reflect differences on the three important parameters. The Object parameter contribution is reflected in the distinction between member and group levels of reference; the Mode parameter role is shown by the distinctions between properties of members and groups as entities or states (e.g., personality, task capabilities, group structure, etc.), and members and groups as acting, behaving objects (e.g., measures of performance, discussion behavior, etc.) The Source-Viewpoint parameter is represented by differential classification of subjective measures, perceptions, etc. and objective measures of member and group properties, behavior and performance. In addition, a final modification of the system, as a descriptive device, was to reincorporate some content language of the everyday researcher, but to have it now contain definitional meaning that attaches to operational properties of the data on which it was based. In a sense then, for purposes of integration, we completed a full cycle from translation of the data into a new language, evaluation of the translation, and then back to a more communicable language, now based on more standard-ized underpinning.

With this lengthy, though superficial exposition of the logic, eval-uation and modification of the classification approach, let us now consider how some of the findings of the small group field may be applied to an understanding of behavior in organizations and, secondly, how an approach of the type here discussed may be useful in integrating and keeping up with research information on behavior in organizations.

IMPLICATIONS FOR BEHAVIOR IN ORGANIZATIONS

As indicated at the outset, it is neither simple nor completely appropriate to generalize from knowledge accrued about small groups to behavior in organizations. This is the case for several reasons. To begin with, organizations are much more complex than the typical small group; they contain many interrelated parts which include numerous "small groups." In addition, organizational functioning often hinges on effective intergroup relations, dependencies and linkages. Research on small groups has been almost completely concerned with intragroup phenomena and has largely ignored intergroup processes. Further, approximately two-thirds of the studies in our review sample, which is probably representative of the field as a whole, were studies done by academic researchers in laboratory situations— which ordinarily involved artificial tasks, groups formed only for the purpose of the experiment and whose life as a group was extremely short, and group members who largely came from college populations. Nevertheless, if such qualifications are held in mind, certain substantive generalizations and fruitful areas of study may emerge from an appre-ciation of major small group research findings. We shall briefly dis-cuss some of these now.

As indicated in Table 1 and in the earlier discussion, the original classification of small group variables was altered to reflect the con-tributions of the three critical parameters: Object, Mode and Source-Viewpoint. The resulting variable classes were further modified to be more communicable and reflective of current content-oriented terminol-ogy, now hopefully more rigorous and tied to operational properties of data. One can conceive of the 31 variables of Table 1 cast in a 31 x 31 matrix of relationships, i.e., each variable class related to each other one. This arrangement would represent, hypothetically, the range of relationship classes that could occur in the small group field, as specified by the classification system. While each relationship so depicted might have relevance to behavior in organizations, space does not permit a discussion of all of them. We shall therefore sharply restrict the following discussion to variables that seem most pertinent to behavior in organizations. Specifically we have selected for discussion certain variables in the 600 series of Table 1, namely, measures of member and group performance effectiveness. Other variable classes are discussed with respect to their association with various performance effectiveness measures, on the presumption that students of behavior in organizations might use such data as a basis for studies in organizational settings.

Performance Effectiveness of Members of the Group

The role of member characteristics. Research results support some common-sense suppositions about the impact of member-level factors on individual performance in groups, e.g., the higher a person's general abilities or intelligence and the greater his task aptitude, the better is his performance in a group. Moreover, there is a positive relationship between job performance and actual job knowledge, training and experience. Thus, if one aims to increase the performance of individuals in a group situation, one should select bright people, those who have relevant aptitudes, knowledge of the job, and who are trained and possess experience. While not seemingly profound findings, they do lend objective credence to institutional wisdom and contrast somewhat with factors enhancing group performance, as discussed later. It is interesting to note that these results demonstrate how the concordance hypothesis was supported by the data of the sample. That is, member abilities, etc. usually are coded as *objective states* of *members* and thus are quite similar to measures of individual performance which are generally classified as *objective actions* of *members.*

One finds that factors such as member personality, attitudes, subjective perceptions, etc., do not have consistently clear-cut relationships to individual performance. In some situations such personal variables are important determinants of performance, but not in other cases. Interestingly, this ambiguity, if further research continues to yield such results, may suggest re-examination of the extreme "human relations" approach to management which has been in vogue in recent years. Some possible reasons for the confusing role of these more "romantic" variables is discussed later. Here again the concordance notion is evident. The personality, attitude, etc. class of variables often involve *different objects* than performance measures, *states* versus *actions,* and *subjective* judgments versus *objective* judgments of performance. This class of variables is conceptually quite different from member performance effectiveness measures and, according to the general hypothesis of the classification approach, should not be expected to relate highly to member performance. In summary, predicting member performance in group situations is more easily and consistently done from knowledge of an individual's intelligence and job-related characteristics than from his personal-social properties.

The role of environmental factors. In examining the role of outside influences on individual performance we again obtain some expected findings. The indications are that individual autonomy has a positive effect on performance. Feelings of participation in decision-making about various aspects of the job (whether it actually takes place or not), and feedback in the form of reward and knowledge of performance enhance member performance. The requirement to make a decision imposed upon an individual also affects his performance favorably. In short, freedom, a sense of involvement, the requirement to act, and feedback enhance member performance—ideas compatible with common-sense notions are substantiated by a scientific approach to behavior.

Performance Effectiveness of the Group

The role of member characteristics. In examining factors which bear on overall group performance rather than individual member performance, some interesting findings appear. Results suggest that member intellectual and task-relevant abilities, e.g., mechanical aptitude, taken alone, are not consistently good predictors of group performance while individual job experience is. Merely having intelligent, high potential people in a group does not necessarily produce an effective team.

Data also suggest that personality and attitudinal characteristics are not consistently related to group performance except that the absence of extreme personality characteristics enhances group functioning. In addition, subjective perceptions of various types, e.g., personal skill estimates or estimates of the skills of others, are not always associated with good group performance. Here again the data of the sample supported the general concordance hypothesis. Group performance effectiveness measures would normally be categorized as *objective* measures of *group action,* while many of the immediately preceding variables represent *subjective* judgments of *member states.* Thus, the variables entering into these classes of relationships are quite different from one another in operational terms.

The role of group characteristics. At the group level results appear to tie in with the preceding. For one, experience as a group (working together for a period of time) has a positive effect on group performance as does a relatively small-sized group. Favorable interpersonal relations in the group, e.g., cohesion and morale, show unclear effects although the trend is for high morale and cohesion to produce better performance. Such results are compatible with those for individual member performance where job-rated factors had a definite impact on productivity while the more social-personal variables played a less precise role.

The role of environmental factors. Outside influences play a similar role for group and individual productivity, with reward and punishment, rather than explanation and illustration alone, tending to enhance performance. In addition, there are differential effects of types of feedback on group performance, e.g., structured having a more enhancing effect than completely unstructured critiques. Other work conditions such as routing of necessary information, direct and rapid access to information, have a positive effect on group performance. The clarity of role definition, i.e., the job each person is to do and relationships between various jobs, aid group performance.

The Role of Personality and Social Factors on Performance

As we have seen, results are not unequivocal regarding the effects of personal-social factors on individual and group performance, a finding somewhat in contrast to the attention such variables have received by researchers. How can we account for such findings and what potential role do the variables play? As already implied, part of the answer may lie in the conceptual "distance," as reflected in the degree of operational concordance, between such variables and performance effectiveness. The relatively smaller proportion of significant relationships may be due to the attenuation that occurs as such factors interact with a host of other variables that are conceptually closer to final performance. It is not that they are unimportant, but that their role is more indirect and more affected by a host of other more salient and directly relevant variables.

It may be that the results are also attributable to methodology. For example, in aptitude and ability measurement psychologists have well-developed tools, whereas in personality, attitude, group cohesion measurement the technology is far less advanced. Let us however consider the role of these variables from another point of departure. When one speaks of abilities and experiences as determinants of performance one is usually arguing that the *more* of the characteristic the better the performance, and this usually is true. But for personal-social variables this monotonic principle may not apply; rather we may be in a realm where either *too much* or *too little* of a characteristic interferes with some optimum in-between point enhancing it.

Another hypothesis related to the role of these variables is that they are mobilizers of individual and group productivity potential. Perhaps individual and group abilities, experience, etc. tend to set limits within which the group can function, as intelligence may have limits set on it by heredity. In the same way the environment may operate only within a fixed band of intellectual capacity, so may it be that social-personal variables can enhance performance only within limits set by abilities, training, and experience. If abilities and experience are present, then desirable interpersonal relations will allow the group to achieve its potential. If not sufficiently present then the member or group may not achieve its performance potential. Without attempting to resolve the possibilities raised here, it should be recognized that personal-social variables cannot be viewed simply within the common-sense adage that "the happy, well-adjusted worker is the good worker."

This, of course, is neither an intensive nor complete review of the small group research literature on performance effectiveness of individuals and groups. The general trends portrayed here, however, may contribute to an understanding of behavior in organizations where many of the same dynamics operate; they also may have broader, strategic implications for such research. Our experience with small group research suggests several potentially important strategic areas of consideration.

The operational concordance hypothesis and the general results presented suggest that if one is interested in understanding and predicting performance effectiveness of organizations as a whole, or subgroups within an organization, one should attempt to use, as predictor variables, those which are similar in terms of Object, Mode and, Source-Viewpoint properties. That is, a best guess would be that group and system level variables bear a more important relationship to group and organizational performance effectiveness than do properties of individual members of the group. Not that the latter are unimportant, but that where one is interested in group outputs a major part of the variance resides with group level variables. Beyond this specific example, our work suggests the general utility of the concordance hypothesis as a predictive device and, because of the overlap of subject matters, it would seem useful to attempt to validate and explore the hypothesis in another setting.

Some General Comments.

An area of consideration which has been grossly overlooked in the small group area and which also has considerable importance for organizational behavior involves the criterion problem. In our work an attempt was made to describe the dependent variable, performance effectiveness, in some detail, but this was only a very crude beginning. Considerable work needs to be done to identify the important properties of performance effectiveness, the varieties of performance involved in group and organizational settings, and the appropriate levels or standards of effective performance. The fact that these issues and related ones have not received very much attention in small group research increases the difficulty of making comparisons among studies, tasks and situations. As another aspect of the criterion problem, considerable effort needs to be expended on the development of a taxonomy or classification of tasks and situations. A major variable affecting performance of individuals, groups and organizations is obviously the task worked on and the general situation in which the group finds itself. Without an appreciation of the dimensions of tasks in terms of performance requirements, or role relationships required between group members, little real progress can be made toward understanding the dynamics of teams and organizations. Because of the complexity of organizational phenomena, the problems created by lack of attention to task and situation definition will be magnified tenfold.

A third aspect of the criterion problem which has hampered progress in understanding small group phenomena and which will similarly generate difficulty in the organizational research area is the overly narrow concept of performance effectiveness held by many researchers. Too often the study of performance effectiveness is limited to analysis of final group outputs with little regard for "process" description and evaluation. Performance effectiveness should be viewed from a much larger perspective, to include so-called "process variables" as intrinsic antecedents of performance outputs. Thus, we reject the approach to small group performance or organizational performance solely from a "black box" point of view, but propose instead a strategy of research that peers into the box and attempts to understand the sequential development of performance as it progresses from input to output. This strategy is also implicit in the operational concordance hypothesis, wherein it was stated that the probability of a relationship between variables "distant" in the multidimensional space of the classification system is low. This suggests that to understand the role of such variables, one must understand how the attenuation of their effect occurs and the nature of their indirect effect on performance.

Finally, we offer a "commercial" for an extension of work on the classification and synthesis of research information to the area of organizational behavior. Research on behavior in organizations is already a productive field. Far beyond what has occurred in small group research, students of behavior in organizations will continue to come from a host of disciplines, each of which will provide varying perspectives, concepts, methods and interests. This is certainly healthy, but it will also lead to difficulties of communication, semantic confusion, etc. in much the same way that diversity among small group researchers has led to much unintegrated and not easily comparable research. For this reason, a research program with the goal to develop a system for systematically organizing research on behavior in organizations, and later development of a central repository of information is urged. Focus should be placed on the development of a multidimensional, exhaustive, predictive system to enable more than description and cataloging of knowledge. The need to systematize the existing accumulated body of knowledge is important now; it will become even more critical as research proceeds in this and the coming decade.

BIBLIOGRAPHY

1. Altman, Irwin, and McGrath, Joseph E. *A Conceptual Framework for the Integration of Small Group Research Information*. Arlington, Va.: Human Sciences Research, Inc., February, 1959. (AFOSR TN 59-252, ASTIA AD No. 212 252)

2. ––––––––––, Jenkins, J. P., and McGrath, J. E. *The Translation of Small Group Research Information for Computer Analysis*. Arlington, Va.: Human Sciences Research, Inc., October, 1959. (AFOSR TN 59-1194, ASTIA AD No. 230 241)

3. ––––––––––, Pendleton, Catherine A., and Terauds, Anita. *Annotations of Small Group Research Studies*. Arlington, Va.: Human Sciences Research, Inc., October, 1960. (AFOSR TN 60-1208, ASTIA AD No. 248 440)

4. ––––––––––, and Terauds, A. *Major Variables of the Small Group Field*. Arlington, Va.: Human Sciences Research, Inc., November, 1960. (AFOSR TN 60-1207, ASTIA AD No. 250 740)

5. Cartwright, Dorwin, and Zander, Alvin. *Group Dynamics: Research and Theory*. 2nd ed. Evanston, Ill.: Row, Peterson and Co., 1960

6. Coombs, C. *A Theory of Psychological Scaling*. Ann Arbor: University of Michigan Press, 1952. (University of Michigan, Engineering Research Institute, Bulletin No. 34)

7. Festinger, Leon. "Informal Social Communication," *Psychological Review,* LVII (September, 1950) 271-282

8. ––––––––––. "A Theory of Social Comparison Processes," *Human Relations,* VII (1954) 117-140

9. Foa, Uriel G. "The Contiguity Principle in the Structure of Interpersonal Relations," *Human Relations,* XI (1958) 229-238

10. Golembiewski, Robert. *The Small Group: An Analysis of Research Concepts and Operations*. Chicago: University of Chicago Press, 1962

11. Guttman, Louis. "A Structural Theory for Intergroup Beliefs and Action," *American Sociological Review,* XXIV (June, 1959) 318-328

12. Hare, A. Paul. *Handbook of Small Group Research*. Glencoe, Ill.: The Free Press, 1962

13. _____, Borgatta, E. F., and Bales, R. F. (ed.) *Small Groups: Studies in Social Interaction*. New York: Alfred A. Knopf, 1955

14. Kelley, Harold H., and Thibaut, John W., "Experimental Studies of Group Problem Solving and Process," in *Handbook of Social Psychology*, ed. by G. Lindzey, (2 vols., Cambridge, Mass.: Addison-Wesley Publ. Co., 1954) vol. II, pp. 735-785

15. McGrath, Joseph E. *A Framework for Integration of Small Group Research Studies: A Pilot Study*. Arlington, Va.: Psychological Research Associates, October 1957. (PRA Report No. 57-20, AFOSR TN 57-87, ASTIA AD No. 136 680)

16. _____. *Systems of Information in Small Group Research Studies*. Arlington, Va.: Human Sciences Research, Inc., April, 1962. (AFOSR Doc. No. 2416)

17. _____. *A Summary of Small Group Research Studies*. Arlington, Va.: Human Sciences Research, Inc., June, 1962. (AFOSR Doc. No. 2709)

18. Petrullo, Luigi, and Bass, Bernard M., (eds.) *Leadership and Interpersonal Behavior*. New York: Holt, Rinehart and Winston, 1961

19. Riecken, Henry W., and Homans, George C. "Psychological Aspects of Social Structure," in *Handbook of Social Psychology,* ed. by G. Lindzey, (2 vols. Cambridge, Mass.: Addison-Wesley Publ. Co., Inc., 1954) vol. II, pp. 786-832

20. Roseborough, Mary E. "Experimental Studies of Small Groups," *Psychological Bulletin,* L (July, 1953) 275-303

21. Terauds, Anita, Altman, Irwin, and McGrath, Joseph E., *A Bibliography of Small Group Research*. Arlington, Va.: Human Sciences Research, Inc., April, 1960. (AFOSR TN 60-365, ASTIA AD No. 237 304)

22. Thibaut, John W., and Kelley, Harold H. *The Social Psychology of Groups*. New York: John Wiley and Sons, Inc., 1959

Field Experiments with Formal Organizations*

STANLEY E. SEASHORE**

A RECENT task of describing a field experiment concerning organizational structure and process (12) has led us to make a review of some other studies of a similar kind, and to formulate some general thoughts on the dilemmas and strategies in such research. This paper is a first rough attempt to organize these thoughts. It seems worth doing because: (a) few people have had any direct experience in conducting field experiments with complex organizations, (b) with increasing financial and methodological resources we are likely to see more work of this kind, and (c) compared with experiments of other kinds, certain issues of strategy and method become of crucial importance and deserve examination.

Let us first state the reference of discourse. We will consider here experiments done in natural settings where the experiment is incidental to the main purposes of the organizations. We will consider as a "formal organization" any relatively stable social system that is complex in the sense of including two or more component groups coordinated through two or more hierarchical levels of leadership. What constitutes an "experiment" is less easy to state. Obviously, there are alternative designs and a continuum of conformance with ideal experimental design. Let us settle, for the moment, on minimum criteria of: (a) definable and measurable change in organizational environment, structure, or process, (b) some means for quantification of variables, and (c) some provision for testing of causal hypotheses through the method of difference.

---

*Some of the work leading to this paper was supported by a grant from the Air Force Office of Scientific Research, Contract AF 49 (638) - 1032. This article was published in the Summer, 1964, issue of *Human Organization* of the Society for Applied Anthropology (vol. 23, pp. 164-170).

**Dr. Seashore is Professor of Psychology, Department of Psychology, and Assistant Director, Institute for Social Research, University of Michigan, Ann Arbor, Michigan.

These definitions exempt from consideration *simulation experiments* (such as the work of Sydney and Beatrice Rome with a computer model of an organization), *case studies* (such as the Tavistock Institute's work at the Glacier metals factory), *correlational studies* (such as those of the Survey Research Center done in many organizations), and most *ex post facto comparison studies* (such as the work of Mann and Hoffman comparing two power plants with differing degrees of automation). These are all highly productive and valuable classes of research effort, but they are not "experiments" even by our suggested minimal standards. Also excluded from discussion are the many *group experiments* that have been conducted within organizations (such as the classic Hawthorne Test Room and Harwood Rate Change experiments). Exclusion is on the grounds that such field experiments concern small groups rather than larger, more complex social organizations, and that the location of the subject groups within complex organizations is, in such cases, only incidental to the purposes, design and conduct of the work.

The reader will recognize that these exclusions are arbitrary, and have no purpose other than to narrow attention to the special problems that arise or become accentuated when one attempts field studies of relatively large and complex organizational units with methods that approach those of classical experimental design.

WHY EXPERIMENTS?

The justification for conducting experiments must rest on grounds of effectiveness and efficiency in generating information and testing hypotheses. The advantages must be sufficient to offset the added costs, which may be great. Two considerations seem relevant.

It is difficult to establish unequivocally a causal relationship between variables without a controlled experiment spanning the period of change in both variables. Organizational theory is becoming sufficiently complex and sophisticated to bring to the fore issues of causality. Therefore, on certain theoretical issues, no other research approach is effective.

The second consideration is one of efficiency and economy. A single well designed experiment can, in principle, produce information of such unequivocal nature that it outweighs any number of case studies or demonstrations.*

---

*An example of the failure of non-experimental method comes to mind. Marriott's review (10) of the research on the efficacy of incentive payment plans in raising individual and organizational work performance led to the conclusion that, in spite of many hundreds of "successful" introductions of incentive pay plans, one cannot know whether the reported effects are produced by the pay plans or by other concomitant factors. There have been a total of three experiments on the matter, but all were done about thirty years ago and all involved N's of less than ten individuals. The amount of useful information from this vast amount of work is remarkably small.

Other reasons one might invoke to justify attempts to use the experimental method are of a different order. For example, an experiment in a natural setting with real organizations is likely to produce results that seem acceptable and persuasive to action-oriented people and therefore to encourage application of the results.

Literature on the Methodology of Field Experiments

The otherwise rich literature on methodology of research on human social behavior is barren when it comes to experiments with formal organizations. The two primary works in the field from the early Fifties (5, 7) contain sections on experimental design and on field procedures, but no special reference to experiments with formal organizations, and only cne example is mentioned—possibly the only one that existed at the time. A later book by Argyle (2) includes an excellent critical review of methodological designs and principles, arguing strongly for the use of experimental methods, but has no reference to the special case of experiments with formal organizations. Etzioni's recent collection of articles (3) similarly is void of examples or discussion in this area.

A scanning of five recent major works on research design in the behavioral sciences uncovered not a single example of experimental work with formal human organizations, and no reference to the problems of conducting such research in field settings.

The picture looks very different when one turns from sources that focus on experimental design to those that focus on field research methods generally. Here one finds a rich fund of example and analytic discussion of procedures for obtaining information about complex social organizations, for inducing change in organizations, and for drawing tentative conclusions from field data. There are numerous reports of anthropological methods in the study of formal organizations, descriptions of participant-observer techniques and of survey techniques, and the like (1). All these have great merit and are highly relevant to the conduct of field experiments, but they do not deal systematically with the special problems of experimental design in conjunction with these methods.

Dimensions for Describing and Evaluating Experiments

A general and inclusive set of dimensions for describing and evaluating field experimental designs would be a very long and complicated one, and probably not very useful at the present time. However, some dimensions of evident importance can be suggested at a start:

Choice of populations: Number and size of organizational units; pre-experimental homogeneity and differences as to membership, structure, function; provision for control populations and for contrasting or variable treatment of experimental units; provision for control of potential confounding variables through randomization, purposive selection, measurement and statistical treatment of population variables not part of the theory.

Approach to change: Natural vs. purposeful change; if purposeful, is the point-of-change at the level of individual members, general organizational policy, internal structure and process, or in the organizations' environment?

Variables for manipulation or measurement: Are the point-of-change variables part of the theory? How many independent variables are there and what are the provisions for treating their relationship? How many are the dependent variables, and do they include both "internal" and "output" variables? What causal chains and interactions are implied if not specified by the design?

Level of theory: Does the theory refer to institutional, organizational, social-psychological, or psychological phenomena? What is the level of abstraction on a continuum from the highly specific and restricted to the highly general and universal?

Duration in time

Analysis plan: Assessment of results through before-after comparisons, through difference between experimental and control units, through analysis of variance, etc. Is analysis at the individual, the group, or the organizational level?

EXAMPLES OF EXPERIMENTS WITH FORMAL ORGANIZATIONS

The total number of research ventures that might be reasonably considered to be field experiments with formal organizations is very small, perhaps from five to ten, depending upon how generous one chooses to be in tolerating deviations from ideal experimental conditions. None of these fulfills the canons of experimental design to the degree ordinarily expected in laboratory or field experiments on small groups. One must view them as rather primitive, pioneering ventures. Three of the better examples are summarized briefly here.

Experiment I concerns the relationship between level of decision-making in an organization and the effectiveness of work performance (11). The population included four parallel divisions (about 500 employees) of a large business firm, all performing similar clerical work under similar conditions. Data on work force composition, past performance, and the like were used to estimate and maximize pre-experimental homogeneity. Divisions were paired for contrasting experimental treatment. The experimental changes involved policy clarification and change, training of individual supervisors and employees, alteration of certain organizational structures and processes. These actions were intended to produce contrasting effects on the independent variable, and measurements were obtained to confirm the success of the change program. Dependent variables included both variables descriptive of internal organizational processes and state and also output variables such as cost of production and member satisfaction. The theory was at the level of social psychology, in the sense of treating the psychological consequences of social structure and processes. The experimental period extended over a full year, with measurements before and after, and with active change program interventions conducted during the six months preceding the experimental period. Results: increasing the amount of involvement in decision-making of rank and file employees led to reduced cost of work performance, increased employee satisfaction, and increased sense of responsibility for work performance. Increasing the amount of involvement in decision-making by higher-level staff and supervisors also reduced cost of work performance, but otherwise led to reduced employee satisfaction, a lowering of individual responsibility for production, and other similar changes.

Experiment II concerns the "feedback" of employee attitude survey data as a means for inducing beneficial changes in the attitudes and "morale" of employees (9). The population included six departments (about 1,000 employees) of the accounting division of a large utility firm, with two departments serving as control units and four having differential amounts of change treatment. The method and amount of feedback activity was voluntary for each department and hence the "experimental" units were self-selected. The several departments were of varying size and membership composition, and performed somewhat different functions. The experimental change program was a combination of natural and purposeful procedures: the units electing to undertake the feedback of survey data did so to the extent possible, in ways that expressed their normal policies and work processes; but the managers and supervisors received coaching and counseling in feedback procedures, and encouragement toward extensive and intensive use of the process. Higher-level management support was obtained to legitimize the experiment. The point of change therefore was internal to the organization, and included policy clarification and change, as well as individual training and alteration of organizational processes.

The independent variable was the amount of feedback activity over a one-year span of time and the dependent variables represented numerous aspects of employee satisfaction and "morale," treated as separate variables and also summed to obtain an over-all index of attitudes favorable to the achievement of the organization's goals. The theory underlying the experiment was social-psychological in character and assumed that unspecified but adaptive changes in the attitudes and overt behavior of supervisors were the principal intervening variables. The elements of the theory were not differentiated or measured separately in the experimental plan. The experiment had a total duration of four years, including two pre-experimental measurements of dependent variables (to set base rates), an active feedback period of about one year followed by a year of time, and a final measurement after the fourth year. Analysis consisted of the comparison of experimental and control departments on the dependent variables at the end of the period, and also before-after change measurements for each department. Results: the amount of the improvements in employee attitudes and "morale" were roughly proportional to the amount of effort allocated to the feedback process.

Experiment III concerns the induction of change in four variables central to Likert's management theory (8) and the consequences with respect to "output" criteria of work efficiency, waste, absence, and employee satisfaction. The population included five production departments (about 500 employees) of a packaging materials firm. One of the experimental departments was selected by the research team, two others volunteered for experimental change treatment, and the remaining two were used as control units. The departments varied in size and in productive function but were similar in composition of force, and exposure to a common plant-wide policy and history. The change procedures included policy change to legitimize the experiment and to permit certain structural changes in the organization, training of supervisory and staff people, and changes in various organizational processes concerning communications and decision-making. The change program was intended to induce, in the experimental units: (a) more employee involvement in decision-making, (b) more use of work groups as a medium for organizational activity, (c) more supportiveness in supervisor-employee relationships, and (d) more mutual interaction and influence within work groups. Measurements before and after the change program in both experimental and control units confirmed the successful induction of the desired changes. Criterion variables were also measured before, at one point during, and again after the change period. The change program extended over a three year period. The theory was social-psychological in character, and (for purposes of this experiment) treated the independent variables as a set, not attempting to differentiate their separate effects. The dependent variables were treated separately. Assessment of results provided for before-after comparisons for each unit, for comparisons for each unit, and for comparison of experimental and control departments before and again after the experimental period. Results: changes in the four independent variables are associated with increased employee satisfaction, reduction in waste, increase in productive efficiency and dampening of a trend toward increased absenteeism.

Some Dilemmas in Experimental Design

The design and conduct of field experiments with formal organizations involve the same methodological, theoretical, and ethical considerations that apply to any research with human subjects, but some are particularly bothersome. Some comments follow on several dilemmas that are apparent from a review of the experiments that have been reported thus far.

1. *Control vs. Representativeness.*

The most common forms of organization tend to be exactly those most difficult to perform experiments upon. Experiment I, above, achieved a fairly high degree of control over unknown confounding variables by restricting its scope to four parallel divisions matched in a number of respects. Experiment III, by contrast, involved a much more commonly prevailing situation with organizational units differing in a number of respects (size, population mix, nature of work, etc.) in such a way as to leave some question whether the experimental results derived from the experimental variables or from other unknown sources. The added precision of Experiment I must be weighed against the possibility that its results derive from some feature of the restricted and exceptional population. There are at least two guides toward resolving this dilemma. Until more is known about confounding factors in field experiments there is a great merit in emphasizing control through the selection of an initially homogeneous population. Those choosing to emphasize representativeness might well compensate for loss of homogeneity by using a larger number of cases, thus allowing randomization of some intruding variables. No experiment known to us so far has an N of organizational units greater than six.

2. *Short-term vs. Long-term Experiments.*

Of five cases of field experiments with formal organizations which have been examined most closely, three required a span of time (years, not months) considerably greater than originally intended, and this permitted the instrusion of personnel changes, technological changes, and other events that may well have confounded the results. The problem appears to be that significant changes in organizational structure and process come about rather slowly; at the same time, the longer an experiment continues in a natural organization, the more likely that there will be some loss of control over experimental conditions. In Experiment III, for example, some organizational units present at the beginning of the experiment simply disappeared under the press of technological change in the course of a three-year change program, and there took place a considerable but normal turnover of membership in the experimental units. The advantages of short-term experimental plans are very great, but rest upon having powerful change methods and upon excluding variables not subject to change in a short time. Long-term experimental plans permit the utilization of natural changes and changes induced with less risk of stressful side-effects which might themselves introduce confounding effects.

3. *Small, Explicit Theories vs. Global, Syndromatic Theories.*

Theoretical development, especially during early years of experimentation, is likely to be optimized to the extent that experiments focus upon small segments of organizational theory and deal precisely with a limited number of variables having a high degree of generality. This assertion argues for experiments designed around small, explicit theories. (But, note that these may be small theories about large phenomena.) On the other hand, preliminary theory testing is likely to be accomplished more easily on a global or syndromatic basis. Natural organizations function not in segments but as totalities, and it is likely that "larger" theoretical systems, necessarily coupled with reduced precision of conceptualization and measurement, are needed to capture the main phenomena that occur. All of the experiments examined by the writer chose the latter course, and in translating theory into design ended by making large and risky assumptions about the interrelations among the elements of theory and by using syndromatic assessments. Experiment II, for example, by-passed entirely the details of its theory and measured only the change input, and also the output at the level of individual behavior. Experiment III deliberately treated as a syndrome four independent variables which in theory are separate and not of the same order; this forceable simplification of theory can be justified only on grounds of experimental expediency. The researcher's choice in this dilemma may well be based on grounds of convenience or esthetics until enough progress is made to permit some better judgment of relative effectiveness of the two approaches.

4. *Massive vs. Controlled Change.*

The dilemma here arises from the conflict between the need to obtain change great enough to sustain measurement while at the same time preserving the possibility of differentiating among change sources and avoiding unintended and uncontrolled change. The experiments conducted thus far appear without exception to have called into play virtually all of the change resources available to the experimenters, and none has attempted to separate in analysis the effects of different sources or kinds of change activities. This dilemma is the counterpart, at the level of change induction, of the preceding point regarding specificity of theory. One known experiment was initially designed to differentiate among three change strategies, but this feature of the initial design failed of realization. Considering the difficulty of inducing a significant intentional change in organizational process, it appears likely that the first successful attempts to differentiate and control the sources of change will take the form of "natural" experiments (which exploit powerful singular events and conditions) or changes induced through modifications of organizational environment and/or formal structure (which require less direct intervention within the organizations).

5. Near vs. Distant Criteria.

Organizational theories of the dynamic variety all involve chains of causal linkages between variables. The differentiation between "independent" and "dependent" variables accordingly becomes arbitrary except for their relative position in the causal sequence. One man's independent variable is another's criterion. The dilemma for the designer of experiments lies in weighing the advantages of "near" and "distant" criteria. His theoretical interests press toward criteria of organizational structure or process that are presumed to be immediately dependent upon his independent variables; at the same time his concerns for enlarging the conceptual scheme press toward criteria representing the output of the organizational system. The first choice maximizes his chances of getting significant relationships and is more likely to illuminate and add precision to this theory. The second choice offers the important gain of proving some link between his independent variables and the ultimate criteria by which the organizations are judged by society. Of the three examples given earlier, all involved "output" or distant criteria, and Experiment I also provided for assessment of certain "near" criteria. An example may be needed to clarify the point: a researcher changing the number of hierarchical levels in his experimental organizations might use a near dependent variable such as change in communication rates within the organizations, or he might choose to use a distant criterion such as change in productivity rates. In principle, of course, one can account for all elements in the theoretically specified causal chains, together with their interactions, but this would be a truly formidable and presently impossible task.

6. Self vs. Independent Selection of Subjects.

A problem that has not been treated as yet in any experimental investigation on organizations, but one which needs attention, concerns the consequences of self-selection of the subject organizations. The dilemma for the researcher is to balance the advantages of working with organizations that are accessible and compliant, against the hazard that these qualities may themselves interfere with control and representativeness in the research operations. Having a manager willing to expose his organization to experimentation is hardly a typical organizational condition, and implies that the outcome may be prejudiced in unforeseen ways. The same dilemma arises in experiments with individuals and small groups, but in a less disruptive degree.

7. *Scientific vs. Ethical and Practical Considerations.*

All of the organizational experiments reported thus far involved a degree of collaboration between the subjects and the researchers which is greater than commonly holds for other experiments with human subjects. This collaboration typically includes a rather great financial investment by the "subjects" with some corresponding expectation of benefit, and the scale of work means that any harm that inadvertently may be incurred will effect many people. It is the nature of useful experiments that they tend to go beyond our confident knowledge and establish experimental skills, with consequent risk, and in the case of organizational experiments these risks are on a large scale. The course of experimentally induced changes is not likely to remain in the immediate control of the experimenter, and he must depend upon many others who may misunderstand or take advantage of the experimental situation. A protection is often available in the way of making the design and conduct of the experiment a truly collaborative matter, with responsibility for consequences located in ways compatible with the structure of the organization, but this in turn limits the change program to matters known to and understood by the participants. A few instances are on record where organizations or members have been harmed by organizational-level intervention for research purposes, and more are bound to occur if experimentation proceeds in a vigorous and venturesome way.

RESEARCH STRATEGIES

At this primitive stage of development in experimentation with formal organizations it is probably desirable to emphasize simplicity of design and opportunism in execution as guides to research strategy. Some suggestions follow:

1. *Search for Optimum Research Sites.*

This writer is much impressed by the difficulties of establishing control over variables which are not components of the research design. The practical approach will ordinarily involve a deliberate search for subject organizations which are stable in their environment, technology, and membership,* and which are accessible in large numbers. Homo-

---

*Unless, of course, these enter directly into the experimental design.

geneity of subject organizations has evident advantage; large N's allow randomization, matching or sampling techniques for removal of some potentially confounding effects. Such populations will be found mainly in activities relatively uncomplicated by changing machine technology (e.g., sales, service, government, education, etc.) and in fields having very large parent organizations with many similar decentralized field units (e.g., armed forces, large corporations, communities, government agencies, and the like).

2. *Availability of Criterion Data.*

In instances when the research design rests upon "hard" criteria of organizational performance, a great value must be placed on locating subject organizations that offer reliable differences in performance. Since high reliability and comparability of organizational performance criteria are *very* rare, it is likely that other considerations in choice of research sites will yield to this essential one, or else the research designs will need to be modified in ways to avoid the problem entirely. The chief way to avoid the problem is to settle for criteria of organizational structure and process, rather than criteria of organizational output; these are often relatively easy to measure, are less contaminated, and for many theoretical purposes are equally or even more useful than the "hard" criteria.

3. *Induction of Change.*

A general principle of experimental design is to avoid introducing any changes in conditions other than those absolutely essential for obtaining the desired modification of the independent variables. The organizational experiments reported so far have all involved a rather large amount of loosely-controlled intervention by outside change agents, and this risks the introduction of "Hawthorne effects" and other effects not accounted for in the design. There appears to be great merit in designs which introduce changes in ways that involve little or no contact between experimenter and subject organization. How is this likely to be managed? (a) Through policy and structural changes introduced via persuasion at the top levels of the organizations, (b) by intervention into allocative processes (e.g., assignment of funds, people, tasks) which purposefully affect the subject organizations without direct intervention into the organizations themselves, (c) by altering the environment of the subject organizations.*

---

*Alteration of the environment or allocative processes of organizations may at first seem an improbable accomplishment for a researcher, but consider these hypothetical possibilities as examples: Through home-office intervention, field (subject) organizations could be subjected temporarily to different degrees of work overload; through home-office intervention some subject units and not others could be subjected to conditions of inter-unit competition or cooperation.

4. *Pre-experimental Assessment of Confounding Variables.*

One way of coming to terms with potentially confounding conditions is to make in advance a realistic assessment of what they are and then to provide some control through population selection or statistical adjustment of the experimental variables. To do this appears to require more thorough "scouting" and preparatory operations than is typically done, and in any case it is a procedure dependent on the insight and judgment of the experimenters rather than upon replicable methods. An ideal situation would be that in which the subject organizations (or others like them) were subjected to a series of preliminary investigations allowing the research team to become intimately familiar with the total situation and thus to have a chance, at least, of knowing the surroundings of the experiment. In Experiment II, described earlier, this was done, and the experiment itself followed after several years of prior research within the organization. In Experiment III, there was a full year of preliminary scouting, but crucial factors were overlooked which later revealed their potency in disrupting the experimental plan. A useful guide in this preliminary work would be the formulation of explicit conditional assumptions implied by the proposed research design, so that points of hazard can more readily be discerned and treated.

5. *Skills in Change Induction.*

Some variables of importance in organizational theory present special problems with respect to the introduction of purposeful change and probably have to be dealt with through direct and intensive interventions. An example would be a variable such as "consideration" (a variable referring to a style of supervisory behavior believed to be conditioned by the actor's "organizational climate") which has its variance sources in individual personality, local group norms, and formal organizational policy, as well as in the "climate" and traditions of the organization (6). To attempt to change such a variable experimentally through indirect, "sanitary" means would probably require a great span of time and considerable uncertainty of outcome. To change it directly through intervention by change agents at the personal contact level is also difficult (failures have been reported) but is known to be feasible. To accommodate the requirements of both experimental change and practical application ventures, there is likely to arise a new professional group devoted to "change agentry," different in important respects from their preffesional colleagues in the fields of training and management consulting. The researcher himself is not likely to have the qualifications or time to perform this essential research function, and in the interests of objectivity he probably should not be involved in it. For such practical reasons, the research plans in field experiments should in many cases provide for some kind of division of labor between those who do the theoretical, analytic, and interpretive work, on the one hand, and those who engage in active and personal interventions in the subject organizations, on the other.

6. *Creating New Organizations.*

One potential means for avoiding many of the foregoing problems has, to our knowledge, never been tried. This is the procedure of linking an experimental plan with the growth of an organization in such a way that new organizational units may be designed from their initiation with contrasting characteristics that permit testing of theoretical propositions. Some lucky researcher will one day be permitted to impose such a plan upon, say, the formation of 100 new welfare agencies, retail outlets, or military units.*

7. *Utilization of Natural Change.*

A prime practical problem for the experiment with larger organizations is the induction of a change that is sufficiently great to permit hypothesis-testing even after the consequences of the change are dampened and confounded by its unavoidable surrounding noise. This calls for an enhanced alertness on the part of both researchers and organization managers so that instances of impending natural change can be exploited. In this manner the experimenter may have the use of change events far greater (for reasons of competence and ethics) than those he could introduce on his own initiative. However, optimum use of such situations requires advance knowledge in order that population controls and pre-measures may be instituted.

BIBLIOGRAPHY

1. Adams, R. N. and Preiss, J. J. (eds.) *Human Organization Research: Field Relations and Techniques.* Homewood, Ill.: Dorsey Press, 1960.
2. Argyle, M. *The Scientific Study of Social Behaviour.* New York: Philosophical Library, 1957.
3. Etzioni, Amitai. *Complex Organizations: A Sociological Reader.* New York, Holt, Rinehart and Winston, Inc., 1961.
4. Evan, William M. and Zelditch, Morris, Jr. "A Laboratory Experiment on Bureaucratic Authority," *American Sociological Review,* XXVI (December, 1961) 883-893.

---

*This paper has excluded consideration of laboratory experiments, which may involve creation of new complex organizations and may in some degree of realism approach field conditions. An example is described in "A Laboratory Experiment on Bureaucratic Authority," by William M. Evan and Morris Zelditch, Jr. (4).

5. Festinger, Leon and Katz, Daniel (eds.) *Research Methods in the Behavioral Sciences.* New York: Dryden Press, 1953.
6. Fleishmann, E. A. "Leadership Climate, Human Relations Training, and Supervisory Behavior," *Personnel Psychology,* VI (Summer, 1953) 202-222.
7. Jahoda, M., Deutsch, M., and Cook, S. W. *Research Methods in Social Relations, with Especial Reference to Prejudice.* Part 2: *Selected Techniques.* New York: Dryden Press, 1951.
8. Likert, Rensis. *New Patterns of Management.* New York: McGraw-Hill Book Co., 1961.
9. Likert, R. and Hayes, S. P. Jr. (eds.) *Some Applications of Behavioural Research,* Paris: UNESCO, 1957.
10. Marriott, R. *Incentive Payment Systems.* London: Staples Press, Ltd., 1957.
11. Morse, N. and Reimer, E. "The Experimental Change of a Major Organizational Variable," *Journal of Abnormal and Social Psychology,* LII (January, 1956) 120-129.
12. Seashore, Stanley E. and Bowers, David G. *Changing the Structure and Functioning of an Organization: Report of a Field Experiment.* Ann Arbor: Survey Research Center, 1963. (Institute for Social Research. Survey Research Center Monograph #33.)

A Social Psychological Approach
to the Study of Negotiation*

JOSEPH E. McGRATH**

THIS paper is about research on negotiation. As a gross definition, a *formal* negotiation situation refers to an occasion where one or more *representatives* of two or more *parties* interact in an *explicit attempt* to reach a jointly-acceptable position on one or more *issues* about which they are in disagreement. This definition obviously includes situations of many kinds—in labor-management relations, in international affairs, in the activities of many political bodies and organizational groupings. A parallel definition of *informal* negotiation situations—which relaxes the representational requirement, and the requirement for explicit awareness of and intent to resolve differences—would subsume an even broader range of interactive situations, including many "conferences" in industrial, military and educational settings, much policy-making at community and broader levels, and even a great deal of interaction within the family.

We are not interested in any one particular substantive area of negotiations (e.g., labor negotiations, international affairs) for its own sake. Rather our interest is in studying the negotiation process itself, as a fundamental form of human interaction.

Like many other social psychological phenomena, the negotiation process is either well-studied or poorly-studied, depending on how you look at the problem. If you define what is directly relevant very narrowly, including only those studies which meet *all* the requirements

*The research is supported by the Behavioral Sciences Division of the Air Force Office of Scientific Research, under Grant AF 69-63 and contract AF 49(638)-1291 (J. E. McGrath, Principal Investigator). The work of many others on the research program, including Dr. James Julian, Mr. Stuart Kanter, and Mr. Neil Vidmar, is gratefully acknowledged.

**Dr. McGrath is Associate Professor, Department of Psychology, University of Illinois, Urbana, Illinois.

of the definition, there are at most only a few studies which would qualify. On the other hand, if you define the network of relevant theory and data very broadly, including all studies which meet any of the requirements of the definition, then a great deal of the research on small groups, decision-making, cognitive processes, interpersonal perception, attitudes, and other areas, bears on the problem. The middle ground of the pragmatist suggests that, while negotiation is a relatively unexplored area, there is a lot of *indirectly* related theory and evidence and we ought to make the most of it.

There are several major methodological approaches which have been utilized to study negotiation or related phenomena. The first major part of this paper will review them—illustratively, rather than comprehensively—with two views in mind: (1) to point up the relative advantages and disadvantages of the different methodological approaches; and (2) to bring out some key findings which we will try to build upon in later parts of the paper.

When we have described and compared the various approaches to the study of negotiation, we shall then present a tentative conceptual model of the negotiation situation which provides a guide for our research. The third part of this paper outlines the main features of several negotiation studies which we have recently conducted, and our general results. Finally, we shall try to interpret our major results and indicate the major directions in which we intend to pursue our negotiation studies.

The reader need be warned that this is, in several ways, a "working paper." It does not attempt an exhaustive survey of prior research. Our own research is, as yet, incomplete; hence, "conclusions" are very tentative. Above all, our "conceptual model" is a tentative "working model," to be changed as we gain new evidence and insights about the negotiation process.

THREE APPROACHES TO THE STUDY OF NEGOTIATION

As with many substantive areas of the social sciences, there are three rather distinct strategies for research on negotiation: (1) the laboratory approach, with its attendant rigor, and often artificiality; (2) the field study approach, realistic but methodologically loose; and (3) a middle ground between these two, which attempts to capture the advantages of both and escape or minimize their weaknesses. We will here designate this third approach as "experimental simulation."*

---

*This term has been specified more precisely elsewhere (21). It is roughly equivalent to Guetzkow's term "man-computer simulations" (13), and to Festinger and Katz's term "field experiment" (11).

The Laboratory Approach

We may begin considering the study of negotiation, via the laboratory approach, with the many studies of (individual) choice behavior and decision-making, under conditions of risk and uncertainty (29). While much of this research is quite peripheral to our concern here, it indicates several key points upon which we can build. First, humans do not necessarily make rational choices—or at least not choices which adhere to some objective, logical criterion of rationality. Second, humans learn—or at least modify their behavior systematically—in choice situations. Third, degree of risk, amount of uncertainty, and other parameters of the choice situation affect behavior. Fourth, utility or value is subjective—"one man's meat is another man's poison." Finally, many *social* aspects of the situation (e.g., conformity pressures) and personality characteristics of the respondent *interact* with the parameters of the choice situation to affect behavior.

It is not necessary for present purposes to describe in detail those studies which show that human decision-makers systematically depart from an "obvious rational" choice strategy or to detail the studies of conformity which show systematic departures from objectively correct responses due to social pressures (1). It is sufficient to refer to this body of data to support the premise that human choice behavior is neither chaotic and unintelligible, nor simple and apparent—rather, it is systematic, orderly, but devilishly complex!

But the laboratory studies which are more germane to our present problem are the studies of behavior in two (or more) person games. Here, at least part of our model of negotiation—though by no means all of it—is operative. There are two (or more) parties, with opposed aims and with interdependent fates. Each exercises a choice or a series of choices, and the "payoff" which each receives is co-determined by the choices of the two players. The most interesting sub-set of games for our present purposes are the non-zero sum games, exemplified by the "prisoner's dilemma" type game.

Consider the following game matrix:

Player A Chooses:

		Black	Red
	Black	A = +3	A = +4
Player B Chooses:		B = +3	B = −4
	Red	A = −4	A = −3
		B = +4	B = −3

If A and B "cooperate"—if each chooses "black"—the *joint* payoff is maximized. However, if A chooses "red" and B chooses "black,"

A's individual payoff is increased, at B's expense. If both choose "red," both lose.

With such a payoff matrix, a large proportion of subject-pairs (Scodel reports 20 of 22 pairs), when faced with such a game, choose red-red. This holds for single trial games. The percentage of red-red trials tends to *increase* for later trials of an extended series (25). Perhaps each player is just trying to get a little extra for himself—+4 rather than +3—with resulting catastrophe. However, consider the game with this payoff matrix:

Player A Chooses:

		Black	Red
	Black	A = +3	A = +1
Player B Chooses:		B = +3	B = −1
	Red	A = −1	A = −3
		B = +1	B = −3

Here, there is no individual advantage to A if he chooses red, *even if* B cooperates by choosing black. In fact, the best that can happen for A, if he chooses red, is that he will gain 2 *less* than he would from a black-black choice; and he may lose 3. Yet here again, a large proportion of subject-pairs end up in the red-red cell (Minas reports 47% for this type matrix) (23) and the percentage of non-cooperative choices increases for later trials of an extended series. Even though *joint* payoff *and individual* payoff for each player is maximized at black-black, a player can get a *relative advantage* over the opponent—although at a *substantial absolute loss* to himself—if he plays red while the opponent plays black. Presumably, the possibility of gaining this relative or competitive advantage (or subsequent retaliation against an opponent who tries to gain such advantage) operates sufficiently for both parties to carry the game frequently to a "stable" red-red solution.

There are many other variants of two person and n-person games, and a blossoming literature which explores them (24). For our purposes, these results illustrate several key points. First, they substantiate the premise that human choice is not necessarily rational, or at least that there are multiple criteria of rationality. Second, although learning —systematic modification of behavior over trials—clearly occurs, it just as clearly does *not* tend toward the "more rational" solution. In fact, things go from bad to worse. Third, while there is a substantial aura of artificiality about these games, results seem to parallel certain real-life situations. For example, if we substitute "disarm-arm" for black-red, and the two major nuclear powers for A and B, results obtained in the prisoner's dilemma game are not unlike the present situation in world affairs.

Several of the obvious "artificialities" of such game situations should be pointed out. Players usually have full information, on both their own and the opponent's payoffs. Moreover, the payoffs are unambiguous, certain, and involve only a single commodity (presumably money). Furthermore, the players represent only themselves, and the only "conflict" is generated by the rules of the game. This is *not* what we set out to mean by negotiation. Finally, the players usually *do not* communicate directly with each other, during or between trials.

Duetsch has studied behavior in some variants of the prisoner's dilemma game which approach our central problem more directly (5, 8). He compared groups who had been given *cooperative* instructions (i.e., to maximize joint payoff), groups with *individualistic* instructions (i.e., to maximize individual payoff), and groups with *competitive* instructions (i.e., to maximize *relative* payoff). The former instructions substantially increased cooperation (black-black choice). (83% of pairs cooperated under cooperative instructions; only 13% and 6% respectively, under individualistic and competitive instructions.) He also permitted some groups to communicate during the game. Communication made those with cooperative instructions only slightly more cooperative (from 83% up to 94%). Communication had a definite cooperative effect on those with individual instructions (13% to 59%), but only a minor effect on those with competitive instructions (6% to 16% cooperation).

In a related study, Loomis found that cooperation was tied to *perceptions of trust,* which were facilitated but by no means guaranteed by communication (20). We will refer again, later, to the basic point that communication, per se, is not a *sufficient* condition for successful resolution of conflict.

Even with the modification introduced by Deutsch, however, the prisoner's dilemma game and similar laboratory situations still seem very far removed from the real-life, concrete, substantively-tinged, complex situations which we choose to denote with the term "negotiation." So let us now turn to the second approach—field studies of real-life negotiations.

Field Studies

Field studies of negotiation, like field studies of any other set of phenomena, have one great strength and one great limitation. The strength is, of course, the realism. Whatever variables are *really* important to the phenomena are operative in the field study, for what is a field study but the systematic observation of a "slice of reality?" Such "realism" offers many advantages. The "issue" is real and presumably important to the actors. The interaction is part of their lives, not an experimenter's "game." Their motivation is "real"— though not necessarily greater. We presume that respondents will not give a "non-rational" response just to break the boredom of consistent responses (as subjects frequently do, in the laboratory games played for "penny-ante" stakes!).

But field studies of negotiation are most often case studies, of one or a few negotiations. And case studies are inevitably trapped in the *particular*. In any case study—however well executed—there is no way to tell to what degree results arose from some generalizable structural property of the group or the situation, or from the interplay of the particular personalities involved. In short, case studies are ideographic; and they do not contribute directly to nomothetic formulations which, after all, are what we are seeking. An example of a well-done, but nevertheless ideographic study of negotiation is Ann Douglas' book on labor-management bargaining (9). She offers many very penetrating insights which might be worthy of empirical test, but by the very nature of her study is not able to subject them to such a test.

As one exception, Landsberger has conducted a study of labor-management negotiations in which the data are both (a) drawn from a real-life setting and (b) treated nomothetically (19). He applied the Bales system for interaction process analysis to tape recordings of 12 actual labor negotiation sessions, and compared features of the negotiation process with (rated) effectiveness of results. Even this study suffers from a serious limitation on the number and comparability of cases. Different negotiation sessions were composed of different people and dealt with different problems. Thus it is also tied to "the particular" although in a somewhat more complex way.

Thus, while the lure of the "realistic situation" is great indeed, especially in the light of some of the anomalous results of the artificial laboratory-game studies, the field study approach seems an inevitably limited path to a full exploration of the negotiation process. Yet at the same time, to limit our methodology to the restricted (though rigorous) laboratory setting seems also to place major constraints on our ability to explore the phenomena of negotiation. Let us turn, then, to consideration of the third approach, one which tries to capture at least much of the rigor of the laboratory, but to do so in a "relatively realistic" context.

Experimental Simulation

By experimental simulation we mean those studies which attempt to recreate or simulate the central features of some set of phenomena which are of interest, and then to study those phenomena under relatively controlled conditions.* This differs from the laboratory experiment in that the laboratory study attempts to investigate fundamental variables which have been *abstracted from* their normal, substantive context. The laboratory study is *deliberately* artificial, in the sense that a physicist is artificial when he studies bodies falling in a vacuum. The experimental simulation, on the other hand, tries to create much of the "realness" and "flavor" of the "real-life phenomena" themselves. Thereby he hopes to gain the advantages of real motivation, and of the operation and interaction of many relevant variables—at some cost, to be sure, in control of variables and precision of measurement.

Experimental simulations differ from field studies in that they permit replication of the single negotiation—by the same persons on different negotiation problems, and/or by different groups on the *same* negotiation problem. In this way they can escape the ideographic trap. They also offer greater leverage in manipulation, control and measurement of variables than do field studies, where the investigator is at best an onlooker rather than controller of the situation.

Some outstanding work on negotiation, and closely related problems, has been done through the experimental simulation approach. Guetzkow's now classic inter-nation game (12, 13), while not intended to be a negotiation game, does yield much relevant evidence on the related phenomena of intergroup decision-making. Sherif's Robber's Cave experiment is a stellar example of the study of intergroup conflict resolution by means of an experimental simulation (26). Campbell created a labor-management bargaining situation as a vehicle for studying negotiation (4), and more recently, Bass has adapted the Campbell situation for further study (3). Deutsch's recent work on interpersonal bargaining is also especially relevant here (7) (as well as his prisoner's dilemma studies noted above).

Results of these studies add to the evidence upon which we can build. Sherif and co-workers, by a series of experimental manipulations (isolation, competition, etc.), generated strong intergroup conflict between two boys' groups at a summer camp. Then they brought the boys into contact, with near disastrous results. Finally, they devised a situation in which the two groups had to *work cooperatively* in order to solve a joint and serious problem (a water shortage). Their results dramatically demonstrate the point—suggested by Deutsch's prisoner's dilemma studies noted earlier (5, 8) and by other social psychological studies (e.g. 6)—that contact or communication between conflicting groups is *not a sufficient condition* for lessening of hostility or resolution of conflict. In fact, they show that contact, in the

---

*See footnote, p. 102.

absence of functional interdependence, can lead to an explosive "acting out" of intergroup hostility; while contact under conditions of functional interdependence can lead to reduction of intergroup hostility.

Deutsch and Krauss used a trucking game as a device for studying interpersonal bargaining (7). Each player attempted to move his "truck" from his "factory" to his disposition point in the shortest possible time. (Time was translated into cost, hence reduced profit.) Part of the direct route for each player was a one-lane strip in common, though each had a much longer (hence costlier) alternate route. For various conditions, one player, both, or neither, could close a "gate" which blocked the common path to his opponent. Deutsch's results show that joint gain is best for the no-threat (i.e., no gate) condition, next best for the unilateral threat condition, and poorest for the bilateral threat condition. Moreover, while the person with the threat did better than his opponent in the unilateral threat condition (though not as well as he did when neither had a threat,) the person who *did not* have the threat in the unilateral condition still did *better* than he did when he also had a threat capability. Deutsch also finds that opportunity to communicate during the game is not effective under threat conditions, though it helps under the no-threat condition. Thus, once again, communication alone is not enough; it needs to be accompanied by functional interdependence and the perception of trust.

Campbell composed two-man negotiation teams in which one person was and another was *not* attitudinally aligned with the views of the reference group which he was assigned to represent (4). These mixed teams were more effective than teams where *both* members were attitudinally aligned with the group they represented. This suggests that a group's most loyal and committed member may not be its most effective representative in a negotiation, perhaps because "too much" commitment may "freeze" one's position so as to preclude further change.

However, these studies also have methodological limitations for our present purpose. Deutsch's studies of interpersonal bargaining, while much more realistic than the laboratory games discussed above (and probably more interesting and ego-involving for participants,) nevertheless fail to fulfill the requirements of our definition of negotiation on two counts: (1) the participants represent only themselves and the only "conflict" between them arises from the game itself; and (2) outcomes are reckoned with respect to a single (monetary,) unambiguous, certain "payoff" dimension. Campbell's study, placing college students arbitrarily in the role of labor or management negotiators, carries some of the artificiality of the strictly laboratory study. Conversely, Sherif's Robber's Cave paradigm, though an "experimental simulation" in form, is ideographic as used—and probably inevitably so. There seems little possibility of generating a substantial number of replicated cases for nomothetic purposes. Guetzkow's inter-nation game, while not intended to be a negotiation game as such, provides a context much closer to our negotiation concept than do the others. Unfortunately for our present purpose, Guetzkow and others who have used his basic game have focused primarily on structural conditions (13) and personal characteristics of the participants (10) with relatively little attention to the interaction process itself.

Our own program of research on negotiation follows the "experimental simulation" approach, but attempts to focus on *process* as well as outcome, and attempts to establish a situation which fits our working definition of negotiation. Before describing the experimental paradigm by which we have attempted to study negotiation, and some results of our first three studies, we shall step back from considerations of research strategy and try to present a conceptual framework of the negotiation situation which serves as a tentative model for our studies.

A Tri-Polar Model of the Negotiation Situation

Definition

A negotiation situation consists of one or more representatives of each of two or more "parties," who are in direct interaction for the purpose of obtaining mutually acceptable resolutions of one or more problems about which the parties disagree. It may or may not include representatives of additional "neutral parties."

The definition of negotiation implies that at least four related sets of factors play a part in the negotiation situation: (a) factors related to the individual negotiators; (b) factors arising from the presence and behavior of a neutral "mediator"; (c) factors related to the specific negotiation task and the operating conditions within which it takes place; and (d) the criteria by which the outcome of the negotiation is to be judged. These four classes of factors are shown in Figure 1 and discussed below.

Factors Operating on the Individual Negotiators

The participants in a negotiation group are necessarily concerned with satisfying multiple, conflicting criteria. Each negotiator must be concerned with achieving a product that will satisfy the goals of his reference group. He must also be cognizant of the goals of the other negotiating parties, for those goals also provide constraints on the possible outcomes of the negotiation. It is assumed that each negotiator also has the goal of obtaining some jointly-acceptable solution

Figure 1

CLASSES OF FACTORS WHICH AFFECT NEGOTIATION

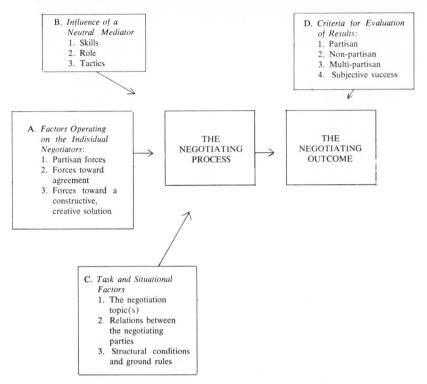

(as opposed to dissolving the session without agreement). The existence of the negotiation situation implies that all parties present have at least something to gain from settlement of the problem. Finally, all parties must take into account certain external criteria, by which the negotiation outcome will be judged within the broader organization or social system in which all parties participate. (For example, in the case of labor-management negotiations, the "welfare of the general public" represents such an external criterion.)

Thus, the negotiation situation can be viewed as a tri-polar "task space" or "force field" within which a number of forces are acting upon each participant. Figure 2 is a diagram of the negotiation task space showing the types of forces acting on each of two negotiating parties and on a third, non-partisan moderator.

Each participant (J and K) is subjected to several forces: (1) a force, R, toward the position held by his reference group; (2) an opposed force, A, toward agreement with the other negotiating parties;

Figure 2

DIAGRAM OF THE FORCES OPERATING IN THE NEGOTIATION SITUATION

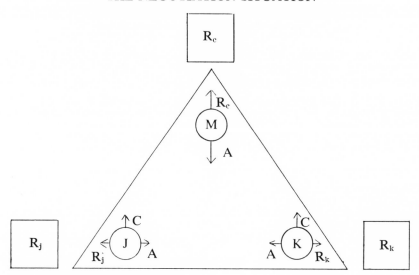

J = Negotiator(s) for Group R_j

K = Negotiator(s) for Group R_k

M = Neutral mediator, representing R_c

R_j = Position of Group R_j

R_k = Position of Group R_k

R_c = Position of general community, R_c

R Forces = Forces toward own reference group

A Forces = Forces toward agreement

C Forces = Forces toward the R_c goal, obtaining a creative, constructive solution

and (3) a third force, C, toward attaining a high quality, creative or constructive solution to the problem as judged from the point of view of the broader social system. Force C is represented as orthogonal to the opposed forces R and A. These three forces produce a resultant force for locomotion of the individual, and of the group, within the "task space." The direction and strength of the resultant depends on the relative and absolute strengths of the composite forces.

Thus, the fundamental forces operating in the situation are those indigenous to the individual negotiators—the R, A, and C forces.

Each of these is itself made up of a number of component forces.

1. *Forces toward the position of the reference group.*

   The "pull" of the reference group's position for the individual negotiator is one important feature of the negotiation situation. The total strength and direction of that pull depends on a number of characteristics of the individual negotiator, J, and upon his relation to his reference group, R_j. Some of these are listed below:

   a. Strength of attraction of J to R_j.
   b. Perceived relevance of Topic (X) to R_j.
   c. Clarity of R_j's position on X.
   d. J's personal belief in R_j's position.
   e. Salience of R_j as a reference group for J.

2. *Forces toward agreement in the negotiation situation.*

   The existence of the negotiation situation implies that each R group has some investment in achieving a solution to the problem(s) to be negotiated. Furthermore, the fact that the negotiation situation is an interpersonal interaction for the negotiator, often involving a continuing set of interpersonal relations, generates additional forces toward agreement in the negotiation situation. A number of the factors which are a part of the over-all force toward agreement are listed below:

   a. J's attraction to K, M, as persons.
   b. J's motivation to reach agreement, based on his perception of R_j's investment in resolution of the problem.
   c. J's understanding of any sympathy with the goals of R_k.

3. *Forces toward obtaining a creative, constructive solution.*

   In addition to the "pull" toward the reference group and the "pull" toward resolution of the problem, there is a third force acting on the individual negotiator, namely, his desire that the problem be resolved in the most constructive form possible. This pull is based on the fact that the negotiator, J, while an agent of reference group R_j, is also a member of and an "ex officio" agent of the broader community within which both R_j and R_k exist. Thus, the force, C, on J is analogous to the "pull" toward the position of a generic or universalistic reference group. Some of the components of the force, C, are listed below:

   a. Salience of the general reference group (R_c) for negotiator J.
   b. J's motivation for achievement in the eyes of the broader community.
   c. J's attraction to the broader reference group, and to its "position" on X as he perceives it.

Factors Arising from the Presence and Behavior of a Neutral Mediator

If a non-partisan mediator is present in the negotiation situation he is also subject to diverse forces. He must be cognizant of the goals of all negotiating parties. His specific goal is attainment of a jointly-acceptable solution. At the same time, he is in a sense the "public's representative." Thus he is concerned with the outcome as judged from the point of view of the external social system. For present purposes, however, the mediator, M, is viewed as a potential *source* of forces on the negotiators, rather than as an individual being subjected to such forces. The mediator potentially generates both a force (A) toward attaining agreement among the negotiators, and a force (C) toward getting the group to attain a constructive, creative solution. The relative and absolute strengths of the A and C forces imposed by the mediator on various members of the negotiating group also affect the resultant locomotion within the "task space."

The mediator's skills and knowledge, his role in the negotiation situation, and the procedures by which he influences the group process, all play a part in determining the outcome of the negotiation. For the most part, the mediator influences outcome by affecting the balance of R, A, and C forces operating on the individual negotiators. Some of the specific factors in the mediator's effect on the negotiation are listed below:

1. *Skill and Knowledge of the Mediator*

The mediator's past experience in similar situations, his knowledge of the background of the problem, his knowledge of the history of the negotiating parties *vis-à-vis* one another, and his knowledge of the goals of R_j and R_k with respect to the negotiation topic(s), all play a part in the effectiveness with which he plays his role, hence in the effect which he has on the outcome of the negotiation.

2. *Manifest Role of the Mediator*

A number of features of the mediator's role may influence the group process and its outcome. In particular, his behavior, *as perceived by group members,* must match their role expectations for him. Some of the aspects of mediator role and role behavior which may be crucial include:

a. The legitimacy of his assignment to the mediator role, the nature of that role (e.g., mediator vs. arbitrator), and his "status" relative to negotiators, as perceived by the negotiators.

b. The degree to which negotiators perceive his manifest behavior as oriented toward achieving interpersonal or "doctrinal" harmony among negotiators.

c. The degree to which negotiators perceive his manifest behavior as oriented toward achieving a creative, constructive solution.

    d. The degree to which his manifest behavior is perceived as being partisan.

  3. *Mediator "Tactics" and Procedures.*

In addition to the mediator's skill and knowledge, and his manifest behavior, a number of specific aspects of his manner as "chairman" may also affect the group process and its outcome:

    a. The degree to which he attempts to exercise control of the group process and of the content of group interaction and the extent to which he is successful in such attempts.

    b. The degree of formality, "affect neutrality," and "professionalism" which he exhibits in his interaction with group members.

    c. The degree to which he guides the group in a search for bases of agreement, for common ground.

    d. The degree to which he guides the group to explicitly establish their point-to-point differences.

    e. The degree to which he uses the "chair" to prevent or attenuate direct clashes, especially those with an *ad hominum* basis.

Factors in the Task and Situation

A number of factors which arise from the particular topic(s) of negotiation, the particular set of negotiating parties, or the particular "ground rules" within which the negotiation takes place, also play a part in determining the process and outcome of the negotiation. As with the mediator factors, the task and situational variables influence the negotiation primarily by altering the balance among the R, A and C forces acting on the individual negotiators. A number of the task and situational factors which seem most likely to affect the negotiation are listed below:

  1. *Factors Related to the Negotiation Topic.*

The topic to be negotiated, in large part, sets the conditions of task difficulty. The "size," "shape" and clarity of positions of the reference groups, and the relations of those positions to one another, all affect the basic "shape" of the task-space, and the potential "solution space." Thus, they affect the direction and strength of forces. Here we are talking about conditions as viewed objectively, not as perceived by the participants.

    a. The importance and relevance of topic (X) to R_j, R_k, and R_c.

    b. The clarity and public-ness of positions of R_j, R_k, and R_c.

    c. The "size" of the region of acceptable solutions for R_j, R_k, and R_c.

    d. The point-by-point "opposition" of R_j and R_k. (That is, do they have directly opposed, mutually exclusive positions on specific aspects of the topic, or is one group for and against certain points while the other group is for and against different points?)

e. The orthogonality of positions R_j and R_k to the R_c "position."

f. The investment of R_j and R_k in obtaining a solution.

g. The power of J and K to bind their respective groups.

2. *Factors Related to the Negotiating Parties.*

Some features of the long-run relation between the two negotiating parties, beyond their differences on the specific topic(s) to be negotiated, affect the process and outcome of a negotiation situation. It may even be the case that the difference between R_j and R_k on the topic is more related to a continuing competition between them than to the specific topic itself. (For example, political parties sometimes seem to have a vested interest in disagreeing with the opposing party, whatever position that party may take on a given issue.) Some of these factors are listed below:

a. The strength and pervasiveness of opposition between R_j and R_k.

b. The degree to which the effective maintenance of R_j depends on continuing opposition to R_k, and *vice versa.*

c. The existence of points of view in the larger social system to which both R_j and R_k are committed, or the existence of forces in the larger social system (e.g., a common threat) which increases both R_j's and R_k's motivation for agreement.

3. *Factors Arising from the Negotiating Conditions.*

A number of structural features and "ground rules" of a particular negotiation session may profoundly affect its outcome:

a. The size and composition of negotiation "teams," the relative size of opposing teams, and the over-all size of the negotiation group.

b. The presence and defined role of a third-party mediator.

c. The public or private nature of the negotiation.

d. The degree to which negotiation of a particular topic takes place at one "sitting" or over an extended series of sessions.

e. The degree to which negotiation is focused on a single topic, or a single topic at a time, versus consideration of multiple topics simultaneously.

Criteria of Negotiation Effectiveness

Success in a negotiation situation can be judged from any of several points of view. First, it can be judged from a strictly partisan point of view, namely: to what extent did "our" group get its position embodied in the negotiation outcome. In a two-party negotiation, there are two different partisan criteria: (1) acceptability of the outcome to group R_j (symbolized as Y_j); and (2) acceptability of the outcome to group R_k (symbolized as Y_k).

The outcome of the negotiation can also be judged from the (presumably non-partisan point of view of the external system (R_c).

Here, the criterion of success is the extent to which the negotiation led to a creative, constructive solution to the problem(s) under consideration: (This will be symbolized as Y_c).

The negotiation situation as here defined, however, requires that there be unanimous (though not necessarily enthusiastic) endorsement of the negotiated solution. A solution which is highly acceptable to group R_j but unacceptable to R_k cannot ensue. Thus a "multi-partisan" criterion is needed to measure the over-all effectiveness of a negotiation.

The model provides a basis for describing the necessary and sufficient conditions for multi-partisan success. Let us represent each party to the negotiation as having a bounded region of "acceptable solutions" within the group's task space, and represent the class of high quality, constructive solutions (acceptable to the external system) as a bounded region in the same "task space." For success, the group must: (a) attain sufficient agreement between the negotiating parties so that there exists a region, JK, which is within the acceptable solution region for *both* negotiating parties; and (b) attain a sufficiently constructive solution so that there exists a region, JKC, which is common to the two negotiating parties and within the acceptable region for the external system. (See Figure 3.) The first is a necessary condition for *any* solution. The first and second together are necessary and sufficient conditions for a "good" solution.

In practice, it is probably more useful to treat constructiveness of negotiated solutions and acceptability to the negotiating parties as matters of degree, rather than as categorically "in" or "out" of an acceptable region. This can be represented by treating acceptability to R_j and R_k as opposed in direction along the horizontal axis of the model, and "constructiveness' as the vertical axis of the model. In these terms, the over-all effectiveness of the negotiation can be defined as the *product* of its acceptability to R_j, R_k and R_c. (This over-all criterion will be symbolized as Y_{jkc}.)

A key point which must not be overlooked in considering criteria of negotiation effectiveness is that results of a negotiation are closely tied to the concepts of acceptability and constructiveness held by the negotiators themselves. It is the degree to which J perceives that a certain outcome will satisfy group R_j, not the subsequent actual acceptance or rejection by R_j, that determines whether J is willing to endorse that outcome. Thus, in addition to the three objective criteria (Y_j, Y_k and Y_c), and their product (Y_{jkc}), we must also take into account the subjective counterparts of these criteria as perceived by the negotiators. These will be symbolized as $Y'R_j$ (J's estimate of R_j's acceptance of the negotiation result); $Y'R_k$ (a parallel criterion for K); and $Y'C_j$, $Y'C_k$ and $Y'C_m$ (estimates of the constructiveness of the negotiation result by J, K and M, respectively).

Both the objective and subjective criteria of success—and especially the degree to which they correspond—must be taken into account if we are to understand the process of negotiation, be able to specify the determinants of that process, and be able to predict its outcome.

Figure 3

DIAGRAM OF NECESSARY AND SUFFICIENT CONDITIONS
FOR NEGOTIATION SUCCESS

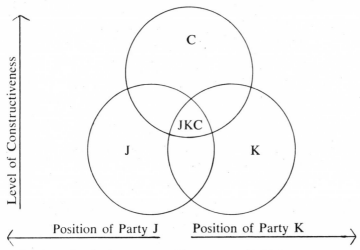

J = Region of solutions acceptable to party J (R_j)

K = Region of solutions acceptable to party K (R_k)

C = Region of "constructive" solutions, as judged by external system (R_c)

JK = Region of solutions jointly acceptable to J and K

JKC = Region of jointly acceptable and constructive solutions

AN EXPERIMENTAL PARADIGM FOR RESEARCH ON NEGOTIATION

The program of research in which we are currently engaged is an admittedly exploratory venture. We are trying to devise ways to simulate the key features of negotiation situations, as here defined, which will meet the following, rather stringent criteria:

    a) The persons involved must be truly representatives of a group, faction, or partisan point of view.

    b) The issue(s) being negotiated must be of importance to the groups, factions or parties represented, and those parties must have dissimilar views independent of the experiment itself.

c) It must be possible to obtain the cooperation of a sufficient number of "legitimate" representatives of each party so that a number (preferably a sizable number) of replicated "runs" can be obtained for any given negotiation topic.

d) The issue(s) must be of a sufficient complexity that there is more than a single, unitary dimension of "payoff"; participants must be able to deal in more than one "coin".

e) It must be possible to obtain reliable evaluations of results (i.e. criterion scores).

The essence of these criteria is that we wish to study the negotiation of issues which are *actually* divisive issues for the people involved and for the groups they represent. They are not artificial or simulated issues. What is "non-real," artificially created, is the actual negotiation—the *confrontation* of representatives of the opposed parties in an attempt to resolve the issue. The methodological "leverage," here, as compared to a field study, comes from the generation of many parallel and comparable negotiation groups dealing with the same issue.

Our research strategy can perhaps best be clarified by illustration. Our first study dealt with the resolution of differences among three religious groups on socio-political issues about which they sharply disagreed (22, 17). The three religious groups (or more accurately, the student foundations of those religious groups on the campus of a large, midwestern, land-grant university) were the Baptist Student Union (Southern Baptist Convention), Newman Foundation (Roman Catholic Church), and Channing-Murray Foundation (Unitarian Universalist Association). We used three different issues, chosen so that each foundation was alone in its position on one issue but in general agreement with one other foundation on each of the other two issues. The issues were: (a) use of the King James Bible as a reading test in public schools (Southern Baptists favoring, others opposed); (b) granting of federal aid to parochial and other private schools (Catholics favoring, others opposed); and (c) granting enforcement powers to F.C.C. to reduce obscenity and violence on TV (Unitarians opposed, others favoring).

Each group consisted of one student representing each of the foundations, plus a graduate student who served as (neutral) mediator. Foundation participants were recruited through the clergymen who headed each foundation, and each sent its most active, interested, and presumably most committed students. Mediators were mainly advanced law students and graduate students in industrial relations.

A "position paper," stating and justifying the group's position, was prepared for each group on each issue. Foundation clergymen signed their respective position papers. These were given to participants before the negotiation session. Mediators had *all* position papers available.

Participants were instructed to act as *agents* or representatives for their foundations, and attempt to get as much of their foundation's position as possible into the negotiation group's product; but they were also warned that each negotiation group must try to formulate a position which all members would endorse. To reinforce these instructions, participants were offered monetary prizes on the following basis. The set of negotiation group products for each issue were rated by clergymen of each foundation, on a scale from 0 to 5, in terms of their acceptability to the foundation. They were also rated by a team of neutral judges, on a scale from 0 to 5, in terms of how constructive they were as an approach to the underlying issue. Each participant was to receive as his prize the number of dollars equal to the *product* of his own foundation's rating times the neutral judges' rating of his group's solution. Thus, if one person abandoned his group's position, he would receive a zero (unacceptable) rating from his foundation and hence a zero product score and a zero prize (even though others in the group might do handsomely). On the other hand, if members of a negotiation group were so immovable that the group failed to come to a joint position, all group members would get a zero rating (on "constructiveness") from the neutral judges. These prizes were offered not so much to motivate participants, who appeared highly motivated because of their commitment to their foundations, but rather to structure the participants' definitions of "success" in a way which simulated the opposition of forces (to compromise and to hold out) existing in actual negotiation situations. These partisan and non-partisan judgments of outcomes also served as criterion data, in accord with our previous discussion of criteria of negotiation success.

It is probably useful to describe the second study in our program at this point, to note certain contrasts between the two. The second study involved negotiation of three labor-grievance cases. Participants were members of an advanced class in labor law, who were arbitrarily assigned to act as attorneys and representatives for the company or for the union, or to act as impartial mediators. The cases were actual labor-grievance cases which had gone to arbitration. They were altered only (a) to disguise the companies involved, and (b) to create a pre-arbitration "last ditch" negotiation situation. Students participated as part of their course activity. Fact sheets and position justifications were prepared for each party and given to participants in advance to permit preparation. The same kind of scoring system as used in the religious group study (i.e., the product of partisan ratings of acceptability times neutral ratings of constructiveness) was used in the labor-law study to provide a structured definition of "success." However, money prizes were not given.

There are several important contrasts between these studies. The obvious one, of different substantive material, may not be too important in and of itself. The difference in negotiation team composition—a one-against-one, with mediator, in the labor-law study, compared to a two-against-one, with mediator, in the religious group study—is a structural difference which is worth further investigation. The really crucial difference, though, is in the relation of the negotiator to the reference group which he represents.

In the religious group study, negotiators were actual (and active) members of the foundations which they represented, and were presumably themselves committed to their own group's views on the issues. In the labor-law study, however, negotiators were "hired representatives," not actual members, of the groups which they represented. While both of these types of relationships occur fairly frequently in real-life negotiation, Campbell's findings (noted earlier) suggest that they may pose quite different situations, social-psychologically, for the participants (4).

One further, and probably crucial, difference between the studies is in the status of the mediator. In the religious group study, mediators were deliberately given high status relative to the negotiators. They were academically senior, older, all male, and we stressed their relevant experience and training in our instructions. In the labor-law study, however, mediators were classmates and peers of the negotiators; and since we arbitrarily assigned persons to roles, the mediator was probably of inferior status relative to the negotiators in at least some of our groups. This difference in relative status of the mediator apparently has a major effect on how, and how much, the mediator participates in the negotiation, as we would expect from other studies of the effects of relative status on communication and influence in groups (e.g., 28, 18, 27, 16).

Further detail about the procedures of these studies can be found in McGrath & Julian (22) and Julian and McGrath (17). Let us now list some of our main findings and make brief comment about them.

The most tempting question to ask of our data is probably: "how does the mediator's leadership ability affect the success of negotiation groups?" It is always nice to "find the man responsible," and to "pin the blame on" (or, here, assign the systematic variance to) that man. In each of our studies, each mediator was involved in negotiations on each of three issues, working with a different set of negotiators on each issue (with appropriate counterbalancing of order of presentation). The first question we asked, therefore, was whether a given mediator was consistent in producing good, or mediocre, or poor negotiation products. In effect, we correlated criterion scores for groups with the same mediator on each pair of topics. *None* of these correlations was statistically significant in either study. (When you consider that, working from a "leadership trait" model of group effectiveness, these correlations represent coefficients of *reliability* or stability of performance, the fact that the correlations were not only low but non-significant is pretty damaging to that position.) However, a grosser analysis (by Chi-square, splitting criterion scores at the median on each topic) did show a significant tendency for certain mediators to have successful groups (top half) on all issues, and others to have unsuccessful groups (bottom half) on all issues. This suggests that, while the behavior of the particular mediator does make a difference the major portion of the variability in negotiation outcomes is by no means attributable to the mediator, independent of negotiators, issues and the situation. This was further indicated by a consistent *lack* of significant correlations between group performance and various mediator characteristics (verbal ability, labor-management attitudes, category width, self-esteem, esteem for least preferred coworker, personal orientations, etc.). None of these measures correlated significantly with group performance, on even two of the three issues, in either study.

If not the leader, then the group? Perhaps, but certainly not the group conceived of as a simple summation or averaging of member characteristics! There was also a consistent *lack* of correlation between group performance and group average scores on all of the characteristics listed above. The "blame," or the systematic variance, does not lie here either (although it is possible, and even likely, that we could account for some of the variance in criterion scores if we had the *right* characteristics and/or the right rules of combination).

A second major "place to look," in the data of our studies, is in the negotiation process itself. All sessions were tape recorded, and careful records of speaker, target, and elapsed time were made by a live observer. The tape recording of each session was divided into four equal time periods or phases (about 7½ minutes each), and each segment was subjected to process analysis.

In the religious group study, we used a process analysis system developed for that study, to bring out what we hypothesized to be the key features of negotiation, namely: the display of positive and negative affect, and the display of structuring or controlling activities (content or process structuring, interrupting, etc.)* In the labor-law

---

*Dr. James W. Julian, now at the University of Buffalo, was primarily responsible for development of the interaction process analysis system (17).

study, we used a more elaborated version of this process analysis system. Our major results for the religious group study are listed below:

(1) Successful negotiation groups show less negative affect than less successful groups; they show more communication which is affectively-neutral, but not necessarily more positive affect.

(2) The same results hold for negative, neutral and positive affect communicated by the mediator.

(3) Successful groups interact more, and have shorter communications than less successful groups. (Confirmed in the labor-law study).

(4) Mediators in positions of high relative status communicate *more* than negotiators (from the religious group study), while mediators in relatively weak status positions communicate *less* than negotiators (from the labor-law study).

(5) The tempo of interaction increases, and the length per act decreases, through successive phases of a negotiation session (confirmed in the labor-law study).

(6) Practically all structuring activity (except interruptions) is carried out by the mediator.

(7) The amount of structuring activity (by mediator) does not correlate with group success, but the *timing* of such activity does. Successful groups are characterized by high structuring activity at the *pre-final* phase, followed by low structuring activity in the final phase; whereas unsuccessful groups have highest structuring activity during the final phase.

(8) The timing of the display of positive and negative affect, as well as the amount, differs for successful and unsuccessful groups. Successful groups show a final-phase rise in positive affect and in affectively-neutral communication, and a final-phase drop in negative affect. Unsuccessful groups show a final-phase rise in negative affect and a final-phase drop or levelling off in positive and neutral communication.

The gist of these results, in broadest terms, seems to be that negotiation groups tend to be successful when: (a) they do not permit interparty disagreement to become manifest interpersonal hostility, and especially when the mediator does not display such hostility; and (b) when at the same time, the mediator focuses the group on its task sufficiently well, and sufficiently early, so that they can grapple with the issue. This sounds very much like a prescription for mediators (and negotiators, too!) who exhibit a high level of *both* Consideration and Structure-in-interaction, as defined by Hemphill (15).

Our analysis also yielded a number of other specific results which seem to have implications for future studies. For example, persons in a minority-of-one expected their reference groups to be less accepting of negotiation outcomes than did persons in the majority. At the same time, the minority reference group was actually *more* accepting than majority reference groups. These results can be interpreted as signifying that minority negotiators felt that they had compromised more, but actually had compromised less, with the reference group's position. This and other specific findings will be discussed further in the last part of this paper.

We have recently conducted a third negotiation study, similar in design but with several major differences (30). The study used fraternity men and independents in negotiations on a campus housing issue on which those two reference groups disagreed. The campus housing study differed from prior studies in three main ways: (1) each participant participated in only one negotiation session; (2) there was no third-party mediator present; and (3) we attempted to manipulate experimentally two structural conditions.

The first experimental manipulation was based on the hypothesis that negotiation groups whose members had developed interpersonal trust, based on prior task success with one another, would be more likely to succeed in negotiation than groups with prior experience of distrust and task failure with one another. Accordingly, half of the groups in the campus housing study were assigned a pre-negotiation task on which they *could not succeed,* designed to disrupt interpersonal relations between members. The other half of the groups had a pre-negotiation task on which they were likely to succeed at least partially, designed to enhance favorable interpersonal relations between members. This manipulation did not produce significant differences in negotiation effectiveness (although results were in the expected direction), although it did produce significant differences (in the expected direction) in member perceptions of whether the pre-negotiation task had helped or hindered their group's subsequent negotiation session. Our present guess is that a similar but stronger manipulation of pre-negotiation experience would show significant effects on negotiation outcomes as well.

The second manipulation in the campus housing study dealt with the relation of negotiators to the reference groups which they represented. Specifically, 20 groups were composed of one independent and one fraternity man, each assigned to represent the views of his own group (the I-F groups). Ten groups were composed of two fraternity men, with one of them assigned to represent the point of view of the independents (the F-F groups). The latter (F-F) groups produced significantly *more constructive* and less partisan solutions than the I-F groups. However, they apparently did so at some cost in interpersonal harmony, and in the case of the fraternity man representing the independent view, some alienation from his own "true" reference group. Results of this study are not yet completely analyzed. They will be presented in detail in a forthcoming report (30), and are discussed further in the final section of this paper.

Rather than presenting further specific findings from our three exploratory studies of negotiation, it is perhaps more useful to step back from these limited data and attempt to assess their broad implications for a social-psychological theory of negotiation. Accordingly, the final section of this paper will summarize and discuss key findings and attempt to interpret them in terms which will provide useful theoretical guidance for subsequent studies. The reader is warned, again, that our speculations go well beyond present data. Our purpose is not to state solidly documented conclusions, but rather to formulate theoretically meaningful hypotheses which are amenable to subsequent empirical test.

DISCUSSION AND IMPLICATIONS

Interpretation of Major Results

Effective negotiation outcomes appear to be associated with certain patterns of interaction in the negotiation session. These, in turn, are influenced by certain structural features of the situation, on the one hand, and perhaps by certain attributes of mediator and negotiators on the other. Effects of these structural conditions and of mediator and negotiator attributes, however, appear to be mediated both through the interactive process which occurs in the negotiation and through changes in participants' *perceptions* of one another and of their own and others' attitudes and behaviors.

The most striking relationship between negotiation process and effectiveness of outcome is that negotiation success is systematically related to an *absence* of manifest negative affect, by all participants but especially by mediators, during the negotiation sessions. It is *not* the case, however, that successful groups display more positive affect than unsuccessful ones. Rather, successful negotiation groups tend to display less negative affect and more affect-neutrality than unsuccessful groups, with about the same, relatively low, amount of positive affect in both successful and unsuccessful groups.

A second notable relationship between negotiation process and outcome has to do with effective *timing* of structuring or controlling behavior by the mediator. This category includes acts which attempt to structure the content, process or communication pattern in the group. Successful negotiation groups do not differ from unsuccessful ones in terms of over-all levels of structuring behavior by the mediator. However, such structuring behavior tends to be at its peak for successful groups at a point in time prior to the final decision phase of the negotiation and to thereafter sharply decrease; whereas mediator structuring behavior in unsuccessful negotiation groups tends to continue to increase up to the end of the session. Furthermore, changes in level of negative affect closely parallel changes in level of structuring behavior through time, which suggests that level of mediator structuring behavior is an index of the occurrence of an internal "control crisis" in the group. The success of effective negotiation groups appears to lie in their ability to bring this control crisis to a focus, and resolve it, in time for successful task completion. We cannot distinguish, with present data, between two possible bases for this effect. On the one hand, it may be that unsuccessful groups err primarily in timing; i.e., their mediators do not "precipitate" the control crisis soon enough for the group to resolve it and still have time for an effective outcome. On the other hand, the unsuccessful groups simply may not be able to resolve the control crisis, whenever precipitated, perhaps because of (prior) high levels of manifest negative affect in these groups. Furthermore, our data do not permit an estimation of whether the "control crisis" can be precipitated *too early* as well as too late — and, indeed, whether such early "over-control" may itself generate negative affect which hinders subsequent resolution of the crisis.

Thus, timely focus upon and resolution of the "control crisis," plus a low level of negative interpersonal affect, appear to be preconditions (though not necessarily either necessary or sufficient conditions) for successful negotiation outcome. How, then, can we predict the occasions and/or groups in which these conditions will occur?

Individual mediators show only marginal consistency in tending to have either successful or unsuccessful negotiation groups. Moreover, none of a series of measures of cognitive skills, value patterns, interpersonal perceptions and attitudes of the mediator are successful and consistent predictors of negotiation outcome. This suggests that the pattern of interaction which is associated with successful outcomes (timely control and low negative affect) is not solely or even primarily a function of the mediator and what he brings with him to the situation. Rather, the "successful" pattern of negotiation—even those aspects which refer to mediator behavior—seems to arise out of a complex of interacting conditions, perhaps including attributes of mediators and negotiators, structural properties of the negotiation group, and features of the task and operating situation.

Characteristics of members of negotiation groups, combined in a simple additive fashion, also do not predict negotiation effectiveness consistently. This statement holds for several measures of cognitive skills, attitudes and interpersonal perceptions. Two such measures of group member characteristics do appear to show some promise as predictors of negotiation success and merit further study. The first is a measure of cognitive flexibility developed for this program. The sum of this test score for group members correlated significantly (r .31) with negotiation outcomes in the labor law study. (However, this relationship did not hold up in the campus housing study, under somewhat different group structure conditions.) The second promising group member characteristic is a measure of personal orientations adapted from Bass (2). While Bass's measure did not show significant relationships with negotiation criteria in the religious group study, we are now developing a modified version which seems likely to be more successful.

It is always possible, perhaps even likely, that an appreciable portion of the systematic variance in negotiation outcomes can be accounted for in terms of mediator and/or member characteristics, if we but had the *right* properties and/or the *right* rules of combination among members. This point of view is indisputable; on logical grounds, no amount of evidence will prove the negative. However, in view of our experience to date, the search for mediator or member attributes which are predictive of success of negotiation groups containing that member does not appear to be an optimal strategy for increasing our understanding of negotiation. Furthermore, a precondition for *any* member attribute to be predictive of group outcome is that certain individuals are systematically associated with (relatively) successful group outcomes while others are systematically associated with poor outcomes. If a given mediator or negotiator is as likely to be involved in an unsuccessful as in a successful negotiation group, then *no* attribute of his (which presumably remains constant for him from one negotiation session to the next) can be predictive of group success. Data from our first two studies indicate that there was not even a significant tendency for particular negotiators to be associated consistently with successful groups, or consistently with unsuccessful groups, in a series of three negotiation sessions (where both topic and combination of members differed), while there was only a slight and marginally significant tendency for mediators to be consistently associated with successful or with unsuccessful groups. On these logical grounds, then, as well as upon our empirical evidence to date, we must hold a highly skeptical attitude toward the proposition that negotiation group outcomes are a function of attributes of the participants.

Perhaps the class of variables most likely to be related to effective interaction patterns and outcomes in negotiation groups are those dealing with structural features of the group. Primary among these is the status of the mediator relative to group members. While our data do not permit a direct comparison, they strongly suggest that relative status of the mediator is positively associated with mediator level of participation. Note, however, that level of mediator participation may be related to the "successful" interaction pattern of negotiation groups in a complex way. The need for timely focusing and resolution of the control crisis implies that at least a moderately high level of mediator participation is favorable to group success, since nearly all structuring behavior is done by the mediator. Since the data does not indicate negative effects of "over control," then perhaps we can view high status of mediator as leading to high participation, which in turn increases the chances of "effective" structuring behavior and thus contributes to the chances of negotiation success.

The other key element of the pattern of successful negotiation process, however, is essentially a negative prescription for the mediator: *not* to inject negative interpersonal affect himself, and not to permit group members to do so. Since it is clear in our data that successful groups do not substitute increased positive affect for negative, but rather minimize negative affect, it would seem that increased participation by the mediator would not directly imply less negative affect. It is likely, in fact, that increased mediator activity, some of which would be "controlling" in nature, might well elicit more rather than less negative affect from members. Thus, the strong active pattern of mediator behavior, which seems to occur when the mediator has high relative status, may both help (by timely structuring) and hurt (by eliciting negative affect) the cause of successful negotiation.

It is also likely that the bases on which the mediator holds his position in the group—the form of legitimization—as well as the "tactics" which he utilizes in the negotiations, affect his "impact" on the negotiation process. Unfortunately, present data does not specifically bear on these questions.

Other structural features of the negotiations, including size and relative size of negotiation teams and the relationship of negotiators to the reference groups which they represent, also appear to affect negotiation process. In particular, a negotiator who is in a minority of one seems to be in a (psychologically) different situation than one who has supportive colleagues present. Our data suggest that the minority of one *feels* that he has compromised his reference group's position more, but actually compromises less, than negotiators holding a majority position. We could say that the minority of one has a psychological disadvantage but an objective advantage. He seems to suffer some of the discomfort of the "deviate" in the classic conformity studies (e.g., Asch, 1). However, he does *not* "yield" to majority pressures as frequently as do the deviates in conformity studies, probably because of his awareness of the support of his position by a salient reference group outside the ongoing negotiation setting. At the same time, he apparently feels as if he has "deviated" from the position he is charged with representing, which may function to "harden" his position and reduce the chances that he will yield further concessions to his opponents.

The relationship between the negotiator's own attitudes on the issues of the negotiation and those of the reference group which he represents is an especially interesting area of investigation. In the religious group study, negotiators were real (and committed) members of the reference groups which they represented. In the labor law study, negotiators were attorneys "hired" to represent the negotiating parties. Our data does not permit direct comparisons between the two conditions, since other differences between the studies (in topic, population and operating conditions) are confounded with this representational difference. However, it is clear that these two contrasting relations of negotiators to reference groups may generate vastly different motivational situations for participants and may lead to different degrees of willingness to compromise.

In the campus housing study, not yet completed, we attempted to explore, experimentally, this question of the relation of negotiator to reference group. Results thus far are rather startling. First, the groups made up of two fraternity men (F-F groups) tended to have more constructive (and less partisan) solutions than did the conventionally structured groups with one independent and one fraternity man (I-F groups). This supports Campbell's (4) findings, under somewhat different conditions of negotiation team structure.

However, this task success for the F-F groups was apparently gained at some cost in interpersonal stress and some alienation. The F-F groups decreased in interpersonal esteem, while the I-F groups increased. The F-F groups were less satisfied than I-F groups with outcomes, and with their own performance.

Moreover, participants showed interesting and differing patterns of change in their own attitudes toward the two reference groups, and in the attitudes toward one another which they attributed to the reference groups. In the I-F groups each member increased in the favorableness of his own attitudes toward the opposed reference group, with no substantial change in his attitudes toward his own reference group. Furthermore each modified (in the favorable direction) his perceptions of how the opposed reference group felt about his own reference group. The F-F groups showed a somewhat opposite pattern. Each member tended to *increase* in favorableness toward the group which he represented and *decrease* in favorableness toward the opposing group (although this finding is statistically marginal). In the case of the fraternity man representing the independent position this implies some alienation from his own "true" reference and membership group. Members of the F-F groups also tended to sharpen rather than reduce differences in their perceptions of reference group attitudes toward one another.

Frankly, we do not yet have a compelling and parsimonious interpretation of these findings. One broad, descriptive interpretation of the overall pattern of results is suggested by our tri-polar model presented earlier in this paper. We can view a successful negotiation as normally requiring two, somewhat distinct stages. The first stage is one of establishing rapport with the opposing negotiators, communicating about and exploring the limits of opposing viewpoints, and searching for common ground upon which possible solutions can be constructed. This is an inter-party integrative stage. The second stage consists of attempts to construct as good a solution as possible within the limits of the common ground, and is likely to include attempts by each party to gain as much for their group's position as possible within the tolerable limits of the opposing group. This may be called a constructive stage, characterized by "distributive bargaining."

In this framework, we can then speculate that the I-F groups focused effort on the first, integrative stage, and with considerable success. They increased interpersonal esteem, gained perspective of each other's reference group positions, and "softened" in their own attitudes toward the other group. However, they did not manage to carry out stage two with as much success as the F-F groups, perhaps because of time limitations.

The F-F groups, on the other hand, began their sessions with stage one more or less completed. They were both actually members of the same reference group, hence shared a common frame of reference on the problem at the outset. In a sense, they began in the second constructive stage; hence they generated more adequate solutions within the fixed time limits than did the I-F groups. However, the second, constructive stage involves distributive bargaining, which may be inherently divisive. Concentration of efforts of the F-F groups on this divisive second stage of negotiation, while leading to more constructive solutions, seems also to have led to disruption of interpersonal relations.

In any case, these data indicate that in attempting to describe the attitudinal structure of a negotiation group we must take into account not only (1) the individual's own attitudes and those of his reference group, but also (2) members' *perceptions* of attitudes of other participants and their reference groups and (3) members' perceptions of the others' "true" relationships to the negotiating parties and the issues over and above the role relationships patterned by the negotiation situation itself. This implication, as others discussed up to this point, highlights the tremendous complexity of even our somewhat abstract and simplified negotiation situations.

Some Implications for Subsequent Research

The touchstone of our guiding model is the proposition that effects of input variables (member, mediator, group structure and situational factors) on negotiation outcomes are mediated through the negotiation process. This proposition seems amply supported by the data from our initial studies. The variables which directly predict negotiation success are indices of interaction process. Group structural and situational variables, although they affect interaction process, do not show direct relationships with negotiation outcome for two reasons. First, there is not a one-to-one-to-one mapping from input-to-process-to-output. Rather, a given input (e.g., mediator status) may affect process in several ways, some of which enhance (e.g., timely structuring behavior) and some of which reduce (e.g., increased negative affect) output effectiveness. Secondly, input variables tend to generate effects *via* changes in member perceptions, and it is these perceived conditions rather than the "objective" conditions which influence member interactive behavior, hence outcome. For example, relative status of the mediator is determined not so much by his expertness and impartiality as by members' perceptions of his experience, his legitimacy in the mediator role, and his attitudes toward the issues under consideration.

The crucial nature of the interaction process in affecting negotiation outcomes implies the need for further study of. (1) patterns of negotiation process characteristic of successful outcomes; (2) input characteristics, member group and situational, which are predictive of key features of negotiation processes; and (3) the extent to which negotiation groups, made aware of the "successful" pattern of negotiations (by instructions and training) can deliberately induce successful outcomes by exhibiting that process pattern. These needs in turn imply the need for further efforts to develop an interaction process analysis system which will highlight those features most crucial in negotiations. It is our intent to give major emphasis in the program to development and use of such an interaction analysis system.

The data collected thus far also suggest that perceptions of participants are crucial in determining the negotiation process and its outcome. This seems to require a vastly more complex conceptualization of the attitudinal structuring of negotiation groups than is often implied by the conceptual models used for studies of negotiation and bargaining (e.g. Bass, 3; Campbell, 4; Minas, *et al.,* 23; Scodel, *et al.,* 25). It would seem that we must consider, *at least*: (1) the participants' own attitudes toward the issues; (2) their perceptions of their own reference group's attitudes toward the issues; (3) their perceptions of the other participant's attitudes toward the issues; (4) their perceptions of the opposing reference group's attitudes toward the issues; (5) several derivative measures such as their perceptions of the degree of disagreement between (a) self and other, (b) self and own reference groups, (c) own and other reference group, and (d) other participant and his reference group; and (6) their perceptions of own and other reference group attitudes toward one another, over and above the specific issues of the negotiation. It would seem to be the *patterning* of these and other participant perceptions, rather than gross lack of "favorableness" or accuracy of any one or several of these, which will influence interactive behavior of participants in negotiation groups. Hence, comprehensive investigation of these (and related) perceptions will also receive major attention in this program.

There seems ample evidence that mediator behavior is central to the pattern of successful negotiation interaction. Yet, the data indicate that mediator attributes, as such, do not predict negotiation outcomes. These results imply that there is a need for specification of *two-stage* mappings by which mediator attributes influence mediator behavior, and how that behavior in turn influences negotiation outcomes. A third major program emphasis will therefore be on the study of the mediator, including experimental manipulations of mediator role behavior, and of negotiator perceptions of mediator status, attitudes and role behavior.

Finally, since this paper began with a discussion of alternative methodological approaches to the study of negotiation, it is probably fitting that it close with a comment about certain limitations of the methodology we have chosen. By choosing to work with issues which are real to our participants and their groups, we have engendered several fundamental problems. From a practical point of view, identifying and securing the cooperation of such "elite" groups, and developing negotiation materials geared to these groups, is costly. Furthermore, such groups tend to have limited numbers willing to cooperate; hence, the number of replications we can hope to achieve for a given negotiation problem is limited. From a scientific standpoint, the need to use a new, and substantively different, set of negotiation problems for each new study limits our ability to generalize findings from one study to another.

One way to escape this problem is to develop a "general game," such as Guetzkow's inter-nation game, Campbell's labor-bargaining game or Deutsch and Krauss's trucking game, all of which were discussed earlier in this paper. The Campbell and Deutsch paradigms have certain limitations which were pointed out in an earlier section. Games like Guetzkow's pose two potential dangers, namely: (1) they can be very expensive, per unit case; and (2) they can be so complex that they require either extensive training or highly select participants. Nevertheless, we are currently exploring the feasibility of developing such a complex, continuous "negotiation game," which could be used with a broad range of participants and would permit manipulation of many personal and structural variables.

Perhaps the key lesson we have learned, from our review of relevant research, from our own findings and our model, as well as from our common sense, is that negotiation is a complex phenomenon. This complexity is such that a long, careful research effort will be needed before we can expect major gains. Therefore, we must set our sights on *long-range* goals, with the expectation that our initial progress will be slow. We should not spend our time casting about to find "the magic variable" which will account for negotiation results, but rather should proceed systematically to assess the effects of a whole set of variables—member, group, situation—which separately and interactively shape the process and outcome of negotiations.

BIBLIOGRAPHY

1. Asch, Solomon E. *Studies of Independence and Conformity*: I. *A Minority of One Against a Unanimous Majority*. Psychological Monographs LXX (1956) No. 9. (Whole No. 416)
2. Bass, Bernard M. *Comparison of Behavior in Groups of Self-Oriented, Interaction-Oriented and Task-Oriented Members*. Technical Report No. 25, Louisiana State University, 1961
3. _____ *Effects on Negotiators of their Prior Experience in Strategy or Study Groups*. Technical Report No. 1 (Contract N ONR 624 14), University of Pittsburgh, 1963
4. Campbell, R. J. *Originality in Group Productivity*: III. *Partisan Commitment and Productive Independence in a Collective Bargaining Situation*. The Ohio State University Research Foundation, 1960
5. Deutsch, Morton. "The Effect of Motivational Orientation upon Trust and Suspicion," *Human Relations,* XIII (May, 1960) 123-139
6. _____ and Collins, M. E. "The Effect of Public Policy in Housing Projects upon Interracial Attitudes," in *Readings in Social Psychology,* ed. Eleanor E. Maccoby *et al.* (3rd ed. New York: Holt, Rinehart and Winston, Inc., 1958) 612-623

7. _____ and Krauss, Robert M. "The Effect of Threat upon Interpersonal Bargaining," *Journal of Abnormal and Social Psychology,* LXI (September, 1960) 181-189

8. _____ "Trust and Suspicion," *Journal of Conflict Resolution,* II (December, 1958) 265-279

9. Douglas, Ann. *Industrial Peacemaking.* New York: Columbia University Press, 1962

10. Driver, M. J. *Conceptual Structure and Group Processes in an Inter-Nation Simulation.* Part I: *The Perception of Simulated Nations.* Princeton University and Educational Testing Service, 1962

11. Festinger, Leon and Katz, Daniel (eds.) *Research Methods in the Behavioral Sciences.* New York: Dryden Press, 1953

12. Guetzkow, Harold S. (ed.) *Simulation in Social Sciences; Readings.* Englewood Cliffs, N. J.: Prentice-Hall, Inc., 1962

13. _____ *Simulation in International Relations*: *Developments for Research and Teaching.* Englewood Cliffs, N. J.: Prentice-Hall, Inc., 1963

14. Hare, A. Paul. *Handbook of Small Group Research.* Glencoe, Ill.: The Free Press, 1962

15. Hemphill, J. E. "Why People Attempt to Lead," in *Leadership and Interpersonal Behavior,* ed. by L. Petrullo and B. Bass. (New York: Holt, Rinehart and Winston, 1961)

16. Hurwitz, Jacob I., Zander, Alvin F., and Hymovitch, Bernard. "Some Effects of Power on the Relations among Group Members," in *Group Dynamics*: *Research and Theory,* ed. by D. Cartwright and A. Zander. (2nd ed. Evanston, Ill.: Row, Peterson & Co., 1960) 800-809

17. Julian, J. W. and McGrath, J. E. *The Influence of Leader and Member Behavior on the Adjustment and Task Effectiveness of Negotiation Groups.* Technical Report No. 17, Group Effectiveness Research Laboratory, University of Illinois, 1963

18. Kelley, Harold H. "Communication in Experimentally Created Hierarchies," *Human Relations,* IV (February, 1951) 39-56

19. Landsberger, H. A. "Interaction Process Analysis of the Mediation of Labor-Management Disputes," *Journal of Abnormal and Social Psychology,* LI (November, 1955) 552-558

20. Loomis, James L. "Communication, the Development of Trust, and Cooperative Behavior," *Human Relations,* XII (November, 1959) 305-315

21. McGrath, J. E. "Toward a 'Theory of Method' for Research on Organizations," in *New Perspectives in Organization Research,* ed. by W. W. Cooper, H. J. Leavitt, and M. W. Shelly (New York: John Wiley and Co., 1964) Ch. 27

22. _____and Julian, J. W. *Negotiation and Conflict: An Experimental Study.* Technical Report No. 16, Group Effectiveness Research Laboratory, University of Illinois, 1962

23. Minas, J. S., Scodel, A., Marlowe, D., and Rawson, H. "Some Descriptive Aspects of Two-Person Non-Zero-Sum Games, II," *Journal of Conflict Resolution,* IV (June, 1960) 193-197

24. Rapoport, A., and Orivant, C. "Experimental Games: A Review," *Behavioral Science,* VII (January, 1962) 1-37

25. Scodel, A., *et al.,* "Some Descriptive Aspects of Two-Person Non-Zero-Sum Games, I," *Journal of Conflict Resolution,* III (June, 1959) 114-119

26. Sherif, M., *et al. Intergroup Conflict and Cooperation: The Robber's Cave Experiment.* Norman, Okla.: University Book Exchange, 1961

27. Strodtbeck, Fred L., *et al.,* "Social Status in Jury Deliberations," *American Sociological Review,* XXII (December, 1957) 713-719

28. Thibaut, John. "An Experimental Study of the Cohesiveness of Underprivileged Groups," *Human Relations,* III (August, 1950) 251-278

29. Thrall, R. M., Coombs, C. H., and Davis, R. L. (eds.) *Decision Processes.* New York: John Wiley and Co., 1954

30. Vidmar, W. J., and McGrath, J. E. *Role Assignment and Attitudinal Commitment As Factors in Negotiation.* Technical Report # 3 (Contract AF 49(638)-1291) University of Illinois, 1965

The Research Team and
Its Organizational Environment

HAROLD B. PEPINSKY, JOHN RINER,
KARL E. WEICK, MARY P. MOLL**

How research is accomplished by teams in organizational settings, how such research activities are assessed within organizations, and how research activities can be modified to increase team productivity are regarded as problems of social as well as scientific significance. The present research project attempts to contribute empirical and theoretical knowledge toward the solution of these problems. This paper will discuss a relevant empirical study, and a theoretical framework to which the research has contributed.

The setting in which data were obtained, which we shall refer to as "X," is a private "not for profit" research organization employing more than two thousand persons. Its chief purpose is to conduct contract research for industry and government. X's research staff is organized into approximately 50 operating sections, grouped under seven divisions of research. Within a division, each section is expected to conduct research in a specialized region of the general area for which the division is responsible; and the division itself is nearly autonomous in its responsibilities for developing fields of research. In this study members of two research teams and their administrative supervisors were interviewed.

The teams, labeled here as "C" and "T," are conducting research considered to be more "basic" than that usually conducted in X.

*This chapter is part of a project supported by the Air Force Office of Scientific Research on Contract AF 49 (638)-373.

**Dr. Pepinsky is Professor of Psychology, Department of Psychology, The Ohio State University; Dr. Riner is Associate Professor of Mathematics, Department of Mathematics, The Ohio State University, Dr. Weick is Assistant Professor of Psychology, Department of Psychology, Purdue University; Miss Moll is a former Research Assistant, Systems Research Group, Engineering Experiment Station, The Ohio State University.

135

Objectives of "C" are to evaluate the intrinsic properties of certain compound materials and to indicate their device applications. Objectives of Team T are very similar to those of Team C except that less is known about the materials selected for study by Team T, and therefore its research is considered slightly more "basic" than Team C's. Its area of device application also is somewhat different. Both teams are sponsored by *groups* of industrial companies—a relatively new procedure in sponsorship, it appears. The reason is that a single company does not elect to be sole supporter for the kind of "basic" long range research that these teams are doing; also, one infers that the two teams' research is too "basic" to interfere with accomplishment of the sponsors' own immediate, competitive goals. Both teams are interdisciplinary and composed of persons belonging to different divisions and sections in X. Figures 1 and 2 display the composition of the two teams.

In the figures team members' regular titles within X are given, and the relative authority and prestige of each title in X's organizational hierarchy is indicated by its superordinate and/or subordinate location on either one or both of the charts. Each position is linked to every other one on a chart by a solid black line, indicating a publicly defined superior-subordinate relationship, with the notable exception of the "Assistant Technical Advisor" and "Consultant" positions. Although within X such advisory positions nominally carry the prestige of equivalent posts on the administrative hierarchy, the non-administrative person is actually responsible for his actions to his administrative counterpart. In Figures 1 and 2 these ambiguous positions are linked by dotted lines to positions in the regular administrative hierarchy. The boundaries of team membership are indicated in the two figures by dot-dash lines. Only persons whose positional titles are enclosed in rectangular, solid line blocks were interviewed in the present study; other immediately relevant positions, however, are illustratively displayed. Tape-recorded interviews approximately 90 minutes in length were held individually and privately with each member of the two teams and with his administrative supervisors. In all, 20 interviews were conducted according to a standardized routine, and every one of the taped interviews was subsequently transcribed.

Data from the 20 transcribed interviews were analyzed from the standpoint of an observer who is not a member of X organization. Such an observer, however, is required to assume that every member of the organization has a theory about himself and his environment, in which he gives phenomenal existence to events in his organization. Thus, an organization member is assumed to have cognitively available *instructions,* which tell him the circumstances under which organizational tasks are to be performed—and who is to perform them.

As the observer attempts schematically to reconstruct a member's instructions, these can be defined at three levels:

Figure 1. ORGANIZATIONAL AFFILIATIONS OF TEAM C

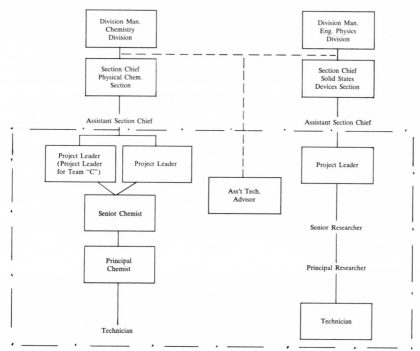

1. In *form,* the instruction is defined at an analytical level, as *a complex sentence comprised of (a) a conditional (independent) and (b) a consequent (dependent) clause.*

2. In *content,* and again at the analytical level, the instruction becomes *a statement containing information of two kinds: (1) a specification (in the conditional clause) of the limiting conditions (guides, constraints) under which (2) certain (in the consequent clause) described action takes place.* Such "described action" may be labeled as a *task.*

3. Finally, the instruction moves to the *empirical* level as *any person is observed to treat it as—or to transpose it into—a directive.* In other words, *a person is observed to give the instructional statement directive or obligatory properties for action.* This transposition involves the observed person's *application* of the instruction to a particular case, such that it *behooves* a performer (who may or may not

Figure 2. ORGANIZATIONAL AFFILIATIONS OF TEAM T

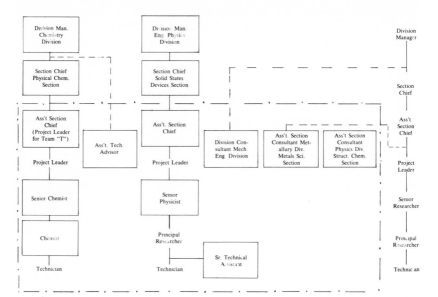

be specifically identified) to execute a designated task ("described action") in accordance with stated conditions. It is only when an instructive statement is observed to be so treated by an identified performer, however, that we may refer to the instruction as *controlling* the actor.

Hence, assuming the *form* of an instruction to be a complex sentence, we could *content analyze* the responses of persons interviewed in X into discrete units such that in each unit at least one described action could be inferred to follow from limiting antecedent conditions. What our informants actually said could now be treated as directives, specifying whom it "behooved" to perform particular tasks in X.

In all, more than thirty-four hundred such instructional statements, made by the persons interviewed in X, were analyzed to yield general task categories which comprised a list of tasks performed by members of X. In every case the person inferred to be the performer of any or all of the tasks specified within the instructional unit was identified, as were inferred problems (difficulties to overcome) in the accomplishment of the tasks.

A summary and interpretation of empirical results are presented in the final section of this chapter. First, however, a set of formal definitions are given as a framework from which empirical results may be viewed.

DEFINITIONS

In this section a set of organizational events, which can be used to describe the research team in its organizational environment, will be given explicit definition. As indicated in our introductory remarks, these definitions were induced from statements made by the inter-viewed members of X about their organization. What is offered here represents the *present* state of our definitions. They have evolved from a number of earlier sets, many times revised to provide a frame-work for our study of organization. Thus it must be realized that our theoretical framework is in a state of change and subject to modifica-tion. Because our primary purpose in making these definitions is to contribute toward a theory of organization, it is well to note that our definitions are consistent with others' attempts to formalize organiza-tions.

In the set of definitions that follows, those of *organization* and *team* are of primary importance. All other definitions are included because they, in turn, define concepts used to define "organization." The concept of *task*, which is highly relevant to our argument, is treated for the moment as an undefined term. Its analytic status, as a cognitive element in the action consequent of any "instruc-tion" that a member may have about his organization, is simply taken for granted. The related terms, "task performance," "task performer," etc., will also be taken as undefined.

If y is a task performing unit, performing task t, we will say that y is paired with t and write (y,t). It should be kept in mind that y might be a set V of persons. To avoid misunderstanding, it will be assumed that, if V is a set of persons and t is a task and if (V,t) exists, then every person in V is contributing to the performance of t. This might mean for a particular individual that he simply gets out of the way. Thus the idea of *subtask* can be defined as follows: DEFINITION 1: Let t be a task and let $\{t_1, t_2, \ldots, t_n\}$ be a collection of tasks the performance of which, in some order, effects the per-formance of t. Then the collection $\{t_1, t_2, \ldots, t_n\}$ is called a de-composition of t and each of the t_i, $1 \leq i \leq n$, is called a *subtask* of t. It is reasonably clear that, given any task t, there are many possible decompositions for t.

Another concept we need in developing our definition of organi-zation is that of *system,* which we now introduce.

Let Y be any set and let U be a set of relations on Y. (If r is a relation on Y, r is a collection of ordered pairs of elements from Y. If the pair (a, b) is in the relation r, we write a r b and say that a is r-related to b.) Given a, b in Y we say that a is chain-related to b if and only if there exist a finite number of relations, say r_1, r_2, . . ., r_k, in U and a finite number of elements, say x_1, x_2, . . ., x_{k-1}, in Y so that:

$$a \; r_1 \; x_1, \; x_1 \; r_2 \; x_2, \; . \; . \; ., \; x_{k-1} \; r_k \; b.$$

Thus system may be defined as follows:

DEFINITION 2: Let Z be a set-valued function defined on a time interval $\tau_o \leq \tau \leq \tau_1$ (i.e., Z (τ) is a set for each τ in the time interval), and let Z* be the set of all elements x so that x is an element of $Z(\tau)$ for at least one τ in the interval $\tau_o \leq \tau \leq \tau_1$. Further let U be a set of relations on Z*. The pair [Z,U] is a *system,* if and only if,

      S1. For every τ in the interval $\tau_o \leq \tau \leq \tau_1$, the set $Z(\tau)$ has a finite number of elements,

and

      S2. For every pair, a, b, of elements of Z* either a is chain-related to b or b is chain-related to a.

In our view, then, a *system* is a set of elements that may change over time with the property that there is a chain of relations relating every pair of elements that exist in the set at any time.

Now we can turn our attention to the concept of *organization.* Preliminary to this we note that, if Y is any task-performing unit performing task T, then T can be considered to induce relations on Y. For example, if t is a task and person x in Y causes person y in Y to perform t, we can say that x and y are related. Or if x and y both are performing subtasks of T we can say that x and y are related. In these and other ways we consider tasks as inducing relations on their task-performing units.

In introducing our definition of organization we shall list three of the properties separately and then recombine them in a formal definition, as follows:

First, we want our organization to be a set of human beings that may change over time. So let O be a set-valued function defined on a time interval $\tau_o \leq \tau \leq \tau_1$ satisfying:

      1.1 For each τ in the interval $\tau_o \leq \tau \leq \tau_1$, O (τ) is a finite set of persons.

Second, we desire that, at every point in our time interval, the set O (τ) be a task performing unit. So suppose that, for each τ in $\tau_o \leq \tau \leq \tau_1$, U $(\tau) = \{T_1 \; (\tau), \; T_2 \; (\tau), \; . \; . \; ., \; Tn_\tau \; (\tau)\}$ is a finite set of tasks satisfying:

      1.2 $(O(\tau), \; T_i \; (\tau))$ exists for i = 1, 2, . . ., n_τ.

This says that for each τ there exists a finite set of tasks for which O (τ) is the task performing unit.

Third, we require that, from some point of view, at each time τ in $\tau_o \leq \tau \leq \tau_1$, the organization is functioning as a single task performing unit. To insure this we suppose now that there exists a task $M = M(\tau)$ (M may change over time) satisfying:

    1.3 for each τ, the pairings $(O(\tau), T_i(\tau))$ effect the pairing $(O(\tau), M(\tau))$.

We will call this task M the mission of the organization. In essence the condition 1.3 points out that the tasks $T_i(\tau)$ may be viewed as subtasks of M. In fact one might well define M to be the collection $T_1, \ldots, Tn_\tau$.

We introduce the notation O^* to denote the set of persons x who are in $O(\tau)$ for at least one τ in $\tau_o \leq \tau \leq \tau_1$. Recalling that any task for which $O(\tau)$ is a task performing unit determines a set of relations on $O(\tau)$ we let M^* denote the set of relations r such that r is induced by at least one T in $U(\tau)$ for at least one τ in $\tau_o \leq \tau \leq \tau_1$.

We define organization, then, as follows:

DEFINITION 3: Let O be a set-valued function defined on a time interval $\tau_o \leq \tau \leq \tau_1$ and, for each τ in this interval, let $U(\tau)$ be a finite set of tasks. Further let $M = M(\tau)$ be a task that varies over time defined on $\tau_o \leq \tau \leq \tau_1$. The triple [O, U, M], where O, U and M satisfy 1.1, 1.2 and 1.3 above is an organization, if and only if:

    01. $[O^*, M^*]$ is a system.

    02. For each τ in $\tau_o \leq \tau \leq \tau_1$, the pairings $(O(\tau), T_i(\tau))$ are sufficient to guarantee the pairings $(O (\sigma), T_1 (\sigma))$ for some σ, $\tau \leq \sigma \leq \tau_1$.

    03. There exists a subset $O_c(\tau)$ of $O(\tau)$ with a task $C(\tau)$ for each τ in $\tau_o \leq \tau \leq \tau_1$ where $C(\tau)$ is the task of effecting the pairing $(O(\sigma), M(\sigma))$ for some σ, $\tau \leq \sigma \leq T_1$.

A few comments on these conditions 01, 02, and 03 are in order. 01 insures that the persons in the organization are chain related to each other by the task-induced relations. 02 is intended to say that the performance of the tasks in $U(\tau)$ insure that the organization will continue in existence. 03 has to do with control. The set $O_c(\tau)$ is the set of persons who at time r set the mission for a later time σ. This set O_c might be called the controller of the organization. The members of this set might change the mission $M(\tau)$, might modify the set $O(\tau)$, might alter the tasks $U(\tau)$, or might modify the pairings $(O(\tau), T_i(\tau))$.

It is in dealing with this postulate 03 that we feel ourselves to be near the heart of organization theory. We feel the necessity for a postulate of this sort—the task categories we have developed from the information given us include seeking resources, assessing, communicating—all of which suggest a change and an expectancy of working more effectively toward accomplishing the mission of the organization. Other tasks, e.g. adapting, indicate that the organization has changed in a purposive manner, and this indicates that the pairing $(O(\tau), M(\tau))$ is different from what it was at an earlier time. Unless this change is accidental it is necessary to explain it in our axioms. Thus our postulate 03.

Since we are interested in research teams in organizations, we need also to define *team*. Primarily the team is a task-performing unit for a particular task. If the task is a research task, we would call the team a research team. Thus we make the following definitions:
DEFINITION 4: Let $O = [O; U, M]$ be an organization. Let A be a set valued function defined on an interval of time $\sigma_o \leqq \sigma \leqq \sigma_1$, where $\tau_o \leqq \sigma_o \leqq \sigma_1 \leqq \tau$ and where $\tau_o \leqq \tau \leqq \tau_1$ is the time interval over which O is defined. Further let $TA = TA(\tau)$ be a task defined for each τ in $\sigma_o \leqq \tau \leqq \sigma_1$. The pair $[A, TA]$ is a team in O if and only if:

     T1. $A(\tau)$ is a subset of $O(\tau)$ for each τ, $\sigma_o \leqq \tau \leqq \sigma_1$.
     T2. $TA(\tau)$ is a subtask of a task in $U(\tau)$ for every τ,
           $\sigma_o \leqq \tau \leqq \sigma_1$.
     T3. $[A^*, TA^*]$ is a system. (Here the notation means the
           same as in def. 5.)
     T4. $(A(\tau), TA(\tau))$ exists for every τ, $\sigma_o \leqq \tau \leqq \sigma_1$.
One may note that this definition agrees with that of organization if we let $TA = M$, $\sigma_o = \tau_o$, $\sigma_1 = \tau_1$ and let $U(\tau)$ contain only the one task TA for each τ. However, no assumption concerning survival or control (02 or 03) is made. So, although a research team may behave like an organization, in general that is not the case.

RESULTS

The foregoing definitions, themselves induced from our interview data, provide a systematic guide for the description of events in Organization X. Three kinds of descriptive information are implied: (1) the tasks that are performed, (2) the pairings of persons with tasks, and (3) pairings between persons that are effected by tasks. Since the data analysis is still being completed, much of our present discussion must be anecdotal.

Central to our identification and description of an organization is the specification that at any given time interval it contains a finite set of tasks (see assumption 1.2 in the preceding section). The tasks inferred from the interviews with members of X are listed in Table 1. These tasks are constructed by categorizing the consequent clauses of interviewee messages. Although we did not analyze the conditional or antecedent clauses of these messages as such, many of these could be treated as consequent to still other antecedent clauses. For example, our informants often seemed to be saying, "If (such-and-such) a task is performed, then my associates or I take (specified) action." This treatment of the data is consistent with our formal assumption that the controlling of action is itself a task.

Table 1

TASKS PERFORMED BY MEMBERS OF X

1. Adapting
2. Assessing
3. Controlling Project Budget
4. Facilitating Problem Solving
5. Problem Solving
6. Supplying
7. Seeking Rewards
8. Communicating
9. Rewarding
10. Seeking and Selecting Extra-organization Resources
11. Teaming
13. Approaching Sponsor's Goal
14. Facilitating Idea Production
15. Maintaining of Appearances
16. Maintaining Continuity
17. Monitoring Interpersonal Behavior
18. Retaining Organization Membership
19. Managing
20. Career Development
21. Seeking and Selecting Intra-organization Resources

When we constructed the task categories, we first grouped them into subsets according to discriminably different circumstances of task performance. These peculiar circumstances became the defining attributes of the task itself. Secondly, we constructed a general definition that subsumed all the special circumstances of task performance. Sample statements that led to the development of the task category of Assessing, for instance, are the following:

(Kinds of standards against which output is assessed:)
"When you go to a technical society meeting where members of the group are sought out, this is a good indicator that they are doing good work, and if other people want to talk with them, this filters up to management in other organizations where there are some good people. And this is what we need."
"It is successful to see other uses for equipment and· ideas other than that which relates directly to a project because when the project is over, then maybe they can seek projects in these new areas."
(Assessor and situational conditions that modify standards of assessment:)
"Being familiar with an area of study increases the likelihood of one viewing an achievement in that area as being successful and good."

"We find that the closer contact we have with government monitors, the more discussion we have with them, the more likely a project is to be successful."

"Quite often when someone who is not a member of X has done research and arrived at a conclusion in a similar area of research that is being done at X, people in X are more likely to believe that the non-X member has a better solution."

(Assessment of one's self and assessment of others:)

"This is pretty much a long term project, the way I look at it. We really haven't accomplished a whole heck of a lot. As far as possitive results are concerned we've eliminated a couple of materials which don't look promising."

The definition arrived at is as follows:

Assessing is the selection and preferential ordering of a set of events regarded as indicators of task accomplishment and their utilization as a standard for judging task accomplishment.

Another interesting task category is one that we have called Maintaining Continuity. We think it is interesting, possibly because the interviewees associated a number of problems with the accomplishment of this task. Statements that have helped to build this category are the following:

(Persons are prevented from completing a project when the funds for the project are depleted:)

"I went out on a limb once. I thought it was worthwhile to go ahead and not write a report on time because I was on to something that looked good, so I spent two weeks more than I should have, and I got reprimanded violently about it. But the result was, it meant another project to the tune of $50,000, renewal of another $50,000 at the beginning of this month, but yet for two weeks—for a lousy two weeks—I was really reprimanded for it."

(Keeping up with the work in several projects at once is demanded, and this is difficult:)

"As the pile of research data builds higher and higher, it becomes increasingly difficult for me to maintain close touch or try to remember what's been done in a certain area, and sometimes I wake up to the fact that I have been negligent in keeping track of what's going on right now, in certain areas."

"It has bothered me, this lack of continuity of efforts on one problem, for a long time. This is from the very nature of research in X. You are liable to have several jobs of diverse nature thrown at you."

(Lack of continuity can be remedied:)

"X is beginning to realize the need for getting completeness or closure on projects terminated prematurely, and is making some funds available."

We define *Maintaining Continuity* to be the task of keeping centered on and carrying through to completion a designated research interest or problem.

Having briefly suggested the nature of the tasks that were inferred, we now wish to call attention briefly to the frequency with which these tasks were mentioned. These data are contained in the first two columns of Table 2. Here the results are quite straightforward. The five most frequently mentioned tasks were 5, 6, 19, 8, 21. These are tasks one might well expect to occur in a research setting, and our respondents strongly confirm this. Tasks 3, 14, 17 were mentioned least often, probably because they suggest action that is somewhat more specific and circumscribed. Nevertheless, there were sufficient mentions of these latter tasks to warrant our inference that they were performed because of instructions cognitively available to members of the two research teams or their supervisors in X Organization.

Brief mention should be made of the data summarized in the last three columns. Respondents frequently mentioned what they regarded to be obstacles or barriers that interfered with the successful performance of various tasks. An example of a statement categorized as a problem is the following:

"Administrators create a hardship on the researcher by expecting him to stay within an unrealistic budget . . . as a result the researcher must cut corners on the research, work after hours, or juggle money from other projects."

It is of interest in columns 1, 3, 4 that the most frequently mentioned tasks do not always show the highest proportion of problems. In fact, some tasks show quite the opposite pattern. For example, task 16 was the 3rd lowest task in number of mentions, yet proportionally it has more problems associated with it than any other task. The 2nd highest proportion of problems is associated with the task of "facilitating problem solving," a task that is the 6th most frequently mentioned. Finally, task 18 has the 3rd highest number of problems associated with it, even though it was ranked 15th in frequency of mentions. We should make clear that the trend toward an inverse relationship between frequency of mention and proportion of problems relative to this frequency, is not nearly as evident with task 4.

If one makes the assumption, which is precarious to say the least, that persons talk most about what is familiar or most important to them, then it is possible to relate these data to the notion of sur-

Table 2

A SUMMARY OF INTERVIEW DATA

Tasks*	Frequency of task mention (t)	% of total no. of task mentions associated with each task (t/T)	Frequency of problem mention for each task (p)	% of task mentions designated as problems (p/t)	% of total no. of problems associated with each task (p/P)
1	290	4.1%	52	17.9%	4.0%
2	349	4.9%	42	12.0%	3.2%
3	52	.7%	12	23.1%	.9%
4	431	6.1%	167	38.7%	12.9%
5	1058	15.0%	102	9.6%	7.9%
6	980	13.9%	198	20.2%	15.3%
7	165	2.3%	51	30.9%	3.9%
8	738	10.4%	163	22.1%	12.6%
9	133	1.9%	34	25.6%	2.6%
10	422	6.0%	58	13.7%	4.5%
11	201	2.8%	10	5.0%	.8%
13	223	3.2%	31	13.9%	2.4%
14	32	.4%	5	15.6%	.4%
15	125	1.8%	24	19.2%	1.9%
16	67	.9%	32	47.7%	2.5%
17	51	.7%	15	29.4%	1.2%
18	90	1.3%	31	34.4%	2.4%
19	846	12.0%	113	13.4%	8.7%
20	73	1.0%	17	23.3%	1.3%
21	730	10.3%	136	18.6	10.5%
Total	7056=T	99.7%	1293=P	—	99.9%

*For titles see Table 1

vival. Our hunch would be that tasks mentioned most frequently are also most important to the continued existence of the organization. Consequently, when problems crop up in these tasks, they are attended to immediately since they threaten this existence. Somewhat more peripheral tasks, judged so on the basis of infrequent mention, may also have associated problems, but in someone's view the occurrence of these problems does not constitute a major threat to X's continued existence. As a result, these obstacles do not receive the amount of attention paid to the obstacles associated with supposedly more central tasks. If we follow this line of reasoning, the central tasks emerge as 11, 5, 2, 19, 10. Thus it may be that the tasks most important to the survival of X, as the interviewees see them (i.e., those with the lowest proportion of problems), are the Solving of Research Problems through Team Effort, the Managing and Assessing of this output, and the attempt to insure the Continuation of this effort by Seeking New Resources. It should be noted that the list of the five most important tasks judged on the basis of lowest proportion of problems differs somewhat from this list of the five most important tasks inferred from the sheer frequency of mention. Only tasks 5 and 19 are common to both lists.

An alternative interpretation could be based on the premise that the lesser mentioned tasks are perhaps more crucial to the continuation of the organization in the sense that persons tend to withhold comment on those activities about which they feel anxious. Thus tasks 3, 14, and 16 may indeed be more important to members of the organization.

Changes in the environment occasioned by task performance are almost always the result of the acts of persons *in combination with* other determinants. However, in an effort to simplify and organize the complex array of things that happen, persons tend to attribute the origin of acts overwhelmingly to persons rather than to capricious situational conditions. By assigning effects to human origins, persons are aided in their attempts to make sense out of what happens to them and in their efforts to identify economically a point at which influence can be exerted to effect changes.

Empirically, assumption 1.1, that an organization is a system containing a finite set of persons, coupled with this notion of "personal causality," suggests the importance of discovering those persons who are identified as the agents of task performance in general and the specific tasks with which they are most often associated. The interviewees identified 53 discriminably different persons or groups of persons, listed in Table 3, as the agents responsible for the accomplishment of the 21 tasks. These designations ranged from as specific an agent as the interviewee himself, to one as global as "Organization X." To make these data somewhat more manageable, a panel of judges combined the 53 different agents into 9 major categories of task performers in X, in order to compare the relative frequency with which each category of agent was paired with the various tasks. These categories include "Administrators," "Organization X," "Teams Generic,"* "Technical People," "Team Leaders," "Research Persons," "Service Group," "T team," "C team."

---

*The word generic is used in opposition to *specific* or *named*. Thus when a research person is said to perform a task but no specific person is named, the task performer is "research person, generic."

Table 3

LIST OF POSITIONS IN X

Position is defined as a pairing of person(s) with task(s), such that "person" designates an intended performer of a task. This pairing may be explicit, as when a task is clearly present or implied; or it may be implicit, as when no task is implied. In the latter case, however, there may be a pairing of person(s) with a condition that is assumed to be logically antecedent to a task. This is not a task category but a category containing response cards in which at least one person is paired with some task.

12.01 Organization X and/or X members (generic—may include positions below but unspecified)

12.02 Division and/or Division Members (generic)

12.03 Section and/or Section Members (generic)

12.04 Project, group, team and/or Team Members (generic)

12.05 Board of Directors, President, Vice Presidents, Trustees (generic and/or specified)

12.06 Administrators, Management, Monitors (generic)

12.07 Chief Technical Advisor, Technical Advisor, Assistant Technical Advisor (generic)

12.08 Consultants (generic)

12.09 Division Managers (generic)

12.10 Sub-Division Managers (generic)

12.11 Section Chiefs (generic)

12.12 Assistant Section Chief

12.13 Project or Team Leader, Project Coordinator, Project Engineer (generic)

12.14 Principal Investigators (generic)

12.15 Principal Engineer (generic)

12.16 Research Persons (generic)

12.17 Technicians (generic)

12.18 Resource Persons or groups (generic and/or specified)

12.19 Service Groups (generic and/or specified) (Special case of 12.18)

12.20 Project Development Personnel (generic and/or specified)

12.21 Secretaries (generic)

12.22 Division (specified) and/or Members (unspecified) of Specified Divisions

12.23 Sections (specified) and/or Members (unspecified) of Specified Sections

12.24 T and C Teams (specified) and/or their members (unspecified)

12.25 T Team (specified and/or its members unspecified)

12.26 T Subgroup—"materials preparation" (specified)

12.27 C Team (specified) and/or its members unspecified

12.28 C Subgroup — "device people" (specified)

12.29 C Subgroup — "material preparation" (specified)

12.30 - 12.50 (Specific Performers named in messages)

12.51 Occupational Groups (specified)

12.52 An X-like Organization (generic)

12.53 More than one task performer designated

Some interesting, although not unexpected, results were provided by this analysis. For example, definitions 3.02 and 3.03 in the preceding section, state formally that one of the central tasks of any organization is that of providing conditions such that at some future time the organization will still exist as a task performing unit. A close look at the data on pairing suggests that several tasks are instrumental in maintaining X's existence, in ensuring its viability as a system of persons and tasks. For example, (See Figure 3) the performance of tasks 1, 9, 10, 18, and 20 was attributed to Organization X more frequently than to any other class of performers. Thus, members seem to regard the organization as responsible for coping with the dual problems of asserting itself against or continuing to exist in a probabilistic environment (tasks 1, 10) and of retaining the human resources deemed necessary for this assertion (9, 20, 18). This suggests a possible extension to organizations of Thibaut and Kelley's notion of "fate" and "behavioral" control. The environment appears to have "fate control" over the organization in that organization actions must either abide by environmental rules of action or fail to accomplish such major tasks as survival. The organization, however, seems to attempt to convert this control into "behavioral control" so that organization actions determine what the environment does in return.

Furthermore, it is interesting to notice some of the tasks that are infrequently attributed to the organization, especially those tasks that seem relevant to survival. For example, Organization X is seldom paired with the tasks of Assessing, Approaching Sponsor Goals, or Maintaining Appearances. Each of these tasks seems to involve maintaining current support for the activities within the organization. Apparently, the interviewees see this responsibility to be mainly that of the research teams, for whom they report the highest frequency of such pairings.

Thus, once a team is assigned a research problem, the team becomes responsible for carrying the problem through to the satisfaction of the sponsor. Such a division of responsibility, however, is seen by team members as creating a number of other problems. The team often feels it has little control over the selection of sponsors and the content of the contract. Despite this, once the contract has been signed, the team is responsible for solving the problem in a way consistent with the sponsor's expectations as set forth in the contract. The team often feels that the problem cannot be realistically solved with the money and time allotted to it. Consequently it becomes somewhat more involved with tasks not directly tied to problem solving; tasks such as 13, 15, 16. The performance of these tasks, as the team sees it, frequently impedes progress in the accomplishment of the task for which it feels mainly responsible: namely the solving of research problems.

Figure 3

PERCENTAGES OF TASK AND PROBLEM PAIRINGS
WITH ORGANIZATION X

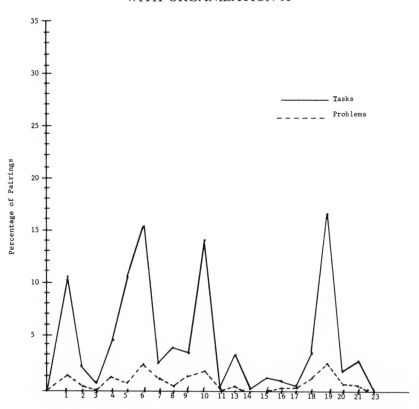

Up to now we have discussed mainly the tasks attributed most frequently to Organization X. Naturally, it is of some interest to know the kinds of tasks attributed to other groups of performers. Samples of these data are shown in Figures 3-7. Immediately apparent are such things as the following: (1) the striking similarities between the profiles of the two teams studied; (2) the more apparent differences between the profiles of Organization X, Administrators, and Team "Generic"; (3) the seemingly low incidence of problems associated with each task. If one attempts to think of these data as suggestive of discrete positions within X, he is struck by the fact that the positions are somewhat more complex, and somewhat less clearly defined, at least by tasks, than might be expected.

Figure 4

PERCENTAGES OF TASK AND PROBLEM PAIRINGS WITH ADMINISTRATORS

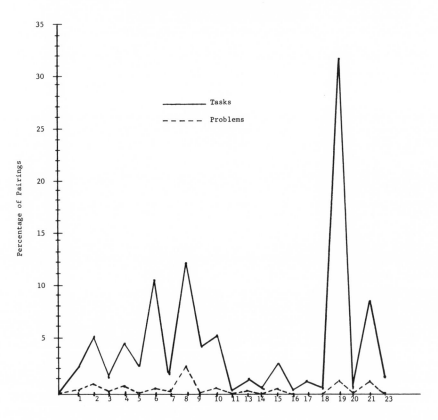

Tasks

So far, we have designated tasks and the persons or groups of persons who are individually paired with these tasks. At this stage, the organization we are representing consists solely of a multitude of discrete person-task pairings. What we need now is to link the members of the organization together in a manner consistent with definition 3.01, "Persons in an organization are chain-related by the performance of tasks."

It is assumed that tasks promote relationships between persons in one of two ways. An actor either is paired with a task, thereby causing another actor within the organization to perform a different task, or two actors perform sub-tasks of the same task. In either case the task accomplishment of one member of the pair is influenced by or under the control of the task accomplishment of the

Figure 5

PERCENTAGES OF TASK AND PROBLEM PAIRINGS
WITH TEAM "GENERIC"

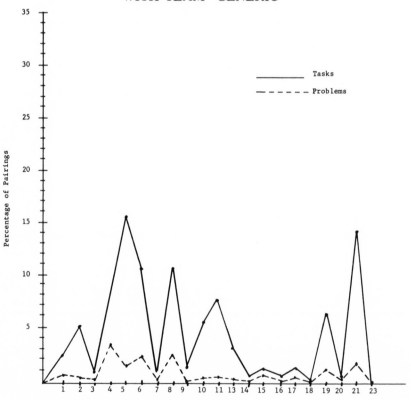

Tasks

other member of the pair. The data that support this assertion of a chain-relationship consist mainly of statements indicating that tasks mediate the relationships between actors.

Figure 6

PERCENTAGES OF TASK AND PROBLEM PAIRINGS
WITH TEAM C

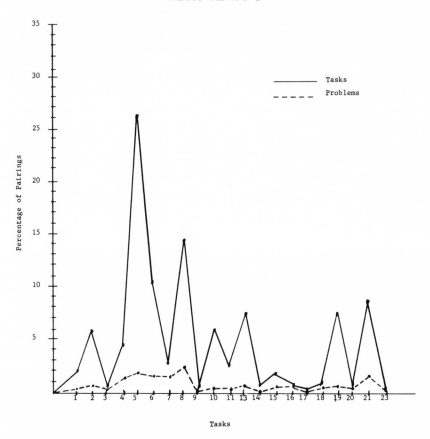

Let us look first of all at statements indicating that a person-task pairing induces or effects at least one other person-task pairing. Note especially, that when a problem is associated with the performance of the logically prior task, this problem frequently ramifies and influences the way in which the subsequent task is handled.

"Now the other people in the division see the equipment I have ordered as being for their use, and it is division property, and

Figure 7

PERCENTAGES OF TASK AND PROBLEM PAIRINGS
WITH TEAM T

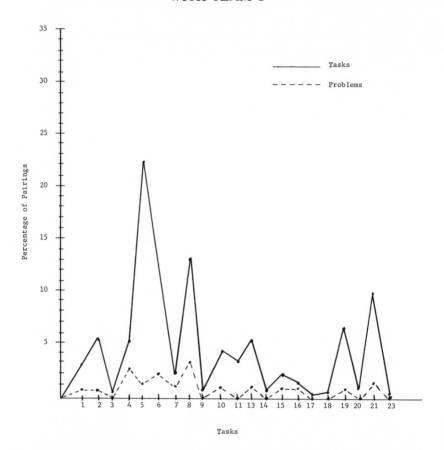

they can demand to use it, and I have no right to say, 'Well, you can't use it, I might use it next week.' So they get it next week. Well, they are using it, something breaks down; they don't know how to use it real well, and when it comes back it's broken, it needs repair, it's wasted time."

Here we see the one set of actors paired with the task of Seeking Intraorganizational Resources induces another set of actors "reluctantly" to supply those resources. The action of Supplying, in turn, seems to induce for the supplier potential difficulty in Facilitating his own Problem Solving. A second example is the following:

"The amount of influence exerted depends on how good the man who's doing the work is. Sometimes they don't have enough confidence in an engineer so they pretty well direct him; other engineers are pretty much free lance and can do just about as they please."

Again we see that an actor, in this case the engineer, paired with the tasks of Problem Solving and Supplying, induces a pairing of the team leader with the task of Managing. The way in which the latter performs his tasks depends directly on the way the former performs his.

"When a division becomes a service unit, the man who likes fundamental research moves on, either gets in a different group or gets into a company."

Here we have the interesting case in which a section paired with the tasks of Adapting and Supplying, induces for certain researchers a pairing with the tasks of Career Development, and in a negative sense, of Retaining Organizational Membership.

So far, we have cited three examples of chain-relationships inferred from reciprocal relationships between the performers of two or more different tasks. A chain relationship, however, also prevails when persons perform subtasks of the same task. Our data abound with examples of this type of relationship. Consider the following:

"There are specific problems in that we are each dependent on the other for either information or material, and if it's not available, then we must re-evaluate what we are doing and work accordingly."

Instances of chain relations induced by the performance of subtasks occur most frequently in association with the task of Teaming. The preceding statement is no exception. Here is a clear example where a team can perform its task of Problem Solving only when subtasks such as Supplying Information and Materials are also performed. Those persons paired with each of these subtasks, are themselves paired in that the way they perform their tasks is contingent upon the needs of the team.

A more explicit statement of pairings between persons induced by their performance of the subtask of a common task, is contained in the following two statements:

"One man may have the responsibility for making a particular material. He would then give it to someone else who would analyze it and give him back the results. Then the two of them would get together and discuss it."

"I think the individual certainly has a somewhat greater respon-

sibility on a team project than he would if he were working alone
. . . particularly if other people's work is dependent on his, e.g., if
the people preparing the materials don't turn out a certain amount
of materials, people who are making the measurements will have
nothing to do, and of course, if the people who are preparing the
materials do a real good job, but the people measuring them don't
feed the results back, why the people preparing the materials don't
know what to do next."

As the last statement indicates, team members become most aware
of their relatedness to others at that point in time when a subtask of
a related actor is not adequately performed.

Another somewhat more indirect way to infer chain relations is
to look at instances of high covariation between tasks. For the moment
we will not be concerned with the specific persons paired with each
task of a frequently occurring pair. We assume only that the persons
paired with each of the tasks probably will be influenced in his task
performance by the way the paired task is performed. As might be
expected, tasks that were mentioned most frequently had the highest
probability of being paired with other tasks. With this in mind let
us indicate a few results.

For each task we listed the three highest and three lowest occurring
pairs. Six of the tasks (2, 11, 13, 15, 19, 21) were associated with
the same cluster of highest occurring pairs. With each of these six tasks,
the tasks of Problem Solving, Supplying and Communicating were
most frequently associated. Thus whenever an instruction required the
action of Teaming, there was about a 50-50 chance that tasks 5, 6,
and 8 would also be required, or at least that their accomplishment
would be affected. The task of Managing, in contrast, was most likely
to occur whenever tasks 1, 3, 9, 17, 18, 20 were also being performed.
One wonders whether frequently occurring pairs of tasks might begin
to indicate potential sequences or chains of tasks such that the accomplishment of one task is prerequisite to the accomplishment of
other paired tasks.

But enough of this speculation. In writing this progress report, we
have been mindful of an aphorism with which we now close: "We are
prone to see what lies behind our eyes rather than what appears before them."

8

Toward an Empirically Derived
Taxonomy of Organizations*

J. EUGENE HAAS, RICHARD H. HALL
AND NORMAN J. JOHNSON**

ORGANIZATIONS are usually viewed as having certain common features. It is also quite obvious that there is great variation among them. It is this variability which challenges the student of organizations. A number of organizational analysts, recognizing this problem, have attempted to bring some order to the phenomena by developing a typology of organizations.*** The view seems to be that a taxonomy would be an aid in the development of knowledge about organizations and could perhaps be a useful tool in the prediction of organizational behavior. To be useful a taxonomy would, of course, have to be empirically validated.

POTENTIAL USES OF A TAXONOMY

Specifically, how might an empirically derived taxonomy of organizations contribute to an emerging science of organizations? Among the probable contributions are the following:

1. It would be strategically helpful for refining hypotheses. It is generally accepted in science that any hypothesis is valid only under certain specified conditions. In the absence of the specified con-

*The study was sponsored by the Air Force Office of Scientific Research under Contract No. AF-AFOSR 41-63. The larger project, of which this research is one part, was begun under the leadership of Professor Carroll L. Shartle, Department of Psychology, The Ohio State University. Special thanks are due Carroll L. Shartle and Gisela J. Hinkle for their contributions in the early stages of the work.

**Dr. Haas is Associate Professor, Department of Sociology and Anthropology, The Ohio State University; Dr. Hall is Assistant Professor, Department of Sociology, Indiana University; and Dr. Johnson is Assistant Professor, Department of Sociology, University of Illinois, Chicago Circle.

***Brown suggests that there are four commonly recognized types of organizations (3, pp. 273-278). For a recent review of the various efforts to classify organizations, see Blau and Scott, *Formal Organizations* (2).

ditions, the law or principle will appear to be inoperative. A major problem for the social sciences is the difficulty we have in stating the conditions under which our hypotheses will hold true. Unless the conditions are first "known" conceptually, it is impossible to test rigorously any hypothesis. Thus, in studying organizations we must recognize that many of our hypotheses will be empirically verified only when we have correctly stated and have demonstrated the presence of certain relevant conditions. Another way of stating the same qualification is to say that a specific hypothesis will be valid only for a certain type of organization, i.e., only for organizations which have the relevant specified conditions (characteristics) in common. A useful taxonomy of organizations would group organizations with similar characteristics together in the same class and thereby point to one set of conditions under which a given hypothesis might be valid. A hypothesis that does not hold for one class of organizations could very well be quite valid for another class of organizations.

2. It would aid the investigation of the validity and utility of existing typologies based on logical and intuitive considerations. Some of the more recently suggested classifications are based on organizational goals or functions*, internal compliance structure (7, esp. Chapters 1, 2, 3), and prime beneficiary of the organization's activities (2, pp. 42-58). It is not possible at this stage of our knowledge to state with certainty which of these schema, if any, will ultimately prove most useful. As Etzioni points out, organizations placed under the same label often differ considerably (e.g., combat military units and peace-time military units), while some organizations placed in different classes reveal more similarity than those grouped together (e.g., the Communist party more closely resembles a combat army than it does an ordinary political party) (7, pp. 23-27). Only by carefully accumulating comparable data for a large number of organizations will it be possible to evaluate the many interesting but as yet untested formulations. An empirically derived taxonomy would facilitate the achievement of this objective.

3. An empirically derived taxonomy could serve as the basis for predicting organizational decisions or change. If the aim were to predict how a sample of organizations will respond to a problem which they all face, the following sequence might be used:

---

*Parsons classifies organizations as: 1) oriented to economic production, 2) oriented to political goals, 3) integrative organizations, and 4) pattern-maintenance organizations (14, pp. 228-29). For an elaboration of this approach, see Samuel N. Eisenstadt, "Bureaucracy and Bureaucratization" (5), Amitai Etzioni, "Industrial Sociology: The Study of Economic Organizations" (6), Frances G. Scott, "Action Theory and Research in Social Organization" (15), and Gordon and Babchuck, "A Typology of Voluntary Associations" (9).

(a) *Specification of the common problem*: An organizational problem is any set of events which may have consequences for the survival of the organization. The statement of the problem would be formulated by the researcher. Members of the various organizations may or may not be aware of the problem, although usually there will be at least some awareness of it.

(b) *Specification of the type of outcome or response to be predicted*: Outcome refers to organizational adaptation or response. Any given response may or may not be a "solution" in the sense of increasing the survival potential of the organization. Since the number of discrete organizational responses could be almost infinite, the researcher would need to categorize possible outcomes so that prediction could be specified in finite terms. For example, if the organizations are facing severe economic competition, the potential responses might be categorized into five types: (1) efforts to purchase one or more competitive firms, (2) efforts to develop collusive agreements in pricing, (3) efforts to destroy or undermine the competitors, (4) attempts to reorganize internally, and (5) no discernible change.

(c) *Delimiting the relatively stable conditions which are directly relevant for the problem*: "Conditions" as used here is a primitive term. It is commonly used to refer to the environmental context within which an organization operates. Here it refers to the internal as well as the external. "Relatively stable" is meant to indicate that the condition has remained constant over a period of time. The minimum length of time used as the criterion of constancy would, of course, be somewhat arbitrary. Examples of stable conditions would be: sources of income (external condition) and highly centralized authority structure (internal condition). Since the number of stable conditions that could be enumerated is so great as to be unwieldy, the analyst would select for consideration only those which, on the basis of current knowledge, appear to have a high probability of influencing the type of outcome which will occur.

(d) *Specification of the relevant situational variables*: In addition to the aforementioned stable conditions, there are usually situational elements which must be considered in prediction. These are internal and external events which are very recent in time. Included would be any recent change in what would otherwise be termed stable conditions as well as new and eruptive events which are relevant to the organizational problem. Examples of situational variables would be: an organization which has been approximately the same size for years is now experiencing rapid growth; the administrative structure of the organization has just been drastically reorganized; a long-time major customer of the organizational product has just cancelled all contracts.

The independent variables needed to predict the organizational response, then, include both the stable conditions and the situational variables. See Chart I for an illustration of the elements in the predictive process.

Chart 1

An Outline of the Elements Involved in Predicting
Organizational Change, with Examples Inserted

(The hypothetical sample is of universities.)

Relevant stable conditions	Relevant situational variables	Task or problem	Outcome or resolution
1. Major sources of income	1. New president appointed	Marked increase in college age population	Type I
			Type II
2. Decentralized authority structure	2. One professional school just lost its accreditation		Type III, etc.
3. Located in a major metropolitan area	3. Competing college being constructed in community		

Stable internal and external conditions may be referred to as organizational characteristics. A taxonomy by definition would have a series of classes each of which represents a unique combination of organizational characteristics (stable conditions). If the researcher had a taxonomy of organizations available, it would permit him to specify readily the universe (a specific class) from which his sample of organizations would be drawn. The list of characteristics on which the class is based could also serve as an initial check list of the stable conditions which might be relevant for the organizational problem being used as the focus of prediction.

A taxonomy of organizations would undoubtedly serve a number of other purposes, but the brief discussion presented above provides some indication of its potential utility.

An Empirical Approach

With the apparent benefits of a taxonomy in mind it was decided to initiate work which would, hopefully, contribute to the eventual development of a useful taxonomic system. Such a taxonomy, it was clear, would have to meet two criteria: (1) It must be multi-dimensional, and (2) it must incorporate significant or crucial variables as contrasted to trivial or superficial ones. The difficulty, of course, is that it is not possible to determine with certainty in advance which dimensions are the significant ones. Various dimensions have been suggested by organizational theorists, but there is no clear consensus among them. In order to preclude the inadvertent omission of dimensions which might later prove highly significant for a taxonomy, it was decided to make the original list as inclusive as possible. An interdisciplinary research team reviewed the literature and attempted to extract and record all those variables which might be relevant for the taxonomy. In addition, a concerted effort was made to list additional characteristics which might need to be included.

Previous efforts to develop a typology of organizations have been largely based on a deductive or an intuitive approach, which is a first and necessary step. With this approach, the author describes the one or few characteristics which seem to him to be crucial for an increased understanding of organizations. He then proceeds to point out that organizations vary on the dimension(s), or that there are relatively discrete categories which fall logically along some dimensional continuum into which any organization can be readily placed. Illustrations are then provided indicating where various kinds of organizations would fit in the typology. It is commonly assumed that the organizations being used for illustrative purposes do, in fact, have the characteristics implied by their location in the typology. Whether or not they do have the imputed characteristics has not been, so far as is known, systematically investigated.*

An alternative approach is to work toward what might be called an *empirically derived taxonomy*. It was felt that if there is to be a useful taxonomy of organizations, it must reflect the characteristics which can, in fact, be found among the myriad of organizations which can be examined. In other words, it was decided to let the data indicate which variables tend to "hang together" in the world of organizational phenomena as we can observe and record it. The aim, then, was to isolate a number of "natural" classes of organizations, each of which represents a homogeneous grouping of organizations. Whether or not

---

*The authors do sometimes refer to official documents for partial substantiation (2, pp. 42-58; 9, pp. 22-29: and 7). The problem in using only official documents is that organizations often do not practice what their official documents "preach," e.g., many social fraternities still systematically practice ethnic and religious discrimination even though they have deleted these restrictive clauses from their constitutions. Secondary sources do provide a partial check where the data reported include the particular dimensions being proposed in a given typology.

organizations could be clustered together into homogeneous classes when a large number of variables is being employed is a question which could be answered only after the data were examined.

Without going into detail, it should be pointed out that the initial "catalog" of variables was very lengthy. The list contained 210 relatively discrete dimensions. It was readily recognized that due to cost and research personnel limitations, it would not be possible to get adequate data on all of these 210 dimensions if the number of organizations to be studied was to be large. An effort was made, therefore, to reduce and refine the variables so that there would be sufficient time to examine a large number of organizations.

Variables which would have required the administering of a questionnaire to all or a large sample of the personnel in each organization were eliminated. This precluded the collection of data on a long list of individual characteristics, and the interpersonal structure. The original formulation called for the collecting of data on both the official (formal) structure and the performance structure as it could be inferred from extensive observation of member interaction. The degree of congruence between the two structures would then provide an additional set of indicators. As finally used, this three-point perspective was reduced to one: the performance structure as described by top executives. Many items dealing with the history of the organization and its various departments were drastically simplified, as were items dealing with economic, social, political, and ideological aspects of the organizational environment. Only gross indicators of the organization's financial condition were retained.

This modification and simplification reduced the number of variables to 99. Listed below are the major headings under which the 99 characteristics are subsumed:

1. Organizational goals and objectives
2. Major activities of the organization
3. Basic organizational character or orientation
4. General levels of workers (members)
5. Major divisions or departments (horizontal differentiation)
6. Vertical and horizontal complexity (combined index)
7. Geographical dispersion of personnel and facilities
8. Interdependency of departments
9. Concreteness of positional descriptions
10. Committees and boards
11. Organizational control (source of major policy decisions)
12. Centralization of authority
13. Formalization of authority structure
14. Communication structure

15. Dependence on written rules and policies
16. Penalties for rule violation
17. Emphasis on status distinctions
18. Manner in which new members enter the organization
19. Orientation program
20. In-service training program
21. Distinctions regarding types of organizational members (non-hierarchical)
22. Number of members, with extent of variation in size of departments
23. Turnover of membership, by level (per year)
24. Planned limit on size
25. Restrictions on membership
26. Dependency on other organizations
27. Other organizations dependent on one studied
28. Competition with other organizations
29. Governmental control and regulation
30. Supply of potential members
31. Share of potential customer market
32. Geographic factors as a handicap
33. Primary sources of income
34. Financial condition of the organization
35. Age of organization
36. Shifts in major activities throughout history of the organization
37. Patterns of growth and decline

An interview schedule containing questions designed to elicit the necessary information from each organization was developed and pre-tested. Tape recorded interviews were conducted in 75 different organizations. Each taped interview was transcribed verbatim and the relevant data bracketed and coded in preparation for punching on electronic data processing cards. Additional information was secured from the records, tables of organization, and other printed material supplied by each organization.

Some mention should be made of the sampling problem. As Blau and Scott point out, the study of organizations poses some difficult research decisions.

A fundamental dilemma is posed for the study of organizations by the double requirement of examining the interdependence between elements in a social structure, on the one hand, and of observing many independent cases to substantiate generalizations, on the other. . . . Treating groups rather than individuals as independent units of analysis permits making generalizations about the internal structure of work groups, but it ignores the interrelations of these groups in the larger industrial organization. And if the investigator analyzes this interdependence among the various groups in the factory—that is, the structure of the formal organization—he is again left with only a single case. General propositions about formal organizations must be based on the investigation of a large number of them. And even when comparable empirical data on many organizations are available, conceptualizing the organizations as independent cases would involve ignoring their interdependence in the larger society, whereas focusing upon their interdependence would leave the investigator, once more, with only one case.

This dilemma cannot be definitively resolved. . . . In short, the important practical implication of the dilemma is that the research design must be adapted to the level of organization to be explained. (2, pp. 11-13)

The aim in this study is to treat each organization as a discrete entity. At this level of analysis individuals and groups are subsumed within the concept of the organization. The relations which each subject organization has with other organizations are viewed as being on the same level, i.e., as being characteristic of the organization under study. The universe, then, from which the sample was to be drawn included all organizations regardless of size, location, or structure. No complete listing of organizations within the United States, or even within a state or city, was available and, therefore, random sampling was not possible. An attempt was made, however, to select the organizations in such a way as to optimize variability within the sample. Size, structure, goals, and type of organizational activity were criteria used as the basis for selection. Listed below are some of the common headings under which these organizations would fall:

Government agencies including federal, state and local, civil and military

Business firms including mining, manufacturing, transporting, processing, selling and providing services

Educational institutions including public and private, elementary, secondary, and college levels

Religious organizations including congregations, convents, community and state organizations

Fraternal and service organizations

Labor unions

Occupational and professional organizations

Social and recreational organizations

Welfare agencies and civic associations

Political and lobbying organizations

Mass communication organizations

Ethnic associations

While the sample includes a wide variety of organizations, it is probably not representative of all organizations in the United States. For example, large organizations which have segments scattered throughout the nation are probably under-represented, and there are no "international" organizations in the sample.

ANALYSIS OF THE DATA

The basic task at this point was to develop a technique to compare each of the 75 organizations with each of the other 74 organizations to ascertain which, if any, have identical or very similar profiles. In addition to the comparisons, two kinds of data must be secured: 1) The degree or level of similarity between any two or more organizations; 2) The specific attributes which the two or more organizations have in common.

Figure 1 illustrates variation and similarity in profiles of organizational characteristics. Organizations I, II, III, although not identical, have four attributes in common. Organizations IV, V, and VI have relatively little in common and show little similarity to the profiles of Organizations I, II, and III. Depending on the degree of homogeneity insisted upon, one might view the profiles in the left column as composing a cluster while those in the right column would probably not be so viewed under any circumstances.

The task of comparing profiles in this study was much more complex, however, than indicated by the above illustration. The comparison involved 75 profiles, one for each organization, composed of 99 characteristics. The number of attribute categories for any characteristic ranged from 2 to 10. Clearly, any kind of manual manipulation and visual comparison of profiles was out of the question, so a new taxonomy computer program for the IBM 7090 was developed.*

The Computer Program

This program is particularly designed for statistical analysis of qualitative information, i.e., data which are more accurately expressed in "yes" or "no" form than in terms of numerical values arbitrarily assigned to describe the same qualities. For example, with this program it is possible to classify statistically information dealing with intangible qualities such as emphasis on status distinctions, growth trends and source of major policies. An illustration appears in Chart 2.

---

*The program is a modification of one originally developed by T. T. Tanimoto and R. G. Loomis of the Data Systems Division of the International Business Machines Corporation.

Figure 1

An Illustration of Organizational Profiles

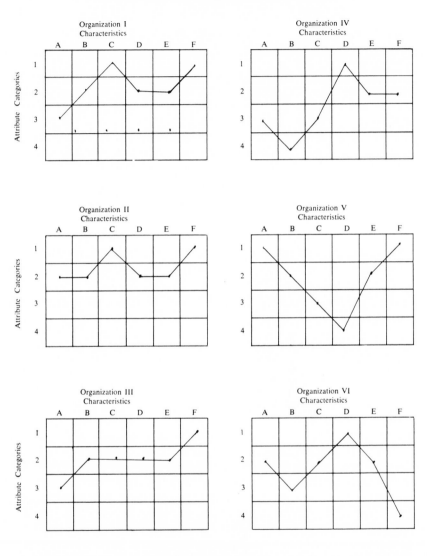

But some data normally appear in numerical form. To prepare such information for computer processing, it is only necessary to divide or partition the range of numerical values into a suitable set of intervals which are then designated as separate attributes. Chart 3 illustrates the point.

Chart 2

An Outline of Qualitative Characteristics, Attributes and Response

Characteristic	Attribute	Presence
Source of official	1. Control by another organization	No
major policy	2. Control by owners through board of	No
decisions	trustees	
	3. Control by a board of directors	No
	4. Control by members	No
	5. Control by the top man in the organization	Yes
	6. Control by management in general	No

Initially the computer makes a count of the matches, i.e., a matching on a "yes" or a "no" response for any given attribute in two organizations. These matches are designated as M's. Then in a similar fashion it makes a count of the non-matches, i.e., cases where one organization has a "yes" and the other a "no" on a given attribute. The non-matches are designated as N's. The computer, then, divides to arrive at the similarity ratio $S_{1,2}$ for the two organizations. Mathematically the operation is expressed as follows:

$$\frac{M_{1,2}}{N_{1,2}} = S_{1,2}$$

Chart 3

An Outline of Quantitative Characteristics, Attributes and Response

Characteristic	Attribute	Presence
Hierarchical Levels	2 levels	No
	3 levels	No
	4 levels	No
	5 levels	No
	6 levels	Yes
	7 levels	No
	8 levels	No

The similarity ratio may be considered as the weighted probability of finding a matching attribute for these two organizations on any characteristic at random. Hence, a very large value of S would indicate a much greater degree of similarity between the two organizations than is likely with random distribution of the attributes. If there are no matching attributes for the two organizations, then the ratio would be zero.

The computer starts by establishing a rough measure of typicality for each organization in the collection. This is done by making for each organization a count, R, of the number of other organizations with which the organization under consideration has at least one attribute in common, i.e., the number of its S values which are not equal to zero. Assume that 75 cases are being analyzed and case 1 has a value of 74 while case 2 has a value of 73. Statistically, case 1 may be considered as having the greater typicality in regard to the total collection of 75 cases.

However, it might happen that a dozen organizations from the collection would have the same value; in this case 74. Obviously, some finer measure of typicality is required. This can be provided by the statistical technique of multiplying together all the R values of S for a given organization. The computer would actually accomplish this by a simple logarithmic method. Expressed quantitatively.

$$H_1 = S_{1,A} \times S_{1,B} \times S_{1,C} \times \ldots \times S_{1,R}; \quad (R = 74)$$

In this sample, H represents the product of 74 non-zero values of S for case 1. Statistically, H represents the probability that, for any characteristic selected at random, the attribute possessed by organization number 1 relative to the chosen characteristic will also be possessed by all of the $R = 74$ other cases. The higher the H value, the less the likelihood that H is the result of chance or random distribution. Hence, H is a suitable measure of typicality, when comparing it with other cases having the same value of R.

Using R and H values, the computer can rank all 75 cases for typicality: first, according to their R values of general typicality within the entire collection, and then, according to their H values of typicality relative to other cases having the same R value. The result is a kind of profile of typicality for the collection as a whole.

The organization which ranks first in the typicality table is considered as statistically the most typical case of the entire collection. (See Table 1 for illustration.) This case is then designated as the *prime node* and around it is formed a cluster of organizations very similar to it; that is, cases having a high S value (the similarity ratio in relation to the *prime node*). Such a primary grouping may be considered to be comparable to a main branch of a family tree in the classification system.

Table 1

An Illustration of Typicality Ranking
with R and H Values

Case No.	R. Value	H. Value
10	74	42.95174456
11	74	43.01696730
29	73	48.77389383
15	72	49.31434918
73	72	49.56528139
1	72	49.72376108

How similar to the *prime node* should another organization be in order to qualify for membership in the cluster to be formed? The limiting S value is determined by the researcher. He must select beforehand the typicality rank of a *secondary node,* deciding that it shall be the case which falls second or third or in some other predesignated rank within the typicality table. The S value of this *secondary node* (actually the *prime-secondary node* S Value), then becomes the measuring stick for deciding which organizations are eligible for the cluster. The cluster thus selected is removed from the collection as a special class of cases to be carefully studied. After removing the first cluster, the computer in the same fashion moves through the residue of cases processing for other clusters.

Each first-level cluster may be further analyzed for any and all subclusters which may exist within it. As each subcluster is located, it in turn may be analyzed for subclusters until all possible subclusters are identified.* By transposing the organization-attribute matrix, the computer can identify which of the many attributes are responsible for the organizations being included in any cluster.

THE FINDINGS

Using the newly developed taxonomy computer program to analyze the similarity of attribute profiles for 75 organizations, ten major or prime classes were found. The classes vary in size from 30 organizations (Class II) to 2 (Classes VI, VII, IX and X). These initial classes are presented in Table 2.

It is clear that in general the larger the number of organizations in a class the smaller will be the number of attributes which

---

*There are a number of options which the researcher must exercise in using this program. For a discussion of these options, see Johnson, *Toward a Taxonomy of Organizations* (10, pp. 94-98).

Table 2

A Listing of Prime Classes Showing the Number of
Organizations and Attributes in Each Class

Prime Class	Number of Organizations in the Class	Number of Attributes in the Class
I	9	7
II	30	4
III	3	34
IV	3	29
V	8	4
VI	2	43
VII	2	33
VIII	14	3
IX	2	34
X	2	27

they have in common. A second pattern also emerges. Where the number of organizations in a class is only two the possibility of isolating subclasses is eliminated because of the nature of the computer program. The analyst could upon examination of the attributes which the two organizations do *not* have in common, decide to view tentatively each of the organizations as a representative of a lower level more homogeneous subclass. It would seem to the authors, however, that an attempt should be made first to increase the size of the sample so that such subclasses could emerge in the same way as they did in classes composed of larger numbers of organizations.

Table 3 shows the various subclasses as they emerge in the initial computer runs.

The same general relation between size and number of attributes appears in the findings for the subclasses. Although there are some obvious exceptions, a subclass composed of a small number of organizations tends to have many more common attributes than one which is larger.

Subclass size is also related to the number of levels which will emerge. The greater the number of cases in a subclass, the greater the likelihood that subclasses at the third and fourth levels will appear.

Finally, the number of second-level subclasses within any prime class is directly related to the number of organizations in the prime class. Class II with 30 organizations is the only one with five subclasses. While it is theoretically possible for any class with ten or more organizations in it to have five subclasses, none appeared. Note that Class VIII with 14 organizations had only four subclasses.

The findings presented thus far make it clear that classes and subclasses of organizations can be isolated through the use of an inductively oriented approach. This in itself would seem to indicate that the approach ought to be utilized in further taxonomic efforts. The significance of these initial findings needs to be more closely examined, however.

Table 3

Prime Classes and Subclasses Showing the Number of Organizations and Number of Attributes in Each

Class	First Level No. of Organizations	First Level No. of Attributes	Second Level No. of Organizations	Second Level No. of Attributes	Third Level No. of Organizations	Third Level No. of Attributes	Fourth Level No. of Organizations	Fourth Level No. of Attributes
I	9	7	2	30	—	—	—	—
			2	36	—	—	—	—
			2	40	—	—	—	—
			2	48	—	—	—	—
II	30	4			3	34	2	51
					3	27	2	50
			11	14	2	49	—	—
					2	39	—	—
					2	46	—	—
			5	10	2	39	—	—
					3	15	2	41
			6	5	2	43	—	—
					3	16	2	37
			6	3	2	42	—	—
			2	32	—	—	—	—
III	3	34	2	45	—	—	—	—
IV	3	29	2	43	—	—	—	—
V	8	4	3	22	2	40	—	—
			2	33	—	—	—	—
			2	42	—	—	—	—
VI	2	40	—	—	—	—	—	—
VII	2	33	—	—	—	—	—	—
VIII	14	3	3	30	2	44	—	—
			4	14	3	24	2	40
					2	32	—	—
			4	13	2	27	—	—
			2	33	—	—	—	—
IX	2	34	—	—	—	—	—	—
X	2	27	—	—	—	—	—	—

Findings Compared to Other Taxonomic Efforts

There appears to be no *a priori* reason why a taxonomy of organizations should necessarily parallel, at least in detail, established taxonomic systems such as those used in zoology and botany. However, if a series of *logical procedures* for developing a fruitful taxonomy has been established in the biological sciences, they ought to be worth careful examination. The procedures and findings of this study will, therefore, be compared to those in zoology.

In zoology the species is the most important taxonomic category. It is defined as groups of actually or potentially interbreeding natural populations which are reproductively isolated from other such groups (13, p. 313). Upon species, higher categories are built which are collective in nature. Based on the relationships of these categories a classification system emerges. Including the species, there are six basic categories or levels into which biological phenomena are grouped. They are in descending order:

1. Phyla
2. Class
3. Order
4. Family
5. Genera
6. Species

Each of these categories which represents a level in the system is comprised of one or more groups from the next lower level. These categories are both objective and subjective. They are objective because they are comprised of objectively definable entities. They are subjective because the categorical level as well as the delimitations of the categories is determined by the analyst. Hence every classification involves the arranging of lower units into groups and then the joining of these groups in an ascending hierarchy of more and more unlike groups. Table 4 illustrates the six basic categorical levels and the grouping of more unlike objects as the ladder is ascended.

In the present study of organizations ten natural classes were located. Within some of the classes which were located, other more homogeneous classes (i.e., subclasses), were found. Each subclass in turn was analyzed until the most homogeneous units were isolated. The maximum number of levels located in this initial study as seen in Table 3 is four. It should be remembered, however, that organizations are but one type of social system; societies, communities, and groups are also social systems. These entities may be seen, then, as subclasses of a higher level called social systems. Table 5 illustrates the levels which have emerged. Since it is probably premature to

Table 4

Level Illustration of Chordata

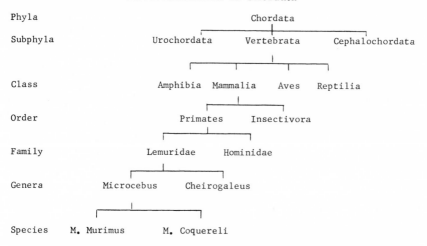

attach descriptive names to the various classes and subclasses, letters
and subscripts are used as designations.*

Table 5

Illustration of Levels in Tentative Taxonomy of Organizations

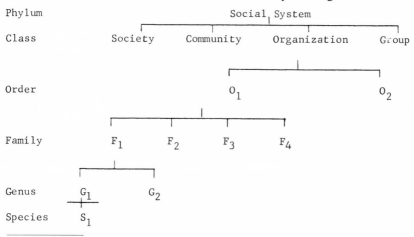

---

*The findings show that organizations which might be expected to appear
in the same cluster from a "common sense" perspective do not always do so.
For example, O_1 includes the following:

Polynesian Restaurant, State Regulative Agency, Motel, Bank, Health Insurance
Agency, Electrical Equipment Firm, Catholic School System, Elite Restaurant,
Commercial Television Station

Contrast the above combination of organizations with those that appear in O_3:
School for Delinquent Girls, Men's Reformatory, Women's Reformatory

A second similarity between the zoological taxonomy and the tentative one developed in this study is the presence of increasing heterogeneity of the groupings as the hierarchy is ascended. The similarity among members of a phylum is less than that among the members of a genus. Table 6 illustrates a similar pattern for the tentative taxonomy of organizations at the various levels. The similarity coefficients, the index of the degree of homogeneity, indicate more heterogeneity at each higher level.(Read from right to left.)

Thus, the organizational taxonomy parallels the zoological taxonomy in that it has, at least for clusters II and VIII, the same number of levels and it shows decreasing homogeneity as the hierarchy is ascended.

Strictly speaking, if a taxonomy represents the joining of taxa in an ascending hierarchy of more and more unlike groups, then the

Table 6

Illustration of Increasing Heterogeneity among Organizations within a Class as the Hierarchy is Ascended*

First Level (Order)		Second Level (Family)		Third Level (Genus)		Fourth Level (Species)	
Org. No.	Similarity Coefficient	Org. No.	Similarity Coefficient	Org. No.	Similarity Coefficient	Org. No.	Similarity Coefficient
57	1.000000**	57	1.000000	57	1.000000	57	1.000000
43	.256578	52	.306122	35	.352112	60	.398496
59	.281879	33	.342657	60	.398496		
52	.306122	65	.350000				
31	.271523	35	.352112				
41	.276315	21	.347017				
33	.342657	67	.342857				
9	.291666	62	.326388				
42	.268456	58	.342657				
67	.342857	60	.398496				
56	.269736	26	.340425				
65	.350000						
62	.326388						
21	.347517						
22	.275167						
35	.352112						
40	.274509						
60	.398496						
11	.277777						
10	.275167						
37	.297297						
26	.340425						
24	.281690						
58	.342657						
23	.268965						
7	.260000						
19	.294520						
53	.292517						
17	.293706						
15	.256944						

*Prime Cluster II used as illustration.
**The Prime Node always has a similarity coefficient of 1.000000.

total number of attributes common to all objects at a given level should be fewer as the hierarchy is ascended. When the top of the hierarchy is neared, the attributes should also take on a more generalized character because there is more heterogeneity as the hierarchy is ascended.

The phylum Chordata will be used to illustrate the principles of a decreasing *number* of total attributes and decreasing *specificity* of the attributes as the hierarchy is ascended. (See Table 7.)

Table 7

Illustration of Decreasing Number and Specificity of Attributes:
Phylum Chordata and Species M. Murimus

Level		*Attributes*
Phylum	Chordata	1. An axial rod-like notochord
		2. A single dorsal tubular nerve cord
		3. Paired gill slits
Order	Primates	1. They have all the characteristics of the levels above.
		2. Unguiculate, claviculate, placental mammals, with orbits encircled by bone.
		3. Three kinds of teeth, at least at one time of life.
		4. Brain has posterior lobe and calcarine fissure.
		5. Four generalized limbs each with five digits bearing nails.
		6. Innermost digit of at least one pair of the limbs is opposable.
		7. Penis is pendulous and the testes are scrotal.
		8. Female has two pectoral mammary glands.
Species M. murimus*		1. They have all the characteristics of the levels above.
		2. Head and body are about 130 mg.
		3. Distinct white medium nasal streak.
		4. The tail is not bushy nor is it washed with black.

*There are 13 characteristics unique to M. murimus but only 3 are presented for illustrative purposes.

It can be seen that the attributes of the phylum Chordata are more gross and general than the attributes of the species M. murimus (an axial rod-like notochord as contrasted to head and body weight of about 130 mg.). This pattern of decreasing specificity of the attributes at each higher level may be seen throughout the entire taxonomy. Also in Chordata there are only three attributes; in M. murimus there are 13. The organizational example, prime cluster II, is presented for comparison. (See Table 8.)

It can be seen that the attributes of the "phylum" social system are more general than the attributes of the S_1 "species" (persistence over time as contrasted to the number of paid employees 2,000-3,999). Similarly, social system has fewer attributes than S_1 (fourth level).

The organizational example seems to suggest that there is congruence with the zoological example on the principles of increasing generality of attributes at each higher level as well as a decreasing number of attributes.

A Core Criterion for Lowest Level Clusters

The basic unit to be classified in the zoological taxonomy is the individual organism. A species is a collection of individual cases that have a large number of relatively specific attributes in common. Unlike higher level categories, each collection (species) is composed of cases where interbreeding does or may occur. This principle of reproductive isolation is a convenient and very significant criterion in that it provides a series of natural groupings which may be used as the basic units or building blocks for the entire taxonomic system. Its significance may be seen in the fact that when a number of cases have the attribute of reproductive isolation, they also have a large number of other specific attributes in common.

No comparable criterion has been discovered so far for organizations. Although this study included 99 relatively distinct dimensions, none of them has emerged as a criterion of comparable utility. Parsons and Etzioni have suggested that organizations can be meaningfully classified according to the type of goals they apparently have (14 and 7). Etzioni thus suggests that there are three basic types of organizations: those with order goals, those with economic goals, and those with cultural goals. If *type of goal* is a basic criterion around which other attributes cluster, it would have appeared as the core of different clusters at one of the levels in the findings. No such evidence was found.

Similarly, Blau and Scott (2, pp. 42-58) present an interesting and reasoned argument for using the concept of prime beneficiary as the basis for a classification of organizations. They suggest that there are four basic types of organizations: mutual benefit associations

Table 8

Illustration of Decreasing Number and Specificity of Attributes:
"Phylum" Social System and "Species" S_1 (Fourth Level)

Level		Attributes
"Phylum"	Social System	1. Functional interdependence of parts 2. Relative stability of structure 3. Persistence over time
"Order"	O_1	1. They have characteristics of the level above them. 2. When organizations of this order are compared to other organizations on geographic factors, they are average. 3. There are no departments engaged in the production of goods for internal use. 4. Persons enter the organization by simple sign up. 5. There are no religious restrictions for membership.
"Species"	S_1*	1. They have characteristics of the levels above them. 2. Three goals. 3. One department is engaged in the production of goods for external distribution. 4. Penalties for rule violation are clearly stated. 5. Penalties for rule violation are stipulated in writing. 6. In-service training is highly formalized for upper levels. 7. In-service training is loosely structured for lower levels. 8. Paid employees number 2,000 to 3,999. 9. Yearly turnover of lower levels is 0-5%.

*Although 17 attributes emerged which are unique to S_1, only 9 are presented for illustrative purposes.

where the members are the prime beneficiaries; service organizations
with the client group as prime beneficiary; business organizations
where the owners are the prime beneficiaries and commonweal
organizations with the prime beneficiary being the public at large (2,
pp. 42-44). These attributes emerged in a number of clusters at various
levels, but there is no evidence that each of the prime beneficiary
attributes is systematically related to a combination of other attributes.
This would seem to indicate that the "prime beneficiary" criterion is
not a crucial or central one since the presence of one of its attributes
(e.g., "mutual benefit associations") does not necessarily coincide with
any particular set of other organizational attributes. The same must
be said, however, for each of the other characteristics or dimensions
utilized in this initial effort to develop a taxonomy. No single characteristic or dimension appears to be a core dimension in the sense
that *it alone* may be used as a starting point for locating a number of
specific natural clusters each of which has a unique combination of
attributes. This fact, however, does not mean that relatively homogeneous clusters of organizations cannot be found; it is clear from
our findings that they can be found. The implication seems to be that
the task of building a systematic taxonomy where the various clusters
are *interrelated in a logically meaningful fashion* may be a very difficult
one. The findings from the initial attempt indicate that such an outcome may be possible, however.

Stability and Change

The individual units (organisms) being classified in a zoological
taxonomy may undergo marked change in attributes during the life
cycle. But the zoologist has discovered that the changes follow a
pattern and, therefore, he is not tempted to shift a particular specimen
from category to category as it changes over time. Indeed the patterns of such changes in the life cycle are utilized as attributes which
define the various classes.

The organizational analyst, however, is apparently dealing with
less stable cases. Organizations also may change drastically over time.
But if a class of organizations has a patterned and, therefore, predictable sequence of changes, it is yet to be discovered. Despite all that
has been said about the tendency for organizations to resist change,
it is manifestly clear that some organizations change so markedly that
it seems entirely appropriate to assert that they are now qualitatively
different social entities from what they were earlier. To the extent
that such changes include alteration of significant organizational attributes (i.e., those which are definitive for taxonomic categories),
the organization would need to be relocated in the taxonomic system.
While the gene structure produces *predictable* changes in organisms,
no equivalent set of forces has as yet been discovered which would

make organizational change predictable and, thus, amenable for inclusion in the taxonomic criteria for classification.

But perhaps the dilemma is more apparent than real. There is no inherent reason why an individual case must necessarily be a member of one and only one class throughout its lifetime. To be sure, it would make our task of systematic classification easier if such stability of attributes did exist. But it is conceivable that we may be able to develop a taxonomic system into which any organization may be meaningfully placed at a given point in time. If at a later point in time its significant attributes change sufficiently, it can simply be "moved" to a more appropriate category. The trick, of course, is to discover what are the really crucial or significant organizational attributes as contrasted to ephemeral ones. Unless that can be accomplished, we are condemned to a continuous game of organizational "musical chairs."

SUMMARY

The development of systematic classification schemes or taxonomies has proved very useful in the physical and biological sciences. Relatively little effort toward that end has been evident in the social sciences, especially in the study of organizations. An empirically derived taxonomy of organizations would be strategically helpful for refining hypotheses, would aid the investigation of the validity and utility of existing typologies, and could serve as the basis for predicting organizational decisions or change.

In an initial effort to develop an empirically based taxonomy, data were collected from 75 organizations on 99 relatively distinct dimensions. A computer program was developed to compare the attribute profile of each organization with that of every other organization in order to ascertain whether homogeneous clusters of organizations could be located. Ten initial clusters of organizations were located, ranging in size from two to thirty. Where possible, each cluster was analyzed for subclusters and each subcluster analyzed in the same manner until no further subclustering was possible.

Among the initial conclusions are the following: (1) The maximum number of levels, six, is identical to the number established in the zoological taxonomy in common use. (2) As in the zoological taxonomy there is decreasing homogeneity within clusters as the hierarchy is ascended. (3) The number of total attributes per cluster and the specificity of the attributes both decrease as the hierarchy is ascended. (4) While the zoological taxonomy is built on the core criterion of reproductive isolation, no comparable criterion was discovered among the dimensions utilized in this effort. (5) The tendency for the attributes of an organization to change over time need not pose an insurmountable problem for the development of a taxonomy of organizations.

BIBLIOGRAPHY

1. Blau, Peter M. "Formal Organizations: Dimensions of Analysis," *American Journal of Sociology,* LXIII (July, 1957) 58-69

2. Blau, Peter M., and Scott, Richard W. *Formal Organizations: A Comparative Approach.* San Francisco: Chandler Publishing Co., 1962

3. Brown, Alvin. *Organization, a Formulation of Principle.* New York: Hibbert Printing Co., 1945

4. Caplow, Theodore. *Principles of Organization.* New York: Harcourt, Brace and World, Inc., 1964, 36-49

5. Eisenstadt, Samuel N. "Bureaucracy and Bureaucratization," *Current Sociology,* VII (1958) 99-124

6. Etzioni, Amitai. "Industrial Sociology: The Study of Economic Organizations," *Social Research,* XXV (October, 1958) 303-324

7. —————————— *A Comparative Analysis of Complex Organizations.* New York: The Free Press of Glencoe, 1961

8. Freeman, Linton C., and Winch, Robert F. "Societal Complexity: An Empirical Test of a Typology of Societies," *American Journal of Sociology,* LXII (March, 1957) 461-466

9. Gordon, C. Wayne, and Babchuk, Nicholas. "A Typology of Voluntary Organizations," *American Sociological Review,* XXIV (February, 1959) 22-29

10. Johnson, Norman J. *Toward a Taxonomy of Organizations.* Ph.D. dissertation, The Ohio State University, June, 1963

11. Lazarsfeld, Paul F. "Some Remarks on the Typological Procedures in Social Research," *Zeitschrift Fur Sozialforschung,* VI (1937) 200-240

12. Lazarsfeld, Paul F., and Menzel, Herbert. "On the Relation between Individual and Collective Properties." In Amitai Etzioni (Ed), *Complex Organizations: A Sociological Reader.* New York: Holt, Rinehart and Winston, Inc., 1961, 422-440

13. Mayr, E.E., Linsley, E. Gorton, and Usinger, R. L. *Methods and Principles of Systematic Zoology.* New York: McGraw-Hill Book Co., 1953

14. Parsons, Talcott. "Suggestions for a Sociological Approach to the Theory of Organization," *Administrative Science Quarterly,* I (June, 1956) 63-85 and (September, 1956) 225-239

15. Scott, Frances G. "Action Theory and Research in Social Organization," *American Journal of Sociology,* LXIV (January, 1959) 386-395

16. Thompson, James D., and Tuden, Arthur. "Strategies, Structures and Processes of Organizational Decisions." In Thompson, James D., *et al.* (Eds), *Comparative Studies in Administration.* Pittsburgh: University of Pittsburgh Press, 1959, 195-216

The Behavior of Leaders, Non-Leader Non-Joiners, and Non-Leader Joiners under Conditions of Group Support and Non-Support*

CHARLES G. McCLINTOCK**

THE phenomenon of leadership has been the object of considerable study within the social sciences. Its importance, both theoretical and pragmatic, to an understanding of the behavior of groups and organizations is unquestioned. Until recently, it was conceived as an attribute or trait of a given individual, as in the statements "he is a good leader," or "he is a 'natural born' leader." However, after many unconvincing attempts to identify particular leadership traits or types, theories about leadership began to stress the role of group needs or expectations in delegating leadership roles.

The present study, while recognizing the importance of the group in selecting and defining leadership roles, attempts to ascertain, in the course of an experimentally manipulated social situation, whether individuals who have had previous experience in filling or assuming leadership roles behave differently from those who have not, under conditions of group support and non-support, given a relatively unstructured group task. Leaders were differentiated from two types of non-leaders, non-leader joiners and non-leader non-joiners, on the basis of their previous memberships and positions of influence within informal and formal groups. The task involved the group's selecting one of several Thematic Apperception Test cards and then constructing a story

---

*This research was supported by the United States Air Force through the Air Force Office of Scientific Research of the Air Research and Development Command, under Contract No. AF 49(638)-794. The author is indebted to Dr. Zajonc and Dr. John Cotton for their suggestions on statistical analysis. Part of the analysis included in this chapter appeared in a previous article by the author, "Group Support and the Behavior of Leaders and Non-Leaders" (15).

**Dr. McClintock is Associate Professor of Psychology, University of California, Santa Barbara, California.

concerning the one chosen. Group support was experimentally created by having the three other members of the group (who were paid participants) strongly reinforce or reward the subject's behavior by stating their agreement with his assertions, and by indicating through various means that he was in a position of considerable influence or control. Non-support was created by having the paid participants negate, ignore, or show incredulity towards the responses of the subject.

A modified Bales' interaction scale was employed to describe the behavior of the subject (1). This scale provided a reliable measure of a number of behavioral dimensions assumed relevant in differentiating the behavior of leaders from that of non-leaders. At the grossest level of analysis, this scale was employed to distinguish between three categories of behavior: task-oriented, positive affect, and negative affect.

THEORY

General Hypothesis

The central hypothesis of this study is that significant variations in behavior between leaders and non-leaders will occur under conditions of group support and non-support. This hypothesis was based upon four general assumptions regarding the acquisition and generality of leadership behavior:

Assumption 1. Achieving a position of leadership is instrumental to the satisfaction of basic individual needs, and thus those behaviors which facilitate the attainment of a leadership position tend to be reinforced, and the likelihood of their repetition increased (18).

Assumption 2. Through the process of secondary reinforcement, the repetition of behaviors associated with the achievement of a leadership position may become rewarding in themselves (13). The basic rationale underlying this assumption is that leadership carries with it certain prerogatives which better ensure the satisfaction of basic or learned needs. Thus, the child who is able to exert the greatest control in a social situation is better able to satisfy his own needs than one who exerts lesser control. For instance, the mere power to control a social situation so as to ensure going first often enables the child to receive more immediate gratification of a number of his needs.

Assumption 3. Due to variations in opportunity for assuming a a leadership position (6), in inherent and acquired capabilities for making appropriate leadership responses (5) (10), and in motivation for attaining the rewards associated with leadership (14), different individuals will exhibit different degrees of leadership behavior. In the present study, it was assumed that individuals selected as leaders on the basis of previous occupancy of formal leadership positions, and their perception of themselves as highly influential in informal groups, had had greater previous opportunity to assume positions of leadership, were more likely to have acquired behaviors which characterize leaders, and were more motivated to assume positions of leadership than those individuals defined as non-leaders.

Assumption 4. The number and variety of situations in which an individual will assume a leadership position is in part determined by the range of the individual's previous leadership experience. If a new situation contains elements similar to past ones in which the individual has achieved leadership, then there is a strong likelihood that past leadership behaviors will be positively transferred. If the new situation is not similar, or in fact calls for behaviors incongruent with previous experience, then transfer may inhibit appropriate behavior, i.e., negative transfer may occur (16). In the present study a relatively unstructured group task was employed to minimize the requirement that the subject possess certain specific knowledge or capabilities to exercise influence within the group, and thereby to increase the likelihood that more generalized leadership behaviors, if previously acquired, could be positively transferred to the experimental situation.

Working Hypotheses for Primary Analysis

The principal hypotheses of the present study concern expected behavioral differences between leaders and non-leaders. Given the above definitions and assumptions, the following two specific hypotheses were made concerning differences in the behavior of leaders, non-leader non-joiners, and non-leader joiners *across* support and non-support experimental conditions:

(1) *Leaders will make more task-oriented responses than non-leader joiners who will make more task-oriented responses than non-leader non-joiners.* This hypothesis followed from the assumptions that (a) leaders will attempt to exert greater influence in determining the course of action of a group than non-leaders since they are more highly motivated and have more experience in exerting influence; and (b) the use of task-oriented responses, i.e., giving directions, asking for directions, giving opinions, etc., facilitates the influence process. Partial support for this hypothesis already exists in the findings of Bass (4), Bales (2), and Gallo and McClintock (9). The latter found that leaders made significantly more task-oriented responses than non-leaders in an experimental situation similar to that employed in the current study.

(2) *Leaders will make significantly more positive affect responses than non-leader joiners, who will make more than non-leader non-joiners.* This hypothesis follows from an assumption that positive affect is one of the more effective means of reinforcing or rewarding changes in another's behavior, i.e., of social influence (22).

Regarding negative affect responses no hypothesis was made concerning group differences across support and non-support conditions, but two hypotheses were made regarding such differences *within* support and non-support situations:

(3) *Leaders will make significantly fewer negative affect responses under group support than non-leader joiners, who will make fewer than non-leader non-joiners.* This hypothesis was founded on the assumptions that (a) leaders are better able to assess the characteristics of their social environment than non-leaders (7), (b) leaders, due to previous experience, are more likely to select responses which increase their potential for social influence, and (c) under conditions of strong group reinforcement or support, negative affect responses are a relatively inadequate means of influence. Thus, leaders would seem more likely than non-leaders to emphasize the use of positive affect and minimize the use of negative affect responses.

(4) *Leaders will make significantly more negative affect responses under conditions of non-support than non-leader joiners, who will make more than non-leader non-joiners.* It was assumed that under conditions of non-support, leaders would suffer greater frustration than non-leaders because they would perceive a greater discrepancy between the influence they expected to exert and that which they actually exerted. This greater frustration would likely cause leaders to continue to attempt to exert more influence than non-leaders through task-oriented and positive affect behaviors. However, when these proved inadequate, the ensuing frustration would result in a more frequent expression of negative affect, i.e., disagreeing passively, showing tension, and antagonism.

The preceding hypotheses were made in terms of a gross classification of the subjects (Ss) behavior into three categories: task-oriented, positive affect, and negative affect. Findings are also reported in terms of ten individual behavioral categories. However, specific hypotheses for each of these categories were not made.

Working Hypotheses for Secondary Analyses

A secondary study involving two different analyses was made to determine the gross effects of social support and non-support.

First, it was hypothesized that the two types of group environments, support and non-support, would produce response differences regardless of the S's previous leadership experience. Several studies—Greenspoon (11), Mandler (17), and Verplanck (19)—have indicated that systematic agreement or non-agreement by one or more persons with another person affects the responses made by the latter. More specifically, it was hypothesized that given group support or reinforcement, the total number of responses made by Ss would substantially exceed those elicited under conditions of non-support or social punishment, i.e., overt ridicule, disagreement, etc. Furthermore, given the gross classification of behavior into task-oriented, positive, and negative affect, it was hypothesized that under group support Ss would make significantly more task-oriented and positive affect responses and significantly fewer negative affect responses than under non-support. The anticipated increase in negative affect under non-support was based upon the supposition that such responses are more likely to occur when others frustrate or punish the S's behavior than when others strongly reinforce or support their behavior.

Second, the response distributions in the present study were compared with those obtained in two studies by Bales and his associates. The first of these studies (2) outlined the behavior patterns of two groups—one in which members report being highly satisfied with the group's task accomplishments, and the other in which members report being relatively dissatisfied. The second of these studies (3) enumerated the combined behavior patterns of twenty-four groups, and serves as a "normative" group in the present analysis.

The principal hypotheses tested in these 'Bales' comparisons were: (a) Group members who are strongly supported, i.e., positively reinforced, by other members of the group will behave differently from those who receive little support or who are actively rejected by other group members. More specifically, as noted above, those receiving positive reinforcement will reciprocate by supporting those who have rewarded them, and by displaying more goal-oriented behavior, than group members who are not supported and/or rejected by the group. The latter will react to the non-supporting group members by displaying greater disagreement and hostility towards them by asking more questions and opinions (9) and by contributing less to the group in terms of goal-oriented behavior; (b) The degree of member satisfaction with a group's success in accomplishing its goals (2) provides an indirect measure of the degree of positive reinforcement afforded group members by the group's activities. Thus, there will be a correspondence between the nature of the responses made in a group situation by individuals who are positively reinforced by other group members and the responses made by individuals who are highly satisfied with the group's performance. A similar correspondence will obtain between responses made by individuals not supported by the group, and those dissatisfied with the group's performance. And finally, the distribution of responses for the norm group will fall between the support vs. non-support, and the satisfied vs. dissatisfied groups. For instance, the greatest proportion of positive affect responses should occur in the support and satisfied groups, the second greatest in the norm group, and the smallest in the non-support and dissatisfied groups.

METHOD

Subjects

In the present study, 348 Freshman and Sophomore males enrolled in compulsory ROTC courses at the University of California, Santa Barbara, were administered questionnaires to determine their past formal and informal leadership experience. On the basis of the responses obtained, three experimental groups of leaders, non-leader non-joiners, and non-leader joiners were selected. Each group was originally composed of 20 individuals but for various reasons of attrition, i.e., not appearing at the experiment, indication of previous knowledge of the experiment, etc., the final experimental groups were reduced to 17 members each, or a total of 51 subjects.

The responses of the three experimental groups to the leadership questionnaire are included in Table 1. Ss within the leadership group were selected because they perceived themselves as more influential in informal groups, and had held significantly more leadership positions in formal groups during their Senior year of high school. Non-leader joiners were distinguished from non-leader non-joiners primarily by their membership in formal organizations, and a tendency to perceive themselves as more influential in informal groups.

Experimental Procedure

Ss were placed in the experimental situation individually. S entered the experimental room in which one paid participant (Pp) was already seated, and two other Pp's joined them immediately. The S and the Pps were seated around a card table according to first name placards. The latter served to ensure that the seating arrangement was constant throughout the entire experiment and enabled all four participants to address each other by their first names. The S was given the impression that all four persons participating in the study were new to the situation.

Standard instructions were read which described the purported purpose of the study. Namely, the group was told that the experiment was being conducted for the Air Force to determine which one of a set of three ambiguous pictures was most conducive to group discussion.* The group was instructed first to select the picture which was

---

*Six cards from the Thomson adaptation of the Thematic Apperception Test were used. The three cards used within the support session were 11, 15, and 17 GF. The three cards used within the non-support session were 14, 13B, and 20. The cards were selected on the *a priori* grounds that they were highly ambiguous, and thus, a number of stories could be constructed.

Table 1

REPORTED INVOLVEMENT IN INFORMAL AND FORMAL
GROUPS DURING SENIOR YEAR IN HIGH SCHOOL, FOR SUBJECTS IN
THREE EXPERIMENTAL GROUPS*

Type of Involvement		*Frequency of Involvement*		
		Leaders (N=17)	Non-Leader Non-Joiners (N=17)	Non-Leader Joiners (N=17)
Informal Groups:				
Frequency of initiating group activity relative to other group members	More Often	17	8	7
	Less Often	0	9	10
Amount of control exerted over group relative to other group members	More	17	5	12
	Less	0	12	5
Behavior you most frequently used if you opposed group's plans	Redirect	8	2	5
	Leave	3	3	5
	Accepted	6	12	7
Own popularity in group	First	7	1	1
	Second	4	1	6
	Third or less	6	15	10
How frequently leader	Most	12	0	1
	Second most	4	3	6
	Third or less	1	14	10
If election were held, what position would you likely get	President	11	1	1
	1st Vice Pres.	5	2	10
	2nd Vice Pres.	1	5	1
	Other	0	9	5
Formal Groups:				
Number of memberships	0-1	0	11	0
	2-3	2	6	0
	4-5	5	0	11
	6 plus	10	0	6
Number of elected offices	0-1	0	17	17
	2-3	8	0	0
	4-5	8	0	0
	6 plus	1	0	0
Number of appointed offices	0	10	17	17
	1	3	0	0
	2 plus	4	0	0

*Data from a Leadership Questionnaire administered to 348 Freshman and Sophomore males enrolled in compulsory ROTC courses at the University of California (Santa Barbara). The three experimental groups of subjects (leaders, non-leader non-joiners, and non-leader joiners) were selected on the basis of these questionnaire data.

most conducive to group discussion, and then to construct a story about it upon which they could all agree. They were further informed that they had 20 minutes in which to complete the task, and that at the end of this period a buzzer would sound. A clock with only a minute hand was started at the beginning of the session so that the participants could assess the amount of time available. The group was also told that its discussion would be recorded so that it could be reviewed again at a later date.

During the first session, S was supported by the Pps. At the end of twenty minutes, a buzzer was sounded, and the group was requested to complete a questionnaire.** Immediately after completing the questionnaire, they were then informed that they were to participate in a second session in which they were to evaluate one of another set of three ambiguous cards in a similar fashion. In this session the S was not supported by the Pps, and at the end of this non-support session, another set of questionnaires was administered.

The S was then taken to a separate room and interrogated concerning his awareness of the manipulation, and requested not to inform other persons of the nature of the experiment. In only two cases were Ss overly suspicious of the nature of the experiment, and these Ss were removed from the experimental group. Most Ss seemed particularly willing not to communicate with others concerning the experiment to ensure that they would undergo a similar "traumatic" experience, i.e., group support followed by non-support.

Paid Participant Training

Three male college students were employed as paid participants throughout the experiment. Considerable effort was expended over a three month period preceding the actual experiment to train the individuals to assume certain standardized roles during the experiment. In the support session, two Pps supported the S's choice for the first 7 minutes. If, during this period, the S shifted his choice of cards, two Pp would continue to support his choice. At the end of the 7 minutes, the remaining Pp shifted over to the S's choice. During the remaining 13 minutes all Pps strongly supported the S's opinions, suggestions, and directions regarding an appropriate story for the selected card.

During the first 7 minutes of the second session, one Pp supported the S's choice and two selected the card which the S preferred least. If the S switched his choice during this period, the Pps followed a predesignated procedure whereby two would still oppose the S. At the end of 7 minutes, the Pp who had been supporting the S's choice switched from the S to the card supported by the two other Pps, and the choice of this card was forced on the basis of a majority

---

**The data obtained from the questionnaires concerned the perceptions and attitudes of the Ss relative to their experiences in the preceding session. Results from these questionnaires are not reported in this paper.

decision. During the subsequent 13 minutes, the Pps disregarded or negated comments, directions, or suggestions made by the S regarding the development of the story. In order to increase the opportunity for non-support responses, the Pps had a set of predetermined bizarre stories which they developed for the selected card. Any attempt made by the S to point out to the Pps discrepancies between the actual structure of the card and the story was ignored or rejected.

It should be noted that although the behavior of the Pps could not be completely standardized, the three months training period produced highly stereotyped behaviors on the part of the Pps so that there was considerably more consistency in the stimulus situation among Ss than one might anticipate. Furthermore, the Pps were not informed until the study was completed that the Ss were drawn from populations of leaders, non-leader non-joiners, and non-leader joiners.

Observer Training

Two observers were trained for three months prior to the experiment in coding behavior into the Bales' interaction system.* The training procedure involved working with tapes collected in a previous study of a similar nature (9), and observing and coding the behavior of Ss in training sessions run for the paid participants.

The Bales system was modified somewhat for this study. Categories "Gives Suggestion" and "Gives Orientation" were combined into a single category "Gives Direction"; similarly categories "Asks for Orientation" and "Asks for Suggestion" were combined into a single category, "Asks for Direction." Thus, the observers classified all behavioral acts made by Ss into one of the following ten categories:

A. Task Oriented:
  1. *Gives Direction:* gives suggestions, information, repeats, clarifies, confirms.
  2. *Gives Opinion:* gives evaluation, analysis, expresses feeling, wishes.
  3. *Asks for Opinion:* asks evaluation, analysis, expression of feeling, wishes.
  4. *Asks for Direction:* asks suggestions, information, repetition, clarification.

B. Positive Affect:
  5. *Shows Solidarity:* raises others' status, gives help, rewards.
  6. *Releases Tension:* jokes, laughs, shows satisfaction.

---

*During the early phases of observer training, an attempt was made to have the observers code the behavior of the subject and the paid participants. This, however, proved to be beyond the capabilities of the observers to do reliably.

   7. *Agrees Passively*: shows passive acceptance, understands, concurs, complies.
C. Negative Affect:
   8. *Disagrees Passively*: shows passive rejection, formality, withholds help.
   9. *Shows Tension*: asks for help, withdraws out of field.
   10. *Shows Antagonism*: deflates others' status, defends or asserts self.

The unit of analysis in the present study also followed from a definition from Bales: "The unit to be scored is the smallest discriminable segment of verbal or nonverbal behavior to which the observer, using the present set of categories after appropriate training, can assign a classification under conditions of continuous serial scoring" (1, p. 37). When observers were faced with a situation where a given behavior unit could be classified in either an affect or a task-oriented category, a decision rule of giving priority to affect categories was adopted.

Toward the end of the observer training session, the observers were given 150 behavioral units to score. The proportion of agreement in placing these units into one of the ten behavior categories was .88. Utilizing a method developed by Guetzkow (12), it was found that the least value which p, the probability that an observer has coded the units into appropriate categories, i.e., the theoretical correctness of classification, might take 99 times out of 100 was .94. In terms of the observations made during the course of actual experiment, it was impossible to obtain an estimate of reliability or theoretical correctness of classification, for there was no way to determine whether the observers were always evaluating the same unit of behavior.

Summary scores for each category of behavior for each individual within each session were obtained by adding the number of acts observed by both observers, dividing by two, and rounding to the nearest even whole number when necessary.

Data Analysis

The behavioral data obtained during the experiment were first analyzed in such a manner as to indicate the effects of previous leadership experience upon behavior across sessions (group effect); they were then analyzed in terms of differences in behavior between groups within each session (group by session effect), and finally, they were analyzed to determine the effects of group support vs. nonsupport upon the S's behavior regardless of previous leadership experience. With the completion of this analysis, the secondary hypotheses were examined.

The data were classified for analysis in two ways: (a) by gross categories, i.e., task-oriented, positive affect, and negative affect, and (b) by individual behavior categories, i.e., gives direction, gives opinion, asks for direction, etc. In the statistical analysis by gross behavior categories, the obtained frequency of responses was used directly. In the analysis of individual categories, the obtained frequencies or actual recorded values were transformed in order to reduce the heterogeneity of variance created by a number of individual Ss receiving scores of zero in several individual behavior categories. The transformation employed prior to running statistical analysis was a square root transformation suggested by Bartlett (8), i.e., $\sqrt{X + .5}$. The fact that gross categories are determined by summing individual behavior categories would indicate, of course, that the two sets of scores are not independent.

The design of the present experiment was not balanced, i.e., 50% of the Ss did not receive support and then non-support, and the remainder the opposite order. Such a design was not employed for two pragmatic reasons: first, it was judged difficult to create a condition of non-support for an individual in a newly formed group without preceding it with some earlier form of support; and, second, the high cost of an experimental procedure, which required three Pps, two observers, and a coordinator, limited the number of Ss that could be tested. To compensate in part for this lack of balance, an analysis of co-variance design was used to evaluate differences between groups in the second session, i.e., non-support, in order to adjust scores obtained within the non-support condition in terms of initial discrepancies occurring under the support condition.

RESULTS

The enumeration of the findings regarding the primary hypotheses will be partitioned into three types of effects: (a) *group effects,* i.e., leaders vs. non-leader non-joiners vs. non-leader joiners; (b) *group by session effects,* and (c) *session effects,* i.e., support vs. non-support. The results of testing the secondary hypotheses will be included in the section on "sessions effects."

Group Effects

Table 2 presents the distribution of acts for gross and individual behavior categories by groups, i.e., leaders, non-leader non-joiners, and non-leader joiners. In terms of the total number of acts across sessions there are no significant differences in group means between groups (Table 3). In comparing group means by gross behavior categories, it is apparent that differences do not exist for eight of the nine comparisons. In the ninth case leaders made significantly more positive affect responses than non-leader non-joiners.

Significant differences between groups in terms of individual behavior categories, as indicated by significant F ratios for group effects in Table 4, were found for the following categories: "shows solidarity," "agrees passively," and "gives direction." Scheffé (s) tests were employed to determine which of the group means differed significantly from one another in each of these categories. The following results were obtained: (a) leaders made significantly more "shows solidarity" responses than non-leader non-joiners; (b) leaders made significantly more "agrees passively" responses than non-leader non-joiners, and non-leader joiners; and (c) non-leader non-joiners made significantly more "gives direction" responses than leaders.

Group by Session Effect

The significant F ratios reported in Table 4 for Session X Group interaction for a number of the individual behavior categories indicates that the groups, i.e., leaders, non-leader non-joiners, and non-leader joiners, made a differential number of responses within sessions, i.e., support vs. non-support. In order to determine where these differences occurred, a simple analysis of variance was run to determine group effects under support, and a simple analysis of co-variance was used to determine group effects under non-support. The results of these analyses are reported in Table 5.

Within the *support* condition, significant F ratios were obtained for the following individual behavior categories: "gives direction," "shows solidarity," "agrees passively," "disagrees passively," and "shows tension." Using Scheffé tests the following significant differences between mean number of responses were obtained: (a) leaders made significantly more "shows solidarity" responses than non-leader non-joiners; (b) leaders made significantly more "agrees passively" responses than non-leader non-joiners; (c) non-leader non-joiners made significantly more "gives direction" responses than leaders and non-leader joiners; (d) non-leader non-joiners made significantly more "disagrees passively" responses than leaders and non-leader joiners; and finally, (e) non-leader non-joiners made significantly more "shows tension" responses than leaders and non-leader joiners.

Under *non-support* condition, the analysis of co-variance yielded significant F ratios for the following individual behavior categories: "releases tension," "agrees passively," "disagrees passively," and "shows tension." Utilizing Scheffé tests, the following significant differences between mean number of responses were found within individual behavior categories: (a) leaders made significantly more "releases tension" acts than non-leader non-joiners; (b) leaders made significantly more "agrees passively" responses than non-leader joiners, and non-leader non-joiners also made significantly more "agrees passively" responses than non-leader joiners; (c) leaders made "disagrees passively" responses than non-leader non-joiners; and (d) leaders made more "shows tension" responses than non-leader non-joiners, and non-leader joiners.

Table 2

DISTRIBUTION OF ACTS BY BEHAVIOR CATEGORIES
FOR TWO EXPERIMENTAL SESSIONS, AND THREE EXPERIMENTAL GROUPS*

Behavior Category	Leaders (N=17)			Non-Leader - Non-Joiners (N=17)			Non-Leader - Joiners (N=17)		
	Support Session	Non-Support Session	Total	Support Session	Non-Support Session	Total	Support Session	Non-Support Session	Total
Task-Oriented									
1. Gives Direction	23	26	49	82	30	112	32	35	67
2. Gives Opinion	2038	922	2960	1919	975	2894	1975	859	2834
3. Asks for Opinion	102	190	292	114	193	307	73	145	218
4. Asks for Direction	22	3	25	21	7	28	20	3	23
Sub-Total	2185	1141	3326	2136	1205	3341	2100	1042	3142
Positive Affect									
5. Shows Solidarity	39	5	44	15	5	20	31	7	38
6. Releases Tension	277	176	453	297	86	383	295	140	435
7. Agrees Passively	710	378	1088	500	320	820	618	228	846
Sub-Total	1026	559	1585	812	411	1223	944	375	1319
Negative Affect									
8. Disagrees Passively	21	334	355	66	227	293	30	287	317
9. Shows Tension	9	98	107	32	49	81	9	51	60
10. Shows Antagonism	0	16	16	1	36	37	2	42	44
Sub-Total	30	448	478	99	312	411	41	380	421
Total	3241	2148	5389	3047	1928	4975	3085	1797	4882

*Data obtained from observer's coding of the acts of Ss during the two experimental sessions that each attended (support session and non-support session).

Table 3

MEAN DIFFERENCES IN FREQUENCY OF ACTS,
BY BEHAVIOR CATEGORIES, FOR THREE EXPERIMENTAL GROUPS; BOTH SESSIONS COMBINED

Gross Behavior Category	Experimental Group Means						Means Difference Test (t)		
	Leaders (L) (N=17)		Non-Leader Non-Joiners (NL, NJ) (N=17)		Non-Leader Joiners (NL, J) (N=17)		L vs NL, NJ	L vs NLJ	NLJ vs NL, NJ
	X	σ	X	σ	X	σ	t	t	t
Task-Oriented	195.7	49.2	196.5	63.6	184.8	39.7	.04	.69	.63
Positive Affect	93.2	14.7	71.9	23.9	77.6	38.3	3.03**	1.52	.50
Negative Affect	28.1	8.1	24.2	10.5	24.8	11.1	.36	.98	.16
Total Acts	317.0	62.3	292.6	82.8	287.2	55.8	.94	1.43	.22

**$p < .01$

Table 4

OVERALL ANALYSIS OF VARIANCE FOR ACTS BY BEHAVIOR CATEGORIES, EXPERIMENTAL SESSIONS, AND EXPERIMENTAL GROUPS[1]

Behavior Category	df	MS	F	Behavior Category	df	MS	F
1. Gives Direction				6. Releases Tension			
Groups	2	2.30	4.34*	Groups	2	1.19	.76
Ss/Groups	48	.53	15.25***	Ss/Groups	48	1.57	
Sessions	1	1.22	24.13***	Sessions	1	36.27	60.31***
Sess. X Grps.	2	1.93		Sess. X Grps.	2	3.23	5.37**
Error	48	.08		Error	48	.60	
Total	101			Total	101		
2. Gives Opinion				7. Agrees Passively			
Groups	2	.25	.08	Groups	2	7.00	4.53*
Ss/Groups	48	3.13		Ss/Groups	48	1.55	
Sessions	1	286.34	295.20***	Sessions	1	72.33	93.71***
Sess. X Grps.	2	.97	1.00	Sess. X Grps.	2	2.48	3.21*
Error	48	.97		Error	48	.77	
Total	101			Total	101		
3. Asks for Opinion				Negative Affect			
Groups	2	2.88	2.02	8. Disagrees Passively			
Ss/Groups	48	1.43		Groups	2	.09	.13
Sessions	1	18.35	43.52***	Ss/Groups	48	.68	
Sess. X Grps.	2	.05	.12	Sessions	1	154.21	416.78***
Error	48	.42		Sess. X Grps.	2	5.65	15.27***
Total	101			Error	48	.37	
				Total	101		
4. Asks for Direction				9. Shows Tension			
Groups	2	.05	.33	Groups	2	1.09	2.73
Ss/Groups	48	.14		Ss/Groups	48	.40	
Sessions	1	4.12	36.63***	Sessions	1	18.55	68.70***
Sess. X Grps.	2	.05	.46	Sess. X Grps	2	2.83	10.48***
Error	48	.11		Error	48	.27	
Total	101			Total	101		
Positive Affect				10. Shows Antagonism			
5. Shows Solidarity				Groups	2	.50	1.87
Groups	2	.66	3.41*	Ss/Groups	48	.27	
Ss/Groups	48	.19		Sessions	1	8.89	45.38***
Sessions	1	6.55	50.39***	Sess. X Grps.	2	.80	4.08*
Sess. X Grps.	2	.73	5.65**	Error	48	.20	
Error	48	.13		Total	101		
Total	101						

*p < .05   **p < .01   ***p < .001

[1]Total subjects = 51

Table 5
ANALYSIS OF VARIANCE FOR ACTS BY BEHAVIORAL CATEGORIES, OCCURRING
UNDER GROUP SUPPORT, AND GROUP NON-SUPPORT; ANALYSIS OF COVARIANCE
FOR ACTS OCCURRING UNDER NON-SUPPORT[1]

Behavior Category	Variance Analysis (Support)			Variance Analysis (Non-Support)			Co-Variance Analysis (Non-Support)		
	df	MS	F	df	MS	F	df	MS	F
Task-Oriented									
1. Gives Direction									
Groups	2	4.15	10.71***	2	.07	.02	2	.61	2.19
Subjects	48	.39		48	.29		48	.21	
Total	50			50			50		
2. Gives Opinion									
Groups	2	.70	.23	2	.52	.48	2	.86	1.21
Subjects	48	3.02		48	1.08		48	.71	
Total	50			50			50		
3. Asks for Opinion									
Groups	2	1.36	1.53	2	1.61	1.64	2	.41	.62
Subjects	48	.89		48	.99		48	.69	
Total	50			50			50		
4. Asks for Direction									
Groups	2	.03	.15	2	.07	1.27	2	.07	1.27
Subjects	48	.21		48	.06		48	.06	
Total	50			50			50		
Positive Affect									
5. Shows Solidarity									
Groups	2	1.38	5.88**	2	.01	.15	2	.04	.49
Subjects	48	.23		48	.09		48	.09	
Total	50			50			50		
6. Releases Tension									
Groups	2	.25	.14	2	4.17	8.14**	2	4.18	9.22***
Subjects	48	1.84		48	.51		48	.45	
Total	50			50			50		
7. Agrees Passively									
Groups	2	4.90	3.25*	2	4.58	5.66**	2	2.14	6.16**
Subjects	48	1.51		48	.81		48	.79	
Total	50			50			50		
Negative Affect									
8. Disagrees Passively									
Groups	2	2.76	11.90***	2	2.97	3.59*	2	5.36	7.30**
Subjects	48	.23		48	.83		48	.73	
Total	50			50			50		
9. Shows Tension									
Groups	2	.99	4.34*	2	2.93	6.66**	2	3.05	6.82**
Subjects	48	.23		48	.44		48	.45	
Total	50			50			50		
10. Shows Antagonism									
Groups	2	Insufficient N		2	.78	1.60	2	.43	.95
Subjects	48			48	.49		48	.46	
Total	50			50			50		

Total subjects = 51

*p <.05   **p<.01   ***p<.001

Session Effects

The distribution of responses across both sessions by gross and individual behavior categories is presented in Tables 6 and 7. A direct difference test confirmed the prediction of more responses in the support condition ($\overline{X} = 183.8$ acts) than in the non-support condition ($\overline{X} = 115.2$). Predictions were also supported for the gross behavior categories: Greater mean numbers of positive affect and task-oriented responses, and a smaller mean number of negative affect responses were made under support than non-support.

The effect of support vs. non-support upon individual categories of behavior also was marked. Within each individual behavior category, there was a significant shift in the response level (see Sessions Effect in Table 4). Although the over-all number of responses decreased from support to non-support, increases in the mean number of responses were found for the following categories. "asks for opinion," "disagrees passively," "shows tension," and "shows antagonism." Significant decreases in the mean number of responses occurred in the remaining individual categories: "gives direction," "gives opinion," "asks for direction," "shows solidarity," "releases tension," and "agrees passively."

Table 6

DISTRIBUTION OF ACTS BY BEHAVIOR CATEGORIES,
IN TWO EXPERIMENTAL SESSIONS;
FOR ALL GROUPS COMBINED*

Behavior Category	Experimental Session		Percent of Acts in Non-Support Session
	Support	Non-Support	
Task-Oriented			
1. Gives Direction	137	91	40
2. Gives Opinion	5932	2756	32
3. Asks for Opinion	289	528	65
4. Asks for Direction	63	13	17
Sub-total	6421	3388	35
Positive Affect			
5. Shows Solidarity	85	17	17
6. Releases Tension	869	402	32
7. Agrees Passively	1828	926	34
Sub-total	2782	1345	33
Negative Affect			
8. Disagrees Passively	117	848	80
9. Shows Tension	50	198	80
10. Shows Antagonism	3	94	97
Sub-total	170	1140	87
Total	9373	5873	39

*Total-subjects $= 51$

An additional analysis was performed to determine the effects of the sessions upon the variability of the responses of Ss within individual

Table 7

MEAN DIFFERENCES IN FREQUENCY OF ACTS
BY BEHAVIOR CATEGORIES, IN TWO EXPERIMENTAL SESSIONS,
FOR ALL GROUPS COMBINED*

Gross Behavior Category	Experimental Session Means				Mean Diff. Test (t)
	Support		Non-Support		
	X̄	σ	X̄	σ	
Task-Oriented	125.9	37.2	66.4	16.8	14.50***
Positive Affect	54.6	22.6	26.4	10.7	9.72***
Negative Affect	3.3	2.9	22.4	9.7	13.58***
Total Acts	183.8	36.9	115.2	28.9	11.38***

*Total subjects =51   ***$p < .001$

categories of behavior. Utilizing a method for comparing variances based on related scores (20), significant increases in the variability of the number of Ss responses from support to non-support were found in two categories (See Table 8): "disagrees passively," and "shows tension." Significant decreases in variability in the number of Ss responses occurred in the categories: "shows solidarity," "releases tension," "agrees passively," "gives opinion," and "asks for direction."

A final evaluation of the session effect (secondary hypotheses) was made by comparing the percentage distribution of responses for each session with a distribution of responses obtained in the Bales' studies (2, 3). The dependent variable in this analysis, the group member's verbal and gestural responses, were classified in terms of an aggregated version of the Bales' interaction profile (1). Four behavior categories were employed: (a) social-emotional: expresses positive affect (EPA), (b) task behavior: gives direction and opinion (GDO), (c) task behavior: asks direction and opinion (ADO), and (d) socio-emotional: expresses negative affect (ENA). It should be noted that the preceding classification varied from that employed for the major hypotheses where three major categories were used: positive affect, task-oriented behavior, and negative affect. For the present classification the task-oriented behavior category was split into: (a) gives direction and opinion, and (b) asks opinion and suggestion. However, for the secondary hypotheses, an analysis was not made of the ten individual categories. Prior to reporting the results of the analysis of secondary hypotheses, the methods employed by Bales in the two studies considered here will be briefly outlined.

In the first Bales' study (2), the response profiles for a group which was strongly satisfied and another group which was strongly dissatisfied with the outcome of their activities were reported. The study employed groups composed of four college students who were

Table 8

DIFFERENCES IN VARIABILITY OF ACTS, BY BEHAVIOR CATEGORIES,
IN TWO EXPERIMENTAL SESSIONS;
FOR ALL GROUPS COMBINED*

| Behavior Category | Variance (S^2) by Session | | t |
	Support	Non-Support	
Task-Oriented			
1. Gives Direction	18.72	13.92	1.19
2. Gives Opinion	144.96	51.84	4.70***
3. Asks for Opinion	42.72	47.52	.43
4. Asks for Direction	10.08	2.88	4.98***
Positive Affect			
5. Shows Solidarity	11.04	4.32	3.70***
6. Releases Tension	88.32	24.48	5.14***
7. Agrees Passively	72.48	38.88	2.27*
Negative Affect			
8. Disagrees Passively	11.04	39.84	5.09***
9. Shows Tension	11.04	21.12	2.36*
10. Shows Antagonism	Insufficient N	23.52	

*Total subjects = 51

*p < .05
***p < .001

confronted with a standardized group task. The behavior of each of the members of the groups was coded into Bales' twelve category system which was subsequently grouped into a four-fold classification. Following the group problem solving situation members were given rating scales on which they expressed their degree of satisfaction with the group's efforts. The response profiles obtained for the group whose members made the highest average rating of satisfaction and the group whose members made the lowest average rating of satisfaction are compared.

In the second Bales' study (3) twenty-four groups of college students of varying sizes interacted in a varied number of sessions working towards the solution of standardized problems. The behavior of each of the individuals in the groups was again coded into Bales' twelve-category system, and subsequently collapsed for the present study into a four-category system. Their collective profile represents a normative group in the present analysis.

The number of responses coded and the number of groups involved in each of the three conditions, i.e., group support and non-support, satisfaction and dissatisfaction, and a normative group, are presented in Table 9. The proportional distribution of responses by condition across the four behavior categories is indicated in Table 10. It is apparent that the distributions of responses obtained across conditions by behavior categories are consistent with the secondary hypotheses advanced earlier. That is, Ss in the non-support and the dissatisfied conditions made proportionately more Asks Direction and Opinion, and

Negative Affect responses, than those in the support and satisfied conditions; Ss in the support and satisfied conditions made proportionately more Positive Affect and Gives Direction and Opinion responses than those in the non-support and dissatisfied conditions; and finally, the proportion of responses in each behavior category for the normative group fell between those obtained for the non-support and dissatisfied conditions and the support and satisfied conditions. Since the distribution of responses for single individuals by condition is unavailable in the reports of the Bales' studies, it is not possible to run individual statistical comparisons between conditions. However, if one compares the rank ordering of the proportion of responses predicted within each behavior category across conditions with the obtained rank orderings, one can estimate whether the obtained distribution of ranks is one which could have been achieved by chance alone (Table 10). A *very conservative* test of whether or not the obtained rank orderings differed from distributions which one might obtain by chance alone can be made by, (1) ranking the proportion of responses for each behavior category across conditions in a direction consistent with the predicted rank orderings and, (2) computing a chi-square statistic for replicated rank orderings (21).

Table 9

NUMBER OF ACTS OBSERVED UNDER
SEVERAL GROUP CONDITIONS

Group Condition	Acts	Groups Involved
Non-support	5,873	51*
Dissatisfied	767	1**
Normative	71,838	24**
Satisfied	719	1**
Support	9,373	51*
Total	88,570	128

*Observations were made on one subject in each group who participated with three paid participants in both non-support and support conditions.
**Observations were made on all subjects in each group (2,3).

Since, in the present analysis, data are reported in terms of proportion of responses for each behavior category within a given condition, and since these must by definition sum to 100, the rank ordering across one behavior category was deleted because orderings within it were *partially* determined by orderings obtained across the remaining

Table 10

RANK ORDERING OF PROPORTIONAL DISTRIBUTION OF ACTS,
BY BEHAVIOR CATEGORIES, FOR EACH GROUP CONDITION

Behavior Category	Group Condition									
	Non-Support		Dissatisfied		Normative		Satisfied		Support	
	Proportion	Rank	Proportion	Rank	Proportion	Rank	Proportion	Rank	Proportion	Rank
Positive Affect	(22.9)	2	(17.2)	1	(25.9)	3	(33.5)	5	(29.9)	4
Gives Direction and Opinion	(48.4)	1	(56.0)	2.5	(56.0)	2.5	(57.3)	4	(64.6)	5
Asks Direction and Opinion	(9.2)	2	(9.5)	1	(7.0)	3	(3.9)	4	(3.8)	5
Negative Affect	(19.4)	1	(17.4)	2	(11.2)	3	(5.3)	4	(1.7)	5
Predicted Rank Order		1.5		1.5		3		4.5		4.5
Total	(99.9)	7.5	(100.1)	8	(100.1)	14.5	(100.0)	21.5	(100.0)	23.5

categories. In this instance the positive affect category was arbitrarily omitted. The X_r^2 obtained in this analysis was significant ($X_r^2 = 14.4$, $p < .01$) indicating that the distribution of ranks, ordered in terms of the original predicted distribution, would have occurred by chance less than one time out of a hundred.

Table 11

PROPORTIONS OF ACTS IN THE
'POSITIVE AND NEGATIVE AFFECT' BEHAVIOR
CATEGORIES, FOR EACH GROUP CONDITION

Condition	Positive Affect (1)	Negative Affect (2)	Percentage Difference [(1) − (2)]
Non-Support	22.9	19.6	2.7
Dissatisfied	17.2	17.4	−.2
Normative	25.9	11.2	14.7
Satisfied	33.5	5.3	28.2
Support	29.6	1.7	27.9

Table 11 presents data which report the differences in the proportions of positive and negative affect responses by conditions. As indicated, in the non-support and dissatisfied conditions, there is almost equivalence in the proportion of positive and negative affect responses made. In the support and satisfied conditions there is a substantially greater proportion of positive than negative affect responses.

DISCUSSION

Leadership Behavior

Task-Oriented Responses. The major hypotheses of this study concerned differences in the behavior of leaders, non-leader non-joiners, and non-leader joiners under conditions of group support. One major hypothesis was not supported. Leaders did not, as predicted, make more task-oriented responses across or within sessions. The only difference within an individual task-oriented category which achieved statistical significance was in a direction opposite to the major prediction. Namely, non-leader non-joiners made a signifcantly higher mean number of "gives direction" responses across sessions than leaders. By examining the 'group by session' effects, it becomes apparent that this mean difference was significant only within the support session where non-leader non-joiners made a significantly higher mean number of "gives direction" responses than non-leaders and non-leader joiners. One possible explanation of this unanticipated finding might be that given social support, the subject is automatically in a position of influence. Consequently, leaders and non-leader joiners, who have a greater familarity with inter-personal situations, may perceive their relative position of power more readily, and thus feel less compelled to use strong directive means to demonstrate this influence. Or it may be that persons who normally perceive themselves as relatively unimportant in a group situation discover under the group support condition that they are being strongly reinforced for active participation. Consequently, they may over-compensate for their usual inability to effectively participate in groups by making a relatively large number of "gives direction" responses. In any case, the observation that leaders did not make significantly more task-oriented responses than either type of non-leaders contradicts, at least for the particular setting of the present study, one of the more frequently stated assumptions in the literature on leadership (4, 2, and 9).

Positive Affect Responses. As hypothesized, leaders did make significantly more positive affect responses across sessions than non-leader non-joiners in terms of the gross category and within two of the individual categories, i.e., "shows solidarity" and "agrees passively." This finding is consistent with the assumption that leaders are more likely to use positive affect or reinforcement as a means of exerting influence within a group than non-leader non-joiners. The predicted relationship between non-leader joiners and the other two groups within the category of positive affect is supported. The frequency of positive affect responses of non-leader joiners fell between the two other groups within the gross category, and within the three individual positive affect behavior categories. In reviewing the results for the 'group by session' effects as relates to the expression of positive affect, we find that under support, leaders made significantly more "shows solidarity" and "agrees passively" responses than non-leader non-joiners. Non-leader joiners, as predicted, within the support condition, fell between the leaders and non-leader non-joiners in terms of the mean frequency of total positive affect responses and the mean frequency of responses within each of the three individual positive affect categories.

In the non-support condition, leaders made significantly more "release tension" responses than non-leader non-joiners, and significantly more "passive agreement" responses than non-leader joiners. Within this condition, the predicted ordering of positive affect response level between the three groups was not supported. Non-leader joiners made fewer responses within the gross category of positive affect under non-support than non-leader non-joiners. This was accounted for in part by non-leader joiners making significantly fewer "agrees passively" responses than non-leader non-joiners.

One possible explanation of this deviation from our predictions is that both leaders and non-leader joiners are more likely to perceive that they have lost status than non-leader non-joiners. The leaders may make a strong attempt to regain their previous position and use positive affect responses in this attempt; whereas the non-leader joiners may not possess the skills or motivations to make as great a number of positive affect responses in the face of a non-supporting, rejecting group. The non-leader non-joiners, because of less experience in groups, may not perceive the group climate as accurately as either of the other groups, and consequently may not be as inhibited in making positive affect responses as the non-leader joiners. Thus, one might speculate that the positive responses made by non-leader joiners under support are more readily extinguished given a condition of non-support, i.e., social punishment, than those of leaders who are more strongly motivated to regain their position of influence, or non-leader non-joiners, who less readily perceive or are less concerned about social rejection.

Negative Affect Responses. The principal hypotheses concerning difference between leader, non-leader non-joiners, and non-leader joiners as regards the expression of negative affect were made for each experimental situation separately. As anticipated, the non-leader non-joiners made significantly more "disagrees passively" and "shows tension" responses within the support environment than leader and non-leader joiners. It seems likely that both leaders and non-leader joiners were more aware of their relative position of influence under strong social support, and/or had learned by previous experience within groups that negative affect responses are not effective means for maintaining a position of influence under conditions of support. Also, as anticipated, non-leader joiners occupied a middle position between leaders and non-leader non-joiners in two of the three individual negative affect categories, i.e., "disagrees passively" and "shows antagonism."

Under conditions of group non-support, leaders made more negative responses than non-leader non-joiners. Within individual behavior categories, they made significantly more "shows tension" and "disagrees passively" responses. However, leaders tended to make fewer "show antagonism" responses than both non-leader joiners ($p < .10$) and non-leader non-joiners ($p < .10$). Thus in general, leaders responded to the loss of influence and the likely frustration generated by the non-support environment with greater negative affect than non-leaders.

However, the expression of this negative affect was limited to more passive and withdrawing forms of behavior. The non-leaders showed less over-all negative affect, but were more likely to respond to non-support by more open forms of negative behavior than were leaders. It may be that leaders expressed more over-all negative affect because they were more perceptive of non-support and/or were more highly frustrated by this form of environment. However, even given a higher level of awareness and/or frustration, leaders were less likely to directly attack other members within the group. This reluctance may have stemmed from their greater awareness that the direct expression of hostility towards members of a group would markedly reduce the likelihood that they would be able to exert influence or rejoin in the activities of the group.

The Effects of Support vs. Non-Support

In the present study it was hypothesized that certain behavioral differences would occur across all Ss under conditions of group support vs. non-support. These hypotheses were based upon the general assumption that reinforcement in a social situation produces a different level and distribution of responses than non-reinforcement or punishment. These hypotheses were confirmed. The total number of responses which the Ss made were significantly greater under the support or reinforcement condition. In terms of gross behavioral categories significantly higher mean numbers of task-oriented and positive affect responses occurred under support than under non-support, whereas a significantly higher mean frequency of negative affect responses occurred under non-support than support.

The changes in individual behavior categories under support vs. non-support corresponded closely to those in the gross categories. Thus, with one exception, significantly more responses were made within individual task-oriented and positive affect categories under support than non-support, whereas significantly more responses within the individual negative affect categories were made under non-support. The one exception was that a significant increase in mean number of responses under non-support occurred within the individual task-oriented category, "asks for opinion."

These findings on the effects of social reinforcement and non-reinforcement are congruent with earlier results obtained by Verplanck (19). Verplanck found that reinforcing statements of opinion affected the content of conversations. The latter variable, conversation, he defined as operant response, i.e., "a part of behavior (1) that is recurrently identifiable and hence can be enumerated, and (2) whose rate of occurrence can be determined as a systematic function of certain classes of environmental events." (19, p. 32) The behaviors observed in the present study under support and non-support can be similarly classified as operant responses: (1) they were identified recurrently, and (2) the rate of their occurrence was demonstrated to be a systematic function of environmental events. Thus, it would appear that the principles of operant conditioning may appropriately be used as a basis for describing differences in response rates under conditions of group support and non-support.

The results also indicated that there were marked shifts in the variability of Ss scores within individual behavior categories from support to non-support. Significant decreases in variability were observed under non-support within two of the individual task-oriented categories, "gives opinion" and "asks for direction," and within all of the positive affect categories, "agrees passively," "shows solidarity," and "releases tension." This decrease in inter-individual variability of response may indicate that the support condition creates an environment which is not only more appropriate and therefore more conducive to a greater expression of these forms of behavior, but also one in which individual differences in the frequency of using these behaviors are likely to emerge. Increases in inter-individual response variability occurred in the non-support condition within the individual categories, "disagrees passively," and "shows tension." This may similarly indicate that these behaviors are not only more likely to occur in a frustrating situation, but also that individual differences are more likely to emerge. As had been indicated previously, part of this greater variability of positive affect responses under support, and negative affect responses under non-support is due to systematic differences in the behaviors of leaders, non-leaders, and non-leader joiners in these conditions.

The comparison of the findings of the present study with those of Bales (2, 3) indicate that there are similarities in the response profiles of persons interacting in social groups as a function of the amount of positive reinforcement they are afforded by other group members, and as a function of the degree of satisfaction they express with the group's activities. Although predicted similarities in the relative proportion of task-oriented behaviors were found, the greatest proportional similarities in response occur within the affective categories. Given the data reported in Table 11, it is apparent that the most striking characteristic of the response profiles of individuals in groups which afford them positive reinforcement and of individuals who are highly satisfied with the activities of the group of which they are a member is the very small proportion of negative affect responses they both make relative to Ss who do not receive group support, or Ss who are dissatisfied with the performance of their group. It is apparent that the major behavioral similarities which attend support vs. non-support, and satisfaction vs. dissatisfaction is in the increased expression of disagreement, tension, and antagonistic responses which characterize both the non-support and dissatisfaction conditions.

Thus, the anticipated congruence between the behavior profiles of Ss who were supported by the group and those expressing satisfaction with the activities of their group was obtained, as was the anticipated congruence between the response profiles of Ss who were non-supported and those who expressed dissatisfaction with the activities of their group. The distribution of responses with the normative group also, as hypothesized, fell between the more extreme distributions of support vs. non-support, and satisfaction vs. dissatisfaction conditions. (See Table 10.) In conclusion, there is indirect evidence that attitudes of satisfaction and dissatisfaction toward the task accomplishments of group provide an index of the amount of group support, i.e., positive reinforcement, experienced by Ss within the group.

It is apparent, then, from this study that support vs. non-support had a marked effect upon the behavior of the group members. Furthermore, the results indicate that there exist behavioral differences between leaders, non-leader non-joiners, and non-leader joiners under conditions of support and non-support. The major differences, given the relatively unstructured group employed in the present study, occurred within the positive and negative affect categories of behavior. This would suggest that leaders selected on the criteria employed in the present study may be behaviorally distinguished from non-leaders in terms of their affective orientation towards other group members. Finally, the results suggest that task-oriented behaviors, i.e., "gives opinion," "asks opinion," "gives direction" and "asks direction" do not as hypothesized provide a means for distinguishing leaders from non-leaders within an unstructured task environment.

SUMMARY

Three experimental groups of 17 leaders, 17 non-leader non-joiners, and 17 non-leader joiners were selected from a population of 348 Freshman and Sophomore male students on the basis of their previous experience in informal and formal groups. The 51 experimental Ss were placed individually in a group with three paid participants (Pps). In a first session, the Pps reinforced or supported the S in selecting one of three ambiguous pictures on the basis of its utility in fostering group discussion, and then in constructing a story about the picture. In a second session, the Pps did not support the S's card preference, and did not support, but in fact discouraged, the subject from participating in constructing a story.

A set of hypotheses was made regarding expected behavioral differences between leader, non-leader non-joiners, and non-leader joiners under conditions of group support and non-support. As predicted, leaders made more positive affect responses across and within both support and non-support sessions than non-leader non-joiners; leaders made fewer negative affect responses than non-leader non-joiners under group support; and leaders made more negative affect responses than non-leader non-joiners under group non-support. Also, as anticipated, non-leader joiners tended to fall between the leader and non-leader non-joiners in terms of the number of positive and negative responses they made under conditions of support and non-support. One major hypothesis was not confirmed. Leaders did *not* make significantly more task-oriented responses within either or both of the sessions than either non-leader non-joiners or non-leader joiners.

The distribution of responses for leader, non-leader non-joiners, and non-leader joiners was also compared on ten individual behavior categories: "gives direction," "gives opinion," "asks for opinion," "asks for direction," "shows solidarity," "releases tension," "agrees passively," "disagrees passively," "shows tension," and "shows antagonism." The results of these comparisons were generally compatible with those obtained within the gross categories of task-oriented, positive affect and negative affect behavior. An attempt was made to offer tentative explanations for the few significant discrepancies which were found.

A secondary set of hypotheses was formulated concerning the differential effects upon all S's behavior of the supporting and non-supporting environments. It was predicted that under support or reinforcement, Ss would make more over-all responses, and would also make more task-oriented and positive affect responses than under non-support. Furthermore, it was predicted that the frustration of non-support would increase the amount of negative affect expressed relative to the support condition. These hypotheses were strongly supported.

Finally, a secondary set of hypotheses was made regarding the similarity of response profiles of individuals under group support and non-support, and those who expressed satisfaction and dissatisfaction with the group's efforts. As hypothesized, there were marked similarities of response between those supported and those who reported satisfaction, and those non-supported and those who reported dissatisfaction with the group's efforts.

BIBLIOGRAPHY

1. Bales, Robert F. *Interaction Process Analysis: A Method for the Study of Small Groups*. Cambridge, Mass.: Addison-Wesley Publ. Co., 1950

2. _____ "Some Uniformities of Behavior in Small Social Systems," in *Readings in Social Psychology,* rev. ed. by G. E. Swanson et al. New York: Henry Holt and Co., 1952, 146-159

3. _____ "Task Roles and Social Roles in Problem-Solving Groups," in *Readings in Social Psychology,* 3rd ed. by E. E. Maccoby et al. New York: Holt, Rinehart and Winston, Inc. 1958, 437-447

4. Bass, Bernard M. "The Leaderless Group Discussion," *Psychological Bulletin,* LI (September, 1954), 465-492

5. _____ *Leadership, Psychology, and Organizational Behavior.* New York: Harper and Bros., 1960

6. Bird, Charles. *Social Psychology.* New York: Appleton-Century Co., 1940

7. Chowdhry, Kamla, and Newcomb, Theodore, M. "The Relative Abilities of Leaders and Non-Leaders to Estimate Opinions of Their Own Groups," *Journal of Abnormal and Social Psychology,* XLVII (January, 1952), 51-57

8. Edwards, Allen L. *Experimental Design in Psychological Research.* New York: Rinehart and Co., 1950; rev. ed. 1960

9. Gallo, Philip S., and McClintock, Charles G. "Behavioral, Attitudinal and Perceptual Differences between Leaders and Non-Leaders in Situations of Group Support and Non-Support," *Journal of Social Psychology,* LVI (February, 1962), 121-133

10. Gibb, C. A. "Leadership," in *Handbook of Social Psychology,* ed. by G. Lindzey (2 vols.). Cambridge, Mass.: Addison-Wesley Publ. Co., 1954, vol. II, pp. 877-920

11. Greenspoon, J. "The Reinforcing Effect of Two Spoken Sounds on the Frequency of Two Responses," *American Journal of Psychology,* LXVIII (1955), 409-416

12. Guetzkow, Harold. "Unitizing and Categorizing Problems in Coding Qualitative Data," *Journal of Clinical Psychology,* VI (January, 1950), 47-57

13. Hull, C. L. *A Behavior System; An Introduction to Behavior Theory Concerning the Individual Organism.* New Haven: Yale University Press, 1952

14. McClelland, D. C., Atkinson, J. W., et al. *The Achievement Motive.* New York: Appleton-Century-Crofts, 1953

15. McClintock, Charles G. "Group Support and the Behavior of Leaders and Non-Leaders," *Journal of Abnormal and Social Psychology,* LXVII (August, 1963), 105-113

16. McGeoch, J. A. *The Psychology of Human Learning.* New York: Longmans Green, 1952

17. Mandler, George W., and Kaplan, Warren K. "Subjective Evaluation and Reinforcing Effect of a Verbal Stimulus," *Science,* CXXIV (September, 1956), 582-583

18. Thorndike, E. L. et al. *The Fundamentals of Learning.* New York: Columbia University Press, 1932. (Prepared by Staff of Division of Psychology of Institute of Educational Research, Teachers College)

19. Verplanck, William S. "The Control of the Content of Conversation: Reinforcement of Statements of Opinion,' in *Readings in Social Psychology,* 3rd ed. by E. E. Maccoby et al. New York: Holt, Rinehart and Winston, Inc. 1958, 32-39

20. Walker, Helen M., and Lev, Joseph. *Statistical Inference.* New York: Henry Holt and Co., 1953

21. Wilcoxon, F. *Some Rapid Approximate Statistical Procedures.* New York: American Cyanamid Co., 1949

22. Wolman, Benjamin B. "Leadership and Group Dynamics," *Journal of Social Psychology,* XLIII (February, 1956), 11-25

The Impact of Technological Change on the Careers of Managers and Professionals in Large-Scale Organizations: Design of an Exploratory Study*

RAYMOND V. BOWERS, ROBERT GUY BROWN
and CLIFTON DOW BRYANT**

BACKGROUND OF THE PROBLEM

ALTHOUGH much attention has been paid to the effect of technological change on the lower status levels of military, industrial, and other large-scale organizations, relatively little is known in any systematic way about the effect of such change on the "organization men" themselves—the career professionals and executives who manage these organizations technically and administratively. Yet as the tempo of technological change steps up, and as the importance of such careers in large-scale organizations continues to grow, it is obvious that the effectiveness of the organizations will depend to an increasing degree on an understanding of how these key functionaries adjust to change, and what happens when they fail to adjust.

The facts regarding these trends in our society are too well known to dwell on here at any length. With reference to the increasing importance of the large-scale organization as employer, our federal government alone has grown to include 10 per cent of the nation's labor force, and three-fourths of all personnel in manufacturing are employed by firms having more than 100 employees. This increasing size of the unit of employment has been accompanied by a shift from self-employment to salaried status. The self-employment segment of

*A behavioral sciences project conducted at the University of Georgia, February 1960 - August 1963 under Contract AF 49 (638) - 804 sponsored by the Behavioral Sciences Division, Air Force Office of Scientific Research, Office of Aerospace Research, Department of the Air Force.

**Dr. Bowers is now Professor and Head, Department of Sociology, The University of Arizona, Tucson, Arizona; Dr. Brown is Associate Professor of Sociology, The George Washington University, Washington, D. C.; and Dr. Bryant is Associate Professor and Chairman, Department of Sociology and Anthropology, Millsaps College, Jackson, Mississippi.

the labor force has declined from 40 per cent to 13 per cent since 1870, while the proportion that is salaried has grown from 7 per cent to 31 per cent. Moreover, the proportion of the salaried group that can be classified as executive or professional increased from 3 to 12 per cent.

With reference to the increasing tempo of technological change, the cause is, of course, the expanding emphasis on research and development in all large-scale organizations. We are, for the first time in our history, "force feeding" the change process, not only to keep ahead of domestic competitors but to maintain and improve our competitive position abroad. The U. S. Air Force, as one example, has changed its weapons systems so frequently since World War II that it is meaningless to talk about the "new" Air Force. And even the bank clerks and country doctors are feeling the hot breath of change as automatic equipment and pharmaceutical advances revolutionize their practices.

"Accelerating change" and "large-scale organization" are two key factors in the conceptualization of our research problem. A third, however, is equally important. It is the fact that career commitments to these large-scale organizations appear to be on the increase. More and more of the middle class is becoming committed to military careers, civil service careers, telephone company careers, or careers in some other large-scale organization. Some of this commitment is undoubtedly due to the greater efforts of the organizations to "involve" the employee in his work, while some is certainly due to the "entrapment" effect of pension plans and other rewards for length of service. Moreover, the salaried worker is brought to this "point of no return" at an increasingly early stage in his career. As one hears so frequently, "I've got too much invested to get out now."

Thus, the factors in our research equation are technological change, large-scale work organization, and career commitment. The problem is what happens to these career-committed organization men when the organizations in which they have invested too much to leave without serious career loss undergo major technological change? What are the coping techniques, and what are the outcomes for the individual and the organization?

CONCEPTUALIZATION OF THE PROBLEM

The considerable amount of writing in the field of management contains much background material for any such new study as this of the people who do the managing. However, the bulk of it concerns the characteristics of, the morale or job satisfactions of, or the development of such personnel, and, while useful as background, does not offer much specific guidance for the study of technological impact.

The conceptualization was drawn up in terms of the independent (change) variables, the dependent (career) variables, and certain intervening variables in the person through whom the change is filtered. The general nature of these categories will be summarized here, but the development of the items representing them in the Schedule will be described below, under "Research on the Problem."

The Independent Variables: Sources of Change.

"Technological change" usually brings to mind images of new products, automated machinery, or an improved method of manufacturing some product, due to a break-through in the physical or biological sciences. However, a broader meaning can and should be given to the phrase. In recent years the behavioral sciences have also begun to provide research results which have led to changes in work systems. The impact on industry and government of new supervisory styles, career development programs, customer and public relations techniques—all aimed at greater organizational effectiveness—are examples of such non-mechanical technological change. Accordingly, we have preferred to define *"technological change" in the more general sense of change which is precipitated by any type of scientific research and development and the engineering applications stemming from them, whether these concern materials, people or organizations.*

The Intervening Variables: Modifiers of Change.

It is, or course, to be expected that there would be differences in behavioral and attitudinal reactions to technological change among career executives and professionals even within the same status level of the same organization in response to the same objective condition of change. Not only did we wish to uncover and classify such differential response patterns, but also to account for them. Certainly among the important considerations are the intervening variables of the person, through whom the impact of the change is filtered.

One class of such intervening variables consists of such factual matters as age, length of work career, when one began working for his present organization, and the amount and type of his educational background. Another class concerns the person's "attitudinal sets," or what has sometimes been called "general life orientations." Two such attitudinal sets were required by the nature of the problem: the amount and type of commitment to the organization, and the person's general receptivity to change. However, we also wished to include one of the more basic orientations presently popular in the literature, and after much consideration, we chose the "inner-other directedness" syndromes first described in detail in *The Lonely Crowd* (9). These would appear not only to have substantial sociological roots but also substantial operational if not conceptual overlap with such competitors for selection as "achievement-affiliation motivation," "work-centered or person-centered orientation," "rugged individualistic or organization-centered orientation "

The Dependent Variables: Things Affected by Change.

The dependent variables are, of course, those factors regarding the per..on's career that have been affected by technological change. For our purposes we classified them as (a) *the person's career in general,* (b) *various aspects of his career,* (c) *the ways in which he attempted to cope with change, and* (d) *his reactions to his affected career status.* These categories of dependent variables will be described below under "The Third Year—Field Research Study."

RESEARCH DESIGN

The culmination of the project was a field survey of samples of managers and professionals in twelve large-scale industrial, govern mental, and military organizations The 35-page research schedule contained 142 items of information, and was returned by 3.970 respondents, or 65 per cent of those on the mailing lists, with an average loss of information per schedule of only 1 per cent. Thus, we have some 550,000 bits of information to process about the impact of change on careers.

Two years of work went into the development of this research schedule. The sequence of events was as follows:

The First Year—Reconnaissance.

The project began with the usual review of the literature to determine what had been done in the past and to obtain leads for what might be done in the future. This was a formidable task, not only because such topics as "Technological Change." "Careers," and "Large-Scale Organizations" are sizeable in themselves but also because the literature on them is scattered in many fields. Professional journals and unpublished dissertations were specially important sources, but it was soon apparent that there was more "talk about" this area of interest than "data."

A separate part of this review concerned a study of the relevant unpublished reports submitted by behavioral science contractors to the Air University Human Resources Research Institute during 1950-54. This resulted in an edited volume of selected items under the title "Studies in Organizational Effectiveness: Contributions to Military Sociology," which was published by the Air Force Office of Scientific Research (3). A second separate part of this review resulted in a master's degree thesis (7).

The Second Year—Development of the Research Design.

Toward the end of the first year it was apparent to the research team that a satisfactory research design would require more knowledge of the change situation than could be obtained from the literature. Thus it was decided to conduct intensive interviews with a number of managers and professionals in some large organization that had undergone considerable change. It was also deemed advisable to begin the search for instruments to measure some of the more complex intervening variables such as "commitment to the organization," "reaction to change," and "inner-other directedness." An opportunity to accomplish both—to interview in depth and to administer tests to executives and professionals—was provided by the Southern Bell Telephone Company through its middle management training program at the University. This was fortunate, for not only is the Bell System one of the nation's largest work organizations, but it has many parallels to such other large-scale organizations as the Air Force Moreover, the principal investigator's previous experience with the training of telephone executives gave him a special background for this organizational case study. The executives and professionals attending the "Athens Program" represented a cross-section of Southern Bell management at the middle levels.

The interview guide was shaped around four main questions: "The kinds of change you have experienced in your work since World War II"; "the impact of such changes on the work you were doing at the time"; "the impact of such changes on the careers of other people in the organization like yourself"; and "the impact of these changes on your own career." One hundred one-and-one-half-hour interviews were conducted, tape-recorded and transcribed.

At the same time existing research instruments to measure "reaction to change" and "inner-other directedness" were selected and tested for their usefulness to the objectives of the project. They were given to three groups: telephone executives, university students, and petroleum landmen, the last as part of a doctoral dissertation (6). On the basis of these results the research team decided to develop its own measures.

During the summer and fall of this second year the research team was concerned primarily with exploiting the interview data. The main job was to extract insights and codes from 3,000 pages of information on the above-mentioned four topics—to uncover the variety of effects that might result from technological change. This turned out to be a most exacting task, but one which paid off not only for the conceptualization of the dependent variables but for the independent variables as well.

The Third Year—The Field Research Study.

The first part of the year was devoted to designing the research schedule for the field study, and pre-testing it. The second part was spent on selecting the sample of organizations and respondents, conducting the field work, and processing the 3,970 returned schedules.

The research schedule is included at the end of this chapter. The reader will find there not only the final choices of items designed to represent the independent, intervening, and dependent variables, but also the detailed context of information about the project, including careful definition of terms, in which the items were set. Moreover, he will note that the study was explicitly stated in terms of basic research, an attempt to extend our knowledge rather than to improve personnel operations of any kind. This approach was also followed by the top managements of the organizations in explaining the project to their samples of managers and professionals. That this effort to involve the respondent in what he could put into the study, rather than what he or his organization would get out of it, did not constitute a "kiss of death" is indicated by the fact that despite the unfortunate timing of the study during the peak vacation months of July and August, 65 per cent of the respondents returned their schedules, with an average loss of information per schedule of only 1 per cent.

1. *Design of the independent variables.* We wished to know *what types* and *how much* change had affected the respondent's work. On the basis of the literature and from our own intensive interviews we decided to codify the types of change under three headings: *Material Technology* (product developments; automation; computerization; etc.); *Ways of Serving or Dealing with People* (new services for customers and the public; new supervisory programs; new personnel appraisal and development programs; new developments in customer relations, public relations, and union-management relations; etc.); *Growth of the Organization* (expanded volume of work; greater diversification of the organization's activities; increase in tempo of work; centralization or decentralization of operations; number and variety of employees; etc.). The first is, of course, that type derived from advances in the physical, biological, and engineering sciences; the second, in good part at least, from advances in the social or behavioral sciences. The third is probably a derivative of the other two rather than a primary type per se. However, we felt compelled to list it separately because of its prominence in the interviews and thus the possibility that respondents, not given the opportunity to select it, might actually be talking about it when they were checking one of the other two. In other words, if not listed separately, it might have been a contaminating factor.

In regard to the "how much change" question, there were two special problems. The first concerned the choice of restricting the stimulus situation to a period of time more or less comparable for all respondents or leaving it open to the different lengths of exposure to change due simply to length of work life. The decision was made in favor of the former, partly at least because it would also lay a more realistic requirement on the respondent's memory. Thus we finally stated the problem in terms of "the impact on your work during the past ten years." The second problem concerned the provision of some outside standard of comparison for judging how much "some" or "considerable" change really was. This is an old and tough problem in studies of this kind, and our attempts to handle it involved two types of items. First, we got respondent's judgment as to how much change had affected his work compared to each of two key reference groups (other people on your level in this organization, and other people your age you know in other organizations); and, second, we got him to rank, in degree of importance, this "change factor" in comparison with other factors, such as his ability, education, "contacts," health, family, luck, etc., which might have had some effect on his career in the organization.

2. *Design of the intervening variables.* The two problems were the selection of the factual items, such as age and education, and the development of instruments to measure the "basic life orientations" or "attitudinal sets." Since the instruments to measure two of the latter— "general receptivity of change" and "inner-other directedness"—had already been developed, only the instrument for "commitment to the organization" remained to be constructed.

The receptivity to change instrument will be found on page 253 of the Schedule. It includes a general self-rating item preceded by one requiring ratings on specific contacts with change, such as on the job, in one's family life, one's church life, etc. It was hoped that these specific ratings would serve to focus the respondents' attention more strongly on the change variable and thus increase the relevance and comparability of the general ratings.

The instrument for "inner-other directedness" is on pages 254-55 of the Schedule. This consists of seventeen pairs of statements, one of each pair being an inner-directed statement and the other, an other-directed one. The pool of statements out of which the pairs were made was taken from Herbert W. Gross's doctoral dissertation, "The Relationship Between Insecurity, Self-acceptance, Other-direction, and Conformity Under Conditions of Differential Social Pressure" (8). The statements in each pair were matched on the "social desirability" dimension to control the influence of that factor. The respondent had to choose one statement in each pair. His score is the summation of his inner-directed choices, and can range from 0 to 17. The actual distribution of the 3,970 respondents turned out to be a bell-shaped and almost normal curve (the mean of 9.5 indicating a slight skew to the inner-directed side).

The items regarding "commitment to the organization" are found on pages 251-52 of the Schedule. We decided to measure not only the amount of commitment, but also the type, that is, the relative inputs of "involvement" and "entrapment." A general self-rating item "how much do you feel committed to this organization as a place of work" contains five statements ranging in connotation from total commitment at one end to no commitment at the other. This was followed by an item regarding how important a part each of nine involvement and entrapment items played in that commitment. On the basis of this item we are able to classify respondents into four groups from "those claiming both high involvement and high entrapment" at one end, to "those claiming low involvement and low entrapment" at the other.

The selection of factual items appears on pages 247-49 of the Schedule. In addition to age and education the reader will find several items on *length* of work history (year of first full time job, year starting management or professional career, year starting to work for the organization) and several items on *type* of work history (management or professional, line or staff, operations or support). This selection was made after considerable consultation with middle and top management people in industry and government.

3. *Design of the dependent variables.* Most of the first part of this third year was devoted to constructing items to represent the dependent variables. The final choices appear on pages 232-46 of the Schedule. They are divided into two parts· first, the impact of change on the respondent's career in general, and, second, on some twenty important considerations in connection with his career

There were three main problems in designing the items. The first was to obtain useful measures of the respondent's success so far, and of the importance of various career considerations to him. The second was to obtain useful measures of the impact of change on his career and on those career considerations that were important to him. The third was to determine how the respondent had attempted to cope with change during his career. Each of these will be discussed in the following paragraphs.

Regarding the first—securing useful measures of career success— a number of them were built into the schedule, and one, performance ratings, was built into three of the samples as a stratification principle.* The first of the measures built into the schedule is a general self-rating: "In general how successful a career do you feel you have had in this organization up to now?—Very successful, fairly successful, not very successful." This is followed by items designed to pin such a rating down by providing some external reference points. This was done by obtaining the respondent's comparisons of his success with that of people in four key reference groups,** and with that of his original aspiration level. Through a combination of these judgments, we hoped to have an index of his career success that would seem to warrant more confidence than the single general item.

Two other means of pinning the career success variable down by some more objective evidence than general self-rating were also included. In our review of the literature we had come across a number of studies which purported to uncover a difference in behavior between more successful and less successful people. We assembled seven of these and made each into a seven-point rating scale, as shown on page 240 of the Schedule. By combining them into an index we have another measure of career success, perhaps more objective than those above, and more comparable from one respondent to another. The final attempt to provide such "objective" evidence through self-reporting appears on page 241 of the Schedule. The respondent is asked to rate his present position, as compared with the other positions he has held in the organization, with reference to five key career considerations: salary, responsibility, authority, opportunity to use knowledge and abilities, and real satisfaction. The hypothesis was that those whose current jobs provided less of these than their previous jobs might judge their careers to be less successful than those who were in positions that provided more (It may be of interest here that whereas over 90 per cent of the 3,970 respondents said they were in positions that provided more salary than they had ever received before, only 60 per cent said that about "authority" or "real satisfaction.")

The design of a list of key career factors or considerations constituted a special task. The literature contains a number of lists of

---

*For most organizations the providing of performance ratings would have been a considerable task and hence was not urged. Cooperation was received, however, from two industrial and one military organization. This provides a comparison of internal with external evidence in three of the samples, even though there is no evidence that the external evidence (performance ratings) is of superior reliability or validity.

**Managers and professionals with comparable length of service in this organization; persons at my level in this organization; my friends from school or college days; my friends and acquaintances in other organizations.

so-called job factors and these were studied intensively for commonalities. Also reference was made to the project's file of intensive interviews. From these sources five categories of "career considerations," as they are called here, were identified. These are: self-actualization considerations, autonomy considerations, status considerations, associational considerations, and security considerations. A number of specific items were selected for each category, the total numbering twenty. This list appears in Part III of the Schedule.

Regarding the second design problem—the construction of items concerning the impact of change on the respondent's career—the final selection appears on pages 235-36 and 245-46 of the Schedule. Included is a general over-all rating of the impact of change on careers from "advanced it considerably" to "retarded it considerably"; separate ratings of the impact of each of the three types of change on careers; and a rating of the relative importance of change as a career factor compared with such other factors as education, family, or luck. Included also are two sets of items which attempt to explore the impact of change on the twenty career considerations. In the first set, the respondent is asked to indicate, for each of the twenty, whether it is important or not to him in his work, and, if it is, whether he has enough of it in his present job or would like more. In the second set, the respondent's choices in each case are whether there is more or less of it in his job now as compared to five years ago, and, if more, whether he judges this to be due to change or to other factors.

Regarding the third design problem—the construction of items concerning coping with change—the final selection is on pages 237 and 238 of the Schedule. These items were developed almost entirely from the interview materials, whose hundreds of statements regarding the handling of change seemed to be classifiable into two dimensions: "techniques" on the one hand, and "agents" on the other. Each statement seemed to represent either a mastering technique, or opposing technique, or avoiding technique. Also, each seemed to be something the person did through his own efforts, or something he did through others or through the organization. This conceptualization provided six "technique-agent" combinations for handling change, from "mastering change through one's own efforts" at one extreme to "avoiding change through the manipulation of others" at the other. Four examples of each combination were selected, making a set of twenty-four items. For each item the respondent was asked to judge how much it had enabled him to cope with change ("little if any," "some," or "a great deal"). Scores can be computed for each of the three "techniques" and two "agents," and indexes based on these scores can be constructed. In addition, the Schedule contains two general items regarding "coping with change." In one, the respondent is asked his judgment as to how successfully he has coped with change up till now; in the other, he is asked how confident he is about coping with change in the future. Thus we can, by relating the "technique-agent" data to these feelings about coping success, learn something more about the process of handling the impact of change on careers.

4. *The selection of organizations and respondents.* Since there is no recognized method of selecting a sample of large organizations that has validity for this type of study, we were on our own. Our decision was to select examples from each of three categories: industry and business, the federal government, and the military services. Originally we also thought it might be useful to sub-stratify these types of organizations by amount of change that they had experienced since World War II. Thus ideally we would have a selection of fast-changing organizations and slow-changing organizations in each of the three categories. This proved too difficult to carry out in practice, partly because it is hard to get agreement about which should be considered slow-moving, and partly because the organizations that we considered in that category seemed less receptive to the idea of being part of the study. Thus we have had to depend on evidence concerning change obtained from the respondents for the most part, although some organizations stratified their own samples in terms of change by selecting part of them from divisions that had undergone considerable technological change and part from ones that had not.

Another factor in selecting the organizations concerned our estimate of how amenable they would be to participation in such a study. It occurred to us that organizations that had an installation in Georgia might be more cooperative than those that did not. Hence the final selection of organizations within each category was determined in good part by this factor, although in only three cases out of twelve were the samples primarily located in the Georgia installations. Lockheed and Westinghouse had plants in Marietta and Athens, Southern Bell's headquarters was in Atlanta, and the Citizens and Southern Bank had branches throughout the State.* The military organizations were located at Robins Air Force Base, Hunter Air Force Base, and nearby Maxwell Air Force Base, although the Continental Air Command sample covered its nation-wide organization.** However, in the case of

---

*The Lockheed and C&S Bank samples were entirely in the state; those for Westinghouse and Southern Bell were chiefly outside the state.

**The military organizations were Air University, the Continental Air Command, Warner-Robins Air Materiel Area, and two Strategic Air Command squadrons.

the federal government sample, the active interest in the study of Mr. John Macy, Chairman of the Civil Service Commission, reduced the importance of the Georgia tie. His staff gave assistance not only in selecting the agencies for the sample but also in validating the project to their top managements.*

The populations to be sampled in each of these twelve organizations were restricted to middle management, defined as GS-11 through 15 for the Federal Civil Service, Captain through Colonel for the Air Force, and equivalent levels for industrial managers and professionals. The organizations were urged to further restrict these populations to persons who had at least five years of service in them. The populations were then stratified into supervisors and non-supervisors (which was the closest we could come to the distinction between managers and professionals), although it turned out that six of the organizations claimed to have only supervisors at this middle management level. Other stratification principles such as performance ratings, length of service and as mentioned above, slow- and fast-changing parts of the organization, were applied by one or more of the organizations, permitting us to explore relationships not otherwise possible.

Numerically the objective was to obtain samples of five hundred from each organization: 250 managers and 250 professionals. In six of the twelve organizations this goal was approximated. Within each cell of the sampling table the respondents were chosen by a random process whenever there were more names than the sample called for. The total sample numbered 6,096 of which 66 per cent were classified as supervisors due to the fact that six of the organizations, as mentioned above, claimed to have no non-supervisors at this middle management level. The returns numbered 3,970, or 65 per cent of those mailed out the proportion varying by organization from 51 to 86 per cent. This wide range was found in each of the three categories of organizations.

REPORTING OF THE DATA

The information on the 3,970 returns was processed and punched on two IBM cards per respondent. Three series of tabulations have so far been run on the IBM 1401 computer. The first consists of tabulations of each item by type of organization, by organization, and by the supervisor-non-supervisor classification. The second explores, for the total sample, relationships among the independent and dependent variables, holding one intervening variable constant at a time. The

---

*The federal samples were parts of the National Aeronautics and Space Administration, the Federal Aviation Agency, the Internal Revenue Service, and the Bureau of Old Age and Survivor's Insurance.

third involves the exploration of special relationships in various seg-ments of the sample, based on findings from the first and second sets. Reports on the first set of tabulations are now being prepared as feedback to the participating organizations. Technical reports to the professions on both substantive and methodological findings are also in process.

BIBLIOGRAPHY

1. Alewine, Jimmie Ray. *An Empirical Investigation of Some Hypo-theses Taken from "The Lonely Crowd."* M. A. Thesis, Univer-sity of Georgia, 1962

2. Bowers, Raymond V. "Lessons from Two ARDC Opinion Surveys, with additional data from a study of career managers and pro-fessionals in twelve industrial, governmental and military organi-zations," a paper presented to the Air Force In-House Laboratory Symposium sponsored by the Directorate of Civilian Personnel, Headquarters USAF, and the Air Force Office of Scientific Re-search, 6-7 August 1963

3. _____ _____ et al. *Studies in Organizational Effectiveness (Con-tributions to Military Sociology).* Air Force Office of Scientific Re-search, Washington, D. C., 1962

4. _____ _____ ,Brown, R. G., and Bryant, C. D. *Reactions to Change: An Informal Report on the Southern Bell District Division Management Development Conference, 1960-61.* University of Georgia, 1962

5. _____ _____ , Brown, Robert G., and Bryant, Clifton D. "Techno-logical Change and the Organization Man: Preliminary Conceptu-alization of a Research Project," *Sociological Inquiry,* XXXII (Winter, 1962), 117-127

6. Bryant, Clifton D. *Petroleum Landman A Sociological Analysis of an Occupation.* Ph.D. dissertation, Louisiana State University, 1963

7. Greenspon, Stanley P. *The Impact of Technological Change on the Structure and Function of Large-Scale Organizations.* M. A. Thesis, University of Georgia, 1961

8. Gross, Herbert W. *The Relationship Between Insecurity, Self-Acceptance, Other-Direction, and Conformity Under Conditions of Differential Social Pressure.* Ph. D. dissertation, University of Buf-falo, 1959

9. Riesman, David, Glazer, Nathan, and Denney, Reuel. *The Lonely Crowd. A Study of the Changing American Character.* New Haven: Yale University Press, 1950

A Confidential Research Schedule

whose Purpose is to Provide Data

to Extend Our Knowledge

of the Impact of Change on Careers

———————

Supported by a grant from the
Air Force Office of Scientific Research
(Contract AF 49(638)-804)

Social Science Research Institute

The University of Georgia

Athens, Georgia

THE UNIVERSITY OF GEORGIA
SOCIAL SCIENCE RESEARCH INSTITUTE
ATHENS, GEORGIA

OFFICE OF THE
DIRECTOR

Request from the research staff:

We need your help. This is Phase II of a
long-range study of management and professional
careers under the impact of change. Two years
of research lie behind the items assembled in
this document. The answers to them provided by
you and others in the sample will enable us to
test a number of hypotheses, clarify some hunches
and pin-point promising avenues for further study.

The level of confidence we can have in these
results will, however, depend upon the completeness of the returns. Your willingness to
participate in this basic research venture will
be greatly appreciated. Rather full explanation
of what we are trying to do appears at various
points below, beginning on the next page.

Raymond V. Bowers

RAYMOND V. BOWERS, Project Director
Robert G. Brown, Research Associate
Clifton D. Bryant, Research Associate

July, 1962

Although considerable attention has been paid to the effect of technological change on the employment of "blue collar" level workers in military, industrial and other large-scale organizations, relatively little is known in any systematic way about the effect of such change on the careers of the managers and professionals who are responsible for running these organizations technically and administratively.

Yet as the tempo of technological change increases, and as the commitment to careers in such large-scale organizations continues to grow, the effectiveness of the organizations will depend to an increasing degree on an understanding of how these key personnel adjust to change, and what happens to them, their careers and their organizations when they fail to adjust.

As social scientists interested in the human factor in industry and other large-scale organizations we have long been puzzled by this gap in our knowledge and began two years ago to try to do something about it. Basic research funds from the Air Force Office of Scientific Research, along with support from the University of Georgia, enabled us to carry out Phase I of the plan and is enabling us to pursue the current Phase II.

Phase I included a review of the research literature for hypotheses or other leads regarding the subject. In addition, we spent a considerable part of the past year conducting and tape recording intensive exploratory interviews with industrial managers, and on detailed analyses of the transcripts. From these Phase I efforts has come this research schedule for Phase II.

This is a basic research project. The main objective is to extend our knowledge in this area of human behavior. However, any success we have should also find uses in the career development and career management programs of our large employers of managerial and professional talent.

This is a "field study". The data cannot be collected in a laboratory or in a library. They must be obtained "live"--at first hand--from a sample of the people like yourself who have had the experience we wish to study.

We would prefer to come to your office or home to ask these questions in person, but this is impossibly expensive. The alternative is to mail the questions to you, hoping that the instructions will be an adequate guide for your participation.

TWO POINTS ABOUT YOUR PARTICIPATION

Your participation will be completely anonymous. There is no code anywhere in this booklet to tie your answers to you.

Your participation will also be strictly confidential. The schedules will remain in the Project's files and no one will have access to them except the research staff. We are interested simply in transferring the information you give us to IBM punch cards so that it can be pooled with that coming from others.

There will be no feed-back to your organization concerning individual schedules. We are interested in statistics not individuals, and our statistical findings will be available to one and all.

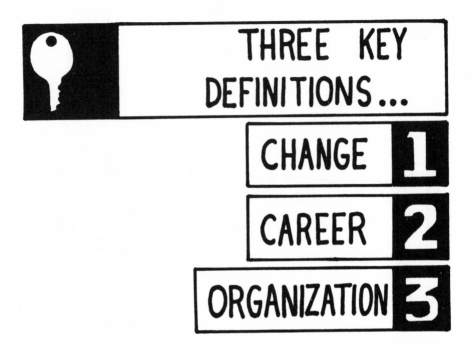

In order to tabulate your answers with those of others we must all have the same thing in mind when we refer to "change", "career", or "organization". We shall define "organization" here, and shall define "change" and "career" at the beginning of Parts I and II.

What we mean and don't mean by "Organization":

When we say "your organization" or "the organization for which you work" we mean the company, agency, or military service that employs you and to which you presumably have some career identification. You might ordinarily think of this in terms of the large organization itself: "the Air Force", "Westinghouse", "the telephone company", or "the Treasury Department". Or you might think of it in terms of some such major segment as "the Strategic Air Command", "the Internal Revenue Service" or "Georgia Lockheed". Either is all right. What we don't want is for you to think in terms of the small unit to which you may be currently assigned--as for example "the engineering section" or "personnel branch".

YOUR CONTACT WITH CHANGE IN YOUR WORK | PART ONE

What we mean by "Change": ┌─────────────────────────────┐
│ This is the crux of the matter. │
└─────────────────────────────┘

When we use the word "change" in the following pages we are using it as short-hand for both "technological change" and the "growth" in volume and variety of business that may have accompanied such changes in your organization. By techno-logical change we mean any change that stems from advances in knowledge in some area of science and technology.

From our studies of change in organizations such as yours we have come to the conclusion that there are two main varieties so far as their effect on jobs and careers are concerned:

A. Changes growing out of advances in the physical sciences and mathe-matics: new product developments; automation; computerization, and other similar <u>Changes in the Organization's Material Technology</u>.

B. Changes growing out of advances in our knowledge of human behavior: new developments in supervision, personnel appraisal, and career development; new approaches to customer and public relations; innovations in the services produced by the organization, and other similar <u>Changes in the Organization's Ways of Serving or Dealing with People</u>.

Thus, whenever you read "change", we shall be asking about your contacts with changes in both the material and human environments of your work -- and with changes in the sheer growth of the job the organization is doing.

CHANGE:

But before you proceed to the questions themselves you might find the task easier and more interesting if you stop for a moment and recapitulate your contacts with changes in each of the three categories during the past 10 years:

> Material Technology (product developments; automation; computerization; etc.)
>
> Ways of Serving and Dealing with People (new services for customers and the public; new supervisory programs; new personnel appraisal and development programs; new developments in customer relations, public relations, and union-management relations; etc.)
>
> Growth of the Organization (expanded volume of work; greater diversification of the organization's activities; increase in tempo of work; centralization or decentralization of operations; number and variety of employees; etc.)

In the following items we are attempting to get your estimate of your experience in this regard.

1. Of the three broad varieties of change we are dealing with, how would you rank them in terms of their impact on your work within the past 10 years? (Please answer by writing "most", "second", or "least" in the blanks in front of the types of change.)

(Do not write in this blank)

(7) _____

_____(1) Material technology

_____(2) Ways of serving or dealing with people

_____(3) Growth of the organization

2. How much have such changes affected your work within this 10 year period? (Check only one of the following)

(8)
(1) _____ little if any
(2) _____ some
(3) _____ considerable

3. How much have such changes affected your work within this period as compared with other people on your level in this organization? (Check only one of the following)

(9)
(1) _____ less than most
(2) _____ more than most

4. How much have such changes affected your work as compared with other people your age you know in other organizations? (Check only one of the following)

less than most _____(1)	(10)
more than most _____(2)	

5. If you could turn the clock back and were able to determine the amount and rate of such changes that would affect your work, what would you say?

    a. (1) I would want: (Check only one of the following)

much more change _____(1)	
somewhat more change _____(2)	(11)
somewhat less change _____(3)	
much less change _____(4)	

       (2) Why do you say this? (Write your answer in the _____ (12-13)
space below)   (Do not write in this blank)

    b. (1) I would want the changes to come at a: (Check only one of the following)

much slower rate _____(1)	
somewhat slower rate _____(2)	(14)
somewhat faster rate _____(3)	
much faster rate _____(4)	

       (2) Why do you say this? (Write your answer in the _____ (15-16)
space below)   (Do not write in this blank)

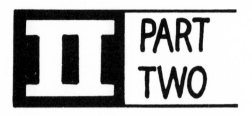

What we mean by "Career".

    When we refer to your "career" we mean your work or occupational career. You may think of yourself as having other careers such as one in community affairs, in lodge work or as a husband and father, but we are narrowing the focus to your "making a living" career. In addition, "career" here usually refers to your work history since you came into the organization for which you are now working. However, the context will always be clearly specified. We shall say "your career in this organization" or something like "your career so far".

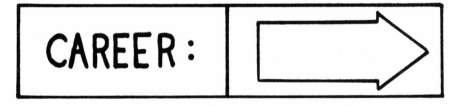

THE IMPACT OF CHANGE ON YOUR CAREER

In Part I above we explored your contacts with change. Now we would like to get your estimates of the impact of this change on your career. There are several aspects of this impact that we need to have information on. They are:

- How you feel about your career in this organization
- Your estimate of the impact of change on your career
- Your ways of handling the impact of change on your career
- Your reasons for your current career status
- Ratings on certain aspects of work behavior
- Your rating of your present position

1. How You Feel About Your Career in This Organization.

Each of us has some impression of how well he has done so far in his work career, and some estimate of what probably lies ahead for him. We need this information from you about your career.

a. In general how successful a career do you feel you have had in this organization up to now? (Check only one of the following)

Very successful _____ (1)	
Fairly successful _____ (2)	(17)
Not very successful _____ (3)	

b. How would you estimate your career progress to date in comparison with the aspirations you had at the start of your career in this organization? (Check only one of the following)

My career has been more successful than I expected it to be _____ (1)	
My career has been about as successful as I expected it to be _____ (2)	(18)
My career has been somewhat less successful than I expected it to be _____ (3)	
I had no specific career aspirations when I started to work for this organization _____ (4)	

c. How successful do you feel you have been in your career so far as compared to those specified in the left hand column? Would you say you have been more, about equally, or less successful? (Circle only one number on each line)

In comparison with ↓	I have been →	Much more successful	Somewhat more successful	About equally successful	Somewhat less successful	Much less successful
(19)	Managers or professionals with comparable length of service in the organization for which I work	5	4	3	2	1
(20)	Managers or professionals at my level in the organization for which I work	5	4	3	2	1
(21)	My friends from school or college days	5	4	3	2	1
(22)	My friends and acquaintances in other organizations	5	4	3	2	1

(23-24) ‾‾‾‾‾‾
(Do not write in this blank)

d. How would you estimate your career progress in this organization from now on? (Check only one of the following)

(25)	(1) _____	I'll progress faster than the average person in my position
	(2) _____	I'll progress about the same as the average person in my position
	(3) _____	I'll probably stay at my present level
	(4) _____	I may have trouble staying at my present level

2. <u>Your Estimate of the Impact of Change on Your Career</u>.

   The primary objective of this research, we have said, is to find out more
about the impact of change on careers like yours. We defined <u>change</u> as the
introduction of changes in the organization's material technology (new products,
automation, etc.), changes in the organization's ways of serving or dealing with
people (employees, customers, public, etc.), and the growth of the organization.

   a. In general, what effect do you estimate such changes have had on your
       career in this organization? (<u>Check only one of the following</u>)

       ```
       little, if any (or none) _____(1)
         advanced my career some _____(2)
          retarded my career some _____(3)       (26)
      advanced my career considerably _____(4)
      retarded my career considerably _____(5)
       ```

       NOTE: If you checked "little, if any (or none)"
              please skip to question b.

              If you checked a "some" or "considerably"
              choice please answer parts (1), (2) and (3) below.

   (1) How much effect do you think that each of the three main types of
        change have had on your career in this organization? (<u>Circle only
        one number on each line</u>)

Type of Change	Effect on Your Career		
	Consid-erable	Some	Little if any (or none)
Material Technology (product development; automation; computerization; etc.)	3	2	1	(27)
Ways of Serving or Dealing with People (new services for customers and the public; new supervisory programs; new personnel appraisal and development programs; new developments in customer relations, public relations, and union-management relations; etc.)	3	2	1	(28)
Growth of the Organization (expanded volume of work; greater diversification; increase in work tempo; centralization or decentralization; number and variety or employees; etc.)	3	2	1	(29)

(2) With reference to the changes that your organization has introduced,
or is introducing, that have affected your career, where do you believe you stand today? (Check only one of the following)

(30)
(1)	_____	I believe I'm keeping up very well with them
(2)	_____	I'm keeping up with them well enough for all practical purposes
(3)	_____	I've had a good bit of trouble keeping up with them
(4)	_____	I've pretty much given up trying to keep up with them

(3) Where would you rank, in degree of importance, this "change" factor
in comparison with all the other factors (such as your ability,
education, contacts, health, family, luck, etc.) which may have had
some effect on your career in this organization? (Check only one
of the following)

(31)
(1)	_____	Such "change" has been the most important influence
(2)	_____	Very important but probably not the most important
(3)	_____	Of some importance but less than many other factors
(4)	_____	Of little or no importance

b. As you look ahead to the future, how confident are you about keeping up
with changes in your organization that may affect your career?

(32)
(1)	_____	Very confident
(2)	_____	Fairly confident
(3)	_____	Not very confident

(1) What are you two main reasons for saying this? (Mark them 1 and 2.)

(33-34)
(1)	_____	Education
(2)	_____	Experience
(3)	_____	Age
(4)	_____	Interest
(5)	_____	Health
(6)	_____	Other (Please specify) _____

3. Your Ways of Handling the Impact of Change on Your Career.

   On the basis of a large number of interviews with middle management and professional people who had undergone or were undergoing considerable adjustment to changes introduced into their organizations, we have drawn up a list of ways used by them in their attempts to handle the changes. These are included in the left hand column. You are asked to indicate in each case (by circling one of the numbers) whether you recognize it as one of the ways that enabled you to cope with change, and to what extent.

Ways of Handling Changes in the Work Situation	Enabled you to cope with change		
	Little if any (or none)	Some	A great deal
Previous work experience	1	2	3
Put in long hours on the job	1	2	3
Took a lower position less affected by change	1	2	3
Made a point of getting information to use against the change	1	2	3
Educational background	1	2	3
Decided to get out of the 'rat race' by transfering to a position not likely to be affected by the change	1	2	3
Defended established methods as tried and proven	1	2	3
Banded together with others who were worried about change, to help one another out	1	2	3
Got others to take responsibility for implementing the change; concentrated on other parts of the job	1	2	3
Took retraining provided by the organization	1	2	3
Just plain refused to go along with the changes for awhile at least	1	2	3
Developed new interests outside of work	1	2	3
Managed to get competent subordinates who could handle the change	1	2	3

Ways of Handling Changes in the Work Situation	Enabled you to cope with change		
	Little if any (or none)	Some	A great deal
Contemplated a job in another organization	1	2	3
Saw the changes coming and got set ahead of time	1	2	3
Used knowledge of 'how to get things done around here' to get the change introduced elsewhere first	1	2	3
Depended more on the boss than usual to give help and advice	1	2	3
Contemplated early retirement	1	2	3
Repeatedly aired complaints about the change, thus managing to slow it down	1	2	3
Got together with others to request postponement of the changes until more could be learned about them	1	2	3
Passively resisted change--attitude was "to heck with it"	1	2	3
Managed to get into a position that was not likely to be affected by the change for a while, but where a valuable contribution to the organization could be made	1	2	3
Expressed resentment at being pushed hard to accept the changes	1	2	3
Convinced superiors that the change should be put off and, thus gained time for meeting it	1	2	3

(35)
(36)   _____   (Do not write
(37)   _____   in these blanks)
(38)   _____
(39)   _____

(Do not write
in these spaces)

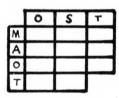

	O	S	T
M			
A			
O			
T			

4. Your Reasons for Your Current Career Status.

There are various reasons to account for the level of success that people reach in life and below are some of the major ones that "white collar career people" find relevant to their situation. Please consider each in terms of how important a part it has played in attaining your present career status and circle the number (1, 2 or 3) representing that degree of importance.

Reasons	An important reason	A minor reason	Not a reason in my case
(1) The good breaks I got--being in the right place at the right time, having good bosses, etc.	3	2	1
(2) Support my family gave me	3	2	1
(3) My own deficiencies in education and perhaps other qualities	3	2	1
(4) The hard work and extra effort I have put in all the way along	3	2	1
(5) My declining health	3	2	1
(6) The tough breaks I got--being in the wrong place at the wrong time, having a bad boss, etc.	3	2	1
(7) My own capabilities, talents, education, etc.	3	2	1
(8) Special family considerations which tied me down	3	2	1

(If you have circled more than one 3 please go back and draw a second circle around the one that you believe is the most important.)

(Do not write
in these spaces)

	S	N	T
C			
B			
T			

(Do not write
in these blanks) _____ (40)
_____ (41)
_____ (42)
_____ (43)
_____ (44)

5. Rating on Certain Aspects of Work Behavior.

    Below are some brief descriptions of certain types of work behavior. They are arranged in scales which have opposite ways of behaving at each end. We are interested in having you rate yourself on each of these scales by circling the number (from 1 to 7) which best describes your behavior.

		1	2	3	4	5	6	7

(45)   a.   Major interests are in the job; almost all energies devoted to participating in organizational tasks and activities.   Finds frequent excuses for being away from the office to pursue such interests as family, hobbies, community affairs and organizations.

               1   2   3   4   5   6   7

(46)   b.   Mainly reminisces about past achievements and contributions to the organization.   Is good at anticipating what lies ahead and making plans for the future.

               1   2   3   4   5   6   7

(47)   c.   Prefers to associate with superiors much more than with subordinates.   Prefers to associate with subordinates much more than with superiors.

               1   2   3   4   5   6   7

(48)   d.   Is usually found right "in the middle" of what's going on in the organization.   Is definitely "off to one side" of the organization's major activities.

               1   2   3   4   5   6   7

(49)   e.   Tends to be highly critical of things and people; tearing down rather than building up.   Always trying to build up and increase their performance and satisfaction.

               1   2   3   4   5   6   7

(50)   f.   Very dependent on others; always bands together with others to get help or to solve problems.   Very self-assured and independent; doesn't mind going it alone if necessary.

               1   2   3   4   5   6   7

(51)   g.   About as hard a worker as there is in the organization.   Gets by with as little effort as possible; never seems to be around when there's work to be done.

6. Your Rating of Your Present Position.

How would you rate your present position in terms of others you have held during your career in this organization? (Circle only one number on each line)

	My Present Position Provides:			
	More of this than any other position I have held	2nd most	3rd most	4th most
Salary	1	2	3	4	(52)
Responsibility	1	2	3	4	(53)
Authority	1	2	3	4	(54)
Use of my knowledge, abilities and experience	1	2	3	4	(55)
Real satisfaction	1	2	3	4	(56)

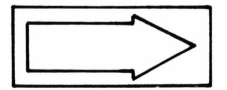

HOW HAS CHANGE AFFECTED VARIOUS CAREER CONSIDERATIONS

PART THREE III

So far we have been concerned entirely with the impact of change on your career as a whole, although we know that careers involve many considerations. These extend all the way from salary and job security to relations with people, opportunity to use one's abilities, and the challenge of the job. Moreover, people don't all want the same combination of satisfactions in their careers, and it seems likely that change would affect some of these career considerations more than others.

We have spent a great deal of time designing the following two questions to get at these matters. The list of twenty career considerations is a consolidation of a dozen or more lists found in the research literature, as well as some growing out of our own research. We believe it meets the logical standards of mutual exclusion and completeness as well as any short list of this kind can.

The responses that we are asking you to make regarding them are complex, but extremely crucial to the project. In the first question we want to know how important each career consideration is to you and how satisfactory an amount of it you feel you have in your present job. In the second question we need to know whether you have more or less of each in your job than you had five years ago and whether you believe this variation is due mainly to changes introduced into the organization or to other factors.

1. Listed below are a number of considerations that people frequently mention in
    connection with their careers. You are asked to judge in each case whether
    it is important or not to you. If it is not important, circle 1. If you
    judge it to be important, then decide between 2 and 3.

Career Considerations	Not important to me in my work	Important to me in my work and	
		I would like more of it in my present job	I have enough of it in my present job
Having an opportunity for personal growth and development	1	2	3	(57)
Having some say in the setting of goals for my job	1	2	3	(58)
A sense of security in my job	1	2	3	(59)
Being with people who are congenial to work with	1	2	3	(60)
Having a job which is respected and considered important by others in my organization	1	2	3	(61)
Having an opportunity to use my knowledge, skills and abilities	1	2	3	(62)
Having some say in selecting my assignments	1	2	3	(63)
My salary	1	2	3	(64)
Having people around me who can rely upon me for friendly and sympathetic understanding of the problems of their job and assistance and advice from me	1	2	3	(65)
Having some say in the way in which I accomplish my work in terms of methods, procedures, routine and pace	1	2	3	(66)
Having an opportunity to undertake interesting and challenging tasks which have variety	1	2	3	(67)

Career Considerations	Not important to me in my work	Important to me in my work and	
		I would like more of it in my present job	I have enough of it in my present job
(68) Having understanding people around me who are sympathetic to the problems of my job and upon whom I can rely for assistance and advice when I am in need of them	1	2	3
(69) Knowing pretty much what to expect in my job day after day: few surprises	1	2	3
(70) Having a job which is respected and considered important by people outside the organization	1	2	3
(71) The amount of responsibility my job carries	1	2	3
(72) Having a job in which it is possible to advance and move ahead	1	2	3
(73) Having an opportunity to make valuable contributions	1	2	3
(74) The amount of authority I have to accomplish the goals of my job	1	2	3
(75) Having a job in which tasks can be satisfactorily completed	1	2	3
(76) Being respected and having my abilities and accomplishments recognized by those with whom I work	1	2	3

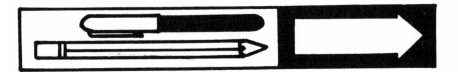

2. Listed below are the same career considerations which were presented in the previous question. This time you are asked to decide first if you now have "less", or "about the same", or "more" of each in your work than you had 5 years ago, and, if you say "more", whether or not this is due mainly to changes introduced into the organization or to other factors. (If you believe you have "less" or "about the same" circle either 1 or 2. If you believe you have "more", then choose between 3 and 4.

Career Considerations	Less of this in my work than 5 years ago	About the same amount of this in my work as 5 years ago	More of this in my work than 5 years ago	
			Due mainly to changes introduced into the organization	Due mainly to other factors
Having an opportunity for personal growth and development	1	2	3	4	(7)
Having some say in the setting of goals for my job	1	2	3	4	(8)
A sense of security in my job	1	2	3	4	(9)
Being with people who are congenial to work with	1	2	3	4	(10)
Having a job which is respected and considered important by others in my organization	1	2	3	4	(11)
Having an opportunity to use my knowledge, skills and abilities	1	2	3	4	(12)
Having some say in selecting my assignments	1	2	3	4	(13)
My salary	1	2	3	4	(14)
Having people around me who can rely upon me for friendly and sympathetic understanding of the problems of their job and assistance and advice from me	1	2	3	4	(15)

Career Considerations	Less of this in my work than 5 years ago	About the same amount of this in my work as 5 years ago	More of this in my work than 5 years ago	
			Due mainly to changes introduced into the organization	Due mainly to other factors
(16) Having some say in the way in which I accomplish my work in terms of methods, procedures, routine and pace	1	2	3	4
(17) Having an opportunity to undertake interesting and challenging tasks which have variety	1	2	3	4
(18) Having understanding people around me who are sympathetic to the problems of my job and upon whom I can rely for assistance and advice when you are in need of them	1	2	3	4
(19) Knowing pretty much what to expect in my job day after day; few surprises	1	2	3	4
(20) Having a job which is respected and considered important by people outside the organization	1	2	3	4
(21) The amount of responsibility my job carries	1	2	3	4
(22) Having a job in which it is possible to advance and move ahead	1	2	3	4
(23) Having an opportunity to make valuable contributions	1	2	3	4
(24) The amount of authority I have to accomplish the goals of my job	1	2	3	4
(25) Having a job in which tasks can be satisfactorily completed	1	2	3	4
(26) Being respected and having my abilities and accomplishments recognized by those with whom I work	1	2	3	4

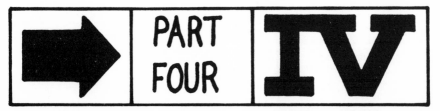

PART FOUR IV
SOME ITEMS ABOUT YOUR BACKGROUND

In all studies of human behavior for which we get the data directly from individuals, such as we are doing here, it is a necessary and standard practice to collect some items about the background of the individual. These are used for statistical control purposes so that "apples are not compared to oranges", so to speak. We have a special reason for including each item.

---

1. In what year were you born?   _____ (27-28)

2. How far did you go in school? (Check only one of the following)

> High school or specialized training _____ (1)
> Some college work but less than a bachelor's degree _____ (2)   (29)
> Bachelor's degree or equivalent _____ (3)
> Work beyond the bachelor's level _____ (4)

3. If you attended college, in which one of the following fields did you take the most work? (Check only one of the following)

> Business administration; economics _____ (1)
> Natural sciences; mathematics _____ (2)
> Humanities; social sciences _____ (3)   (30)
> Engineering _____ (4)
> Other (please specify) _____ _____ (5)

4. How much time do you put in on hobbies now as compared to two or three years ago? (Check only one of the following)

> Much more _____ (1)
> Somewhat more _____ (2)   (31)
> Somewhat less _____ (3)
> Much less _____ (4)

5. How active are you in community organizations now as compared to two or
    three years ago? (Check only one of the following)

(32)
> (1) _____ Much more
> (2) _____ Somewhat more
> (3) _____ Somewhat less
> (4) _____ Much less

(33-34) 6. _____ In what year did you hold your first full time job? (Please exclude
            military service unless you are now on extended active duty)

(35-36)   _____ In what year did you begin your management or professional career?

(37-38)   _____ In what year did you start working for this organization?

(39-40)   _____ In what year did you receive your last promotion?

7. Do you think of yourself as having a management career or a professional
    career?

(41)
> (1) _____ Primarily a management career
> (2) _____ Primarily a professional career

8. Which of the following describes most closely the types of positions you
    have held in your organization during the past 10 years? (Check only one
    of the following)

(42)
> (1) _____ I have been in line positions all of this time
> (2) _____ I have been in line positions most of this time
> (3) _____ I have been in staff positions most of this time
> (4) _____ I have been in staff positions all of this time
> (5) _____ I have spent about equal time in line and staff positions

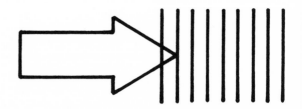

9. What part of the organization have you been primarily working in during the
    past 5 years?

> Operations (the parts of the organization
>   responsible for the products
>   or services the organization
>   is in business to produce) _____ (1)
>
> Support services (e.g. purchasing, personnel,   (43)
>   (Supply budgeting, management
>   services, etc.) _____ (2)

10. Is your present job defined by the organization for which you work as a
    supervisory one?

> Yes _____ (1)
> No _____ (2)   (44)

11. What is your present level in the organization? (Answer only (a), (b)
    or (c))

a. If you are in the Civil Service	b. If you are in the military	c. If you are in business or industry (Please write it in)	(45) (Do not write in this blank)
GS 11 _____	Capt. _____	_____	
12 _____	Major _____	_____	
13 _____	Lt. Col. _____	_____	
14 _____	Col. _____		
15 _____			

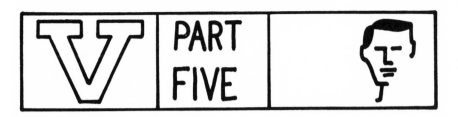

SOME ITEMS CONCERNING PERSONAL ORIENTATIONS

It is reasonable to suppose that people's reactions to change are affected, to some extent at least, by certain of their basic attitudes and orientations. We have selected three of these for use here: commitment to the organization for which you work; general reaction to change; and general life orientation. Measures of these will be obtained from the following three items.

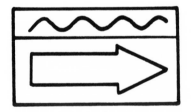

1. One of the factors about belonging to any organization is the strength of
   the ties that bind us to it. Moreover, in every organization some members
   are more committed to it than others, and some have different reasons for
   feeling committed to it than others. Work organizations are no exception.
   Hence, we are interested in determining how much, and in what way, each
   person answering this research schedule feels tied to the organization for
   which he works. The following questions attempt to get at this.

   a. How much do you feel committed to this organization as a place to work?
      (Please circle one of the numbers below)

1	2	3	4	5	(46)
I'm so committed to it that I don't think I would even talk to other employers about working for them. There is little doubt at all but that I will be here until retirement.	I am more committed to it than the average person at my level. It would take a very good offer indeed to interest me in moving	I have the average amount of commitment to it for a person in my position. I certainly would not leave except for a better job.	I am less committed to it than the average person at my level. I think I would leave if an equivalent job came along.	I have no commitment to it. In fact I'd probably leave tomorrow even at ε reduction in salary.	

b. If you circled 1, 2 or 3 in the preceding question, how would you rate
   the following factors as influences tieing you to this organization
   as a place to work? (Please circle one of the numbers on each line.)

		Quite Important	Of some Importance	Of little or no Importance
(47)	Pride in and respect for this organization	3	2	1
(48)	Involvement in community and civic affairs	3	2	1
(49)	Pension rights, seniority, etc.	3	2	1
(50)	Family considerations	3	2	1
(51)	Opportunity and general atmosphere provided by the organization	3	2	1
(52)	The trouble involved in moving	3	2	1
(53)	The job I have in the organization	3	2	1
(54)	My age, health, etc.	3	2	1
(55)	Difficulty of finding as good a job elsewhere	3	2	1

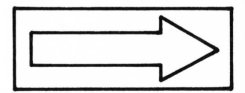

2. We are living in a world of change, and we are all changing to some extent.
Some of us are undoubtedly more receptive to change than others, and all
of us are more receptive in some areas of our lives than other areas. It
would be helpful if we could get your evaluation of your own receptivity
to change--hence, please answer both a and b.

    a. Here are several areas of your life that are subject to change. Please
indicate how receptive you believe you are to change in each by circling
one of the numbers on each line.

	I almost always support changes	I support changes more often than I oppose them	I support changes about as often as I oppose them	I oppose changes more often than I support them	
In my job	4	3	2	1	(56)
In my hobbies	4	3	2	1	(57)
In my church life	4	3	2	1	(58)
In my local gov-ernment	4	3	2	1	(59)
In my family life	4	3	2	1	(60)
In my local school system	4	3	2	1	(61)
In the organization for which I work	4	3	2	1	(62)

    b. Where would you rate yourself on this scale? Statements are included
at the extremes simply to give you two 'fixes'. (Please circle the
number from 1 to 5 that seems to fit your own reaction pattern best.)

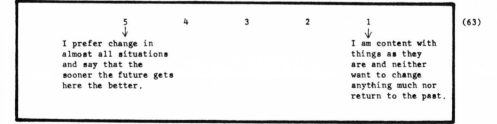

	5	4	3	2	1	(63)
	↓				↓	
	I prefer change in almost all situations and say that the sooner the future gets here the better.				I am content with things as they are and neither want to change anything much nor return to the past.	

3. This is a specially designed test of basic orientations which we have con-
    structed for this study. It is composed of 17 pairs of statements and your
    answers are scored and totaled, giving you a total score. We do not use the
    individual answers for anything other than giving you this score.

    These statements are about things you may or may not like; about things with
    which you may or may not agree. Look at this example:

    A. Ambition should be moderate.

    B. One should get ahead by work.

    Which of these statements do you agree with more? Circle its letter, either
    A or B. If you agree with both, choose the one you like better. If you
    disagree with both, choose the one you dislike less (the one you agree with
    more). Your choice should be a description of your own personal likes and
    feelings. Be sure that you circle the letter A or the letter B in each
    pair of statements. You cannot be given a score unless you make a choice
    for each pair. So please do not skip any.

    1. A. What matters is what one can accomplish.

        B. It is desirable to be more cooperative than competitive.

    2. A. If a man is trying to accomplish something it is necessary to
            gamble "all or nothing".

        B. A secure job is better than a risky one which involves high stakes.

    3. A. A person should be able to fit into any kind of group.

        B. People like to be able to do things better than other people can.

    4. A. Wasting time shouldn't particularly bother a person.

        B. Anyone who doesn't take work seriously should be disliked.

    5. A. Being "people-minded" is preferable to being "job-minded".

        B. A person should like to find out what great men have thought about
            various problems in which he is interested.

    6. A. Being like certain people whom one admires is an important aim in
            life.

        B. It's all right to be an individual, but a person shouldn't want to
            be very different from those around him.

    7. A. Anyone who doesn't take work seriously should be disliked.

        B. Ambition should be moderate.

8. A. Teachers should be more concerned with the child's social adjustment than with his academic progress.

    B. The teacher is supposed to see that the children learn a curriculum, not that they enjoy it or learn group cooperation.

9. A. A person should judge people by their traits--not by what they actually do.

    B. It's more important to get the job done than worry about hurting people's feelings.

10. A. To have security is better than the chance for great achievement.

    B. It is better to be famous than well-liked.

11. A. It's a good idea to have a strong point of view about things.

    B. When planning something one likes to get suggestions from his friends.

12. A. In sports one should rather be thought of as a good team member than a star player.

    B. A person should like situations which are demanding.

13. A. A person should like to have strong attachments with his friends.

    B. Success against odds is the best of American ideals.

14. A. What matters is what one can accomplish.

    B. It's all right to be an individual but a person shouldn't want to be very different from those around him.

15. A. People like to be able to do things better than other people can.

    B. Being "people-minded" is preferable to being "job-minded".

16. A. A parent shouldn't want his child to get very far "out of step" with other children.

    B. One's ambition should be to get to the top.

17. A. Wasting time shouldn't particularly bother a person.

    B. If someone "delivers the goods", it doesn't make much difference what kind of person he is.

VI PART SIX THE WIND-UP

If you have any additional comments to make on the impact of change on your career, we would appreciate having you write them here.

Leviathan: An Experimental Study of Large Organizations with the Aid of Computers

BEATRICE K. ROME and SYDNEY C. ROME*

WE are engaged in the study of large social groups and seek empirically testable knowledge of their complex behavior. Since social scientists have, until now, lacked adequate techniques to obtain such knowledge, basic to our task has been the development of a novel scientific method. Accordingly, we shall begin by describing the kinds of large organizations in which we are interested and some of their principal properties. Then we shall describe the Leviathan experimental technique, including its present status, possible applications, and directions for further development.

The type of large organization of concern to us is any system composed of more than two or three hundred people which produces a product or renders a service. Examples of such large organizations are a civilian industry, a government agency, a university, or a military organization.

There are certain recurring and perhaps even defining characteristics of large productive organizations that make such organizations at once challenging and extremely difficult to study. One is their *complexity*. Unlike small groups, where members meet face-to-face to conduct their business, large groups necessarily depend upon go-betweens; they operate through many intermediaries. Another feature is their *hierarchical structure.* They are built level upon level and consist of multiple systems and subsystems.

Again, in large groups there is an element of *anonymity* or face-lessness. It really makes very little difference to the group who it is that answers the switchboard telephone or who makes out a certain

---

*Dr. Beatrice K. Rome and Dr. Sydney C. Rome are with the Decision Processes Staff, Research Directorate, System Development Corporation, Santa Monica, California.

form. The important thing is that the operation or activity gets accomplished. This aspect entails complicated and formalized *standard routines,* operating procedures and communication channels. Interestingly enough, despite this depersonalized or impersonalized atmosphere, large groups have tendencies to develop sub-collectivities—subordinate, small, face-to-face, informal groups or units—within them. The latter characteristic leads to the growth of informal, that is, *unofficial, personalized structures,* which sometimes become more powerful and effective than the formal structures.

Another crucial element of large social systems is their tendency to *specialization and proliferation of functions.* This feature, on the one hand, often separates the lines of formal authority from those of professional or technical competence. On the other hand, it frequently necessitates an extra-formal network of power-skill interdependencies that seem to defy principles of order. A final element intrinsic to large productive social groups is, of course, their sheer size.

THE LEVIATHAN APPROACH

The foregoing features of large organizations and their attendant problems merit attention and study. They bear importantly on policy formation and its implementation, strategy manipulation, decision making, negotiation, initiation of change, information flow, the language of communication, the procedural net, and the many other problem areas of large social organizations. A comprehensive survey of the scientific literature shows that some theoretical and a small amount of empirically grounded work has been accomplished. But even this small output has, in the main, used tools and concepts appropriate to small, face-to-face or medium, hierarchically under-developed groups.

The tools that have been developed for the scientific study of large groups include direct observation, statistical surveys, interviews, realistic or imitative simulation, rational gaming and analytic mathematical modeling. Each of these techniques is, or may be, used to support the Leviathan research. But none of these tools, and no combination, we feel, is quite adequate for the experimental study of large social organizations. The Leviathan technique, on the other hand, was specifically designed to supplement these tools. It was designed especially to focus on the central aspect of large organizations —their hierarchical complexity. It also provides for the study of such complexity under dynamically changing conditions and in a rigorously controlled laboratory environment.

What, exactly, is the Leviathan? It is an experimental technique consisting, first, of a conceptual model of large-scale organizations which, second, becomes translated into laboratory operations by means of the following seven elements:

Computer: A modern digital computer.

Laboratory Equipment: Special pushbutton and display equipment, tied by buffers into the computer.

Computer Programs: A system of general, content-free computer programs which can be applied to many types of organizations—military, civilian, and industrial.

Artificial Agents: The option to include in an experiment several hundred artificial agents—robots—who implement policy, make subordinate decisions, and carry on the technical work of the organization.

Live Subjects: Live subjects interacting with the computer.

Artificial Language: Specially designed artificial languages by which live subjects communicate with one another and with the automated robots in natural English over the computer.

Automatic Observation: Computer programs to record and interpret all experimentally relevant observations of the behavior of the subjects and the operations of the artificial agents.

THE CONCEPTUAL MODEL

The Basic Paradigm

This is the basic paradigm underlying our research: STIMULI enter an ORGANIZATION which transputs the stimuli through any number of transforms, eventuating in an output or RESPONSE. The RESPONSE is EVALUATED against previously established CRITERIA (of organizational achievement) and an error signal is generated and fed back to the ORGANIZATION. In real life, the stimuli and the environment are constantly changing. New demands and challenges continually confront it. Hence the purposes of the organization must be adjusted accordingly. The organization is constantly altering the criteria of performance in view of anticipated future events. This paradigm may be represented diagrammatically as shown in Figure 1.

Only a few years ago, this paradigm would have been incomprehensible to many behavioral scientists. At that time, it was fashionable to regard a social group in terms of a stimulus, some intervening but essentially inaccessible variables—the black box or the social group itself—and a response. This attitude was compatible with an old notion that to be scientific one needed causes that acted on things to produce effects, or that one needed independent variables, functional relationships among them, and dependent variables.

This position was modified by cyberneticists, notably Norbert

Figure 1

BASIC PARADIGM FOR LEVIATHAN RESEARCH INTO
LARGE-SCALE PRODUCTIVE ORGANIZATIONS

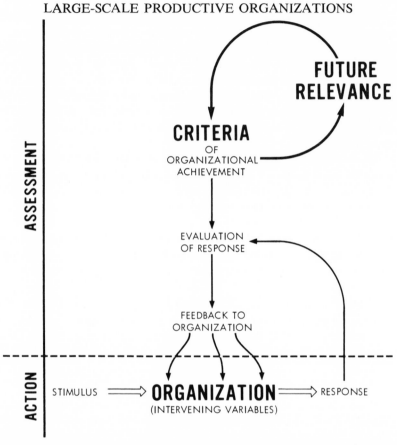

Wiener, who pointed out that a group, person or machine that produces a product can be understood in terms of feedback. In a feedback
model, as is now well known, there are criteria of achievement with
which the actual performance of the system can be compared. As
a result of comparing actual with desired performance, orders are
given to the system, which cause it to better adapt to the pre-existing
criteria.

Feedback designs brought value back into the world of mechanisms.
For cybernetics, contrivances, striving persons, and achieving groups
are all devices that seek to maximize utility; that is, they are devices
that seek to increase their own usefulness or their power to satisfy
human wants.

But the theory of cybernetic models does not usually include the next step. It does not treat with the key questions: Whence come criteria? What makes criteria change? How do they change? These questions are not important for machines. Machines are contrivances or inventions brought into existence in order to serve human wants. The utility that they seek to maximize is prescribed for them by their designers. Live persons and social groups, on the contrary, if they are mechanisms, are the kind of mechanisms that can specify their own standards. They form their own criteria for defining suitable performance, for evaluating their own responses. When they compare their actual performance with desired or ideal performance, they prescribe what is desired or ideal.

In social groups that produce products or render services, the kind in which we on the Leviathan project are interested, the problem of criteria formation is central. This means that evaluation—the establishment and development of systems of values—is a principal function of such groups. It also means that, in order to evaluate a result or to appraise utility, the criteria already must be on hand when the assessment is made. If there is going to be any change in criteria, one must look ahead into the future. Any change in a criterion will take effect only after it happens, that is, in the future; and therefore the relevance of any change is only to some future time. The consequence of this is that temporal "futurity" is of the essence in changing criteria. Hence our basic paradigm (Figure 1) has three elements: (1) the system of stimulus, intervening variables, response, (2) criteria, and (3) futurity.

The Policy, Control and Technological Systems

We now adapt this paradigm to large-scale organizations. We construe large productive or servicing organizations as consisting primarily of three main systems. First, there is a *technological system* (Figure 2) into which raw material or raw data are poured and through which this material gets processed into a final product or service. The materials may be intelligence messages, iron ore, or enemy forces; or we may even think of them as students being processed through a school system and fashioned into a finished product.* The technological system does the basic productive work of the entire organization and actually renders the services that the organization provides to its consumers. It is an input-output or implementing system, and we properly think of it in terms of transputting stimuli

---

*See "Automated Learning Process" (chapter 12). This formulation is of special interest, because in it the artificial agents in the technological system have important decision-making mechanisms.

Figure 2

TRIPARTITE SCHEMA OF LARGE-SCALE
PRODUCTIVE ORGANIZATIONS

(Adaptation of Basic Paradigm Shown in Figure 1)

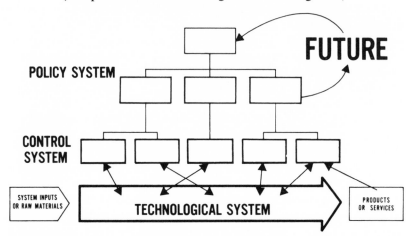

through transforms or in terms of a dynamic network of queues and service stations.

Over this technological system we postulate a higher implementing group or *control system*. The individuals of this system direct and manipulate the technological system by interpreting decisions and policies developed and ratified from the top. The control system monitors the criteria of accomplishment for the entire organization. Each individual in the control system has a limited domain of power in the technological system. He receives feedback information concerning the performance and problems of the technological system primarily within his own restricted area of responsibility.

Over both the control and the technological systems, we place the *policy-formation* system. The policy makers provide the controllers with standards. They say what should be done, and they prescribe criteria in terms of which accomplishments can be evaluated. Whereas the controllers attempt to track and predict inputs to the technological system, the policy makers have to sense and anticipate demands placed on the entire organization by the consumers. In the face of these varying challenges, the policy makers are responsible for providing relatively stationary environments for the controllers, that is, micro-worlds in which the controllers know what they ought to do and what they ought to achieve.

The controllers and the policy makers together face two related internal operating problems. One is to devise local strategies for the respective individual controllers. When taken together, these local strategies form a grand strategy for the management of the technological system and enable this system to accomplish the results required of it by the governing systems. A second, related problem is to predict the performance of the technological system, given knowledge of alternative local strategies that can be employed by the individual controllers.

The sharply-drawn threefold conceptual schema of policy, control, and technological systems is deliberately oversimplified. In actual large organizations, outside the laboratory, each of the three systems is a complex maze in its own right. Each is a system of systems, containing on its level its own elements of executive command, managerial control, and technical skill. Within each subsystem there is the greatest diversity in the exercise of the control and policy-making functions. Appearances and official statements often are at variance with real distributions of power, and officials on different levels in a chain of command may actually form policy and exercise control. For purposes of classification and exposition, however, it is useful to consider large organizations as consisting primarily of these three clear and distinct levels. Analytically and in the laboratory, we on the Leviathan project carefully separate policy and control from the technological system, and we isolate control and policy formation from each other.

With this approach, certain key notions concerning organizational structure and researchable problem areas can be formulated in such a way that their experimental investigation can be undertaken. The first of these is the interrelation between policy formation and control in large organizations. Why is this a problem area?

POLICY FORMATION VERSUS CONTROL

Policy Formation and Futurity

In Figure 2 the word "future" appears at the right top corner. It was placed there deliberately to draw attention to the salient difference between policy formation and control. The control system, close to day-by-day problems, often is little more than a rule-following system. Moreover it lives almost entirely in the present or in the immediately foreseeable future. For the most part, the control system is almost wholly preoccupied with the inner, domestic guts of a given organization—with its operationally on-going demands and processes. It jealously monitors and controls the evanescent, but concrete, factually given, present. Its role, under such conditions, is largely that of a watchdog—to follow accepted, set plans and prescribed, specified goals. When this happens, it tends to view the external environment as no more than a means to its organization's goals and to regard the organization itself as a closed system, an immediate environment that remains relatively stable or stationary through time.

Now the top-level policy system may also be concerned with the inner workings of the entire system; and that means that it too may be heavily concerned with what is actually going on in the present. But it is often forced, willingly or unwillingly, knowingly or not, to become deeply involved in areas of uncertainty and contingency, relating to distant future planning. It is planning how to cope not only with tomorrow's external environment but with tomorrow's internal organization as well.

But futurity brings us face to face with something strange and challenging about policy formation. The future not only is uncertain and contingent, but in fact it is *not;* that is, by nature, the future does not exist. Yet top-level policy must deal with the future and its possible options and alternatives as if each one *were really now.* In other words, those options, even when mutually contradictory and incoherent, are not illusory; they are each very real; and in making long-range plans, policy makers must concern themselves with the possible consequences of any given alternative. Hence, top-level managers are in the paradox that while they are living in the present, in point of fact it is the future which is dictating their complex decisions right now. Top executives, commanders, or strategy and policy planners dwell in a strange unrealized universe, real but nonexistent. Firmly rooted to the past and present, their plans are nonetheless directed to a future that *is not* yet a real thing.

Formulation of Alternatives

It follows that developmental planning or top decision making can be an initiatory, creative process. Top-level managers and decision makers can be theorizers and inventors. In this role, they do not merely solve problems (essentially the task of middle managers); they create problems. They do not simply adapt to change; they can anticipate and initiate change. There are times when they hypothesize strange universes—even colonies on the moon, underground cities, an "inter-dependent" Atlantic alliance—and only later do they make the further decisions that will realize specifically selected plans.

Needless to say, not every top-level policy maker lives in this exalted world, and more often than not his initiatory contribution consists in appraising and ratifying proposals that bubble up from within his organization or from his outside accidental encounters. Thus we should view top-level policy making as a double form of inventiveness or creativity: first is the formulation *of* alternatives, second is the choice *from* alternatives. Of the two, the formulation of alternatives is the more challenging and critical. Failure to imagine "still another possible choice" can be disastrous. Until recently, for example, our foreign policy was guided almost exclusively by the strategy of all-out nuclear war. Concepts of limited wars, guerrilla warfare, para-limited operations are instances of an enlarged vision in the inventiveness of strategic possibilities.

Creating hypothetical situations, problems or plans is similar to an artistic creation. It implies the carving out or cutting off from a tree of infinite possibilities a set of finite options. But these must be *live.* The term *live,* borrowed from William James, indicates that the executive, creative decision process is neither irrational nor whimsical. The situations, problems, and plans conceived must be significant and genuine possibilities—those that may really take place, those which can reasonably be anticipated or can honestly be realized. Thus the executive planner is bounded by the constraints of fitness, relevance, concordance of his future plans with the demands of the present and past environment.

Yet, the fact remains that to be creative, a planner must be time free and space free. When inventing alternatives, his is the region of pure possibilities. Furthermore, as we said, however live his future plans and policies are, however anchored to the real world of today, these live plans are in the non-existent future. They are hypothetical, conditional, uncertain. Thus, when the top-level decision maker is formulating new alternatives, he does not and cannot live in a universe restricted by a two-valued, extensional logic of truth *vs.* falsity. His world encompasses *degrees* of truth and reality. He treats with what exists, can be pointed to, recognized as concretely on hand and to be counted; but he goes beyond the already realized and statically existent. For, once made, policy does not remain statically fixed. It is a continuing engagement with a nonstationary environment and with novel possibilities. It projects the future of an organization into the organization's developing environment; and the choices of the policy makers can contribute to, even at times make, the very environment into which the emerging organization fits. Policy formation thus reaches beyond the existent and even beyond the instrumental. It employs a logic of projection, one that can adequately express what it is to reach beyond what has already been accomplished. This latter logic is a logic of human intention.

Choice from Alternatives

Policy formation does not, of course, remain exclusively on this high plane of purpose or goal, projected realizations, and anticipation of counter thrust by a reacting environment. Once a finite set of possible alternative contingencies, plans or goals has been elaborated, a subsequent paring down is required. The top manager now makes his choice *from* alternatives. This is a process of arbitration, of deliberate rejection and denial, of affirmation and selection, or of compromise. It is a process of conflict and competition, resolution and sacrifice. Festinger explains it in terms of dissonance (1). He points out that whenever you choose a policy, whenever you opt for one alternative plan, you benefit by avoiding the negative values but also sacrifice whatever positive values may exist in any of the other options. This is a fact of our finite kind of existence. We cannot realize all good options; we must make a choice; and when we do, we give up something positively valuable in the others. Crucial, therefore, to this phase of decision making is the manipulation of strategies aimed at achieving first a nearly optimum, flexible set of goals and then, second, a nearly optimum set of means to realize the goals.

This process of choice from among alternatives, even though it necessarily entails at any given moment the sacrifice of innumerable alternative values, nevertheless is not always inevitable or irreversible. As the effects of a choice from alternatives become known and as intelligence formerly inaccessible becomes available, previously neglected values can become realized. Better ways to achieve the alternative become clearer. These possibilities of correction, of course, have limits. There are situations wherein a set of enacted consequences, like selecting a wrong mate or allowing even a small war to break out, are hard to reverse.

Implications for Laboratory Experimentation and Conceptual Formulation

These characteristics concerning high-level policy formation have the following implications for the Leviathan laboratory experimentation. They require the kind of system environment and hence computer programs that can operate in real time in such a way as to permit drastic changes in system performance during the course of an experiment. The system must be capable of embarking on a series of actions and in due course, during simulated time, the policy makers must be free to change, modify or even reverse their earlier decisions. In some experiments it must be possible to carry this even to the point of reorganizing the entire simulated large organization, in order to permit the policy makers to institute fundamentally new goals and radical innovations in basic strategy.

The foregoing characteristics of high-level policy also have implications for another part of the Leviathan program that will supplement laboratory experimentation. Part of the long-range Leviathan program is to automate the top-level decision makers, that is, to produce fully computerized operating Leviathan models without live subjects. Such decision makers will substitute a Bayesian kind of behavior for human intention and planning when they form and institute policy.

THE SOCIAL CHARACTER OF DECISION MAKING

For purposes of scientific investigation and laboratory experimentation, we have sharply distinguished among technology, control and policy formation. This acute dissection applies only to functions; it does not apply simply to the individual decision makers themselves. In real life, creating and perceiving live alternatives and choosing from among them seem to us to be shared or social decisions—group decisions, rather than individual decisions. By this we mean several things. We mean that in large organizations decisions are often made in concert by numerous specialists or interdisciplinary teams. We also mean that even when the decision is that of a single lone individual, for example that of the President of the United States, that individual is nevertheless operating very much in a social role and for a social purpose.

Again, within an organization every top-level decision serves to generate a sequential, cascading series of social or group goals and sub-goals. A top-level policy choice becomes the goal and guide line, the bound and limit, for the next-lower-level decisions. These, in turn, shape the next subordinate level of decision-making. In a sense, then, every top decision (like the axioms of a deductive system) exfoliates or pre-figures the entire chain of choices down the organizational pyramid. Conversely, every top decision, however novel and spontaneous, may be viewed as a reflection and distillation of decisions moving up the pyramid. From this vantage, each lower-level decision becomes a determinant, the occasioning instrument for shaping, penetrating and permeating the next higher-level choice. Going up the pyramid, then, we find a chain of social processes culminating in a comprehensive and often deliberate and even clear choice at the top. Consequently, we affirm that in large organizations, the decision process is shot through and through with a social role and a social concern.

Huntington, for example, says:

Vertical bargaining in the upper reaches of the American executive reflects what might be called the principle of the inverse strength of the chain of command. On the organization chart, the lines of authority fan out from the top executive down level by level to the lowest subordinate. Actually, however, the lines at the bottom of the chart usually should be darker than those at the top, which might well be dotted or light gray. As one moves up a hierarchy, the links in the chain of command weaken and even tend to dissolve. Hierarchical control becomes less important; bargaining relationships more important. . . The President may be the most powerful man in the country, but relatively speaking he has less control over his cabinet than a lowly VA section chief has over his clerks or a corporal over his squad. Consequently, at the higher levels of government, relationships, even among hierarchical superiors and subordinates, tend towards egalitarianism and usually involve substantial bargaining (3, p. 148).

We agree that major policy decisions are seldom the product of a lone decision maker. Overtly or covertly, explicitly or implicitly, major policies reflect chains of controversy, negotiation and bargaining among officials and groups up and down the social hierarchy.

Implications for Laboratory Experimentation and Conceptual Formulation.

The implications of these views for the Leviathan conceptual model and laboratory experimentation include the following. First, the fact that we use a relatively large number (21 in our initial policy experiments, as we shall explain below) of live subjects in the leadership roles is a necessary feature of large-group investigations. Were one to substitute a rational model of decision making without negotiation and many-way interaction, one would lose the social character of the decision process on the policy levels of large-scale organizations. Secondly, the subjects are not expected to develop optimal strategies under any simple expression of goals. Goals and values are to be capable of complex inter-involvement, including conflict and contradictions from level to level and time to time. Thirdly, we require the ability to observe the processes of conflict and negotiation, both in detail and on the level of coalitions. Just to observe a complex process like this, even though the live agents represent only about five per cent of all agents in the simulation, requires that the computer perform all observations and that it be capable of automatically converting its own raw observations into experimentally meaningful interpretations.

COMMAND LANGUAGE

The social character of decision making and policy formation in large organizations has implications for the flow of information in such organizations. Obviously, what a policy maker needs to know is very different from what an official requires in order to make a control decision. This distinction holds on level after level and in the various subsystems. Because knowledge is needed for such very different purposes, there are radical discontinuities in the kinds of knowledge needed for the different system levels. A large organization seems, from this point of view, to be a collection of islands or separate principalities, each solving its own problems and each viewing the entire operation in distinctive ways. And yet, of course, there are also basic identities as one rises and descends from one system level to another. If in an organization there are squads, groups of squads, and branches containing the groups, the branch chief shares responsibilities and authority with his group heads, and these in turn have certain interests in common with their squad leaders. And so we have a paradox: there are autonomies, independencies, self-dependencies in the several units of a large organization; and there are also formal identities. This paradox poses serious problems for the provision of information within a large organization.

First, since system levels are both disjoined and conjoined, autonomous and integrated, the kinds of information any one level needs in order to carry on its business may be both identical with the kinds needed above it or below it and also unique.

Secondly, at every stratum in a pyramid of social control and of deliberate command, intelligence has to be ordered, patterned and made relevant. Information is useless if it is simply collected. It has to be interpreted, filtered, evaluated, assessed. Even the decision to pass raw data upward is a selective choice. While an implementer of policy may have use for raw radar returns or for a plotting board displaying each enemy and friendly weapon, higher-level officials, executives and military leaders need to know something more and something different in kind from unselected or undigested raw facts, namely, their significance.

In the third place, normally, as knowledge rises up the system pyramid, it becomes aggregated or, to use a recent term, it becomes cognitively simplified. It also, of course, becomes cognitively amplified, because by the time a top policy-maker reaches his decision, he needs not only simpler, but conceptually (and in scope) more comprehensive information. On the other hand, as directives come downward, they tend to become expanded, more and more detailed, and at the same time more and more specialized. These upward and downward flows again pose questions concerning the kinds of information which any system level requires. This we call the problem of a command language.

Fourthly, knowledge at the lowest level is ordinarily in a declarative mood. It is concerned with description, with particulars, with details. But the kind of knowledge that faces a policy decision maker is forward looking. On this account, it is in an entirely different mood. The latter concerns himself with hypothetical, subjunctive, contra-factual possibilities—if this plan then this plan, or if such and such is the situation then so and so *could* or might happen. Declarative knowledge structures and hypothetical or contra-factual knowledge structures are very different one from the other. We want to know whether there are any general principles concerning the kinds of evaluated data and the kinds of language which are relevant on different system levels.

Implications for Laboratory Experimentation.

The problems of command language have these implications for Leviathan laboratory investigations. First, it must be possible for the subjects to obtain different kinds of feedback concerning the areas in which they are responsible. They must be able to obtain both raw and interpreted information, and they must be able to have this information continuously and progressively while an experiment proceeds. The computer programs have to be designed to provide such information as specified by the experimenters for different experiments. Thus, it must be possible to design an experiment in which the principal independent variable is kind and flow of information. Secondly, it must be possible for the experimenters to control the kinds of interpretation the subjects can make of the data they receive and for the computer to observe their interpretations automatically as the experiments proceed. Thirdly, it must be possible to categorize the entire corpus of communications from subject to subject under headings as commands, requests for ratification, passing of raw information, interpretation of directives. When thus categorizing, the computer must be able to observe which kinds of communications occur at which point in each experiment and from each decision making node in the social structure. Finally, it must be possible to control and observe the evolution of command language as an experiment proceeds.

HIERARCHICAL DIVERSITY

Except in mob action or in passive audiences, large organizations that produce products or render services invariably possess a complex and highly articulated structure. This structure almost always takes on a hierarchical pattern. There are levels of status, of authority and of responsibility; and across these levels there are many sub-collectivities, that is, subordinate groups. Yet an integral part of the notion of organizations is that a large group becomes unified through its organizing structure. Even though system levels and functional subsystems break out everywhere in a large group, higher systems absorb and in a very intimate sense contain systems on the lower levels. We do not agree that higher system levels are simple aggregates. They are *not* fully explained by events and patterns on the lower levels.

On the contrary, we believe that containment is a unique relationship that holds among system levels. Through this relationship, absorption of a lower system level in a higher-level synthesis results in novel integrations on the higher level (6).

Hence we tend to regard a large organization as an open-ended, self-organizing system, in which each higher level feeds, so to speak, on the lower levels. We say that each lower level is self existent, possessing its own goals and interests and carrying on its affairs autonomously, yet all the while it is contributing to the higher levels and therefore making essential reference to the purposes and goals of these higher system levels. This means that we may look upon the whole system of systems in a large organization as a hierarchy of structures, and also as hierarchies of tasks, purposes, realizations, and goals.

Now it might seem to follow from our views concerning the hierarchical articulation of large social groups that maximal unity and harmony are essential characteristics of successful system performance. This conclusion would be encouraged by the fact that, until very recently, there has been a strong tendency in the theory of large organizations to regard fundamental differences and cleavages within an organization as necessarily detrimental. This tendency has appeared in two forms or two allied positions. One position is that of the environmentalist. He looks on an organization as primarily a passive instrument adaptive to external demands. The environmentalist attempts to develop rational criteria of system performance, regardless of the interplay of forces within the social hierarchy. He attempts by calculation to discover, like an engineer or an economist, what forms of organization or what patterns of operation make for optimal group performance.

A second related position views both the environment and the organization as instruments for manipulation to achieve goals for the organization as a whole. Usually these are the goals of the top-level administration. This position assumes that what is of concern to the governors of the entire system is per se directly relevant to the good of the whole. Plato was an early and leading advocate of this position, and it appears in his writings in a very pure form. Every level or component of an organization has for him its functions, and when each performs its proper functions, without trespassing on any other component, the whole achieves its highest perfection and works with maximum integration and harmony. Plato even calls this condition "justice."

Both of these positions are still highly influential. They offer the attraction that were real groups amenable to analysis like this, a simple science of manipulation could be devised. Often when writers yearn for a science of large social organizations, they equate knowledge with power, and power becomes the ability to control and subordinate large organizations to the will of the leadership. These two positions also offer the attraction that were they tenable, one could rationally optimize the structure and coordination of large organizations. One might even dream of using the resources of computing machinery to reveal the "best" forms of organizational government.

These positions seem to us to have been highly reinforced in recent years by small-group studies. With small groups, resources are often lacking to support specializations, differences, plural points of view, contrary objectives. Their limited size often makes conflict either superfluous or a luxury they cannot sustain.

In large groups, on the other hand, these considerations are far less relevant. Large-scale organizations are characterized by multi-level goals and level-specific interests. They are mazes of criss-crossed, pluralistic values, points of view, objectives, and efforts. The several system levels and functional specializations elicit highly differing sets of values and objectives among the different officers, especially on the control and implementing levels. Where an executive is placed in a pyramid of command, and what his functional responsibilities are have a great deal to do with what he advocates, strives for, believes to be good for the organization. His placement in a web of social interactions can deeply influence his private beliefs. A corporal over a squad may seek to have his squad excel, even at the expense of other squads in his platoon, while his platoon leader may have other ideas concerning the wise employment of the total resources of the platoon. And such differences of view can continue upward over many links in a chain of command.

For these reasons, one wonders why organizational conflict is ever regarded as necessarily pathological or why one should advocate a simple-minded organizational "integration," "harmony," "unity" which, if it could be realized, would obliterate all distinctions of level, task and viewpoint. On the contrary, the very concept of large-scale organizational hierarchy emphasizes intra-level and multi-level specializations, differences, pluralities and contrarieties. These spell disagreements, competition, dissent, and conflict. Conflict, therefore, seems to us intrinsically neither evil nor disease. It becomes such only at the critical boundary, where divergence becomes strife and strife threatens annihilation. Indeed, far from being disruptive, conflict may be the very cohesive force that stabilizes an organization and provides it with resources for change and growth. In the pregnant words of E. A. Ross, "society is sewn together by its inner conflicts" (8, p. 165).

Implications for Conceptual Formulation and Laboratory Experimentation.

Our position concerning the consequences of diversity and conflict in large organizations has direct implications for our conceptual formulation and our laboratory experimentation. First of all, we are compelled to add an important theoretical element to our basic paradigm (Figure 1) and to our tripartite organizational structure (Figure 2). On the technological level, we leave the vestiges of the stimulus, intervening variable and response levels. We allow the control system to remain self-confined, as it is in the cybernetic model. It looks toward the inner operations of the entire organization But on the policy level, we acknowledge *demands* of the environment. (See Figure 3) These demands originate with and among the consumers.

Figure 3

TRIPARTITE SCHEMA OF LARGE-SCALE PRODUCTIVE
ORGANIZATIONS PLUS ENVIRONMENT
OF CONSUMER DEMANDS

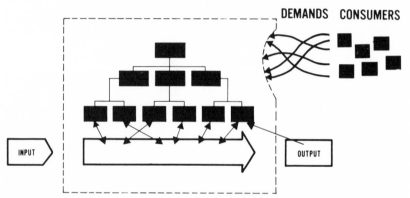

In laboratory operations, the consumers can be represented by live subjects, thus providing a larger system nexus in which multiple interactions and exchanges can take place between the consumers and the focal organization. In other experiments, the experimenters can fully control the nature, magnitude and timing of demands. In response to the demands, the policy makers formulate forward-looking alternatives and choose from among them. We control the extent to which policy makers can restructure policy and control systems, and we control the ways in which they can do this.

We will not, however, try to develop optimal organization or operating procedures. We feel that the question sometimes put by managers, "What's the best kind of organization?" is intrinsically not a significant question. We feel it is much more meaningful to ask what a social group does in order to live with its organization or operating procedures, just as we would ask what a person does to live with his body and with his emotional and intellectual endowments.

From these considerations it will be clear why we have chosen for our first major full Leviathan experimentation the investigation of alternate forms of functional and territorial organization. (See below, Simulation in a Dual (Live and Artificial) Mode, p. 42.) Rather than seek to develop optimal forms of organization and procedure, we seek to determine how our organizations inhabit the structures that intrinsically characterize them. We seek to determine whether functional responsibility and organizational level can elicit specific value structures, objectives, needs for knowledge of results, interpretations and evaluations in the different offices, different for each office.

THE 1961 AUTOMATIC-MODE SIMULATION

We have called attention to crucial aspects of policy formation and control, social decision making, command language, and hierarchical diversity in large social groups. We have done this, because we believe that an important part of our task is to recognize where the significant problems of large-group study lie, before we propose techniques for their investigation. We now turn to the question, how should we study the complex interplay of multi-level structure and multi-level process, of pattern and change through many autonomous yet organically unified subsystems, of command policy referent to an unfinished future and control rooted in the present?

The Leviathan technique consists of two major components: (1) We represent the complex operations of entire classes of technological systems by the operation of a digital computer. (2) We use live subjects and shall use artificial subjects to exercise control over and to govern the technological systems.

Obviously, the realization of such a twofold technique in the laboratory is a large task, requiring extensive resources; therefore we are realizing it in discrete phases. The first phase has been to represent the technological system on a computer. This we have done on the IBM 7090 computer. The program system became operational in June of 1961. It is described in pages 527-547 of the article, "Computer Simulation toward a Theory of Large Organizations" (5). (We call the 1961 computer runs "simulation in an automatic mode," in order to distinguish them from simulations which involve live subjects.)

Design Principles and Key Results.

One guiding principle in the design of any Leviathan system of computer programs is that they have a high degree of generality. The

Leviathan project is aimed toward establishing some propositions that can be included in a pure theory of policy formation and social control regardless of any specific large-group applications. A second principle is that any Leviathan technological system shall be so designed and executed that its performance be highly amenable to control and to policy-formation by higher-level decision makers. This permits us to explore the effect of various middle management and top management policies, decisions, rules and actions on the work of the technological system.

The 7090 computer programs do not imitate any specific productive system in the real world, nor are they an image of some projected system of the future. On the contrary, they represent a large variety of such systems, depending on how the programs are interpreted by the experimenters. The programs were so designed that the experimenters define many features of the simulated technological systems prior to each run on the computer. The defining descriptions specify characteristics of the technological system. Such specification does not entail reprogramming; it is accomplished by cutting IBM cards prior to a computer run and associating these cards with the other cards that carry the computer programs. Thus major program parameters are completely under the control of the experimenters. These parameters define the specific configuration of the technological system that the experimenters elect for that run on the computer.

Placed beyond experimental control, however, are the contingent, dependent response characteristics of the operating programs. Experimenters can specify and control constellations of inputs or stimuli. They can also set various internal production controls. And they can determine the social organization of the artificial agents incorporated in the program. To each of these independent sets of conditions the operating program system reacts in its own many characteristic and specific ways. In the 1961 tests made with the 7090 programs, a number of significant responses were dramatically altered by changes in social organization and in production control settings. In particular, in a test of system sensitivity to priority policy, the experimenters induced a spread of over 100 times in average transit time through the system between two classes of inputs that in a previous run had taken approximately the same average transit time.

In addition to responding in characteristic ways to input and to the experimenters' government and control, the operating program system also automatically provides appropriately aggregated information. Of special importance is information relative to hierarchy. The experimenters superimpose over the technological system a pyramid of executive offices. They define the structure of this pyramid at will, and they associate the lowest-level offices with specific "territories" in the technological system. Then, in accordance with these specifications, information concerning the contributions of the artificial agents in the technological system is automatically assembled and aggregated by epochs of simulated time (5, p. 534).

The 1961 Leviathan programs are valuable as tools for investigating large-group processes and information flow in hierarchical structures. In addition to this intrinsic value, however, they have utility of another kind. They demonstrate that many of the challenges for computer simulation posed by the Leviathan approach can be met and overcome

The 1961 simulation was confined to the technological system. The 7090 computer programs produced at that time did not allow for intervention in real time. Once placed in operation, all the various control settings and the social organization remained fixed until the end of a set run on the computer. It was not possible for a policy-formation or a control system to supervene *during* a simulation run. Nor was any control or policy system implemented at this time.

THE 1962 LIVE SIMULATION

At this juncture, in July of 1961, two paths opened for the Leviathan research. One was to complete the computer programs for control and for policy formation sketched in pages 547-551 of the article "Computer Simulation toward a Theory of Large Organizations" (5). The result would have been a radically automated Leviathan, with artificial controllers and artificial policy makers. The other path was to introduce live subjects in the leadership roles. This alternative was to be accomplished on a new, but far more limited, computer, in a pioneering kind of laboratory, one in which live subjects could interact directly with the computer. While such interaction has existed for some time in a number of applied settings, for example, in the United States Air Force's SAGE (Semi-Automatic Ground Environment) system, laboratory facilities for pure research have not been available, to our knowledge, until SDC's Systems Simulation Research Laboratory became operational in early 1962.

To realize a semi-automatic Leviathan simulation, it was necessary to devise ways for the managers to communicate with each other over the computer and to communicate with the artificial agents in the technological system. Further, we wanted the live managers and the robots to communicate in an idiom that would approximate natural English. To these ends, we had to design and to test special equipment, a special type of natural language, and special computer programs. Then, after obtaining the equipment, the computer programs and the special idioms, we wanted to try these out as an operating system, to see how well they worked. In order to make this trial, a simulated current intelligence center was created and placed into operation. Unlike the Leviathan system toward which we are working, this Center is manned entirely by live people. Live technological workers (analysts) as well as live supervisors are involved. Only the means by which the live subjects communicate with each other are automated.

We employed an intelligence vehicle, because a simulated current intelligence center combines these properties: It is an organized social group; it is complex; it has hierarchies and subsystems; its principal function is that of solving a limited number of problems, which are themselves complex, hierarchically structured, and dependent on organizing the solutions of subordinate problems into systematic wholes; inputs to the center can be completely known; inputs can be controlled and timed; it is not a simple stimulus-response model; demands on the system can be controlled by the experimenters; the problems are imposed on the group; time available for solution is limited and imposed on the group; the problem-solving techniques are applied methods of logical induction; it solves its problems as a social unit or organism; with suitable computer and paper and pencil techniques, all observation of group interaction can be operational and self-generated (that is, all observation can consist of observing the products of the members of the group); group accomplishment can be identified and time to accomplishment measured; it stresses control functions far more than policy-formation functions.

The Current Intelligence Interpretation Center

For the initial trial, a war game involving five fictitious Mediterranean countries was created, as shown in Figure 4. The countries are Antonia, Benton, Conland, Danton and Eltonia. The purpose of the game is to sense Benton's aggressive intentions and involvement in its three target countries. In one version of the scenario, the first few weeks end with a takeover of one of the states by Benton. The game is so devised that we can stop playing at the end of a five-week period, or continue the game to a limited war, or even to the outbreak of a total nuclear hostility.

The U. S. intelligence center is situated in Eltonia; its function is to gather information on all the countries described. How is the center organized? As shown in Figure 5, the organization has a Center Chief or head of the unit. Reporting to him is a General Analyst, specializing in economic intelligence. The General Analyst is in turn responsible for the activities of a Librarian and a Routing Clerk. Directly under the Center Chief are two area chiefs, namely, a Civilian Area Chief and a Military Area Chief. Responding to the Civilian

Area Chief are three civilian analysts. They have three counterparts in the military responding to the Military Area Chief. In each area, one analyst is responsible for Eltonia, a second analyst is responsible for Benton and Conland, and a third analyst is responsible for all data coming in from Antonia and Danton.

Figure 4

1962 LIVE-MODE EXPERIMENT: Geographic Environment for Simulated Current Intelligence Interpretation Center

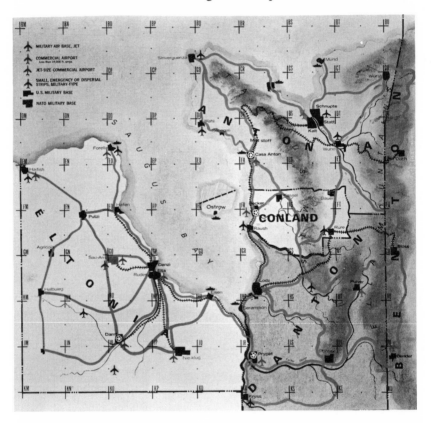

Figure 6 shows the typical complexities of a large-sized, hierarchically structured organization, thus reflecting our conceptual model. Over the unit chief, we have added the commanding officer. He commands the U. S. base at Sau Ami in Eltonia, and he represents the next-larger system context in which is embedded our relatively autonomous intelligence center. At the left, we indicate the external environment that furnishes inputs to and imposes demands upon the

Center. These are shown respectively at the lower and upper left of the figure. At the base of the figure is represented a man-machine interface. This is the result of adding a computerized system to the Center.

Different forms of organization are, of course, also possible. In the organization shown in these Figures 5 and 6, analysts are divided according to military and civilian interests. One could organize instead in terms of geographical areas and then separate out for each area functions such as technological, political, economic and military.

Again, organization could be influenced by certain demands that we might make on the system. We could, for example, demand that the military analysts never submit any report, unless there is complete concurrence among them. This could create strain and friction and consequent need for negotiation at this level. We might, if it were of interest to us, demand that the military group of analysts concur with the civilian group before any communication is sent upward. An interesting possibility would be to demand concurrence among three officers—the civilian and military heads, who report in line to the unit chief, and the deputy chief, who stands in staff capacity

Figure 5

1962 LIVE-MODE EXPERIMENT: Organization Chart for Simulated
Current Intelligence Interpretation Center

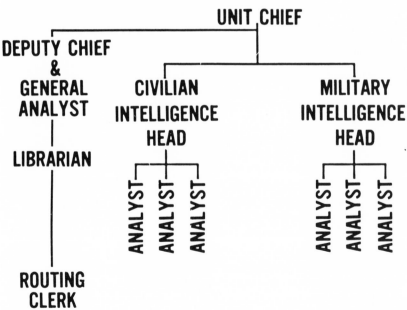

to the unit chief. The game clearly permits wide flexibility for organizational studies. It must be borne in mind, though, that at this point in time and for the very immediate present, we are not primarily studying either organization or intelligence. What we are trying to do is to check out a special type of language for communication.

Figure 6

1962 LIVE-MODE EXPERIMENT: The Simulated Current
Intelligence Interpretation Center Plus Embedding System Environments

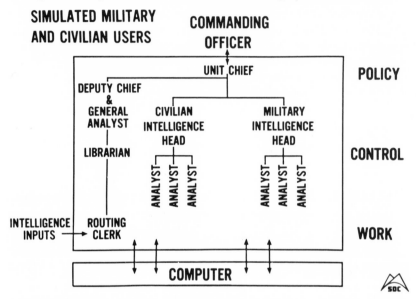

The members of this center must interact among each other as far as possible through the computer. The inputs, that is, the intelligence messages, which come to this center are delivered manually on paper. These inputs—nearly a thousand have been created—represent typical intelligence messages that might come to any real center, such as reports from the press, radio, defectors, agents, tourists, ambassadors and military attachés. A goodly number of them are entirely irrelevant. All messages are under strict experimental control. In addition, the Center is required to submit various kinds of reports, for example, a Weekly Intelligence Summary, or a Special Item Report, or a Monthly Intelligence Digest, or from time to time, Special Area Briefings for visitors. And, of course, all reports concerning imminent hostilities or special stressful situations in the political and economic picture have to be sent at once to the Commanding Officer.

Now the center can make two kinds of responses to these demands.

One is methodological or managerial and the other is substantive. All problems involving the assessment of data or the generation of substantive reports entail the manual activity of writing them out on paper. Problems of a managerial type are handled over the computer. That is, subjects taking the various roles are required to speak to one another through the computer when concerned with a managerial issue. How is communication through the computer accomplished?

The General Operator-Computer Interaction (GOCI) Program.

Picture the following situation: an experimental run is about to begin. Twenty-four subjects can be involved. In our run in April, 1962, we worked with 14 subjects. As shown in the photograph of Figure 7, each of these subjects occupies his own private booth. He sits before a display scope and intervention control equipment. These are interconnected with a Philco 2000 computer. The display scope is an ordinary, medium-sized television tube. The intervention unit,

Figure 7

1962 LIVE-MODE EXPERIMENT: Subjects Operating the Simulated
Current Intelligence Interpretation Center

a little larger than a telephone handset, has 30 buttons and 4 keys. (Shown in idealized form in Figure 8.) This equipment is general-purpose, useful for many games.* When subjects are ready to talk with each other, they take action by pushing appropriate buttons on the control units. In response to these actions, the computer causes natural English phrases to appear on the scopes.

Figure 8

INDIVIDUAL DISPLAY AND INTERVENTION UNITS
EMPLOYED BY SUBJECTS IN LEVIATHAN EXPERIMENTS

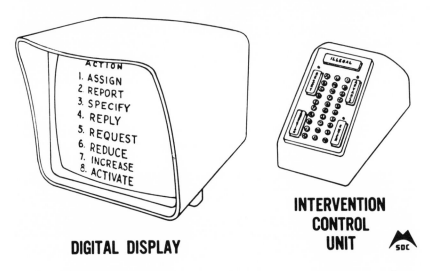

DIGITAL DISPLAY   INTERVENTION CONTROL UNIT

As we begin the session, no messages have yet been sent from one subject to another. Now a chime sounds. On each scope or television tube a display appears, saying:

START OF
PERIOD

After a brief moment, during which the computer is being fed appropriate program cards, a second display appears with the query:

DO YOU WISH
1. TO SEND A
COMMUNICATION

Assume that one of the military analysts wishes to communicate

---

*Although the equipment and laboratory booths were designed especially for the Leviathan experiments, they are also being used in SDC's SSR Laboratory for studying decision making by individual subjects, pattern recognition, artificial intelligence and small-group research.

with one or more of his colleagues. He then presses button 1 and the "enter" key. Instantly another display appears on his scope, saying:

TO WHOM

The analyst now addresses his message. He punches in the proper code name of each addressee, such as AL, DL, AM, BM, DM. (Each subject can address any or all of the 23 others.) Now he presses the "advance" key, then the "enter" key, and is ready to compose his message. A new display appears. It says, "Action," and reads as follows:

ACTION

1 REQUEST FOR
2 REPLYING
3 REQUEST THAT
4 REQ APPROVAL
5 ASSIGN

The player must make a choice. Assume that he presses button 1, meaning "I am making a request for. . . ." This action forces the computer to display the following:

REQUEST FOR

1 REPORT ON
2 ASSIGN DOC NO
3 SEND DATA RE

Suppose that he elects the third option. He presses button 3, requesting "data re"; this action induces the computer to exhibit a list of topics (Figure 9):

TOPICS

1 MILITARY
2 ECONOMIC
3 POLITICAL
4 SOCIOLOGICAL
5 SCIENTIFIC
6 TECHNOLOGICAL

Perhaps the analyst is concerned over rumors about interruptions of transport by air in Benton during the previous week. He takes a series of pushbutton actions. In response to these, the computer successively exhibits appropriate displays. The sequence of displays is shown in Figure 10 and diagramatically mapped in Figure 11. The interventions in Figure 10—"request for," "technological," "specific country"—appear only to the analyst while he is composing the message. They are suppressed on the recipients' displays.

Figure 9

OPERATION OF GENERAL OPERATOR-COMPUTER INTER-ACTION (GOCI) PROGRAM DURING A LEVIATHAN EXPERIMENT

Figure 10

SEQUENCE OF DISPLAYS EMPLOYED TO GENERATE A LEVIATHAN EXPERIMENT MESSAGE:

"Send Data re Interruption of Transport by Air, Benton, Past Week"

```
ACTION
① (REQUEST FOR)→ REQUEST FOR
2 REPLYING        1 REPORT ON
3 REQUEST THAT    2 ASSIGN DOC NO
4 REQ APPROVAL  ③ SEND DATA RE→ TOPICS
5 ASSIGN                        1 MILITARY
                                2 ECONOMIC
                                3 POLITICAL
                                4 SOCIOLOGICAL
                                5 SCIENTIFIC
                             ⑥ (TECHNOLOGICAL)→ SCINTIF TECHNCL
                                1 PRES STATE OF
                                2 RATE GROWTH OF
                                3 DEVELOPMNTS IN
                                4 DEVELOPMNT OF
                                5 CUTBACK IN
                                6 RESEARCH ON
                             ⑦ INTERRUPTN OF→ SCI TECH REFRNCS
                             8 JAMMING OF     ① TRANSPORT BY→ TRANSPORT BY
                             9 PERSONAGE S IN 2 COMMUNICATN BY  1 RAIL
                                              3 SCIENCE         2 ROAD
                                              4 INDUSTRY        3 RIVER
                                                                4 CANAL
                                              ⑤ AIR→ WHERE
                                              6 SEA          1 SURVEILL AREA
                                              7 ALL MEANS    2 ADDRESSEE AREA
                                              8 SPECIAL MEANS 3 WESTERN NATION
                                                             4 UNITED STATES
                                                             5 SOVIET
                                                             6 SOVIET BLOC
                                                             ⑦ (SPECIF COUNTRY)→ SPECIFIC COUNTRY
                                                             8 SPECIF GEOREF   1 ANTONIA
                                                                            ② BENTON→ WHEN
                                                                               3 CONLAND    1 PAST YEAR
                                                                               4 DANTON     2 PAST MONTH
                                                                               5 ELTONIA  ③ PAST WEEK→ END OF MESSAGE
                                                                               6 USA         4 CURRENT     PRESS YOUR
                                                                               7 SOVIET BLOC 5 COMING WEEK  ADVANCE BUTTON
                                                                                             6 COMING MONTH
                                                                                             7 COMING YEAR
```

Figure 11

DIAGRAM OF TREE STRUCTURE USED TO CONTROL
THE SEQUENCE OF DISPLAYS SHOWN IN FIGURE 10

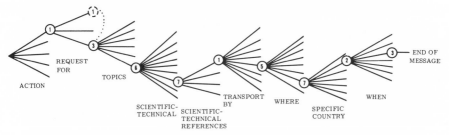

A receiver of the message sees the following on his display scope:

027 DM
SEND DATA RE
INTERRUPTN OF
TRANSPORT BY
AIR
BENTON
PAST WEEK

The top line of the received display indicates the number of the message, in this case 27, assigned sequentially by the computer during an experimental run, and the coded name of the sender of the message.

Should the subject composing a message make a mistake or change his mind while pressing the buttons, he can press the "reset" and "enter" keys. This action permits him to start all over again, without transmitting what he has composed.

The Artificial Experimental Language

The foregoing is an example of how participants in the simulated Current Intelligence Interpretation Center talked with each other through the computer. The total number of different kinds of messages that could and can be framed by the participants is extensive. We call this totality a language. Its scope and power will now be briefly assessed.

As suggested by Figure 11, the language is structured as a tree. The root of the tree is the common display, entitled "Action." Once any message is addressed by a subject in an experiment, composition of that message always begins with this root display. The selection of any one branch of this display then leads to another predetermined display or category of requests which the subject can make. This process of selection is repeated, until a well-formed message has been completed. Thus all possible routes through the entire collection of displays generate a tree, the leaves of which are the terminations of the respective well-formed messages.

The actual tree is defined to the computer in a condensed form. It is not exfoliated branch by branch or leaf by leaf. Suppose, for example, that an analyst in the intelligence center were to ask for a report, rather than merely for *data,* on the interruption of air transport in Benton last week. Then the entire development of the tree issuing from the branch, "Send data re," would be grafted on the branch, "Report on." (See dotted arrows in Figures 10 and 11.) This means that the tree is actually specified to the computer in the form of a net which then in turn defines an ultimate tree.

The net used for the intelligence center simulation has only 81 distinct displays and less than 150 nodes or junctures. (The nodes are the pencils of rays emanating from the circled interventions in Figure 11.) This net does not seriously tax even the limited capacity of the Philco 2000 computer that we are using. The actual tree that results, on the other hand, has over 2,000,000 distinct, well-formed expressions.

This entire language, furthermore, is completely present in the direct-access core memory of the computer. In consequence, the subjects can, first of all, employ the intercommunication equipment in parallel. As many as 24 subjects can independently yet simultaneously compose messages or receive them. Secondly, they can operate the equipment very rapidly. As the subjects became accustomed to the equipment and the operating GOCI programs, during the April 1962 operations, many messages were composed at speeds approaching that of direct verbal discourse. (As we saw above, the entire sentence formulated in figures 10 and 11 requires only nine successive interventions in order to be completed.) To observers watching the participants through one-way glass, displays often succeeded one another too quickly to be recognized. Often displays seemed to be almost subliminally present to the participants.

What Was Accomplished by the April 1962 Simulation

We indicated above that during these laboratory runs, procedural matters, such as requesting reports and assigning priorities, were transmitted over the computer. Substantive matters were carried on by means of handwritten reports. The work of a crew of 14 graduate students was compared with that of a crew composed of subjects with many years of intelligence or other relevant military experience. The experienced analysts operated their center in a purely manual mode. (We had them engage in this activity in order to generate typical messages that we then incorporated into our GOCI vocabulary.) The graduate students worked with the computer. We determined in an intuitive way the loads that the experienced analysts could handle without symptoms of overload. Similar loads were given to the graduate students, who used the computer for procedural intercommunications. Every message they composed over the computer and every message they received was immediately printed and delivered to them within about two minutes. As a result, all procedural matters went over the computer, and it was not necessary for the graduate students to make written records of these matters.

We found that the inexperienced graduate students were not overloaded by the inputs previously imposed upon the experienced intelligence analysts. Their system performance, moreover, was at least equally good. The students' center diagnosed the threat as it developed about as accurately and about as rapidly as did the center operated by the experienced analysts. During one entire simulation session, representing one day in the five simulated weeks of play that comprised the simulation for both crews, we gave the graduate students four times as heavy a load as that previously given the experienced analysts. We still could not overload them. Our intuitive impression was that the students' crew was capable of handling far heavier loads than could the experienced crew operating in the purely manual mode. By relegating procedural matters to the computer, it appears that we left only one task to the crew that operated over the computer—to solve substantive problems.

We wish to emphasize, however, the extremely tentative character of these results. Our objective at the time the simulation was run was not to test the efficiency of the General Operator-Computer Interaction (GOCI) language, but only its feasibility. We sought to determine whether artificial GOCI languages could be constructed that would at once fit into the limited core capacity (16,384 48-bit words) of the Philco 2000 computer that we were using and yet prove practically useful. This we demonstrated. We found, as a matter of fact, that our artificial GOCI languages can be very rich indeed, since hierarchy provides great leverage. As noted above, hundreds of thousands of well-formed expressions can be produced with less than a hundred displays.

The GOCI language proved to be a practical mode of communication in still another way. We had feared that the method of successively presenting displays which had to be read by the subjects would cause the subjects to lose the gist of their intentions before they could complete their sentences. We had intended originally to provide them with teletype printers to record the sentences they were composing step by step as they composed them. We found that this was not necessary. The successions of displays proved to be excellent mnemonic aids. It is almost impossible to be lost during the composition of a message, even when the depth of intervention is as great as twelve levels.

The GOCI programs code the subjects' utterances into highly compact form. Despite this deep coding, the subjects, as we said, did not get lost. Our inference is that the formulation of the GOCI languages benefited greatly from the fact that the subjects' interventions follow a hierarchical structure and that people can comprehend rather tall linguistic hierarchies.

Because the specific vocabularies used in any experiment are parameters to the basic artificial language programs, the actual language trees used in experiments, like their biological counterparts, can evolve or devolve. New branches and leaves can be grown, and obsolescent ones chopped off, without altering the basic computer program. Hence a number of developmental or practical kinds of research become possible. (1) It is possible to evolve languages that are "natural" or efficient or effective for particular command situations and for different levels of command. This can be done by allowing the computer to record what experienced officers say under specific circumstances. The computer, recording who says what to whom under which circumstances, can automatically expunge those sentences which both are rarely used and when used are of minor import. If a new supply of alternative forms is furnished as these excluded sentences are purged, languages can be "grown" in the laboratory. (2) One could use the Leviathan model to explore intelligence information handling. For example, one might run an experiment contrasting the effectiveness of free language with fixed structured language in the area of intelligence. The fixed structure language would be developed from the one now operating for the Leviathan. The experiment would use the intelligence materials already developed for the Leviathan system. In this experiment the criterion of effectiveness would be the time required to sense the various stages in the crescendo of hostility pre-built into the scenario and into the intelligence reports. The question would be: Does the use of a fixed-structure language impede or actually improve system operations? (3) Another practical application arises from the fact that the actual vocabularies used are coded interpretations of the successions of interventions via push-buttons. The same responses, in well-structured control situations, might be interpreted in diverse languages, for example simultaneously in French, German and English. Hence applications for multi-lingual commands, as in NATO, seem feasible. One commander might employ English displays and the sentences composed in English might be directly displayed to other commanders in a basic French and basic German, without further translation. (4) A most important application lies in any field of top-management control: GOCI provides simple and direct interaction in subsets of natural English between executive officers and large, complex computer program systems. With GOCI it is possible to exploit great stores of data and to elaborate tactical plans in highly compressed real time. (5) Applications in the fields of document and fact retrieval are promising, because it is possible to employ retrieval trees that are direct projections of classification trees. (6) Highly interesting applications also exist where physical channel width is very limited or channels are very noisy, since GOCI works *very near the theoretical limit* for translating semantic information into and out of physical carrier information. Where semantic information is composed and transmitted a phrase at a time, GOCI encodes nearly the greatest amount of meaningful communication into the least amount of physical bits.

SIMULATION IN A DUAL (LIVE AND ARTIFICIAL) MODE

Our decision in July of 1961 was to create in the laboratory a simulation in a dual mode, in which a fairly large number of live subjects would be placed in leadership roles over a far more extensive number of artificial agents. Later this year, or perhaps early in 1963, this will be accomplished. The vehicle for this simulation is an Intelligence Communication Control Center. Several hundred artificial agents will be included in the technological system, and up to 24 live subjects will occupy the roles of managers. The live subjects will give guidance to and manipulate the technological system.

How the Live Subjects Communicate with the Artificial Agents

The first basic laboratory problem that naturally arose when we considered live subjects and artificial agents related to designing the link between the live and the artificial agents. How should they intercommunicate? Two separate issues appeared to be at stake. One concerned the question: how should live subjects converse with each other over the computer? The other problem concerned the question: how should live subjects talk to artificial workers represented in the computer? Happily, the solution to both questions was the same. We saw how in the intelligence interpretation center simulation the Leviathan equipment, combined with the GOCI programs and an artificially constructed experimental language, enabled live subjects to communicate with one another over the computer. Exactly the same combination of elements permits live subjects to speak to artificial workers. How is this possible?

Any message composed by Leviathan subjects is completely equivalent to the interventions that are entered into the computer via the pushbuttons. For instance, the message, *Send data re interruption of transport by air in Benton last week,* is translated into the following sequence of nine button pushings: 1, 3, 6, 7, 1, 5, 7, 2, 3. (See

Figures 10 and 11.) When a subject wants to give this order to another live colleague, he expresses it via this set of nine specific interventions, and causes the message to appear on the addressee's display scope.

Now suppose that a live subject wants to send a message, not to a live individual, but instead to an artificial subordinate designated JP. First, the live subject addresses his communication exactly as before. Each artificial subordinate has a coded name: JP, FT, GY, etc. The computer is programmed to identify uniquely each such designation and to cause the designated agents to carry out commands that can be expressed in the experimental language. Assume that the content of the message from the live subject to JP is the following: "Transfer agent CT4 to squad B3 as soon as possible." This message can be composed by the live subject exactly as before. It can be understood as a set of answers to a series of questions posed by the computer in a succession of displays:

Question	Answer
- WHICH ACTION? Request for, replying, request that, request approval, assign?	- REQUEST THAT
- WHICH REQUEST? You send copy, you reply, you investigate, you comply, you send, you transfer?	- YOU TRANSFER
- TRANSFER WHAT?	- AGENT
- WHICH AGENT?	- CT4
- WHERE?	- TO SQUAD
- TO WHICH SQUAD?	- B3
- WHEN SHOULD THE ACTION BE EFFECTED?	- WITH MINIMUM DELAY

Which answers the subject makes to these questions are identified by the pushbuttons he elects to press. For the first question, the answer is *3*. For the second question, it is *6*. Each answer elicits an appropriate question to succeed it as the subject traces his route through the language tree. The last question, when answered, results in a well-formed expression. The computer now has a unique set of interventions made by the live subject and addressed to a specific artificial subject. The computer can be programmed to interpret this unique set and to effect the transfer of the specified agent to the specified squad. This technique of coding and communication between man and machine can be used to transmit intelligence in either direction, from man to computing machinery or in the reverse direction.

The Intelligence Communication Control Center.

We have sketched the manner in which the live managers will address and communicate with the artificial agents in the technological system of an Intelligence Communication Control Center. Now it is appropriate to speak of the simulated center itself. Its function is to receive intelligence messages from worldwide sources, to identify them, and to transmit them to appropriate consumer agencies. It is immaterial where this center is located. Nor does this simulation require any myth of fictitious countries or any synthetic cold war predicament. This center will address itself, not to the intrinsic contents of the individual intelligence messages, but rather to their bulk handling. Its mission is to process very large quantities of messages and to deliver them with minimum delay to the consuming agencies. This task may not always be easy to accomplish. There may be inadequate manpower available; the messages may arrive in unexpected sequences; and the serviced agencies may impose highly conflicting demands.

The organization of this communication control center follows the familiar pattern of our conceptual model. It is a pyramid at whose base is a technological system. Superimposed are the governing systems. The technological society is composed of hundreds of artificial enlisted men and noncommissioned officers. The control and policy offices are manned by live managers, the commissioned officers.

Policy and Control Decisions for the Technological System.

What will the managers in the control system be doing with the technological system? Live controllers will institute fundamental decisions which the robots will interpret and implement. Under the supervision of the policy makers, the controllers will lay down decisions concerning the sorting of messages and their routing over the traffic lanes. They will decide the rate at which messages should be processed over the respective lanes and will have the option to assign priority values. They will also govern the distribution of messages out of the center to the consumers. And, finally, the live controllers will be able to assign and reassign their automated manpower to cope with production requirements.

To appreciate the nature of these decisions and the manner in which the live managers instruct the squads of automated personnel, let us glance at the technological organization (7). What do the automated workers do? They implement decisions. They route, process, and distribute messages, and their artificial squad leaders reallocate personnel.

1. Sorting and Routing. Intelligence messages flow into the center. Each arrives classified according to these eight basic categories (see

Table 1): Subject, Sender, Area, Expedition, Classification, Confidence, Time, Addressee. The numbers of arrivals in each interval of simulated time are set by the experimenters. The kinds of messages arriving during these intervals are determined by probability distributions, also set by the experimenters.

When messages arrive, they enter a storage queue or waiting line. The first tasks of the artificial agents are to inspect them, to sort them, and to decide how to route them over the internal processing lines of the center. The automated personnel, then, have to know how to route. But strictly speaking, as we shall see, the decision rests with the managers—the live managers.

The robots have to sort the messages, in order to route them within the organization. On what basis do they do this? This task is comparable to sorting letters in a post office. To sort mail, distinctions have to be made among the letters that enter a post office. The letters have to be classified. Various schemes of classification are possible. One is by destination—Canada, Oregon, Kentucky, Mexico, and so on. Another basis is urgency—special delivery, airmail, registered, regular mail. Still another basis is type of material—first-class letter mail, educational material, bulk distribution, advertising mail, magazines, and so forth.

Table 1

1963 DUAL-MODE EXPERIMENTS: An Example of a Set of Categories for Classifying Intelligence Messages Entering the Simulated Intelligence Communications Control Center

Field I (Subject)	Field II (Sender)
A = Missiles B = Airplanes C = Space D = Communications E = Industry F = Transportation G = Political H = Forces	A = Military B = Diplomatic C = Electronic D = Scientific E = Agent
Field III (Area)	Field IV (Expedition)
A = Europe B = N. America C = S. America D = N. Asia E = S. Asia F = Africa G = Pacific H = Space	A = Flash B = Operational 　　Immediate C　　Priority D = Routine E = Deferred

Table 1

Field V (Classification)	Field VI (Confidence)
A = Q Secret B = Top Secret C = Secret D = Confidential E = Unclassified	A = High B = Medium C = Low D = Neutral
Field VII (Time)	Field VIII (Addressee)

A = 00-03 hours
B = 03-06 hours
C = 06-09 hours
D = 09-12 hours
E = 12-15 hours
F = 15-18 hours
G = 18-21 hours
H = 21-24 hours
	A = Executive
	B = Diplomatic
	C = Intelligence
	D = Military
	E = Executive, Diplo-
	      matic, Intelligence
	F = Executive, Diplo-
	      matic, Military
	G = Executive, Intelli-
	      gence, Military
	H = Diplomatic, Intelli-
	      gence, Military

The basic fields (shown in Table 1) by which the incoming intelligence messages are classified provide the basis of initial sorting and routing by the robots. There are eight fields and up to ten classifications under each. Thus, multiplying the eight fields together, 10^8 or one hundred million combinations are possible. The scheme represented in Table 1 provides for 2,048,000 combinations (8 x 5 x 8 x 5 x 5 x 4 x 8 x 8). Sorting into this many distinct combinations would be troublesome even for computing machinery, for one would have to do something different with each different sort. Such complexity would be impossible for live managers to comprehend in detail.

We reduce the game to comprehensible and manageable, yet challenging, proportions, by forcing a limited number of policy and control decisions on the live managers. At the very outset, the managers have to make two kinds of decisions. These two relate to routing. First, they have to choose one of the eight fields to be the basis on which routing decisions are made. Second, within the given field they have selected, the live managers must decide which sorts of messages should be routed to which of the possible traffic lanes. Once these decisions concerning routing have been taken by the live managers and communicated to the automated personnel, the in-

structions will be carried out and decisions of implementation will
be made by the artificial enlisted men. The decisions can be changed
by the managers as an experiment proceeds. Specific managers, furthermore, can be given specific responsibilities for choosing the sorting
field and for routing within that field.

Routing policy, or routing decision, can be exceedingly critical.
For example, suppose the live managers instruct the automated personnel to route according to field four, called *expedition*. Suppose further that they decide that all *flash* messages should be routed over line
one, *operational immediate* messages over line two, *priority* messages
over line three, and so on. In effect this might, in times of stress
particularly, create havoc within the center. It is conceivable that the
route carrying the flash messages might become overloaded, as the
Los Angeles freeway system often does with automobiles, with the
unexpected consequence that routine and deferred messages might receive quicker attention than higher priority messages.

Again, should the live managers decide that the automated workers
should proceed to route by field three which defines geographical
area, and should they determine that all messages from Europe go
over line one, those concerning North America over line two, and so
on, then in effect the system would be operating according to a geographical distribution. As a result, in times of sudden critical shifts
of urgency from one area to another, the center might not be able
to react sensitively enough. This would be especially the case if one
consuming agency, perhaps the diplomatic, should require priority
treatment of messages from specific geographical areas, while another
agency, perhaps the intelligence, should require special treatment for
messages relating to specific classes of subject matters, such as space
and communications, and a third, the military, should request minimum
delay for all kinds of messages sent by military senders.

Sorting and routing decisions are important in a distribution system.
The bases for sorting and routing become matters for high-level
policy decision. They can affect how many times an item has to be
inspected before it reaches its destination, through how many different
channels it flows, which parts of the system have to do what, and how
much effort will have to be exerted by each part of the system. And
all this can change as the patterns of incoming items change. Hence the
organization of the technological system is deeply affected by the initial
sorting and routing.

These considerations all entered into the design of the Intelligence
Communication Control Center. We want policy to be made by the
live managers and to be implemented by the artificial agents. We
require a high degree of flexibility in organizing the technological system.

It has to be capable of drastic reorganization at the decision of the live managers during the course of play. A further characteristic that had to be built into the simulation is that any existing organization of the technological system and any reorganization both have to be readily visualized by the live managers, because human decision makers in large social environments have to form intellectual maps of the contexts in which they operate.

    2. Processing. After routing, the second major function of the center is its processing activity. The processing lines of the center are assembled out of unit modules (see Figure 12). The modules

Figure 12

1963 LEVIATHAN DUAL-MODE (Live-Artificial) EXPERI-MENTS: Modular Unit for the Technological System of a Simulated Intelligence Communication Control Center

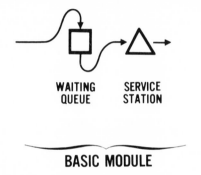

WAITING   **SERVICE**
QUEUE   **STATION**

BASIC MODULE

consist of a waiting queue and a service station at which the messages flowing through the center are processed after they have been routed. Processing is analogous to such organizational activities as recording, stamping, filing, indexing and classifying. The stations are the places where tasks such as these are said to be performed.

    For any specific experiment, the processing modules can be assembled like an erector set (see Figure 13). Several modules are arranged to follow one another in a linear series. Each series constitutes a single processing line. The experimenters can specify how many processing lines shall be available for operation. From one to ten are possible. Each processing line is completely independent of any other. Once any message has been routed to any one line, it cannot leave that line until completely processed. Along each of the parallel processing lines, the experimenters can provide from one to five successive modules. Hence the total modular array can have up to ten parallel processing lines with five modules in each—a

Figure 13

1963 DUAL-MODE EXPERIMENTS: Assembly of Modular Units in the Technological System of a Simulated Intelligence Communications Control Center

SIX BY THREE ARRAY

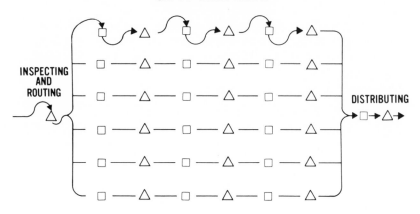

total of fifty unit modules—or any lesser number of modules, even only a single module. The modular array is specified by the experimenters for each Leviathan simulation effort.

The artificial agents man the initial routing station and the processing lines over which the intelligence messages are routed. Obviously, it is important for the automated workers to process and dispatch messages as expeditiously as possible. For this purpose, the live managers must make two further decisions, this time concerning how the robots are to inspect and to evaluate the messages at the various stations. Once more, the managers *select message fields,* one for each station, to which they wish the technological system to pay attention. Then, within the chosen fields, the live managers *assign priority values* to the various component classifications. These priority values range from 1 to 4 in descending order of importance.

Suppose, for example, that messages endorsed by their senders as meriting a high degree of confidence are segregated and routed over a special, high-confidence processing line. At the first stage, the managers might elect to expedite space messages with a priority of 1, political with priority of 2, and so on. Here the robots would be sorting by subject matter. At the second station along the same line the robots could be instructed to sort by expedition assigned by sender, according to the table:

Expedition	*Priority to be Assigned*
Flash	1
Operational Immediate	2
Priority	3
Routine	4
Deferred	4

Further priority treatment could be given at subsequent stations along the high-confidence processing line.

Both the priority control fields and the priorities assigned to their subordinate classifications can be changed at the will of the live managers during an experimental run. Thus, as with changes in routing, changes in the assignment of priority values during processing can take place in the automated society as it operates. The third function, namely distribution, is similarly activated and guided by living managers as were the previous two.

3. Manpower Allocation. Critical to an operating system is the managerial power to allocate and to reallocate manpower according to the challenge of the system's environment and according to its human resources. Hence one may ask what is the character of the artificial, automated agents in our Leviathan simulations? They man the technological system; they provide the source of energy for effecting the routing, processing and distribution function. But how shall we picture them? Strictly speaking the artificial agents are not treated as unique individuals, but rather as prototypes. Just as the human organism from the point of view of a chemist may be looked upon as a mixture of minerals, carbohydrates and protein molecules, so each artificial agent may be considered to be a mixture of four types of skills or aptitudes. These are interpreted to be clerking, coordinating, testing, and computing. And like the chemist, we ascribe to each agent specific quantities in each category of ability. For example, one artificial agent may have an ability profile like the following: He may consist of 500 units of clerking ability, 950 units of coordinating skill, 1500 in testing, and 3500 units in computational ability (see Table 2.) The model provides for up to 25 classes of such profiles, that is, 25 kinds of mixes or job classifications. Table 3 shows a typical squad of seven workers, their respective skill or aptitude mixes, and the combined over-all resources of the team as a whole.

This quantitative method allocates aptitude resources in specific measured units to the squads of artificial agents. It permits the system to expend energy and suffer depletion and thus be charged for work performed. These units of energy we call taylors. The amounts as-

Table 2

1963 DUAL-MODE EXPERIMENTS:

An Example of Aptitude Profiles of Artificial, Automatic Agents

ID of Profile	Aptitudes				Total
	Data-Coordinating	Message Clerking	Testing	Computational	
01	950	500	1,500	3,500	6,450
02	3,741	700	1,000	900	6,341
03	475	400	700	600	2,175
04	575	600	500	750	2,425
05	5,000	700	1,500	500	7,700
06	9,500	1,500	700	5,000	16,700

Table 3

1963 DUAL-MODE EXPERIMENTS:
The Manpower Resources of a Typical Squad
of Seven Artificial, Automatic Agents

Profile	Quantity	Aptitudes				Squad Total
		D-C	MC	T	C	
01	4	3,800	3,000	6,000	14,000	26,800
03	2	950	800	1,400	1,200	4,350
06	1	9,500	1,500	700	5,000	16,700
Totals	7	14,250	5,300	8,100	20,200	47,850

signed to given workers, their rate and place of depletion are determined by the experimenters.

Artificial agents can be grouped into varying squad configurations. For example, Figure 14 depicts a modular 8-by-3 array of traffic lines. The circles are the waiting queues, and the elongated oval areas are the service stations.

The artificial agents can be given responsibility over these various routing lines. As shown in Figure 15 they can be organized into 32 squads. The various markings indicate which ones fall under some one managerial responsibility. In the example in Figure 15, squads 1, 2, 3 and 4 come under the supervision of manager AAA. Squads 9, 10, and 17, on the other hand, fall under manager AAB. Squads 27, 31, 28, and 32 fall under the supervision of BBB.

At any time during the course of an experiment, when deemed necessary or appropriate, the live managers can make personnel rearrangements or transfers. An individual artificial agent may be taken

Figure 14

1963 DUAL-MODE EXPERIMENTS: Example of Modular (8 x 3) Array in the Technological System of a Simulated Intelligence Communications Control Center.

(Waiting queues (circles) and service stations (ovals) assembled as eight three-stage traffic lines)

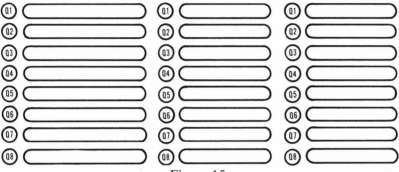

Figure 15

1963 DUAL-MODE EXPERIMENTS: Possible Configuration of Live Command and Artificial Manpower in a Simulated Intelligence Communications Control Center.

(Artificial agents are grouped into 32 squads. The squads are allocated to specific regions on traffic lines in 8 x 3 modular array and assigned to live managers in a pyramid of command)

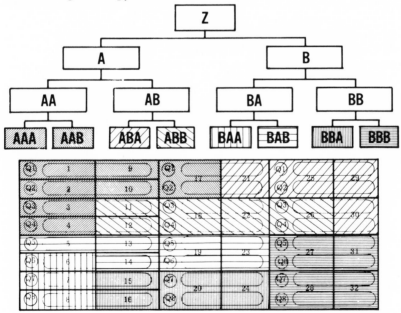

from a squad, put into a reservoir or a pool, and then reassigned to another squad. These changes are made depending on the amount of artificial human energy available within the various squads. And here, obviously, an opportunity for conflict can arise, unless the managers make appropriate provisions to avoid such conflicts. For example, if the squads are so arranged that some come under the supervision of a personnel manpower supervisor, some under the guidance or control of a traffic supervisor, some under a production supervisor, then, as in real life, problems can arise unless handled with patience and wisdom by the managers.

The ability to group artificial workers into squads means that both hierarchical organization and territorial arrangements are strictly defined to the computer programs. Who reports to whom through the entire chain of command is specified in detail. No agent, whether live or artificial, can enter into a simulation unless socially located in a pyramid of authority and responsibility. These prerogatives are monitored by the computer; illegal actions and unauthorized attempts to extend individual power are automatically brought to the attention of the live subjects whose authority, rights and privileges are violated. All managerial negotiations, of course, will be conducted over the computer with an experimental language evolved from the April, 1962, Current Intelligence Interpretation Center vocabulary.

The Dual-Mode Simulation in Operation.

What will a trained observer's eye see, when the dual mode simulation is in operation? As in the prior, April 1962, simulation, he will first observe many subjects sitting in individual, curtained booths in the Leviathan laboratory. One may be smoking a cigarette, another doodling on paper, or a third scowling at the ceiling. Others may be pushing buttons on the Leviathan EXCOM intervention boxes while casually glancing at successions of digital displays. Still others may be intently reviewing files of data. Moving about among the booths will be couriers. The couriers will be operating in their own live logistic support organization, most probably developed by themselves as a subculture.

Out of sight, in other rooms, but also visible, will be operators, programmers, engineers and maintenance personnel. These will be tending a modern digital computer installation, special electronic buffering equipment between the computer and the subjects, and a high speed printer. All this equipment will be working in concert. Supporting these operations will be an intercommunication system, a public address system, and microphone monitoring equipment. Under the floor, out of sight, will be a maze of cables and wiring. And between the laboratory room and the equipment areas will be messengers bearing the output of the on-line printers to the laboratory courier system.

What does all this elaborate activity mean? The observer is given to understand that an experiment is in progress. The live subjects are not just lone individuals. They are occupying structured leadership roles, appropriate to a large social group. In this case, their group is interpreted as the Intelligence Communication Center. Three sorts of pressure are impinging on the subjects: the external demands of the consumer agencies, the internal demands of the center, and the incoming work units—said to be messages emanating from all parts of the world. The subjects are devising strategies for resisting, reconciling, integrating and compromising these demands. They are negotiating, arguing, consulting and thus arriving at critical social decisions.

These decisions are not always harmonious. Often they conflict and are even incoherent. This is so for many reasons. First, the subjects are placed hierarchically in separate levels of command. They thus enjoy and exercise different degrees of power and are solving problems different in kind and in scope. Secondly, they have responsibility and authority over different territories in the technological system. This means that the information which they receive, the rate at which they receive it, and the timing of the information varies from subject to subject. Accordingly, subjects are making different judgments concerning internal operations and are predicting differently concerning the kinds, amounts, and timing of the loads expected to burden their areas. Moreover, as this information is rising in the pyramid of command, it is becoming variously interpreted, evaluated, and aggregated in response to policy directives and specific orders filtering downward. Thirdly, the resources at the subjects' command, both physical and artificially human, are differentially apportioned. Finally, the subjects are struggling to arrive at policy decisions concerning the conflicting demands of the consumers. These decisions will inescapably reflect their own individual propensities, their abilities to cope with crises and uncertainty, their continuing conceptual assessment of the internal organization, and especially the character of their collective managerial initiative.

What else will the observer see? This depends on the particular experiment which happens to be in progress and its stage of development.

The First Dual-Mode Experiment: Group Organization

In the initial dual-mode experiment, the principal independent variable will be group organization. Four types of organizational structures will be realized in the laboratory. All four will have the following characteristics in common: they will consist of five echelons of command. The upper three levels of each of the pyramids will be manned by live subjects, the lower two by artificial agents. At the apex of each pyramid will be a center commander. Reporting to him will be four officers, in the role of branch chiefs. Each branch chief will in turn be responsible for four group heads. Thus each pyramid will have 21 live subjects—one of the highest rank (at Level V), four of the next rank (at Level IV), and 16 of the third level (Level III). (See Table 4). These 21 will enact the leadership roles in their respective organizations.

Table 4

1963 DUAL-MODE EXPERIMENTS:
Proposed Hierarchy and Manning for Initial 1963 Experiment

Level	Span of Control	Number of Personnel by Level	Number of Personnel by Kind	Total Number of Personnel
V Command	4 Branches	1	21 Live	More than 700
IV Branch	4 Groups	4		
III Group	4 Squads	16		
II Squad	8 Members or more	64	600-700	
I Operation	None	More than 500	Artificial	

Descending now to the artificial levels, four squads of artificial agents will report to each of the 16 third-level live officers, making 64 squads in all (at Level II). Every squad will be headed by an artificial squad leader, interpreted as a non-commissioned officer. Each of the 64 squads will be manned by eight or more artificial enlisted men. Thus there will be more than 500 artificial enlisted men (at Level I). Together with the 64 squad leaders, the organization will contain some six or seven hundred artificial agents.

So much for the common characteristics among the four organizations. How are they different? Two generating principles dictate the specific differentiations among the four organizations. These generating principles are *territory* and *function*. Territory consists of the modular assembly of nine traffic routes, each route consisting of a cascade of five successive modules, thus yielding an array of 45 modules at which processing occurs. At the entrance to the entire modular assembly is an initial routing module, and at its exit is a distributing module, making a grand total of 47 modules. At each of the 45 processing modules, four distinct *functions* are exercised. These are directed by the live subjects and implemented by the artificial agents. The functions are:

- Priority administration
- Production control
- Traffic control, including routing and sorting
- Manpower allocation

From the interplay of functional rights and territorial jurisdictions, four distinctive types of organizations emerge (see Figure 16).

Type I is an omnifunctional system. Neither on the branch nor on the group level is there any division of labor. Put differently, in this organization, each of the four branch heads performs all four functions: each one administers priorities, guides production, directs traffic and governs manpower. (This is indicated by the four large black circles.) Similarly, within every branch, each of the four group heads has multifunctional duties (this is indicated by the 16 small black circles). Each, if you will, is a jack-of-all-trades. As one would expect, such complete lack of functional specialization forces the system into an extreme territorial pluralism. That is to say, precisely because each branch and each group is fully self-sufficient in the exercise of power, necessarily their artificial subordinates will be analogously autonomous and self-contained; but as a result, the geographic span of control for the artificial agents becomes severely bounded and fragmented. Interestingly, then, the greater the concentration of functions on the third and fourth organizational levels, the less the territorial control on the lowest levels.

In the second system, type II, there is no diversification of functions on the branch level. Here, too, each of the four branch heads exercises all four functional roles (indicated by the four large black circles). On the group level, however, diversity does enter. Each member of a set of four group heads, reporting to a given branch, is performing one and only one role. This is indicated respectively by the distinctive markings: $\odot$ $\oplus$ $\pmb{\mathbb{C}}$ $\bigcirc$. They stand respectively for priority, production, traffic, and manpower. This functional arrangement will compel both territorial overlapping and territorial division— but not fragmentation—on the lowest levels. For example, each of the four groups (designated by the symbol $\odot$) exercising the priority

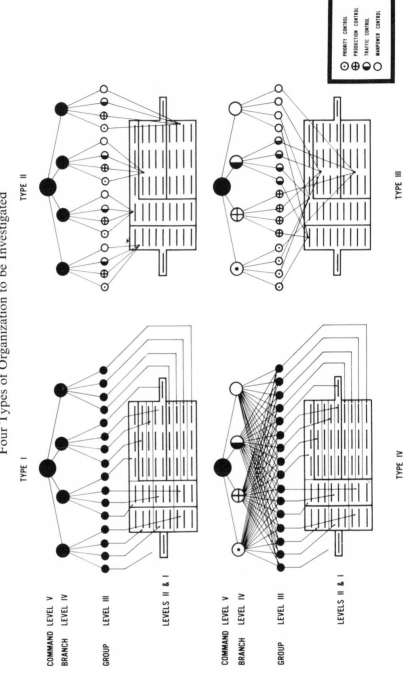

Figure 16

1963 DUAL-MODE EXPERIMENTS:
Four Types of Organization to be Investigated

function does so over an identical area in which one of the four groups (designated by the symbol ⊕) is controlling production. In each case, each of the respective groups has authority, limited to its function, over a given and restricted region within the technological system. In this system, perforce, each branch head has his own limited territorial domain, which, indeed, exactly coincides with that of each of his group heads.

The third type of organization is characterized by complete functional diversity on both branch and group levels. One branch head, ○, is in charge of manpower allocation; the second, ⊙, authorizes priorities; a third, ⊕, determines production roles; and the fourth, ◑, governs traffic. On the group level, in turn, each set of four group heads is performing the same unique functions as their respective branch heads. This functional arrangement leads to a complete overlapping of territory among the four branch heads. Indeed, here territorial distinctions on the branch level are meaningless. On the group level, by contrast, within each of the branches, territorial distinctions are significant.

Finally, in the fourth type of organization, there is functional diversity on the branch level, but none on the group level. This means that each branch head exercises his particular functional authority over all 16 group heads. This arrangement again makes territorial division insignificant on the branch level. But on the group level, territory becomes assigned in fragments and precisely as in type I.

Control of Stress in Dual-Mode Experiment.

Each type of organization will be subjected to identical sets of stimuli, repeated from one experimental run to another. The stochastic composition and timing of the input messages to the entire organization will be controlled by the experimenters, with respect to:

- Load: Quantity of messages entering the technological system within each epoch of simulated time.
- Predictability: Degree to which successive sets of messages entering the system are similar from epoch to epoch. Based on this measure, the subjects in any experimental run are more or less able to predict how many and what kinds of messages will arrive next at the communication center as an experiment proceeds.
- Impingement: Differential loading of the several traffic lines in the technological system from epoch to epoch.

Varying these three controls will affect the kind, degree and timing of the stresses imposed on the entire communication center by the stimuli-messages. Stimuli, of course, are not the only means by which the experimenters can control the environment in which the laboratory

organization operates. Our conceptual paradigm (see Figure 3) recognizes another element in policy formation and system control,
namely, demands imposed on a total system by its consumers. Accordingly, each of the four types of organizations will be subjected to
identical sets of demands, presented in the same sequence. These
demands will be timed and controlled with respect to:

- Load: Quantity of messages requested by each of the four
  consumer agencies (diplomatic, military, intelligence, and executive) impinging upon the governing system during each epoch
  of simulated time
- Predictability: Regularity in the quantities, and kinds of demands
  imposed from epoch to epoch by each consumer agency.
- Coherence: Degree to which the demands imposed by the different consumers are compatible at any given epoch of simulated
  time.

The uncontrolled or problematic element in our experiments will
be reaction to crisis. "Crisis" itself, of course, can be precisely defined in terms of the messages entering the communication center and
the demands placed upon it by its consumers. The sequences in which
these occur, their specific kinds, their duration, their over-all composition and their manner of easement all serve to constitute what the
experimenters view as crises. As each of these elements is specified, the
kind, duration and magnitude of such a critical episode is controlled.

Automatic Data Recording, Interpretation, and Analysis.

The computer does more than simply effect the simulation. It also
performs all experimental observations. The experimenters are not
employed as observers during experimental runs. Some observations are
direct or first order. Others may be called second order. The latter
consist of a combination of direct recording and computer interpretation by means of data analysis programs designed by the experimenters. At this time, these data interpretation programs have not
been completely formulated; as a matter of fact, they will continue to
be developed as the Leviathan project progresses.

Among the first-order data that will be directly recorded are
those that relate to the performance of the technological system.
These include:

- *Elapsed time* (simulated time) of messages through the system,
  by categories of messages.
- *Order of messages* entering the system *vs.* order leaving the system,
  as indicative of the effects of priority filtering disciplines and
  policies.
- Times when *overload* conditions occur and kinds of occasions of
  overload.

- Utilization of artificial human *energy*.
- Unused *production capacity*.
- *Counts of messages* at various stations in the technological system at various epochs of simulated time.
- Degree to which *demands* imposed on the system are satisfied by the total system. Nature and timing of imbalances.

The foregoing first-order data recording programs are not un-expected when one reflects that a computer is being used to stage the experiments. Two important facts about the Leviathan simulation and their implications must be kept in mind: first, that all interactions among the subjects take place over the computer and, second, that an artificial language, tailored to the specific needs of each experiment, is imposed by the experimenters on the subjects. The first fact of com-munication over the computer means that the computer can record all conventional sociometric data: who talks to whom, how often, direction over a possible two-way communication channel, and when, in experimental time, each message is sent.

The second fact of an artificial or contrived experimental language promises to be even more significant. Since every possible response allowed the subjects is defined in advance, and since only the responses specified by the experimenters can be employed by the subjects, a major element in the study of social groups, namely, what is expressed and communicated by the individual members of any group, is there-by brought under laboratory control. By using a restricted, artificial, structured language, the experimenters completely specify the domain of possible responses involved in the design of every experiment. They control what the subjects can express, including redundancy, scope, generality, mood, syntax, semantic content, relevance, reference and many other major features of verbal expression. All this semantic content, moreover, can be recorded in the context of a struc-tured, dynamically active social group. Subjects are identified by social role and formally allocated authority and power. The actual web of intercommunication which such subjects evolve over such hierarchies can be recorded, and its development followed in experi-mental time. Because each response is defined by the specific push-button interventions elected by the subjects while they use the artificial language, first-order or direct data recording can automatically be effected by the computer on the levels of the live control and policy formation systems. To eliminate the danger of excessive or over-refined accumulation of data, special data reduction programs are necessary. The very computing machinery that collects data can be used to sift and reduce them to simple patterns of formal power and authority, of intercommunication, and linguistic expression. There is never need to allow raw data to leave the magnetic tapes that record it. Instead, the hypotheses being tested are employed to specify how the data shall be automatically interpreted, and the computer directly yields aggregated and interpreted results.

The interpretation programs that we have in mind are not conventional statistical programs. Rather, we are in process of formulating programs that will provide information in the following areas:

1. Performance of the Control System:
   a. Sensitivity to loads in the technological system.
   b. Sensitivity to policy-commands.
   c. Extra-formal arrangements and their effects.
   d. Communication patterns among the live subjects on the group and branch levels.
   e. Kinds of expressions employed by group and branch leaders.
2. Performance of the Policy System:
   a. Sensitivity to performance of the technological system.
   b. Quality of knowledge of results at the technological level.
   c. Sensitivity to policy proposed by the control system.
   d. Sensitivity to performance of the control system.
   e. Knowledge of the nature, timing and extent of demands imposed by the consuming agencies.
   f. Sensitivity to such demands.
   g. Quality, timing, and relevance of command decisions.

It should be readily apparent that when placed into laboratory operation this fall (1962), the dual-mode simulation will not be confined to providing information concerning the communication net among the subjects. It goes beyond such conventional studies of group organization and performance. Important elements in the experimental design are hierarchy, function, and imposition of a policy formation system over the technological and cybernetic control systems.*

Hierarchy provides the large-group setting of systems and subsystems in complex organization. Individuals occupy roles that interinvolve one another, and each speaks as an officer of an organization, located in a particular office. *Function* serves to differentiate the offices and their social tasks. It provides for subsystems (think of an autonomic or sympathetic-nervous system, a blood circulation system or a hormone system) defined by class of actions. *Policy formation* introduces a structure of criteria and values; in terms of policy, information

---

*Operations research scientists are just beginning to extend the study of interplay of processes of productivity with processes of control beyond the area of communication switching systems like telephone networks. The study of policy formation and its interplay with control processes is not amenable to conventional optimization techniques.

has meaning, system performance receives direction, and evaluation becomes a basic element of system operation.

The experiments designed for dual-mode operations exercise all three basic elements. Hierarchy and functions are defined and controlled by the experimenters. Policy formation and implementation are the responses of the live subjects. What will be observed will be the growth and function of extra-formal patterns of authority, coordination, rivalry and conflict. The four types of organization that we shall investigate will channel these activities in different ways. In each, the branch heads and the group heads have radically different outlooks from what they have in the other three forms of organization and the problems they have to solve are different. But each of the four organizations has to solve the same over-all problems in the same order. It has been said that people can make almost any pattern of organization viable. Leviathan will enable us to observe how they do this.

Results Sought in the First Dual-Mode Experiment.

The key questions for which answers will be sought in the first dual-mode experiment are of two kinds:

1. System Effectiveness. Does a shift to any one of the four official forms of organization make a very noticeable difference in the ability of a group of individuals to cope with imposed demands and input loads? Are there large and repeated differences in the ways the several organizational structures sense new conditions, discriminate them, react and adjust to them, track their continuance, detect their relaxation, and adjust to their removal? Do the specific patterns, durations and magnitudes of the imposed conditions result in characteristically different responses from the several organizational structures?

2. System Adjustments. What are the internal patterns of adjustment to the changing imposed conditions? These internal adjustments are extra-formal patterns of authority, communication and interaction. Are these internal adjustment patterns peculiar to different forms of organization? Can their effects be observed? Are there large and repeated effects peculiar to specific organizational structures?

As of August, 1962 these questions are solely guide lines for the first experiment. All current planning, including basic design of the first experiment, is tentative.

SUMMARY

Leviathan is a unique experimental approach to the study of large-scale organizations. Leviathan is a concept, a laboratory facility, and a set of computer programs.

The concept provides an idealized framework for such large social groups as a military command, a government bureau, or an industrial corporation. In real life, these groups manifest a varied, conflicting and confused interplay of power, policy, decision, authority, communication and procedure. By means of our conceptual schema, we translate this chaos into a multi-dimensional topology amenable to investigation in a computerized laboratory. Thereby we achieve the simplicity and clarity of computer-coded expression and formulation, while preserving the hierarchical and functional complexity that characterizes social behavior in large groups.

The result is an artificial society operating in the laboratory. The society combines live subjects with artificial agents. The live subjects enact leadership and managerial roles. Their policy decisions and strategies are implemented by the artificial agents. The computer serves four purposes. It represents or simulates the productive skills and behavior of the artificial agents; it provides the artificial language and communication facility for the live subjects to speak with each other and with the robots; and it provides automatic measurement, recording and data reduction of all the behavior of managers and of the accomplishments of the robots. It also automates the analysis and interpretation of the data that it accumulates.

Three simulations have been discussed in this paper. Two have been realized: an automatic-mode simulation in June of 1961 and a live simulation in April of 1962. The automatic mode demonstrated to us the feasibility of operating a complex technological system on a large modern computer. This was the productive facility that our live executives were to direct and manage. The live simulation demonstrated the practicality of operating a control system in a computerized laboratory. The live subjects were required to communicate through the computer. In this way an artificial language is imposed on the subjects of an experiment, forcing on them a restricted and controlled set of responses. The computer at the same time records all interactions.

The third, dual-mode simulation will combine live subjects and artificial agents. The computer programs for the simulation are being developed and checked out.

Looking ahead, a fully automatic mode of operation will eventually be undertaken incorporating within it the lessons to be learned from the experimental study of large organizations in the Leviathan laboratory. By 'fully automatic', we mean the representation on a computer of all three system levels—the technological, the control and the policy formation. These will be operating in concert on the computer and will be manned exclusively by artificial agents. Necessarily, such an automatic society will explicitly embody a theoretical, albeit limited, formulation of social behavior in large organizations.*

BIBLIOGRAPHY

1. Festinger, Leon. *A Theory of Cognitive Dissonance.* Evanston, Ill.: Row, Peterson Co., 1957

2. Herold, Virginia Parry. *Bibliography of Project Leviathan Documents.* Santa Monica, Calif.: System Development Corporation, November 2, 1964 (TM-983/000/01)

3. Huntington, Samuel P. *The Common Defense; Strategic Programs in National Politics.* New York: Columbia University Press, 1961

4. Rome, Beatrice K. and Sydney C. *Communication and Large Organizations.* Two Lectures Presented at the Air Force Office of Scientific Research Summer Scientific Seminar on Communication Cybernetics, Cloudcroft, New Mexico, June 17-18, 1964. Santa Monica, Calif.: System Development Corporation, September 4, 1964 (SP-1690/000/00). Somewhat shorter version published under the title, *Programming the Bureaucratic Computer,* in IEEE *Spectrum,* December, 1964, pp. 72-92.

5. _____ "Computer Simulation toward a Theory of Large Organizations," in *Computer Applications in the Behavioral Sciences,* ed. by Harold Borko (Englewood Cliffs, N. J.: Prentice-Hall, Inc., 1962) 522-555

6. _____ "Formal Representation of Intentionally Structured Systems," in *Information Retrieval and Machine Translation,* ed. by Allen Kent. Proceedings of the International Conference for Standards on a Common Language for Machine Searching and Translation (New York: Interscience Publishers, 1960) vol. III, part I, pp. 468-476

7. _____ *The Leviathan Technological System for the PHILCO 2000 Computer.* Santa Monica, Calif.: System Development Corporation, 1962 (TM-713)

8. Ross, E. A. *The Principles of Sociology.* New York: The Century Co., 1920

---

*Although our principal interests are in the theoretical and experimental domains, nevertheless the practical or developmental applications of Leviathan should be noted. These include:
- Evaluating effective patterns of organization.
- Evaluating system efficiency at the policy level.
- Developing logistic problems.
- Improving management of limited system resources.
- Studying large-group decision-making processes.
- Training and testing managers.
- Exploring inter and intra-system communication.
- Developing a structured intelligence language.
- Developing command language.

Automated Learning Process (ALP)

BEATRICE K. ROME and SYDNEY C. ROME*

Conceptual Scheme

THE topic of this paper is Automated Learning Process. In the course of this paper, we will describe a plan or design for modeling a real college or school system on a digital computer. The pivotal notion here is the combination of live people and automated students. We will trace the step-by-step formulation of this model to the point where it is ready for incorporation into computer programs.

Our initial point of departure is a conceptual scheme or map as illustrated in Figure 1. Actually, this is three-fold.

First of all, we recognize and assert the need of a model in order to model. Consequently, our first schematic representation (Figure 1a) is the most general and abstract. It represents the over-all domain of all possible human knowledge. It is an expression of the goals of human knowledge - similar to Bacon's *Great Insauration* or to his *Novum Organum,* or to Plato's plan in the *Republic* for the education of the guardians and the philosopher-king, or to Descartes' tree of knowledge. Turning to more recent examples, one could cite Whitehead's *Aims of Education* (8) or John Dewey's *Reconstruction in Philosophy* (5). Each of these is an example of a universal and comprehensive schematic representation of human knowledge. It encompasses humanities, sciences, mathematics, logic, etc., but always from a given perspective or point of view. Thus, while Figure 1a is broad and abstract, it remains moored to the demands of culture and time.

---

*See page 257.

Figure 1

CONCEPTUAL MAP, FROM GENERAL TO SPECIFIC, FOR THE
FORMULATION OF AN AUTOMATED LEARNING
PROCESS MODEL

AUTOMATED LEARNING PROCESS MODEL

CONCEPTUAL SYSTEM

1a. Schematic Representation of the Goals of Human Knowledge

CONCEPTUAL SYSTEM

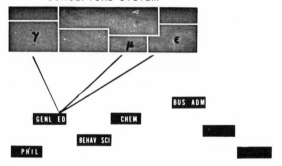

1b. Schematic Representation of the Goals or Desired Intellectual
Image of a Given Institution

CONCEPTUAL SYSTEM

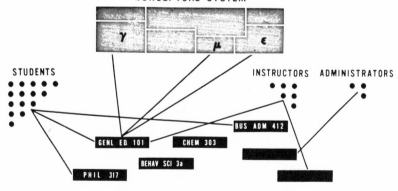

PROGRAM OF COURSES

1c. Concrete Expression of an Institution's Agreed-Upon Plan for
Realizing Its Goals or Intellectual Image

The second map (Figure 1b) is also abstract but less so than the first. It symbolizes the ideal intellectual image which a given college or university seeks to project of itself. St. John's College, for example, with its Great Books Program is quite different in objective and intent from Haverford or Queens. MIT offers a different profile from Swarthmore or the University of Chicago. In each case, however, the college image of intellectual objectives represents a compromise; it is a mix, a pattern carved from the first map to suit its own needs and mission.

The third map (Figure 1c), also is a view of an idealized abstract form. It represents a college's agreed-upon plan as embodied in the school's catalogue. Given the general goals of knowledge in the first map, then the specific image or mission of a school carves for itself in map 2, it then further expresses its goals in a particular curriculum of courses, concerts, and honors and in the selection of students, faculty and administrators.

COURSE ORGANIZATION

This is our next major step in the formulation of ALP. This involves eight substeps as follows:

1. *Course-Plan.* Once a general curriculum has been agreed upon and established, then each course must be carefully structured. A decision or plan has to be made concerning:

    a) The main topics or ground to be covered;

    b) The sequence or the order for the presentation of topics;

    c) The major points, concepts, or principles to be stressed in each topic;

    d) The materials—men and texts—to serve as the vehicles of instruction;

    e) The level at which the course will be presented, that is, freshman, upper-division graduate; and,

    f) Finally, the amount of time to be devoted to the various parts of the course.

Thus, were we to plan a course in seventeenth-century philosophy, we might decide to present it on the junior level; the main topics and the order of presentation might include scientific method, the nature of substance, causality, followed by prototype theories of value in ethics, politics, and aesthetics. In the area of methodology, we should want to treat both the empirical-inductive and deductive approaches, using perhaps such cases as Keppler's laws of motion, Galileo's principle of the pendulum, and Descartes' *Rules for the Direction of the Mind.* These few examples suffice, we are sure, to explain what we mean by planning a course.

2. *Syllabus of Items.* The next substep, however, may be novel to

you. Remember that we are formulating a plan for automating the learning process on a digital computer. Accordingly, this requirement demands that we now construct a syllabus of items. This syllabus must consist of a minutely-detailed list of statements or propositions in natural language. For example, a course in logic would include items such as the following under the topic, "The Nature of Propositions" (6, pp. 5-6):

    a) Certain combinations of words comprise sentences;

    b) Sentences have meaning;

    c) Meanings of sentences are propositions;

    d) Some sentences are true, others false; and,

    e) Propositions can be the objects of belief and disbelief, etc.

Note that we have chosen a relatively easy area, namely, logic. Were this to be a course in the philosophy of education, or in English literature, the effort to construct a syllabus of items would require much labor and ingenuity.

Nor is this all. Following the painful ordeal of syllabus construction, each item is now assigned a code name, e.g., HA, AB, LG. These code names will subsequently be entered into the computer. Finally, these items are then ordered sequentially or like a tree with branches and looping.

3. *Categories.* The next substep in formulating our course organization is to impose a categorical learning structure within which the items will be embedded. We have selected the following six categories:

    a) Knowledge or Acquaintance with Specifics;

    b) Comprehension;

    c) Application;

    d) Analysis;

    e) Synthesis; and,

    f) Evaluation.

As will be readily recognized, these categories are borrowed from the handbook, *Taxonomy of Educational Objectives* (3). These categories define the six principal *cognitive* goals of education. Within each category, there exist several subclasses. However, the capacity of the large digital computers that we have used to guide us in limiting the scale of our proposed simulation is such that no finer breakdown can be employed than the six major categories listed above. Larger machines may become available in the future.

This particular taxonomy, of course, is only one way of ordering knowledge. There may be other, perhaps even superior, taxonomies. The one we have chosen appeals to us because of its somewhat hierarchal, systematic character. The six categories to some extent fall into a hierarchal order of complexity and interconnectedness, i.e., the goals represent something of an ascent from the simple to the complex, and each subsequent goal depends upon and presupposes the behavior of its predecessor.

4. *Component Scaling of Items.* The fourth substep in our course formulation is to scale the items in terms of component difficulty and significance. We believe that any one lesson or item always involves all six categories, but it does so in varying degrees of significance and in varying amounts of difficulty. For example, an early session of an elementary language course or one in physiology may contain far more emphasis on detail or knowledge (whether specific facts or specific concepts) than on the categories of analysis and evaluation. At the same time the degree of difficulty in the category of knowledge may be very low compared to that in the analysis category. Thus, a given item may be high in significance (s) and low in difficulty (d) for any one of the six categories, or vice versa.

We thus introduce two component measures: one for assessing the difficulty of each item within each cognitive category; the other, for expressing the relative significance of an item within each of the respective categories. In other words, each item is always accompanied by two sets of tags: *six* difficulty tags and *six* significance tags. The significance numbers express relative significance. Their sum is always 1: $\sum_{i=1}^{6} s_i = 1$. Each difficulty number, on the other hand, may have any value from 1 to 100.

We further assume that the significance and difficulty levels for a given item can and will vary depending on the item's *location* in the course. Individual items may appear and reappear at different stages of the course. *Where* an item appears makes a great deal of difference to that item. For example, a notion such as the Trinity in religion or entropy in physics may be presented at the beginning of a course. It may occur in the middle or at the end. Its location in time will affect its *difficulty* and also its *significance*. Furthermore, we also assume that a given course, as a whole, will become progressively harder as it proceeds from one major stage to another. Consider, for instance, Plato's notion of justice in the *Republic*. As first presented, justice is defined as paying your debts, doing good to your friends and evil to your enemies, etc. For purposes of illustration, it may be said that these statements are not very difficult with respect to the category of knowledge or acquaintance; even less difficult in the category of comprehension; about the same in application; a little more with respect to synthesis; much more in the category of analysis; and very high in evaluation.

The zigzagging pattern of categorical difficulty is pictured in Figure 2a by the height of the bars. These heights may be interpreted as representing the assignment of the following difficulty weightings:

knowledge	19
comprehension	8
application	18
analysis	37
synthesis	21
evaluation	75

In this same figure, on the other hand, a very different picture emerges along the significance dimension. Here the categories of evaluation and synthesis are relatively low in significance, as shown by the cross-hatches; analysis and acquaintance with specifics are of moderate significance (vertical shading); but application and comprehension are of great or high import (solid color). We may interpret the significance ratings as follows:

Category	Significance Weights
Evaluation	.05 (Cross Hatching)
Synthesis	.07 (Cross Hatching)
Analysis	.15 (Vertical Shading)
Knowledge	.18 (Vertical Shading)
Application	.25 (Solid Shading)
Comprehension	.30 (Solid Shading)
TOTAL	1.00

Now proceed to the final stages of the *Republic*, where justice is seen to involve such other concepts as wisdom, courage, temperance; both the state and the individual; both temporal and eternal existence. A great transformation now takes place. As depicted in Figure 2b we see that:

a) A progressive rise or step-up in the over-all difficulty level has taken place from the first to the third stage;

b) The difficulty level in Stage 3 rises sharply as we move from knowledge to evaluation—a much steeper and more uniform ascent than in the first stage; and,

c) Finally, along the significance dimension a marked shift has taken place. In this stage, evaluation and synthesis possess far more significance than do application and analysis (medium), and far far more than does the category of comprehension or knowledge of specifics (low).

Figure 2

EXAMPLE OF COMPONENT SCALING OF AN ITEM IN THE SYLLABUS OF A COURSE: ITEM IS WEIGHTED FOR SIGNIFICANCE AND DIFFICULTY

2a. Example of Weighting for Significance and Difficulty at First Stage of the Course

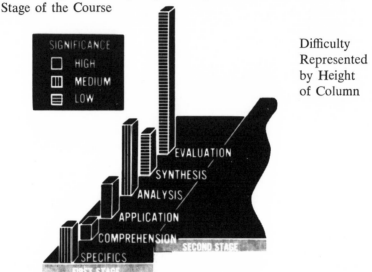

2b. Example of Relative Significance and Difficulty of the Same Item at a Later Stage in the Progress of a Course

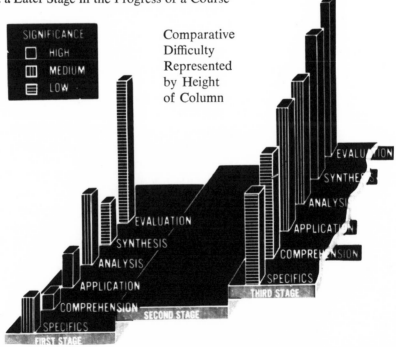

The new difficulty and significance values may read somewhat as follows:

Category	First Stage		Third Stage	
	d	s	d	s
Knowledge	19	.18	48	.05
Comprehension	8	.30	53	.08
Application	18	.25	64	.13
Analysis	37	.15	64	.16
Synthesis	21	.07	74	.28
Evaluation	75	.05	80	.30
TOTALS	178	1.00	383	1.00

Note that the difficulty ratings in the third stage are net values and are independent of the uniform increase in difficulty for all items from stage to stage.

Once the 12 value numbers, six for difficulty and six for significance, have been established for each item of the syllabus at each stage of the course, these are then entered into the computer.

5. *Sequential Scaling.* The analysis of items in terms of component difficulties and the relative significance of the components at various stages of a course applies to the internal structure of the items. A major feature of any course, however, is the architecture of the items. Where an item occurs in a course—at which stage of the course it is mastered—can make a great deal of difference in the over-all impact of the course on the students who master it. A badly designed course can include items, even very difficult items, offered in such a sequence that their mastery hardly advances a student at all.

In a well-planned course, on the other hand, ideas or concepts grow and change. This they do in at least two ways:

a) A given item may become so enriched through association with other ideas as to become wholly different by the end of a course from what it was at the beginning. For example, justice in the later stage of the *Republic* is intrinsically a more potent or fecund notion than it was at the beginning.

b) Some ideas—hence items—are per se more inclusive and powerful than others. Plato's idea of the good is ever more comprehensive, profound and potent than is justice. Hence, its introduction at a later stage of the course renders that stage of learning more important.

In deference, thus, to the organic or achitectural quality of the educational process, we introduce a potency or importance value, I, to each item as a whole at each stage of the course. This value ranges between 0 and 10. The set of all these values in the course is subject to this condition: that the sum of all the importance values taken over all the items and over all the stages of the course is equal to the number of items in the course times the number of stages into which the course is divided. Another way to express this condition is, obviously, to say the average value of I for any item at any stage of a course is 1.

Two useful consequences follow as a result of introducing the potency values.

a) One teacher can select a sequence of items for presentation to his students so that each student advances only a little way toward mastery of his subject no matter how well he does with his items, while another teacher can be a far better organizer. The better organizer picks items at the several stages of the course that, in aggregate, contribute a greater total potency to the learning process.

b) Similarly, two students can select items by diverse strategies and one selection strategy can be much better than another. (Selection of items by students will be described below.)

But the crucial question arises: Who will determine the specific numerical values? Who will assess the potency, significance and difficulty ratings? This brings us to the next substep in the ALP course formulation.

6. *Assessment of Syllabus*. No computer thinks for itself. It requires detailed, specific and precise instructions. Nothing occult or ambiguous is permissible. Not only, moreover, must the computer be programmed down to the most minute operation that it will perform, but, in addition, every logical symbol or variable characterizing the process must be given a particular value or quantitative expression. This implies that our list of items must be translated from their natural language into determinate numbers. These numbers will represent the significance and difficulty values for each specific session **during which the** items can be presented by the teacher to the artificial students. But the moment numbers are used we are, in fact, introducing a process of evaluation: we are assessing the significance and difficulty of items under the six categories. Now there is no known program, at present, or computer formulation that can be trusted to do this. For these reasons, it is mandatory that the live teacher himself, or a jury of colleagues versed in his subject, review the list of items and assess them preparatory to their use by the computer. This is an essential requirement of system design. It will be familiar to anyone acquainted with the methods by which any current industrial or military data processing or executive command system is adapted

to operation on a computer. This process of system analysis and design is not without pain to those upon whom it is imposed, but its advantages are very great, for it compels a Socratic self-examination.

Thus, our proposal is that an actual school system or college be employed in a pilot study. We suggest that a large number of representative courses and actual students be analyzed, formulated and represented in operating computer programs. This approach is being effectively used for understanding and evaluating the flow of traffic over roads and skyways, the processing of patient data in our hospitals, and the process of command, communication and control in military organizations. A similar approach to the educational process, we believe, would bring similar benefits.

Assume, now, that this kind of preliminary system analysis has been realized, and that we are in possession of a complex, agreed-upon inventory of assessments of items for each given course. What next?

7. *Course Composition.* Now let us concentrate on one particular course. In your imagination choose one of your own favorites. But remember, you are not in an ordinary classroom with the familiar blackboard and chalk and two-legged creatures sitting in front of you. Rather, you must picture yourself in a large semidark area, dimly lit by fluorescent light. Your students are there, but intangible, inaudible, and invisible as befits their artificial character. You can, however, communicate with them by means of a small pushbutton console and cathode-ray digital display system or television tube. This permits great latitude in the composition of a course.

We plan that our course should accommodate from one to about 200 artificial students. From one to about 16 live teachers can offer independent courses simultaneously. This setup of 200 students and 16 courses can be repeated up to about five times. Thus, our present model can service a total of about 1000 artificial students and about 80 units consisting of one real teacher and one course. About 8 live administrators can service the 80 units.

8. *Time.* Finally, with respect to time, we suggest that the course cover a standard semester of work, that is, about 15 weeks with three sessions per week. This is, of course, quite arbitrary. Other forms of time-units are possible.

So far, two major steps of the ALP model have been presented: namely, (A) the three-fold conceptual map and (B) the eight-fold substeps of course organization.

MECHANISM OF OPERATIONS

We turn now to the mechanism for teacher-student interaction, the mechanism, that is, for describing the student's progression through the course. This is the third major step in the formulation. It, in turn, involves the following substeps or decision rules:

a) At the beginning of the course the teacher will have a listing or printout, briefly indicating in ordinary English all the items planned for the course. Not available to the teacher, but recorded in the computer, are the 13 difficulty, importance, and significance values of each item at each stage of the course.

b) At his or her discretion, the teacher may select up to, but no more than, ten different items for a given session. (This constraint of ten is due to the computer and display equipment for which this model is planned.)

c) The teacher presents these items in groups or clusters—two or three or five—up to seven—to a cluster. (This limit of seven stems from the decision rules regulating the selection of items from clusters by our artificial students. See next part, "The Student," Section 2, "Choice of Item from Cluster.") Figure 3a exhibits a variety of clusters and temporal intervals. In the first interval, a cluster of five items is presented; cluster two contains three items; there are no items in the third interval; and a cluster of four items is presented in the fourth interval.

d) Items may be repeated from cluster to cluster. But clustering will not affect the difficulty or significance values of an item. In other words, while we permit these values of an item to change from stage to stage, we say that there is no group or gestalt effect. We take an atomistic approach for the sake of convenience and simplicity—that is, out of reluctant respect for the limitations of the digital computer. Thus, if during a session an item SC appears first in cluster a, then in cluster b, item SC retains the identical s and d values in the two clusters, regardless of the values of the other items in the respective clusters.

e) All students may be presented with the same cluster; or the class may be divided so that: a group of selected students is presented with a single cluster for that special group; another single cluster for another special group. This class division may occur either at the judgment and initiative of the teacher or, to go beyond the present formulation, through mechanisms that simulate the informal natural associations of students.

f) Once an item has been chosen and mastered by a student, he may not select it again within that session.

g) If time between presentation of clusters permits, a student may select more than one item from that cluster. In Figure 3b, for example, student X is shown choosing two items from the first cluster, one from the second, and two from the third. Lengths of arrows represent the amount of time consumed in mastering selected items.

h) Students may fail to select any item.

i) Any item is available for a limited temporal portion of the course—i.e., it may not necessarily continue throughout the course. But, on the other hand, it may. If it is repeated, then the repetition is not wooden; it appears at a later stage with new values in a new context, as we saw above with the example of Plato's justice.

j) Completion time for a given item will or may vary from student to student. Hence, the rhythm of presentation is most important. Shortly, we shall indicate how the rate of completion time can be measured. Figure 3c, for example, illustrates a marked contrast between students X and Y. While X is moving rapidly forward, Y is progressing very slowly. This situation may be variously interpreted. It may mean that X is the superior scholar, a quiz-kid who is fast outrunning his mate. It is conceivable, however, that X is working in a slipshod manner, perhaps on a D or C level, while his slow colleague Y is the profound, painstaking A student.

These observations lead us to investigate the object of our solicitude, namely the student, and thus, naturally, to the fourth major step in the formulation of our model. Thus far the formulation has covered three principal themes: (A) The Three-fold Conceptual Scheme or Map; (B) The Course Organization (with its plan, syllabus of items, six categories, difficulty and significance scales, sequential scaling, assessment of syllabus, composition and time); and (C) The Mechanism of Operations between teacher and student. Now we shall concentrate on the formulation of the artificial student.

THE STUDENT

Despite the fact that our students are artificial automata, nevertheless, like the prophet Ezekiel who tried to breathe life into the dead bones, we endow our student machines with a limited set of recognizable and measurable human traits. Imagine that *you* are an artificial student confronted with a cluster of items during a session of a course. On what basis would you be inclined to choose or reject any given item?

Figure 3

INTERACTION BETWEEN LIVE TEACHER
AND ARTIFICIAL STUDENTS

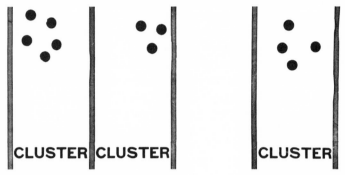

3a. First Step: Teacher Presents Clusters of Items to Students at Selected Intervals of Time

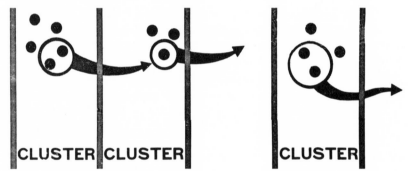

3b. Second Step: Student Selects Items from Cluster. (Length of Arrow Indicates Amount of Time Consumed in Mastering Selected Items)

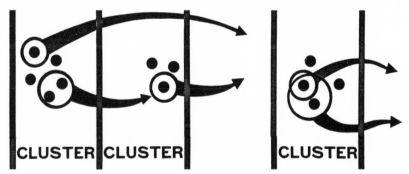

3c. Third Step: Two Students Choosing and Mastering Different Items

It would be possible to endow our creatures with subjectivity and perceptual fallibility. We could introduce a mechanism which would project the student's value structure into the perceived item. However, were so refined a mechanism introduced, then would arise the problem of educating and reconstructing a student's value system. This process can be readily modeled and would have great value in the humanities. But, at this juncture we omit deliberately the subtle dimension of subjectivity lest our variables become too unmanageable and our programs too ambitious. We wish to avoid the danger of confounding the variance arising from subjectivity with that arising from preferences. Accordingly, in the present formulation, we adopt the simplifying hypothesis that the student can evaluate accurately and realistically the difficulties and significances of the items in any cluster. But, we do endow him with preferences or tendencies.

1. *Tendencies.* A tendency is similar to a Leibnitzian inclining force or the principle of sufficient reason. Faced with a choice among alternatives, the student is disposed to turn in one direction rather than in another. The direction of choice is his tendency.

Each tendency is viewed as a serial order. As far as the computer is concerned we have numbers 1 through 7 that define locations along a scale. When a specific continuum ranges from a negative extreme through a central point to a positive extreme, the value 1 is defined as the negative extreme and 7 as the positive. Ordinarily, 4 is treated as the neutral point. For example, a student's tendency to choose along the *easy-difficult* dimension may be so scaled. See Figure 4.

Figure 4

THE NINE COMPONENTS OF THE LEARNING PROCESS,
AND AN EXAMPLE OF THE SCALES DEVELOPED TO
MEASURE A STUDENT'S TENDENCIES TOWARD THEM

CHOICE ACCORDING TO DIFFICULTY

+	7	STRONGLY FAVORS DIFFICULT
	6	MODERATELY FAVORS DIFFICULT
	5	SLIGHTLY FAVORS DIFFICULT
NEUTRAL	4	INDIFFERENT
	3	SLIGHTLY FAVORS EASY
	2	MODERATELY FAVORS EASY
—	1	STRONGLY FAVORS EASY

Each student in each course is endowed with nine principal tendencies. Six of these relate to the respective six categories. For each cognitive category, a student is given a rating between 7 and 1. The rating expresses the degree to which he favors or disfavors that category. For example, a rating of 6 in the category of knowledge would represent a high interest in or preference for that cognitive dimension.

In Figure 5b we contrast the profile of an altogether neutral type of student (X) whose six categorial preferences all fall along the central point 4—indifference—with a student (Y) who has fairly high interest ratings in the categories of knowledge and comprehension, moderately low in analysis and synthesis, and very low in evaluation.

In addition to the six preference ratings for the six categories, three other tendencies affect the student's choice of items from a cluster. One relates to the over-all difficulty of an item; another to

Figure 5

STUDENTS' TENDENCIES TO SELECT ITEMS ACCORDING TO NINE BASIC COMPONENTS OF THE LEARNING PROCESS

		COGNITIVE CATEGORIES					
INCLINATION		KNLG	COMP	APPL	ANAL	SYNTH	EVAL
+	7						
	6						
	5						
N	4	X	X	X	X	X	X
	3						
	2						
—	1						

5a. Tendency Profile of a Student Neutrally Inclined Toward All Six Cognitive Categories

	COGNITIVE CATEGORIES					
INCLINATION	**KNLG**	**COMP**	**APPL**	**ANAL**	**SYNTH**	**EVAL**
+ 7						
6	X	X				
5			X			
N 4	X	X	X	X	X	X
3				X	X	
2						
– 1						X

5b. Tendency Profile of a Student Neutrally Inclined Toward All Six Cognitive Categories, compared with that of a Student Who Has Definite Inclinations Toward Them

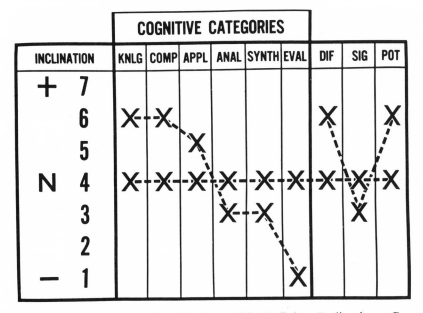

5c. Tendency Profile of a Student with Definite Inclinations Contrasted with That of a Neutrally Inclined Student with respect to the Nine Components of the Learning Process

the significances attributed by the teacher; and the third to the student's aptitudes or potentialities. See Figure 5c.

These three tendencies are scaled along the following serial orders. First is the easy-to-difficult dimension. For example, students who favor easy tasks will tend to choose an item from a cluster on the basis of those categories for which it has a low difficulty rating.

A second dimension is that which ranges preferences from low-to-high significance. For example, students who favor relatively trivial tasks will tend to choose an item with relatively low significance value.

The third dimension orders preferences in accordance with the degree to which a student favors an item on the basis of those cognitive categories in which he excels. This particular tendency depends on his aptitudes or potentialities—a concept we shall presently develop.

Figure 6 shows two items selected respectively by a neutrally inclined student and one with definite inclinations. Note how in item I the difficulty (d) level rises steadily in each category; so does the relative significance (s); and their product or moment (m). In item II, on the other hand, the difficulty descends in fairly uniform decline; the absolute difficulty values average much higher than those in item I; the difficulty values in the first three categories are far higher than any in item I; and the relative significance values remain the same for the first three categories, with a gradual decrease in the last three categories. The neutrally inclined student selects item I, the student with definite preferences, item II. The decision model is explained in the next section.

A final remark concerning our model of tendencies deserves mention. Our model provides nonparametric numerical representations to characterize these individual variations in tendencies among students. It permits us to employ the tests and interest inventories available to the deans and counselors of an existing college or school system, and thereby to represent major tendencies of actual students— up to about 1000—in the computer programs.

2. *Choice of Item from Cluster.* Faced by a number of items (up to and no more than seven) in a cluster, how will a student's selection go? *Assume that all nine of his tendencies are neutral* (each is scaled at 4, as for the neutral student represented in Figure 5c). Under this assumption, we postulate that his choice will be determined by the following decision rule: He chooses the item for which the sum, $\sum_{i=1}^{6} s_i d_i$, is the minimum, which we shall call "the fundamental rule of choice." For example, suppose that an artificial student is presented with a cluster consisting of three items, α, β, γ, with the

Figure 6

AN ITEM SELECTED BY A NEUTRALLY INCLINED STUDENT
(Item I) COMPARED WITH AN ITEM SELECTED BY A
STUDENT WITH DEFINITE INCLINATIONS (Item II) TOWARD
THE SIX COGNITIVE CATEGORIES.

(Items are rated for each cognitive category with respect to significance,
difficulty, and product or moment of significance and difficulty.)

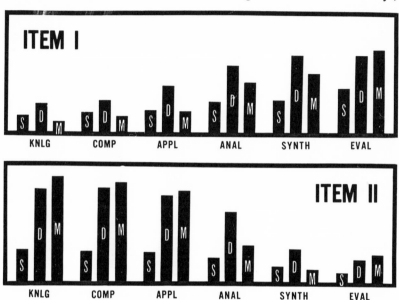

significance and difficulty values defined in Table I. These values
are given respectively in lines (1) and (2) for item α, in lines
(4) and (5) for item β, and in lines (7) and (8) for item γ.
Moments for the respective items are shown in lines (3), (6), and
(9); and $\sum\limits_{i=1}^{6} s_i d_i$ for α, β, and γ respectively is as follows: $\alpha = 65$,
$\beta = 80$, $\gamma = 67$. A completely neutral student, following the
fundamental rule of choice, selects the item for which the sum of the
moments is least, namely, item α.

Assume, on the other hand, that the student is biased in his tenden-
cies towards the six categories, in the manner previously shown in
Figure 5b. His tendencies to prefer the six categories are scaled
respectively at 6 (knowledge), 6 (comprehension), 5 application),
3 (analysis), 3 (synthesis) and 1 (evaluation). These biases may be
called the vector {6, 6, 5, 3, 3, 1}. They surely will affect this

Table I. Difficulty and Significance Values for a Prototype Cluster of Three Items. (Student chooses item for which the sum of moments is least, in the present case, item α.)

Item	Line	Characteristic	CATEGORY						Sum of Moments
			Knowledge	Comprehension	Application	Analysis	Synthesis	Evaluation	
α	(1)	Significance	.10	.10	.10	.20	.20	.30	
	(2)	Difficulty	20	30	50	75	80	80	65
	(3)	Moment	2.0	3.0	5.0	15.0	16.0	24.0	
β	(4)	Significance	.30	.20	.20	.10	.10	.10	
	(5)	Difficulty	70	80	90	80	75	95	80
	(6)	Moment	21.0	16.0	18.0	8.0	7.5	9.5	
γ	(7)	Significance	.30	.10	.30	.20	.05	.05	
	(8)	Difficulty	80	80	75	50	30	20	67
	(9)	Moment	24.0	8.0	22.5	10.0	1.5	1.0	

student's evaluations of items α, β, and γ and could affect his preference for one of these items. Thus, to reflect biasing, our model requires an appropriate loading rule. This rule will generate a factor to be applied to the moment, $s_i d_i$, for each value of i (for each of the respective six categories). A convenient set of such factors for the tendency values is shown in Table II.

Table II. Loading Factors for Tendency Values

	Tendency Value						
	—			N			+
	1	2	3	4	5	6	7
Loading Factor	2.0	1.6	1.3	1.0	0.8	0.6	0.5

Consulting this table, it may be seen that, for a student whose categorial tendency vector is {6, 6, 5, 3, 3, 1}, the loading values are as follows:

Tendency rating:	6	6	5	3	3	1
Loading:	0.6	0.6	0.8	1.3	1.3	2.0

The moments given in lines (3), (6) and (9) of Table I are multiplied in turn by these loading values. Resultant products of moments and loading values for items α, β, and γ are shown respectively in lines (3), (6), and (9) of Table III. Note that the sums of the resultants are: 95.3 for α, 75.8 for β, and 54.2 for γ. For the present, we deliberately attend only to the student's categorial tendencies and ignore his significance, difficulty and potential tendencies.

The fundamental rule of choice is now restated: The student chooses the item in the cluster for which the sum of the resultants over the six categories in the minimum—in this case item γ.

The loading factors presented in Table II are illustrative only. The model is so formulated that alternative sets of values may be ascribed at the experimenter's discretion.

Now assume that the student is biased with respect to the difficulty dimension. In this situation, we want to apply appropriate loadings to the six $s_i d_i$ moments of each item. Rules are therefore required to specify how the moments are to be affected by this bias.

First of all, we rank the six difficulty values of an item in order of their magnitude. Let A designate the highest value, B the next highest, . . . and F the lowest value. For the three items, α, β, γ, characterized in Table I, the rankings are as shown in Table IV. When two values are equal, ranking letters are assigned from left to right, the value on the left being given the higher rating.

Table III. Resultant Sums for Student with Tendency Vector, {6, 6, 5, 3, 3, 1} . (Student chooses item γ.)

Item	Line	Computation	CATEGORY							Sum of Re-sultants
			Knowl-edge	Compre-hension	Appli-cation	Anal-ysis	Syn-thesis	Evalu-ation		
α	(1)	Moment	2.0	3.0	5.0	15.0	16.0	24.0		
	(2)	Loading	0.6	0.6	0.8	1.3	1.3	2.0		
	(3)	Resultant	1.2	1.8	4.0	19.5	20.8	48.0		95.3
β	(4)	Moment	21.0	16.0	18.0	8.0	7.5	9.5		
	(5)	Loading	0.6	0.6	0.8	1.3	1.3	2.0		
	(6)	Resultant	12.6	9.6	14.4	10.4	9.8	19.0		75.8
γ	(7)	Moment	24.0	8.0	22.5	10.0	1.5	1.0		
	(8)	Loading	0.6	0.6	0.8	1.3	1.3	2.0		
	(9)	Resultant	14.4	4.8	18.0	13.0	2.0	2.0		54.2

Table IV. Rank Order of Difficulty Values for Items α, β, γ.

Item	Line	Rating	CATEGORY					
			Knowl-edge	Compre-hension	Appli-cation	Anal-ysis	Syn-thesis	Evalu-ation
α	(1)	Difficulty	20	30	50	75	80	80
	(2)	Rank	F	E	D	C	A	B
β	(3)	Difficulty	70	80	90	80	75	95
	(4)	Rank	F	C	B	D	E	A
γ	(5)	Difficulty	80	80	75	50	30	30
	(6)	Rank	A	B	C	D	E	F

Table V. Loading Factors Associated with Tendency Ratings.

Tendency Rating.	RANK					
	A	B	C	D	E	F
+						
7	.5	.6	.8	1.3	1.6	2.0
6	.6	.5	.6	.8	1.3	1.6
5	.8	.6	.5	.6	.8	1.3
N 4	.8	.6	.5	.5	.6	.8
3	1.3	.8	.6	.5	.6	.8
2	1.6	1.3	.8	.6	.5	.6
1	2.0	1.6	1.3	.8	.6	.5
—						

The next step is to associate the loading factors given in Table II with the student's difficulty-tendency rating. This is done in Table V. Note that a student with a difficulty-tendency of 7 will bias the difficulty ratings, d_i, of an item with progressively larger loading factors. This will have the effect of making the higher difficulty ratings lower and lower ones higher. A student rated 1 biases with progressively smaller factors. For this student, the "harder" ratings are amplified, while the lower ratings are decreased. Students falling between the highest and the lowest difficulty-tendency ratings tend to favor the intermediate difficulties. Consider once again the biased student represented in Figure 5c. He has a tendency of 6 with respect to the difficulties of an item. How will he respond to, say, item α? Its difficulty ratings are respectively 20, 30, 50, 75, 80, 80, as shown in line (1) of Table I. For this biased student, the loadings for item α are the following:

Difficulty Rating:	20	30	50	75	80	80
Loading:	1.6	1.3	0.8	0.6	0.6	0.5

Table VI. Rank Order of Significance Values, Items α, β, and γ.

Item	Line	Characteristic	CATEGORY					
			Knowl-edge	Compre-hension	Appli-cation	Anal-ysis	Syn-thesis	Evalu-ation
α	(1) (2)	Significance Rank	.10 D	.10 E	.10 F	.20 B	.20 C	.30 A
β	(3) (4)	Significance Rank	.30 A	.20 B	.20 C	.10 D	.10 E	.10 F
γ	(5) (6)	Significance Rank	.30 A	.10 D	30 B	.20 C	.05 E	.05 F

(Because the two ratings of 80 are equal, the ratings are applied from left to right. As a result, the first 80 is considered to be the higher of the two.) The difficulty loadings for items α, β, and γ are shown on lines (2), (9) and (16) respectively of Table VIII.

Loadings for bias along the significance dimension are generated precisely as are those along the difficulty dimension. Significance rankings for items α, β, and γ are shown in Table VI. For the

Table VII. Ranking of Potentialities, and Loading Values for Student with Potentialities Rated as Shown.

Line	Characteristic	CATEGORY					
		Knowl-edge	Compre-hension	Appli-cation	Anal-ysis	Syn-thesis	Evalu-ation
(1)	Potentiality	50	55	60	65	40	30
(2)	Rank	D	C	B	A	E	F
(3)	Loading	0.8	0.6	0.5	0.6	1.3	1.6

biased student represented in Figure 5c, who has a significance-tendency rating of 3, the loadings for item α are:

Significance Rating: .10   .10   .10   .20   .20   .20
            Loading: 0.5   0.6   0.8   0.8   0.6   1.3

The loadings for items α, β, and γ are shown in lines (3), (10), and (17) of Table VIII.

In our ALP model, the artificial students are endowed with aptitudes or potentialities, as well as with tendencies. These potentialities will shortly be discussed in detail. Meanwhile, let us assume that our biased student represented in Figure 5c is possessed of the following potentiality ratings: 50 in knowledge, 55 in application, 60 in comprehension, 65 in analysis, 40 in synthesis, and 30 in evaluation. These potentialities are ranked as shown in Table VII.

This particular student is rated 6 on the potentiality-tendency scale (Figure 5c). From Table V we obtain the loading factors that are to be applied to $s_i d_i$ moments of items α, β, and γ. These are included in line (3) of Table VII and lines (4), (11), and (18) of Table VIII.

To determine the effect of the combined biases on the choice of which item our artificial student selects from the cluster that contains α, β, γ, we must multiply the four loading values—for category tendencies, difficulty tendencies, significance tendencies, and potentiality tendencies respectively—together for each category of item α. In Table VIII the resultant products are labeled "Product of loadings," and are listed on line (5) for item α. Similar products are obtained for items β and γ; see lines (12) and (19). Next the $s_i d_i$ moments of the three items listed in Table I [lines (3), (6) and (9) respectively] are multiplied by these products of loadings. The resultants are shown in line (7) for item α, line (14) for β, and line (21) for γ in Table VIII. Finally, the sums of the latter resultants are taken. These sums are: α = 68.1, β = 39.7, and γ = 23.7. The student chooses the item with the least value of the three, namely, he chooses item γ.

3. *Aptitudes or Potentialities*. Educators are fully aware how some students always select the easiest path, a good majority falls in the middle range, and some few are invariably attracted by challenge and resistance. Then, too, some pupils always favor their long suits; they lead from their best strength or aptitude. Others deliberately strive to overcome their weaknesses. How shall we adapt this notion to the computer?

Commensurate with the six difficulty ratings and the six significance ratings that characterize each item at each session of a course, we postulate six kinds of potentialities for each student for each subject matter. The six aptitudes are each scaled from 1 to 100. Each aptitude is relative to a specific course.

Recall that we asserted that each course becomes progressively harder as it proceeds from one stage to another. Now we postulate that the students generally increase in aptitude as they succeed in mastering the specific items in the progression of the stages of a course. The problem now becomes: How can we model the specific increments of student potentials? To do so, we shall shortly consider the temporal aspect of a student's accomplishments in each course. But first, attention must be paid to two additional attributes of a student's character.

4. *Effort and Aspiration*. A student, we saw, selected items on the basis of nine fundamental tendencies. He tends to favor or disfavor an item in terms of the degree of his interest or leaning towards one or another of the basic six categories, in terms of their respective difficulty and relative significance, and also in terms of his own aptitudes or potentialities. Tendencies thus relate to the student's capacity for

Table VIII. Resultant Sums for Students with Tendency Vector, {6, 6, 5, 3, 3, 1; 6, 3, 6} for Potentiality Vector {50, 55, 60, 65, 40, 30} . Student chooses Item γ.

| Item | Line | Characteristic | CATEGORY | | | | | | Sum of Re-sultants |
			Knowl-edge	Compre-hension	Appli-cation	Anal-ysis	Syn-thesis	Evalu-ation	
α	1	Category Loadings	0.6	0.6	0.8	1.3	1.3	2.0	
	2	Difficulty Loadings	1.6	1.3	0.8	0.6	0.6	0.5	
	3	Significance Loadings	0.5	0.6	0.8	0.8	0.6	1.3	
	4	Potentiality Loadings	0.8	0.6	0.5	0.6	1.3	1.6	
	5	Product of Loadings	0.38	0.28	0.26	0.37	0.61	2.08	
	6	$s_i d_i$ Moments	2.0	3.0	5.0	15.0	16.0	24.0	
	7	Resultants	0.76	0.84	1.30	5.55	9.76	49.92	68.1
β	8	Category Loadings	0.6	0.6	0.8	1.3	1.3	2.0	
	9	Difficulty Loadings	1.6	0.6	0.5	0.8	1.3	0.6	
	10	Significance Loadings	1.3	0.8	0.6	0.5	0.6	0.8	
	11	Potentiality Loadings	0.8	0.6	0.5	0.6	1.3	1.6	
	12	Product of Loadings	1.00	0.17	0.12	0.31	1.32	1.54	
	13	$s_i d_i$ Moments	21.0	16.0	18.0	8.0	7.5	9.5	
	14	Resultants	21.0	2.72	2.16	2.48	9.90	1.46	39.7
γ	15	Category Loadings	0.6	0.6	0.8	1.3	1.3	2.0	
	16	Difficulty Loadings	0.6	0.5	0.6	0.8	1.3	1.6	
	17	Significance Loadings	1.3	0.5	0.8	0.6	0.6	0.8	
	18	Potentiality Loadings	0.8	0.6	0.5	0.6	1.3	1.6	
	19	Products of Loadings	0.37	0.09	0.19	0.37	1.32	4.10	
	20	$s_i d_i$ Moments	24.0	8.0	22.5	10.0	1.5	1.0	
	21	Resultants	8.88	0.72	4.28	3.70	1.98	4.10	23.7

choice. The six aptitudes relate to his rate of mastery of items and thus to his rate of growth. Now, adhering even more faithfully to the dynamics of the learning process, we further bestow upon our students the attributes of *effort* and *aspiration*. These also relate to a student's mastery of items. By effort we mean to represent his striving or conational drive. By aspiration we mean the level of achievement, the level at which he elects to master items—A, B, C, or D level.

5. Δt *Formula—Temporal Measure for Item Mastery.* Suppose a student selects a given item from a cluster. How long does it take him to master it? (In the present model we do not provide differential de-

cision times for choosing items from clusters.) This interval of time is a function of the following variables:

      a) Six difficulty ratings of the item;
      b) Six significance ratings of the item;
      c) Six potentialities of the student;
      d) Level or grade on which the student is normally working (aspiration); and,
      e) Amount of effort he exerts (conation).

Now, the interval of time to complete an item depends directly on the grade, g, to which he aspires, and the sum of the difficulty-significance moments for all six categories of the item:

$$\Delta t \propto g \sum_{i=1}^{6} s_i d_i \tag{1}$$

This formula says that, all other things being equal, the greater a student's level of aspiration and the greater the aggregated significance and difficulty ratings of an item, the longer he will take to master it. However, his effort and potential also enter the picture. The more he exerts himself and the more aptitude he has, the shorter the time. Hence, Δt is inversely a function of effort and of the sum of the individual aptitudes or potentials:

$$\Delta t \propto \frac{1}{E \sum_{i=1}^{6} p_i} \tag{2}$$

The complete formula is:

$$\Delta t = k \frac{g \sum_{i=1}^{6} s_i d_i}{E \sum_{i=1}^{6} p_i} \tag{3}$$

where $\sum_{i=1}^{6} s_i = 1$. Grade and effort are both scaled: $A = 19$, $B = 16$, $C = 10$, $D = 4$, $E = 1$; but these values are parameters for the computer program and can be altered at the experimenters' will. k is a constant.

    6. *Δp Formula—Measure of Student's Change in Potential.* Now we are able to determine a student's rise in aptitude or potential. What

we need is a percentage number to represent the change in a student's aptitude or potential as a result of his performance during a class session. This percentage number, which we call Δp, will be multiplied into a student's potential as it stood at the beginning of the session. Then the resulting product will be added to, or subtracted from, his beginning potential. Thus, if p_o is the beginning potential, his potential at the end of the session is $p_o + (\Delta p)(p_o)$. Δp depends on two basic elements: one, a student's actual performance, and two, a standard of achievement or expected performance. The increment is directly proportional to the difference between a student's actual accomplishment and the standard:

$$\Delta p \propto \text{ACTUAL - STANDARD} \qquad (4)$$

How shall we measure actual performance? Answer: Actual performance is a ratio or comparison between delivered and expected performance:

$$\text{ACTUAL} = \frac{\text{delivered}}{\text{expected}} \qquad (5)$$

How shall we measure standard performance? Answer: A performance is up to standard when the delivered equals the expected:

$$\text{STANDARD} = \frac{\text{expected}}{\text{expected}} = 1 \qquad (6)$$

Hence,

$$\Delta p \propto \frac{\text{delivered}}{\text{expected}} - 1 \qquad (7)$$

And what is expected performance? Answer: Expected performance varies directly with two factors: first, the student's aptitude for a specific category and subject matter, and second, a quota, q, of items mastered during a class session. This quota is a number specified by the faculty for specific subject matters and course levels:

$$\text{expected} = qp \qquad (8)$$

And what is the delivered performance? Answer: This plainly derives from the significance and difficulty of the items, as well as their relative importance:

$$\text{delivered} = \sum_{j=1}^{n} I_j s_j d_j \qquad (9)$$

where n is the number of items mastered by the student in one session of the course.

Using k_o as a factor of proportionality, Δp becomes:

$$\Delta p_i = k_o \left[\frac{6 \sum_{j=1}^{n} I_j s_j d_j}{q p_i} - 1 \right] \qquad (10)$$

We write Δp with subscript i, because Δp is computed separately for each of the six cognitive categories. The number 6 is included as a scaling factor to account for the fact that the average value of s_j is 1/6, since the significance values over the six categories add up to one.

As we said, Δp_i is a percentage number to yield a student's change in potential as a result of his mastery of items during a class session. This formula, therefore, is basic for a theory of the learning process—it converts accomplishment into aptitude.

7. *Modifiers.* ALP is a dynamic model. Thus far we have stressed a student's capacity to improve and to develop his potentialities or aptitudes. And we showed how the rise in a student's potential can be precisely measured. We now suggest that a student's tendencies, level of aspiration, and effort or conative striving can also be affected or modified by a number of factors. The computer side of such dynamic, contingent change has been developed, but we feel that the number, kinds, and quantitative relationships of the complex feedback loops should be left to the discretion of the experimenter. In our opinion, 25 or more such modifiers per artificial student can be provided by the programs.

Suppose, by way of example, that a student's tendency along the difficult-easy scale is affected by the grades he receives in a course. Suppose too that he is stimulated by encouragement to attempt harder and harder items. The relation, however, is not linear, and it falls off if encouragement is carried too far.

Grade:	A	B	C	D
Modification points:	+1	+2	0	−1

Depending on the grade the student receives, his difficulty tendency will become modified. How much? Each modification point is multiplied by a constant for that modification and that student. Let us set this constant to 1/10 for the student. Assume that he receives ten grades: A, A, B, C, B, B, A, D, B, B. His increments (or decrements) are respectively .1, .1, .2, 0, .2, .2, .1, −.1, .2, .2. These total 1.2. We round off to the nearest integer; his tendency to select difficulty is increased by one in the scale from one to seven.

One important class of modifiers is the student's higher-level reflexive tendencies. After each major stage of the course, the student rates the course in terms of:

    a) His expectations concerning the nine principal tendencies;
    b) Its efficiency (dead time) for him;
    c) The effort he is expending;
    d) Its effect on his potential;
    e) His grade;
    f) The questions raised by the teacher during a post-session conference.

Figure 7

MODIFICATION OF DIFFICULTY TENDENCY
AS RESULT OF GRADES RECEIVED

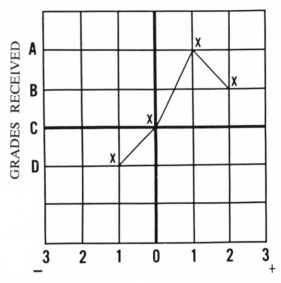

MODIFICATION POINTS   MODIFICATION POINTS

These ratings are relative to the constellation of courses he is taking and has taken. As a result of these ratings, his initial tendencies, aspiration, and striving are modified. The over-all pattern of modification is in terms of subject matter, e.g., natural science, not in relation to specific courses. Again we leave to the experimenter the number, kinds, and functional relationships for these higher-level reflexive modifiers. For technical reasons concerning the computer programs, this group of modifiers can be almost as complex as the experimenter desires.

8. *Testing.* Tests can be administered at selected stages of a course. For the tests, the items of the course are employed. It is not necessary for a student previously to have mastered a test item. Again we have to restrict the number of items in a single test to ten on account of hardware limitations.

Two testing procedures are available. One alternative is to require each student to master every test item, freeing him, however, from any time constraints. A second method is to restrict the test to a given time-span, but permitting the students the freedom to elect fewer than the total set of items. Either option is a useful diagnostic tool, the first stressing accomplishment regardless of time, the second focusing on content over time. In the second procedure, the number of test items mastered depends on the same variables as does the Δt formula for the temporal progress of the student through the course.

With either testing procedure, an artificial student's performance, G, for each item is expressed simply as:

$$G = k'' \frac{\sum\limits_{i=1}^{6} p_i}{6 \sum\limits_{i=1}^{6} s_i d_i} \qquad (11)$$

The relative grade, Γ, for the guidance of the live teacher is simply.

$$\Gamma = \frac{\sum\limits_{i=1}^{n} G_i}{n} \qquad (12)$$

where n is the number of items mastered in the time period. Actual grade is given by the live teacher.

TEACHER-STUDENT INTERACTION

1. *Class Behavior.* You may be wondering, perhaps, how the teacher remains cognizant of her automated students' responses to the items presented from session to session. The fact of the matter is that any time in the conduct of the course, the teacher can, upon request, obtain from the computer a display showing over-all class performance Each display is a time-structured histogram that tells how the class as a whole is behaving during two successive sessions. Three such histograms are exhibited in Figures 8a, 8b, and 8c. The letters indicate the names of the items. In the upper left corner of each display are shown the time and the number of the session or cluster now in progress. The oblong symbols to the left of the lettered items indicate what the class has cumulatively achieved in the preceding sessions; those on the right of the lettered items indicate how the class is behaving in the current session. Reading from top down, the oblong symbols represent, respectively, the grade levels of the students—A, B, C, D. Finally, each oblong ordinarily counts for one student

By way of illustration, let us examine the data on the three histograms. In Figure 8a we note that cluster 4 is being presented to the students. The time is 22. How, we may ask, did the class behave in the previous session? Turning to the left array of oblongs. we note that item AP was selected by one A student; five B students; twelve C students; and eight D students. Item AM was chosen by four A students; two B students; one C and one D student. None of the D students bothered with AS or BW. And no one at all selected CS or FT.

Turning now to the right array of oblongs, we see that an interesting change is taking place. Now, as the session with cluster 4 is just developing, items AP, AM, and FT are being bypassed. Six A students are grappling with AS. The B's and C's ignore AS.

To see what finally happens by the time this fourth session is over, let us consult the left side of Figure 8b. Now, four minutes later, we find, for example, that no student, in the interval between 22 and 26, attempted items AP and AM. AS was mastered by the six A students. An interesting item to note is CS. In period four, it was entertained by one A and thirteen D students (see Figure 8a). Period four ended with one A and two D's mastering it. Similar comparisons can be traced for

Figure 8

COMPUTER-GENERATED DISPLAYS SHOWING CLASS PERFORMANCE DURING A SERIES OF PRESENTATIONS OF ITEM CLUSTERS

8a. Class Performance during Presentation of Fourth Cluster Compared with Performance during Third Session.

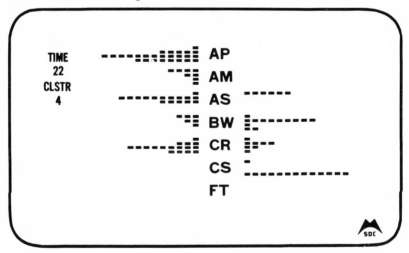

The rows of blocks alongside each item (AP, AM, etc.) indicate the selection of these items by A, B, C, and D Students in the previous session (to the left), and in the present session (to the right) of the item column.

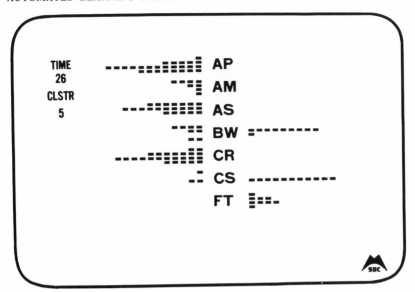

8b. Class Performance during Presentation of Fifth Cluster Compared with Performance during Fourth Session

and

8c. Class Performance during Presentation of Sixth Cluster Compared with Performance during Fifth Session.

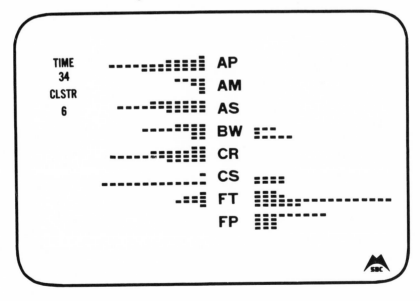

the beginning and end of session 5 by studying Figures 8b and 8c respectively.

2. *Individual Student Behavior*. Suppose now that the teacher wants to concentrate upon the performance of some one particular student rather than on general class performance. For this purpose, the teacher will, upon request, be provided by the computer with two reports, or printouts, at the end of a particular session. These printed reports can be suppressed, or aggregated over several sessions. Printout I will present an analysis of the entire class. Printout II will relate to the student in question

The first will provide data such as the following:

- Item names accompanied by descriptions in natural language, that is, in English;
- The items' difficulty and relative significance values,
- Names and grades of students who selected specific items;
- Times of cluster and item presentation.

The second printout will provide the teacher with an analysis of a given student's performance during a particular session. It will include the following kinds of data:

- Student's name and grade history;
- The numbers of the clusters presented, the names of the items on the clusters, and the times of presentation;
- Items actually selected from each cluster by the student;
- Time for student's mastery of each item.

3 *Teacher-Student Conference Session*. Given these two printouts, it is now possible for the teacher to conduct a "face-to-face" counseling session with the selected student. Imagine the following "dialogue." The teacher presents the student with one or several pairs of items. The student is then asked a series of questions such as:

- Which item would you choose on the basis of your preferred content-interests?

  (This question is designed to elicit a student's tendencies towards the six content categories.)
- Which would you select on the basis of difficulty?

  (This query would elicit a combination of content and difficulty ratings.)
- Which would you choose on the basis of significance?
- With which item do you feel more competent to cope?
- Is your grade too low?
- Have you been working harder lately?
- For what grade are you working?

This set of seven questions is, of course, no more than a sample. Others can be devised. Moreover, different questions could be asked of different students.

The importance of this type of conference is that it affords the teacher guidance in the subsequent conduct of the course. Sampled feedback responses from representative numbers of students allows for course restructuring at the teacher's option. As important, the very questions raised by the teacher in such a conference may directly affect the student and thus modify his subsequent behavior in the course. Of course, as in real life, the teacher's interrogations need not have the effect on the student which the teacher hopefully intended. See Fig. 9.

SUMMARY AND CONCLUSION

Artificial reproduction on a computer is no mean task. To design an automated student, it has been necessary to endow him with a special, but normal, set of idiosyncrasies, subject to quantitative treatment, as follows: nine tendencies; a selective or biased capacity to choose items from clusters; six aptitudes; effort and aspiration; specific abilities for item mastery, for growth or decline in potentiality, for general change or modification, and for test-taking. Finally to guarantee the teacher access to this automated creature, we have had to devise special techniques for indicating class performance and individual student performance, and for holding teacher-student conferences. This student design constitutes the final major step in the ALP formulation.

It is time now to take stock and reappraise this proposed model for automating the learning process. Let us emphasize that it is not our intention to preside over the dissolution of the educational process, but to offer a research tool for its study and improvement. No more than William James' automatic sweetheart, which posed the threat of being indistinguishable from its human counterpart, ALP is *not* offered as a substitute for the air-breathing student. It is *not* our intention to propose automation as a substitute for the vital, palpable teacher-student dialogue. Our model does *not* aim to eliminate the living adventure of the teaching-learning situation. It is offered only as an aid to teaching and learning. In what ways, then, can ALP be useful? First of all, in a purely practical way.

1. The ALP model can be used by a school or college for preparing and quickly testing a variety of curriculum mixes before adopting a settled plan.

2. ALP can be used for exploring and analyzing the various styles and strategies in the art of teaching. We can have *different* teachers conduct the same courses for the same students and thus compare the dynamics of diverse teaching techniques.

3. We can study the effects which different groups of students or different course materials may have on the same set of teachers.

Figure 9

INDIVIDUAL DISPLAY AND INTERVENTION UNITS THAT
CAN BE EMPLOYED BY TEACHER FOR INTERACTION WITH
AUTOMATED STUDENTS.

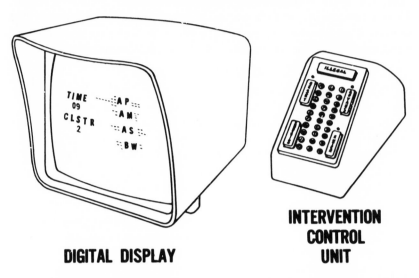

DIGITAL DISPLAY

**INTERVENTION
CONTROL
UNIT**

4. Similarly, we can study the effects of different course-materials
or of different teachers on the same students, or;

5. The effects of the same materials or the same teachers on different students.

6. Again the model can be used to study the effects of breaking
the "lock-step" in learning; that is, allowing different students to set
their own pace of learning.

7. ALP could benefit harried school administrators in structuring,
for example, admissions policy; student placement; curriculum design and administration; faculty development and selection: college or
university organization; advanced planning of specific divisions, departments and interdisciplinary efforts; extension schools for adult
education; extra-curricular and community relations; and facilities and
equipments.

In addition to the practical aspects of serving as an aid in administration, in curriculum planning, teacher training and as a diagnostic
tool, ALP has theoretical utility as well. ALP implicitly represents
a theory of learning. The very attempt to automate the learning process
on a digital computer carries theoretic implications. It encourages,
even compels, educators to consider the dynamics of education in
terms of the basic, universal elements in learning and their interaction.

The model, further, allows the experimenter to treat any of these universal elements or variables as dependent or independent. Now, if this approach, this anatomy of learning, is sound and adequate, it should have some correspondence to the real world. It should yield both new understanding of the learning process and predictive control. On the other hand, should the model be deficient or inadequate, then it would serve to generate novel approaches and hypotheses. Thus, as Bacon would say, ALP offers both fruits of light and fruits of profit.

BIBLIOGRAPHY

1. Bacon, Sir Francis. *Novum Organum.*
2. _____ *Great Instauration (Instauratio magna).*
3. Bloom, Benjamin Samuel, ed. *Taxonomy of Educational Objectives; The Classification of Educational Goals. Handbook I: Cognitive Domain.* New York: Longmans, Green and Co., 1956.
4. Descartes, René. *Rules for the Direction of the Mind.*
5. Dewey, John. *Reconstruction in Philosophy.* New York: H. Holt and Co., 1920.
6. Fitch, F. B. *Symbolic Logic, An Introduction.* New York: Ronald Press Co., 1952.
7. Plato. *Republic.*
8. Whitehead, Alfred North. *The Aims of Education and Other Essays.* New York: The Macmillan Co., 1929.

13

Putting Organizational Research to Use

CECIL E. GOODE*

THE Federal Government is by far the largest organization in the country. It is the largest sponsor and user of research, and it probably has most to gain from the use of organizational research findings. In the final analysis, the Government's gain is the country's gain in improved public service.

The role of the Bureau of the Budget is one of leadership and help in advancing the science of management. The departments and agencies, of course, have the original responsibility, the Bureau's being one of encouragement and central concern. At the present moment, within our limited staff resources, we are advancing and seeking out knowl edge on the principles of large scale organization, planning of programs and work, the measurement and improvement of productivity, means for organizing work for maximum effectiveness and personal satisfaction, the effects of automation on work and people, planning for change, and appraisal of program results In all of these we must depend on behavioral research for help in finding the answers, even though we must go ahead as best we can until these answers are available.

PROBLEMS IN UTILIZING BEHAVIORAL SCIENCE

A study the writer made almost seven years ago, with Ford Foundation support. identified two great needs relative to social science research as applied to working organizations.

---

*Mr. Goode, special guest of the conference, was invited to lead a discussion of this important topic. His prepared remarks are presented as the parting con ribution in the volume, to emphasize that the utilization of research results 's a worthy and final objective of the federal support of science and technology Mr. Goode is in the Office of Management and Organization, Bureau of the Budget, Executive Office of the President.

1. The need to develop means for correlating, interpreting, disseminating, and using in working organizations the knowledge uncovered by social science research.

2. The need to develop means for getting more research done, particularly by application not only to the special problems of Government, but also to the problems of all segments of the working world (2).

During the ensuing seven years there is indication that the amount of behavioral research as applied to working organizations has materially increased. For example, it was estimated in 1957 that the social science research sponsored by the Federal Government would be $35 million or 1.5% of the total devoted to all research (2). The most recent estimate (1963 and 1964) indicates that the Federal Government spends about $210 million each year for such research, including predominantly the fields of economics, statistics, sociological and psychological studies, demographic and manpower studies, and administrative studies. However, due to the very large increase in Federal research funds in recent years, this social science total is still only about 2% of the total Federal research dollar (6,7).

Perhaps there still is not enough organizational research performed but that is not our main problem as I see it. The main problem is the other great need that my study identified in 1957: that of correlating, interpreting, disseminating, and using the results of behavioral science research. This is no doubt a problem in any science but is particularly so in the behavioral or social sciences because the practitioners are not as closely identified with the scientists as they are in the "hard" sciences. Moreover, everyone feels he is an expert in human nature and feels competent to second guess the social scientist.

The problem is acute, also, because of the great mass of material that is available. For example, it has been estimated that, in 1960, there were enough technical papers produced by the world's laboratories and research centers in the "hard" sciences to fill 60 million pages—the equivalent of 1400 man years of reading, eight hours every day (9). The problem may be as great or even greater in the behavioral sciences not only because of the mass but because the machinery is less orderly. The behavioral sciences are characterized by many fragmented bits of research conducted by many individual researchers in widely diverse institutions and settings, representing a variety of disciplines, the results of which are largely uncorrelated and uninterpreted in any meaningful and usable sense.

The problems of synthesizing and using behavioral science research are broadly these:

1. Directing research resources to the principal needs that exist and toward filling the gaps of knowledge.

2. Preventing needless duplication of research efforts.

3. Synthesizing research results into meaningful and understandable bodies of knowledge.

4. Communicating the results of behavioral research to the action agents—those who will apply it.

Relating Resources to Needs

We have no really effective system at present for relating organizational research needs to the research resources available. Perhaps we are doing better than we used to. With some $189 million a year going into psychological and social science research sponsored by the Federal Government and with the great foundations providing large sums of money, there is probably more research being done on a planned or program basis than ever before.

There needs, however, to be some central thinking-through of the behavioral research that should be done, so that the resources available can be directed where they will do the most good. Many of the respondents in the study to which I referred earlier expressed a need for a central planning and coordinating agency for behavioral research. Such central planning and coordinating needs to be accomplished in such a way that researchers are not encouraged to pursue funds instead of new frontiers of knowledge. This is by no means an easy problem.

The Behavioral Sciences Sub-Panel of the President's Science Advisory Committee has declared that the behavioral sciences have received modest but increasing support in recent years but that this support has not been as effective as it might be because it has not met certain underlying needs (8).

Reducing Needless Duplication.

There is need, also, for promoting and sponsoring research to meet identified needs and for steering researchers away from areas where much effort is already being exerted or where a project might unnecessarily duplicate what has already been done. It is possible that just a little bit of research in a particular area will place a capstone on a great body of already accomplished research. We may expect breakthroughs in the behavioral sciences similar to those in the physical and biological sciences which may throw into perspective existing findings.

In my own study, I encountered numerous researchers who were contemplating studies in particular areas because they had identified a need or felt that there were glaring gaps. Since I visited 60-odd research organizations and conferred in depth with more than 200 behavioral researchers, I was in a position to know of others who had similar aims. If all of these were carried out, there would be duplication. Of course, in science some duplication is a good thing. The question is merely where can we *most afford* or where *should* we have duplication?

Another problem is one of the sheer magnitude of becoming or keeping informed on what has already been done in order to keep from duplicating research. Any good researcher spends a considerable period of time before he begins a given piece of research in searching the literature for what has already been done and what the findings were. A certain amount of literature study is essential for the education of the researcher but the present system places too great a burden on him. Besides, he has no way of being sure that he has covered all significant studies, and this may be an unduly expensive way to do it.

There are currently some attempts to fill this need. An example is the Sciences Information Exchange operated by the Smithsonian Institution, which hardly touches the behavioral sciences. Other examples representing efforts by professional societies are the Psychological Abstracts, Sociological Abstracts, and Annual Review of Psychology. A few years ago, the American Psychological Association was promoting the formation of a new corporation—Apex—to be an information exchange in applied psychology. Apparently this venture did not get off the ground. The National Science Foundation has recently published an inventory of on-going research efforts on the economic and social implications of science and technology (5).

Synthesizing Research Findings

There is a great need for the synthesis of the many bits of behavioral science research that have been conducted, in almost as many specialized areas. It is characteristic of science to atomize problems for study. Behavioral scientists do this, too. They dissect and isolate certain factors for study, attempting to control or exclude from consideration all others. For every hundred social scientists who are busy breaking human problems into atoms for study, there is barely one interested in synthesis—bringing the findings of hundreds of social scientists together into a fabric of meaningful principles and truths for application by managers of people and programs.

Some few synthesizing efforts are now being made, some as an integral part of research itself, some as a part of textbook writing and theory development, and some in specific recognition of the need for greater integration of knowledge. At present the principal integrative activities are the literature searches made by researchers themselves as a prelude to their own research and the synthesizing that is done by textbook writers. Beyond these efforts there are beginning to be special efforts to develop bodies of knowledge, theories, or models for better understanding of the principles and forces affecting human behavior in organizations.

A noteworthy effort in this direction is the work done by Chris Argyris to synthesize the emerging behavioral science insights into a body of theory with respect to people in working organizations. Said Argyris: "I began to wonder if it would not be helpful for someone to attempt the necessary first step of assembling as much of the existing empirical research as possible, preferably on some sort of framework, in order that more meaningful patterns could emerge. This book represents my first step at integrating the existing research literature relevant to understanding human behavior in on-going organizations" (1, p.ix). Further he pointed out that the extension of knowledge can be increased by the recognition of relations between formerly unconnected groups of phenomena. Harold Guetzkow of Northwestern University has said that: "The transformation of social science knowledge into social technology is an undertaking of the first importance," because such knowledge cannot be used easily without translation (3).

Another example of integrative study is that conducted on job attitudes or job satisfaction by Frederic Herzberg of the Psychological Service of Pittsburgh (4). This was a five-year study involving 2,000 separate research reports. More research resources need to be directed toward studies of this kind.

Keeping Practitioners up to Date

Correlation of knowledge on organizational behavior is just the first step. Next, it must be interpreted and made available to those who will apply it to actual organizational situations. There are some meager but encouraging efforts in this direction such as the following·

The Foundation for Research on Human Behavior at Ann Arbor considers as one of its principal missions the interpretation of social science knowledge for actual use. In addition to the sponsorship of human research projects, the Foundation sponsors seminars of behavioral scientists and managers for the presentation of the latest knowledge in selected areas.

The University of California at Los Angeles has conducted several conferences on research developments in personnel management.

Some societies and professional journals are moving toward providing an over-view of the state of the art in the fields with which they are concerned. Examples are the *Annual Review of Psychology,* the publication of the *Behavioral Scientist* magazine, and the inclusion of state-of-the-art summaries in professional journals. An example of the latter is "Developments in Public Administration" appearing as a regular feature in the *Public Administration Review.*

As will be seen, efforts to reach the practitioner are rather spotty and not at all an integral part of the behavioral science scheme. Means for the translation of social science knowledge into actual practice is itself a suitable subject for research—this is virtually unexplored territory. Carefully designed research on this problem should be both interesting and helpful.

Another possibility is the development of a profession of information scientists or interpreters, such as has been started relative to the physical and biological sciences. Companies have found that research is essential to their continued progress, as well as the progress of mankind, but the cost of science is so great that it is necessary to have an intelligence service to keep up with what is being done elsewhere. There is probably a place for a new profession of behavioral science interpretation, the members of which would be trained in several behavioral science fields and also in the communicative arts. They would need to learn several languages: the languages of the research fields to be interpreted and the languages of the practitioners who would be expected to apply the research knowledge.

Our interest should not be to try to make social scientists out of managers; they are really social engineers rather than social scientists. The mental discipline of the two must be quite different. The social scientist's concern is with the study of human behavior over a long period without the necessity of solving immediate problems. The practitioner's concern, on the other hand, is *right now* as well as the long run; and he has to make decisions even though he may not have all the facts he needs. In the course of reaching his decision he needs all the help science can give but he cannot ignore such practical matters as the traditions of the organization, its previous history, and the personalities who, after all, can make or break the decision once arrived at. Our purpose should be to make the management practitioner aware of the best that is now known about human behavior in organizations. Based on this knowledge, he can, then, take whatever risks the situation requires in spite of a lack of facts.

A Program for Increasing the Use of Behavioral Science

My suggestions for putting the results of behavioral or organizational research to practical and effective use fall into three broad categories:

1. *Provide machinery for planning, coordinating, integrating and disseminating information on the behavioral sciences.* As a result of the study mentioned earlier, I suggested the formation of a Personnel Research Council. This could be broadened perhaps to an Organizational Research Council which would be broadly supported by research, professional and user organizations.

Since the Federal Government supports such a large share of behavioral science research, more planning and coordinating could be done within the governmental sphere. The recent report on behavioral sciences by the President's Science Advisory Committee suggested that (1) the structure of the National Academy of Sciences— National Research Council be broadened to include the areas of behavioral and social science, and (2) the Government should make more effective use of the Social Science Research Council and other national professional organizations of the behavioral and social sciences (8).

Pending the development of more effective machinery, additional research conferences of behavioral scientists, such as this one at the University of Georgia, would probably be fruitful. In that way we can focus on organizational problems many capable minds representing a variety of experience and several behavioral science disciplines. Such seminar groups might include insightful practitioners as well.

2. *Make management practitioners more knowledgeable of the findings of behavioral science.* There are various possibilities for making managers more research conscious, more interested in finding out what knowledge behavioral science has to offer, and more interested in improving practice by using the findings of research:

a. Develop a closer relationship between researchers and practitioners. This can be done by including more social scientists on the staff of working organizations. Already there is a move in this direction in the spread of operations research and the use of industrial psychologists and industrial sociologists. Moreover, there can be a closer tie-in between research personnel and managers in the research conducted on live organizations. By joint participation, researchers will be made more aware of real problems and managers will become more appreciative of the methods and potentialities of science. Moreover, research projects can be conducted so that a feedback of results to the employees as well as the management is an integral and expected part of the plan. The Institute for Social Research at the University of Michigan has found that this procedure facilitates social and organizational change.

b. Conduct state-of-the-art conferences sponsored by professional societies, universities and working organizations. Such conferences would correlate research findings in important areas and discuss new findings that show promise.

c. Include more research topics as a part of regular conferences and meetings of professional associations. Instead of taking so much time in exchanging notes on experiences and "how we do it," they should devote at least *some* more attention to the emerging knowledge of the behavioral sciences.

d. Prepare more state-of-the-art summaries; these can be contracted for by foundations, user organizations, or other sources of funds in specific organizational problem areas. In addition, the professional journals can profitably devote more space to articles bringing together the findings of research on various problems and drawing conclusions on them. Too often, now, professional magazines devote most of their space to didactic, how-to-do-it discourses or reports of isolated and fragmented pieces of research.

e. Exchange personnel between research and operating organizations for periods of up to a year for purposes of mutual orientation and training. In this way the practitioners would be exposed to the inquisitive and analytical thinking of the behavioral scientist and the behavioral scientist would have the opportunity to observe and attempt to solve on a practical basis real human and organizational problems.

3. *Take steps to improve the art of communicating behavioral research findings.* These may include:

a. Making researchers more appreciative of the importance of communicating their findings to those who must apply them. Too often, now, behavioral scientists are mainly interested in communicating with each other. On the other side, it must be said that many practitioners are not interested in being communicated with—they think they have the answers already.

b. Developing a middle man profession between the researchers and the practitioners. The purpose of this profession would be to keep informed on research efforts and findings, and to disseminate them in a meaningful and understandable way to management staff and operating people. Some of these middle men can be on the staff of working organizations as behavioral scientists, management analysts, or operations researchers; or they may be employed by professional societies, professional journals or central research organizations.

c. Conducting research on the most effective means for translating behavioral science knowledge into practice. This will include questions of communication and purposeful social change.

d. Increasing efforts to develop a workable system of information storage and retrieval so that central exchanges of behavioral science information will be feasible. Current Government efforts along this line may help us reach this objective.

CONCLUSION

No one doubts the importance of science to continued progress in the world. There may be some who question the importance of behavioral research to the betterment of mankind in general and to the effective functioning of organizations in particular, but there is little question to those who have given the subject serious thought. While to some the primary reason for conducting behavioral research may be intellectual curiosity, the really important reason is to increase human understanding and to make organizational and social purposes more reachable. *We need to concentrate some attention on the big problem of how to translate the findings of behavioral research into practice.*

BIBLIOGRAPHY

1. Argyris, Chris. *Personality and Organization.* New York: Harper and Brothers, 1957.
2. Goode, Cecil E. *Personnel Research Frontiers.* Chicago: Public Personnel Assn., 1958.
3. Guetzkow, Harold. "A Model on the Application of the Social Sciences to Management Practice." An address before the Operations Research Society of America, San Francisco, November 1956.
4. Herzberg, Frederick, Maunser, Bernard, Peterson, Richard L., and Capwell, Dora F. *Job Attitudes: Review of Research and Opinion.* Pittsburgh: Psychological Service of Pittsburgh, 1957.
5. National Science Foundation. *Current Projects on Economic and Social Implications of Science and Technology.* Washington: National Science Foundation, 1962.
6. _____ *Federal Funds for Science XI,* Fiscal Years 1961, 1962 and 1963. Washington: National Science Foundation, 1963.
7. _____ *The Federal Government in Behavioral Science: Fields, Methods, and Funds.* Washington: American Enterprise Institute for Public Policy Research, 1964.
8. President's Science Advisory Committee, The Behavioral Sciences Sub-Panel. *Strengthening the Behavioral Sciences.* Released by the President, April 20, 1962.
9. Stanton, Ted. "'Information Scientists' — Industry's Link with Outside Research," *The Management Review,* L (March, 1961) 33-35.

Name Index

Subject Index